D1484179

# The Originals

## The Women's Auxiliary Ferrying Squadron of World War II

### by Sarah Byrn Rickman

Disc-Us
Books

The Originals: The Women's Auxiliary Ferrying Squadron of World War II
ISBN 1-58444-263-8 Hardcover
ISBN 1-58444-264-6 Softcover

Copyright ©2001 by Sarah Byrn Rickman
Library of Congress Control Number: 2001089605

Published in the United States.

Book Design by Renée Pocock-Cotter
(daughter of Colonel William "Wild Bill" Pocock, Ret.
of The Burma Peacocks, who flew The Hump in the CBI Theater)

For information contact:
Disc-Us Books, Inc.
4010 Sawyer Court
Sarasota, FL 34233
books@disc-us.com
www.disc-us.com

**Cover photo:** WAFS pilots at the Fairchild Aircraft Company, Hagerstown,
Maryland, 1943: Kathryn (Sis) Bernheim, Gertrude Meserve, Dorothy Fulton,
Betty Gillies, Helen McGilvery, Teresa James, Nancy Batson.

From the Teresa James Collection

# *Praise for the Women Pilots of World War II*

"The WASPs and WAFS are role models of mine. They are greatly respected for their services to our country."

Eileen Collins, NASA Astronaut

"I knew at the moment I pulled the trigger on the collective and watched the rotor blade start turning on my medivac helicopter that history for all women was about to change in military aviation. We were all going to make history. I thought about the WASPs I had read about towing targets during WWII to train our young male pilots, hopefully giving them a fighting chance to win and survive. Now, me, three wars later and a long generation since WWII, would carry the hope for all those women and this task I was about to perform would show our country 'yes' women can do this job of flying and be superior at it, too. I prayed not for my safe return to my family, but I prayed like those many, many, young male pilots before me that I would have the courage to do my duty."

LTC Ann Hollingsworth Patrie, USAR
Veteran Desert Storm, UH-1MedivacPilot
Cousin of WASP Lois Hollingsworth Ziler (43-W-3)

# INTRODUCTION

I am thrilled to have the real story of Nancy Love and the WAFS finally told. This is a dream come true.

So much of the emphasis, up to now, has been on the WASPs' story, that the other WAFS and I felt our story had been eclipsed if not forgotten. It is a different story, even though, eventually, we all were melded under one name. Not to take away from their story, but to have ours told, has been my goal for many years.

Those years that I was a member of the WAFS changed my life and for that extraordinary opportunity, I am eternally grateful to Nancy Love. I hope people reading this will grasp what an incredibly capable and smart — as well as gracious — woman Nancy Love really was. And I hope the true mettle of the first 28 women who flew for her — The Originals — is evident.

Sarah Rickman and I have worked on this book since June 1999 and, with the help and cooperation of the other surviving WAFS, it is now a reality.

*Nancy Batson Crews*

Nancy Batson Crews
December 22, 2000

# FOREWORD

I didn't grow up with an airport in my backyard. I didn't fly as a teenager, or even in my twenties. When I piloted an airplane for the first time, I was past fifty. But long before that, at the impressionable age of thirteen, I discovered Amelia Earhart, fell in love with airplanes and the whole idea of women in flight, and, with that, the course that led to this book was set.

Our ninth grade English text book contained stories of famous Americans. The only woman — amidst the likes of Walter P. Chrysler, George Washington Carver and Thomas Edison — was Amelia, that lost daughter of the sky, "Lady Lindy" who so captured the imagination of 1930s, Depression-weary, hero-worshipping America. The title of her chapter was "The Girl in Brown Who Walks Alone." I've never forgotten that telling portrayal of the painfully private yet conspicuously public woman who helped set my feet, and those of so many other young women, on the path to flight.

For Halloween that year, I dressed as Amelia — my riding jodhpurs and boots (both appropriately brown), a borrowed World War II-vintage leather flying helmet and goggles, a newly purchased cloth imitation of a leather flight jacket that I wheedled out of my mother, and a nylon scarf — a run-of-the-mill square (fashionable in the early 1950s), not the long, elegant, flowing white silk number worn with such panache by the early aviators.

I read everything I could find on the ill-fated Amelia but, alas, there wasn't a lot back then. Not like today. Her mysterious disappearance off remote Howland Island in the Pacific Ocean in July 1937 was never solved. Rumors circulated that her around-the-world flight was a cover for a spy mission. Was she checking out Japanese defenses under orders from President Roosevelt? Had she been shot down? Was she taken prisoner by the Japanese? Was there a clandestine romance between Amelia and her navigator Fred Noonan who disappeared with her?

World War II intervened, but after the war the curious started to look for her again, to no avail. She, Noonan and the Lockheed Electra were gone without a trace — other than an occasional questionable artifact that some searcher claims is hers. Today, everybody has a theory. Books have been written. Amelia would be one hundred four years old now.

But to a thirteen-year-old, Amelia's life was the stuff of which adventure and romance were made. For a long time I hoped she might be found alive. Some forty years after my fateful encounter with Amelia between the pages of a book, within the space of a few hours and a meeting of minds, I moved, irrevocably, into that world of women in aviation.

Joan Hrubec, administrator for the International Women's Air and Space Museum (IWASM) — then located a mere three blocks from my home in Centerville, Ohio, a Dayton suburb — approached me when she heard I had left the local newspaper. In June 1989, after twenty-plus years in print journalism, I resigned my position as editor of the twice-weekly *Centerville-Bellbrook Times* to pursue a career as a freelance writer. Before I did that, however, I had covered the birth of IWASM in "my town" and had written several newspaper and magazine articles on the museum and the women who made it fly.

Joan, museum board president Nancy Hopkins Tier, and executive vice president B Steadman took me to lunch and offered me a job. By coincidence, I had met B in Michigan twenty-six years earlier when I was a reporter doing a story on women in aviation for *The Detroit News*. That encounter had further whetted my interest in aviation, but the time to pursue it was not yet at hand. In January 1990, the time had come.

I agreed to do some writing and promotion work for the museum and, in doing so, changed my life. A little over a year later, I started flying lessons because I felt the need to prove myself, to walk the talk — to be and feel a part of these women in aviation, women who, like Amelia before them, had so captured my imagination. I joined the 66s, more recently known as Future Women Pilots — women who hope someday to become Ninety-Nines, the international organization for licensed women pilots founded November 2, 1929, by Amelia Earhart and ninety-eight other pioneer women pilots.

One of my innovations, working for the museum, was to

encourage them to videotape the modest lecture series they sponsored to acquaint the Dayton-area with what IWASM had to offer. I went to aviation buff Dave Gordon, then program director for the Miami Valley Cable Council (MVCC) — public access TV in the south Dayton suburbs. We formed a team — he, Joan and I. We planned three lectures a year — the second Monday of November, January and March — to be taped at the Cable Council studios for showing to the general community on the Public Access channels.

We did twelve shows in all. The first, November 12, 1990, featured IWASM's indomitable president Nancy Hopkins Tier, then eighty-one, one of the founders of the Ninety Nines, and still flying. MVCC still airs our programs. "They're oral history," the current programming supervisor told me recently when I inquired as to their timeliness. "They never go out of date."

Because of people's innate fear of the television cameras, we had our best success with panels — safety in numbers — bringing together three or more women pilots with a similar story to tell and using a moderator to keep the questions and answers moving. Overcoming my own aversion to the probing eye of the camera, I personally moderated several such discussions — in themselves incredible learning experiences.

In January 1992, we organized a panel of seven Women Airforce Service Pilots (WASPs) and one member of the Women's Auxiliary Ferrying Squadron (WAFS). These are the women who flew as civilians for the U.S. Army during World War II. In 1992, both groups were celebrating the fiftieth anniversary of their founding, but they were still relatively unknown to the American public. Nadine Nagle, a WASP and a museum trustee, served as moderator. For an hour, the eight women shared their experiences, to the delight of a sizeable studio audience and for the general public via videotape.

That was how I met Nancy Batson Crews, the representative WAFS on the panel. Though we didn't realize it then, this book was born the night Nadine and I picked Nancy up at Dayton International Airport prior to the lecture. Nancy and I hit it off, struck up a friendship. Later, I asked if I might write her story. She suggested, instead, that I write the story of WAFS founder and squadron commander Nancy Love. Not long after that, while I was still considering Nancy's request, Joan Hrubec asked me to consider writing the history of the WAFS. Though their story has been included in several books about the WASPs, no definitive book exists that tells the story of the WAFS. Nor has a book been written about Nancy Love. Both circumstances were mine for the remedying.

*Sarah Byrn Rickman*
*February 2001*

# PROLOGUE

On May 29, 1941 — when the United States was still seven months from its abrupt entry into the war — the unit that would eventually be known as the Air Transport Command (ATC) of the United States Army Air Forces was born. The major component of the ATC was the Ferrying Division. To ferry an airplane means to move it from one place to another. As reported in General William H. Tunner's World War II memoir, *Over the Hump*, up until three o'clock that afternoon in May 1941, no organization existed in American military aviation to provide for either the delivery of airplanes or the transport of materiel by air.

President Franklin D. Roosevelt had just told his Secretary of War that something needed to be done to speed up the number of deliveries of bombers to England via Lend Lease, which had been in existence only two months, dating from March 1941. Colonel Robert Olds — a World War I pilot who had, according to Tunner, "made a great name for himself in military aviation" — was assigned to set up the ferrying operation. He chose the young Major Tunner for his team — a fortuitous move. Lieutenant Colonel Tunner almost single-handedly created the ATC's domestic ferrying division and, through it, an efficient means of delivering airplanes from one point to another.

Tunner began to recruit pilots for his new service — first from National Guard and Reserve units, some of which he had helped build through aggressive recruitment in the late 1930s. Then he began to borrow them from other tactical units. However, the safe and timely delivery of an airplane takes a different mindset and utilization of piloting skills than taking a plane into combat when that airplane driver is intent solely on destroying the enemy. So Tunner's former barnstormers, crop dusters, and air race circuit cowboys had to be retrained.

"The mission of our pilots was to move their planes along toward their ultimate destination, which for many planes was combat. Our pilots were not supposed to risk their lives or their ships, but to fly skillfully and safely and deliver those planes in good condition. The ferry pilot was not expected to be a hero, but just to do his job," Tunner said.

Then came Pearl Harbor and the declaration of War. Immediately, all ferrying stopped. All but 386 of Tunner's pilots were ordered to report back to their units in preparation for combat. Airplane production went into high gear. Trainer planes were coming off the line, but there weren't enough pilots to ferry them from the factories in the Northeast and the West to newly-established Army Air Forces flight training bases in the South. Combat airplanes, desperately needed at the front, were rolling off the lines as well. Pilots were needed to ferry them to the docks for shipment overseas. Tunner was back to square one. He had to rebuild his ferrying operation almost from scratch.

Desperate, Tunner looked for pilots anywhere he could find them. Most pilots who could meet his high standards, and who weren't already in the Army, were certified flight instructors and every certified flight instructor was by now under contract teaching future combat pilots how to fly. Some of those flight instructors were women. But the truth was, there weren't that many pilots in the United States, period. His pickings were slim. On top of that, in spring 1942, the United States was losing the war. Everything seemed to be going wrong at once.

Several times in 1940 and 1941, the possibility had surfaced of using experienced women pilots to ferry airplanes, thus freeing male pilots for more hazardous duty. But in early 1940s America, this was a revolutionary idea and the Army brass rejected it almost to a man. The experienced male pilots who had been around women flyers in the Golden Age of Aviation, as the 1930s were called, knew how good some of them really were. They had flown with and against them in air races. But most of the old guard military men were saddled with a "good ol' boy," myopic, regimental mentality and envisioned no such notion. They didn't understand women and they most certainly didn't want to deal with them.

But Bob Olds was different. He didn't totally reject the idea, he simply put it on the shelf until the time was ripe — the need more pressing. By spring 1942, that time, as well as the need, had arrived.

At first, Bill Tunner wasn't in favor of using women ferry pilots either, but then fate dropped a woman pilot by the name of Nancy Harkness Love into his midst and the opportunity for women to fly for the Army was at hand. Tunner was about to get his chance to listen, to change his mind, and to make a difference — not only to the war effort but to the future of women in the military and in aviation in general.

Twenty-eight women, averaging approximately 1,400 hours of flying experience, answered their country's wartime call and joined the Women's Auxiliary Ferrying Squadron (WAFS). Their original assignment was to ferry small single-engine trainer and liaison-type aircraft and, thereby, release male pilots for combat duty.

Nancy Harkness Love, age twenty-eight, was named director of the squadron which was organized under the Ferrying Division of the Air Transport Command, U.S. Army Air Forces.

On September 5, 1942, she sent telegrams to eighty-three American women, ages twenty-one to thirty-five, known to have logged at least 500 hours in the air, to hold commercial licenses and a 200-horsepower engine rating, and to have recent cross-country flying experience. "Advise if you are immediately available to join a group of women pilots under the Air Transport Command to perform domestic ferrying duties," the telegram read.

In addition to being an elite corps from the standpoint of skills, ability, and experience, the women who became WAFS were guinea pigs. Nothing like this had ever been tried before. The future of women in military aviation hung on how these select women pilots performed professionally and conducted themselves socially and morally.

This is the story of those women. . .The Originals.

**Nancy Harkness Love**

# 1

"I'm going to quit school and become a pilot, Daddy," sixteen-year-old Nancy Harkness told her father when they sat down to dinner one late August evening in 1930.

The Harkness family lived in the town of Houghton in the northernmost part of Michigan's Upper Peninsula. Much of the year, the area — 47⁺ degrees north latitude — is locked in ice and snow. When summer comes, the snow melts and the light of the high northern sun lingers until ten o'clock at night, creating silver shadows that play hide 'n' seek among the towering pines.

That day, while Nancy was out riding her horse Daisy, she saw a sleek airplane landing and taking off from a field outside of town. She watched, fascinated. The aircraft seemed to dance in the sun, catching and reflecting golden rays on its silver wings and turning the world into a shimmering metallic fairyland. Never had she seen anything quite so graceful, so lovely, so exciting.

It didn't take her long to wangle a ride in that marvelous winged machine. The barnstormer pilot was looking for business at five dollars a crack and the prospect of taking up a pretty young girl was far more pleasant than flying the town's business and political leaders around. With that first flight, Nancy was hooked. And when Nancy made up her mind, she acted. The mature, focused woman she would become was beginning to emerge even then.

"Nancy, why can't you learn to fly, become a pilot, *and* stay in school?" her father suggested, well aware of his daughter's determined nature. Nancy thought about that and, possibly with logic beyond her years, agreed. Her mother, however, was utterly opposed. But, with her dad on her side, she got her lessons. Between August 26 and August 30, 1930, she accrued four hours and thirty minutes of flying time with her instructor, Jimmy Hansen of Milwaukee.

On August 31, she soloed in a Fleet Biplane and by September 10, she had ten flying hours to her credit.

She was born Hannah Lincoln Harkness on February 14, 1914, in Houghton, the daughter of Dr. Robert Bruce and Alice Chadbourne Harkness. "My grandfather hated his sister-in-law — Hannah Lincoln Chadbourne — and told my grandmother she could name their daughter after her sister, but that he was going to call her Nancy," Margaret (Marky) Love, Nancy's middle daughter, relates. "There's always been a Hannah Lincoln in the family. That's my older sister's name and also her daughter's name."

Though young Nancy enjoyed the blue waters of Lake Superior and the dark green forests of Michigan's Keweenaw Peninsula as a summer playground, the family had roots in old Boston. When Nancy was in her mid-teens, the Harknesses opted to send her to school in Massachusetts. So after a summer of horseback riding and flying lessons, Nancy dutifully returned to Milton Academy, the prep school where she was a boarding student, and, in the fall of 1930, fulfilled her part of the bargain with her father.

Two incidents soon altered any carefree attitudes Nancy might have harbored about flying. With a mere fifteen hours of solo time under her belt, she took off on her first cross-country trip — with two passengers and luggage in tow. They were headed from Boston to Poughkeepsie, New York, to visit friends at Vassar. She hadn't yet learned to read her compass. Then the weather turned bad. Finally, the oil gauge broke and the novice pilot realized she was in trouble and had to get the aircraft down.

She called it "a precarious landing." Fortunately, neither plane nor passengers nor pilot were any the worse for wear, but the incident taught her a lesson she would never forget. Nancy knew she had made a serious mistake.

On another afternoon, while flying some friends around, Nancy decided to buzz the neighboring boys' prep school. She flew low down the quadrangle and tried to pull up at the far end to avoid hitting the chapel. "My mother still hadn't learned much about physics," says youngest daughter Alice (Allie) Love. "She didn't realize that though you pull up, the plane doesn't immediately go up. She nearly hit the bell tower and did rattle some slates loose so they fell off the roof.

"Well, someone got the tail number of the airplane and called the airport. Two local boys, the Fuller brothers, were known for such stunts. The irate headmaster of the boy's academy rang the airport manager. 'Which one of those Fuller boys just buzzed the school?' The manager dutifully answered that the pilot of that particular airplane that afternoon was Miss Nancy Harkness.

"My mother was off campus that day with her older brother, Robert. He drove her back to school and when she walked in the door at her residence hall, the headmistress, the house mistress, and a couple of the members of the board of trustees were waiting for her. Her brother took one look and bolted, leaving her to make the explanations by herself. But the school had no rules about flying. Students couldn't drive cars, but nothing said they couldn't fly, so she wasn't suspended. Instead, my mother was severely reprimanded and told to stay out of airplanes for the remainder of the semester.

"I went to Milton, too," Allie continues. "Nancy Harkness was still a legend all those years later. Turns out, I roomed with Emily Fuller, daughter of one of the Fuller brothers."

Nancy emerged from those two youthful escapades a more cautious student of flying. Never again, throughout a flying career that lasted more than forty years, would she overestimate her flying skills. At a very young age, she began to upgrade her knowledge and her proficiency.

Fall of 1931, Nancy Harkness entered Vassar College in Poughkeepsie, New York. She had her eye on a career in education and declared French and French history as her majors.

Little did she know that, a few years later, she would make history herself.

By 1932, she was an eighteen-year-old on the brink of woman-hood and her eyes already were turned on the stars. Gaining that much-sought-after college degree was important to her, but school paled beside the lure of Bernoulli's principle of flight, lift and angle of attack. Her classroom of choice became the cockpit of a single engine trainer airplane. She continued her flying and made the most of what precious hours aloft she could steal. Soon she was dubbed "The Flying Freshman" by the local press when they noticed the young woman who hung out at the Poughkeepsie airport on weekends.

She earned her commercial license in 1932 and her transport license in the summer of 1933. She was not yet twenty.

While at Vassar she heightened the school's interest in aviation by organizing a student flying club — a process she then repeated for other New England college campuses the following year. On weekends, she gave airplane rides — just like the barnstormer had once given her — to earn money to pay for flight time.

A reversal in the Harkness family's financial fortunes required that Nancy leave Vassar in January 1934. Her father had not invested her mother's inheritance wisely and the Depression economy had caught up with the family. Nancy once told a friend that she left school because, "It occurred to me that the people of the world were making history, not studying it, and the airplane was in the very center of it all."

Marky is convinced that leaving school was one of the most difficult things her mother ever had to do because she truly believed in the advantages of education and would not have left willingly had the choice been hers. "But she would never have told anyone that she left because the family no longer had the money to send her to college."

So what does a young woman in need of a job and in love with aviation do with herself and those skills she has managed to acquire? Five years later, a young woman from Nebraska by the name of Evelyn Sharp — who was destined to fly with Nancy's WAFS — faced the same dilemma. She, too, earned her license at sixteen. She too, set out to find a way to make a living flying.

Evelyn did it barnstorming — flying around the countryside giving people airplane rides — and later by instructing. Nancy, now with three hundred hours to her credit, landed a job in Boston operating a sales agency out of East Boston Airport for Beechcraft, a manufacturer of small airplanes. Beechcraft, founded in 1930 by Walter and Olive Ann Beech, was located in Wichita, Kansas. Nancy continued to build her flying time demonstrating Beechcraft's wares on a commission basis.

Using young, attractive women to sell airplanes was no different than using them to sell automobiles or any other wares for that matter. Not only did they attract male buyers, if a man saw that a woman could fly an airplane, then surely flying must not be that difficult. Nancy saw this ploy used successfully again several years later when the country was immersed not in an economic depression but a war.

Nancy once tried to sell an airplane to millionaire Joe Kennedy. Though unsuccessful at that venture, she learned later that Kennedy was so taken with her that he had her checked out by private detectives as a possible marriage candidate for Joe Jr.

"She wasn't even Roman Catholic, so that put her out of the running anyway," Marky says, relating the story as her mother told it years later. "And she was furious."

The intensely private Nancy Harkness emerged early on.

Then, chance meetings with two men set her feet on the path to her date with destiny — the history she would eventually live and help make. She married the first one and the second became her mentor and her wartime commander.

"When my mother and father met in 1934, it wasn't love at first sight," Marky relates. "She told us that she was sitting perched on his desk at Inter City Airways one day when he walked in. He wasn't happy to find her there. She envied him being around airplanes so much. He was doing something she really wanted to do."

Robert M. Love — five feet eleven inches with sandy hair and a wry sense of humor — owned a rival aircraft agency. The initial animosity between them eventually receded and a mutual attraction took over. Friends recount that they began courting "on the wing of an airplane over a cup of hot dope." Dope is a sticky, thick substance used to protect, waterproof and make tight the cloth surfaces of airplane wings. Nancy was applying the gooey stuff to the wing of a needy airplane one day when Bob Love happened by and, naturally, stopped to chat. After that, more than the dope began to heat up.

Romance was one thing, but Nancy Harkness wasn't ready to settle down and get married just yet. She was too busy establishing her name in the world of aviation. In 1935, veteran aviatrix Phoebe Omlie — Special Assistant for Intelligence of the National Advisory Committee for Aeronautics (NACA), the forerunner of the National Aeronautics and Space Administration (NASA) — chose Nancy to work with the Airmarking Project at airports around the country. Selected to be field representatives along with Nancy were 1930s aviation luminaries Louise Thaden, Blanche Noyes, and Helen McCloskey.

Omlie had convinced the chief of the Airport Marking and Mapping Section of the Bureau of Air Commerce of the need for making towns and cities more identifiable from the air. Few pilots in those days flew over established airways, nor did they have radios. Getting lost was frighteningly easy, even for an experienced pilot. Omlie's solution was that the states would be marked off in sections of twenty square miles. A marker with the name of the nearest town — at each fifteen-mile interval — would be painted on the roof of the most prominent building in the town.

State grants were awarded through President Franklin D. Roosevelt's Works Progress Administration (WPA) to pay for the airmarking project. The cost was close to one million dollars. Not only was the program designed to help private pilots and to provide a permanent benefit to the airways in the U.S., it also was intended to provide jobs for the unemployed of the Great Depression. By mid-1936, thirty states were involved in the program. Approval had been given for sixteen thousand markers.

Nancy's job entailed traveling around her territory, the eastern part of the U.S., convincing city fathers that the name of their town painted on the roof of a prominent building would serve as an aid to pilots. Originally, the government promised its representatives airplanes, but then reneged. Occasionally Nancy had a government plane to fly, otherwise she traveled by train or bus. She worked for Omlie and the Airmarking Project for nearly two years. She left in the fall of 1935 to help take care of her mother, who was ill, and to plan her upcoming wedding. Omlie replaced her with Helen Richey, who would go on to fly with the Air Transport Auxiliary (ATA) in England in 1942, and eventually ferry airplanes in the United States under Nancy's command.

In January 1936, Nancy and Bob Love were married in Houghton, Michigan, and took off for a flying honeymoon to California. Now the press called her "The Flying Bride." The Loves' vastly different flying styles almost caused a divorce before the marriage could get off the ground, figuratively speaking. According to Marky, "Dad was a hot pilot. A bit of a cowboy. Mom was careful, deliberate, exacting. They didn't fly a lot together after that, each preferring their own skills and style in the cockpit."

Bob Love had earned his pilot's license in 1929. Initially a student at Princeton, he eventually transferred to Massachusetts Institute of Technology. He left school before graduation, bought the Curtiss-Wright Air Terminal at East Boston Airport, and started his own company, Inter City Airways. In the late 1930s, he joined the Army Air Corps as a reserve flying officer, a move that would have considerable impact on both their lives a few years later.

In September 1936, Nancy and Bob went to California for the National Air Races. Beechcraft surprised Nancy with the news that they had entered her in the Amelia Earhart Trophy Race. She had never flown a pylon race before, but still managed to come in fifth, though she was more than forty-five minutes behind Betty Browning, the winner. Nancy's prize: $75. Later that month, in Detroit, Nancy came in second in a race flying a Monocoupe. And that was the sum total of her racing career.

As Marky pointed out, Nancy was a careful and deliberate pilot. She disliked the haste and confusion that were part of air racing. She had begun to establish her own methodical approach to flying that eventually evolved into a routine of carefully written checklists for her pre-flights and close attention to the overall details of flight. These were traits that would benefit her greatly several years later when she was ferrying strange and sometimes balky new aircraft across the country with a minimum of check out.

Late that fall of 1936, Nancy returned to the Airmarking Project to check up on the results of her previous work and get information on what additional air-marking work was needed. Then in August, 1937, yet another aviation challenge awaited her. She thought she was being hired, once again, to sell a new aircraft — this one equipped with a revolutionary type of landing gear. Instead, she became a test pilot for the Gwinn Aircar Company in Buffalo, New York. There, she tested the tricycle landing gear (nosewheel in front of the main wheels) that would eventually replace the tail-wheel or "tail-dragger" planes of the '30s and become the standard in aviation.

Nancy flew with Joe Gwinn, her boss and owner of the company, on several test flights — she in the left seat operating the only set of controls and he in the right seat. While she flew, he worked a slide rule and did his engineering calculations, apparently unconcerned about the orientation of the aircraft relative to the horizon (known in aviation as "attitude"). His mind was on numbers, not where the plane was in the air. At one point, Joe told her to land the plane from 2,000 feet with the control column full back, flaps down and engine throttled. Though the maneuver violated Nancy's every flying instinct, she did as Joe instructed, holding the wheel back as they approached the ground at 980 feet per minute, to a smooth landing.

Finally, in 1938 she went into the business with Bob at Inter City where they ran flying classes and charters and did aerial surveying. She also demonstrated and sold airplanes.

By 1940, Nancy had earned a Civil Aeronautics Administration (CAA) instrument card as well as a seaplane rating. She now had logged more than a thousand hours. Inter City was being called upon to ferry airplanes to Canada. These aircraft were bound for England — now locked in a life and death air war with Germany. They had to be landed and pushed or towed, not flown, across the US-Canadian border. Nancy ferried a Stinson 105 to Maine, pushed it over the border, and flew it on to Halifax, Nova Scotia, to be shipped abroad. It was Nancy's first crack at ferrying. It also gave her an idea.

On May 21, 1940 she wrote to Colonel Robert Olds, Army Air Corps Plans Division, that she knew of forty-nine women pilots — possibly another fifteen — who were capable of ferrying aircraft, just as she had done, for the Army Air Corps. Many of the women pilots she knew were fellow members of the Ninety-Nines, the International Organization for Women Pilots which Nancy joined after she earned her private pilot's license.

"I really think this list is up to handling pretty complicated stuff," Nancy said in her letter.

At this point, the United States was not in the war. So Olds filed her suggestion away for future reference. He didn't completely discount the idea because he thought she might be on to something. But, in May 1940, the U.S. Army was not ready to consider women ferrying its airplanes, and so the matter was shelved.

Two years later, in June 1942, the idea resurfaced — quite by accident. By then, the United States was in the war, thanks to the Japanese surprise attack on Pearl Harbor on December 7, 1941. The war was not going well for the American military in June 1942. The Army was hurting for pilots. There just weren't enough of them and the ones they had were being groomed for combat. The Ferrying Division of the Air Transport Command, whose job it was to move airplanes around, began 1942 with a grand total of 384 pilots. In June 1942, its newly named commander, Colonel William H. Tunner, was on the hunt for more — a lot more, and fast.

After Pearl Harbor, all airfields within fifty miles of both coasts were shut down. That included East Boston Airport and, consequently, Inter City Airways. Bob Love, already in the Reserve, became Major Love (eventually Colonel) and was placed on active duty with the ATC as deputy chief of staff at headquarters in Washington, D.C. He and Nancy immediately moved to Washington.

Using the business skills she had honed working at Inter City with her husband, she found a job working in the northeast office of the ATC's Ferrying Command in Baltimore. Because it was easier for an employee to get gasoline for an airplane than for an automobile, Nancy flew the sixty miles from Washington to Baltimore daily in their high-winged, single-engine, four-seater Fairchild 24 in order to get to work.

IWASM

Bob Love's office was in close proximity to Colonel Tunner's in the dingy basement of the old munitions building where the ATC was temporarily housed. At a chance meeting over the watercooler, the fact that Bob Love's wife flew to work daily came out. That particular June morning was a stormy one and Bob Love was wondering aloud if his wife had gotten to work safely.

"Your wife flies?" Tunner asked.

"Yes," Bob answered.

"I'm combing the woods for pilots, and here's one right under my nose. Are there many more women like your wife?" Tunner asked.

"Why don't you ask her?" Bob suggested.

At that moment the idea of women ferrying airplanes for the Ferrying Division of the ATC was firmly implanted in Bill Tunner's mind. Yet another chance meeting had set in motion events that, once again, would change Nancy Love's life.

෴

At this point, Nancy Love's story has to pause and allow "the other half" to be told — the rest of this true-life conflict that shaped the future of American female flyers in the armed services. No novelist could dream up a better plot of intrigue, political jockeying, jealousy, thwarted patriotism and blind ambition, seasoned with bureaucratic insensitivity.

**Nancy Love**

IWASM

# 2

Jacqueline Cochran — that very name was her own creation — became a beautician at thirteen and, by the late 1920s, had worked her way out of north Florida canebrake poverty all the way to Antoine's famous beauty salon at Saks Fifth Avenue in New York City.

A story from her autobiography, *The Stars At Noon*, perfectly conveys the drive and determination that dominated Cochran's life. It seems that the Christmas she was six, the little barefoot ragamuffin who became the glamorous, world-renown aviatrix, was ordered to give up something that was very dear to her. She had bought two chances on a doll with fifty cents that she earned by drawing well water for women to do their washing — a task that made her hands bleed — and by serving as midwife to a young mother. On Christmas Eve, the little girl's name was drawn and, wonder of wonders, she won the doll fair and square, only to be told by her foster mother that she had to give it up. Her fifteen-year-old foster sister had a two-year-old daughter and the little ragamuffin was ordered to give the doll to baby Willa Mae.

Years later, when she was a success and money was hers to do with as she wished, the woman who was now Jacqueline Cochran brought Willa Mae — now, herself, a struggling single mother — to New York to live. She provided Willa Mae and her child with a new start in life. But she did make one stipulation — that they bring the doll with them and return it to its rightful owner. They did, and for the rest of her life Cochran kept the doll in a special place in her home — first in her New York apartment and later at her ranch in Indio, California.

Cochran met millionaire Floyd Odlum in 1932 and, after he divorced his first wife, married him. The first Mrs. Odlum got the New York department store Bonwit Teller in the divorce settlement.

Floyd then helped Jackie set up her own beauty business, Jacqueline Cochran Cosmetics, and eventually convinced her to learn to fly in order to get around the country more easily to call on her customers. Jackie Cochran was a born saleswoman and she made it her business to learn every aspect of the beauty business. But she had her eyes on bigger things and she saw aviation as the way to get it.

Whether it was the heady sensation of power she experienced in flight or the feeling that she was in control of her destiny, once she got behind the controls of an airplane, Cochran set her sights on the stars — not only those seen from the cockpit, but the star power that came with fame and recognition. Winning air races and setting aviation records were the ways to achieve both celebrity status and credibility — the acclaim she craved.

Cochran and America's most famous aviatrix in the 1930s, Amelia Earhart, became friends when they met in 1935. Amelia and her husband, publisher George Palmer Putnam, spent time on the Odlum's California ranch. In her second book, *Jacqueline Cochran an Autobiography*, Cochran describes the following exchange with Putnam:

> He was always patronizing me. "Well, little girl," he said to me, "what's your ambition in flying?"
>
> That was like waving a red flag in front of a bull. "To put your wife in the shade, sir," I answered. But I never felt competitive with Amelia. I could be positively fearsome when it came to putting real competition in the shade, but Amelia was different. She was such a gentle lady.
>
> My home was her home — a home that offered her horseback riding, swimming, pilot talk, quiet walks in the desert but especially peace and privacy. God, the world hounded that woman after she became famous. During the last year of her life, I was closer to Amelia than anyone else, even her husband, George Putnam.

There is little doubt among those who have studied Jackie Cochran's life and accomplishments that she felt Amelia's torch had been passed to her.

In *Those Wonderful Women in Their Flying Machines*, Sally Van Wagenen Keil wrote:

> Five months after Amelia Earhart vanished without a trace, about two hundred people huddled near a wooden speaker's platform by the administration building of Floyd Bennett Field in Brooklyn. The skies were a dismal November gray and the crowd tightened their winter coats against the freezing west wind which whipped through two American flags mounted at each end of the platform. The Women's National Aeronautical Association was paying tribute to Amelia Earhart, but the speaker, Jacqueline Cochran, conveyed the feelings of everyone that, whether or not Earhart still existed somewhere in the flesh, her spirit was very much alive.
>
> "If her last flight was into eternity, one can mourn her loss but not regret her effort," Cochran said, somberly. "Amelia did not lose, for her last flight was endless. Like in a relay race of progress she has merely placed the torch in the hands of others to carry on to the next goal and from there on and on forever."

Cochran began her assault on aviation's history books when she was one of two women to enter the 10,000-mile race from Suffolk, England to Melbourne, Australia in 1934. The other woman was Great Britain's Amy Johnson Mollison. Cochran's plane was forced down in Rumania due to engine trouble and defective flaps. The following year, she attempted the prestigious Bendix Transcontinental Race from the West Coast to Cleveland but was unable to finish. Earhart placed fifth in that race.

Two years later, in 1937, Cochran placed third in the Bendix and immediately turned her eyes toward the 1938 competition. Alexander de Seversky was trying to sell his revolutionary aircraft to the U.S. military. His 1,200-horsepower P-35 was fast and capable of long range flying to accompany bombers, protecting them while in the air. This is the plane that evolved into the P-47 pursuit that helped Uncle Sam win the war. When de Seversky offered Cochran the chance to fly a P-35 in the 1938 Bendix, she jumped at it. Floyd Odlum helped finance the venture. Jackie flew the 2,042 miles from Los Angeles to Cleveland in eight hours, ten minutes and thirty seconds, non-stop. She won.

Now having been firmly established as a pilot to be reckoned with, a businesswoman of considerable acumen, and the wife of an influential millionaire, Jackie Cochran was ready to conquer new horizons. She went after aviation records, breaking old ones and setting new ones. She offered herself as a test pilot for medical data as well as airplane equipment. She was awarded the women's Harmon Trophy, aviation's highest award, for achievements in aviation in 1938, 1939 and 1940.

On the occasion of one of those awards presentations, Jackie met Eleanor Roosevelt. When war broke out, she wrote to Mrs. Roosevelt and offered to organize a group of women pilots to be used for war service, thus freeing up male pilots for more hazardous duty. Nothing came of it. Men still could no more fathom the intelligent use of women in such a non-traditional undertaking than their counterparts fifty years earlier could fathom women voting. But Mrs. Roosevelt commented in her column, "My Day," that it was an idea whose time had come.

Considering her success in the aviation world — coupled with her husband's money and the added impetus of their friendship with, and political support of, Franklin and Eleanor Roosevelt — Jackie found it a short leap into bed, figuratively speaking, with Washington's military establishment when war raged in Europe and seemed imminent on this side of the Atlantic.

In June 1941, Cochran attended a luncheon with General H. H. "Hap" Arnold, chief of the U.S. Army Air Corps, and Clayton Knight who was recruiting American ferry pilots to fly for the British. Jackie asked what she could do for the war effort. The Battle of Britain had left the island nation battered and reeling. The Lend Lease program was sending everything from airplanes to food to shore up the sagging country. Either Arnold or Knight suggested she might ferry a bomber to England, as a publicity ploy to get more male pilots to volunteer for what was then considered extremely hazardous duty.

Jackie went to Montreal to check out in a twin-engine bomber. The male pilots responsible for checking her out "didn't want a woman in their midst." The way she tells it in her second book, operating the hand brake on the big airplane was her downfall: "At least a half-dozen takeoffs and landings using that damned difficult hand brake sored up my right arm. . . . My hand was red and my arm was aching. . . the hand brake turned out to be a major millstone."

Cochran finally did qualify, conditionally, and did help ferry one Lockheed Hudson bomber to England, but she served as co-pilot to a male pilot who did the takeoff and landing. She had not satisfactorily demonstrated the physical ability to operate the hand brake in an emergency. The crew took off from Gander, Newfoundland, on June 17, 1941 and successfully delivered their twin-engine bomber to Prestwick, Scotland.

Unfortunately, this one flight by Cochran — before the U.S. ever entered the war — eventually was blown way out of proportion with the result that today, sixty years later, many people have the mistaken idea that Cochran and a whole squadron of American women pilots ferried airplanes to Britain before and during the war as a matter of course. The truth is, they did not!

While in England, Cochran met with Pauline Gower, chief of the British women's group ferrying airplanes for England's Air Transport Auxiliary (ATA). Cochran said she hoped to get ideas for forming a similar group on this side of the Atlantic. Upon her return to the States, she met with President and Mrs. Roosevelt. The President gave her a note to take to Secretary of War Henry Stimson stating that the President had asked her to look into a plan to have American women pilots perform a similar service in this country. The note later disappeared.

But General Arnold wasn't buying it. He had plenty of men, he said, and no need to involve women in flying duties. He still didn't think women could handle the Army's airplanes, even the small single-engine ones.

Cochran's overtures got nowhere, but she didn't give up. The next time she accosted Arnold with her idea, he suggested she recruit some of the American women pilots to go to England since a woman's flying program in the U.S. was not in the cards. So Cochran got the go-ahead from the British to recruit twenty-five American women pilots to come to England and fly for the ATA. Less than two months after Pearl Harbor, Cochran was immersed in that project.

The previous summer (1941), in hopes of starting a women's flying program for the U.S. Army, Cochran had members of her personal and business staff search the Civil Aeronautics Administration (CAA) files for names of women pilots who might qualify. They found 2,733 licensed women pilots in the United States, one hundred fifty of whom had more than two hundred hours of flying experience. She sent telegrams to those she thought could meet her qualifications. When the girls she interviewed asked about the potential for a similar program in the United States, Cochran told them there would be no such program.

Nancy Love's friend Robert Olds nearly threw a monkey wrench into Cochran's plans at that point. Olds was now a Brigadier General and, in January 1942, was the head of the Ferry Command under the Army Air Forces (previously the Army Air Corps). He decided to resurrect Nancy Love's idea for using women to ferry airplanes. The Army Air Forces (AAF), under Hap Arnold's command, was taking every available male pilot it could lay its hands on to fight the war in which the United States was now embroiled. Olds and the Ferry Command suddenly had a number of new aircraft to deliver and no pilots to ferry them. He was ready to hire women pilots, immediately, as civilians — the same way he was hiring male pilots where he could find them.

Olds let his plan slip to Cochran. Furious, because of her now unbreakable commitment to the British, she wrote the following note to AAF Commanding General Hap Arnold:

> General Olds has informed me that he is planning on hiring women pilots for his Ferrying Command almost at once. His plan, as outlined to me, is not only bad in my opinion from the organizational standpoint, and contrary to what you told me yesterday but is in

direct conflict, in fact, with the plans of a women's unit for England. In addition, it would wash me out of the supervision of the women flyers here rather than the contrary as we contemplated.

Arnold, aware of Cochran's political clout with the Roosevelts, in turn wrote to Olds and told him: "You will make no plans or re-open negotiations for hiring women pilots until Miss Jacqueline Cochran has completed her present agreement with the British authorities and has returned to the United States."

Finally, spring 1942, Cochran set sail for England with commitments from twenty-three of Uncle Sam's best women pilots. The last of them arrived in London on September 2, 1942. Cochran stayed there to help them get settled, then prepared to return home.

That same week, back "across the pond" in Washington, events took a turn that changed forever the lives of 1,102 American women pilots — and the lives of all those who came in contact with them. Likewise, when Jacqueline Cochran landed on U.S. soil a few days later and got wind of those events, she made a beeline for Hap Arnold's office full of undisguised fury and further changed the course of history.

**Teresa James, 1934**

# 3

***March 2, 2000, Lake Worth, Florida***

"How are ya, honey," the gravely voice greets me through the screen. "Come on in. I just got back from Mass and the coffee pot's on."

Shelves bulging with books bearing aviation titles line the narrow, enclosed porch. Stacks of magazines with glossy pictures of airplanes top every table. The house is abloom with flowers. Religious icons, symbols and statues of the Virgin Mary fill every remaining cranny.

Eighty-six-year-old Teresa James and I sit in the small dining room at a Formica table and stir our coffee. Photos from the 1930s and '40s line one wall. Teresa as a nineteen-year-old, clad in jodhpurs, a zip-front leather vest over a long-sleeved blouse, and a leather flying helmet, stands beside a Travel Air OX-5 biplane flanked by a couple of adoring young male pilots. Teresa as a member of the Women's Auxiliary Ferrying Squadron, World War II, taxis a P-47 away from the flight line. The face in both pictures wears the same devil-may-care look that the woman sitting across from me wears. Only now the face is lined with character and age.

The unruly black curls evident in the vintage photos have given way to unruly blonde ones — "they said blondes have more fun; I decided to find out for myself" — but the merry brown eyes miss nothing and the smile that broke men's hearts from Long Island to Hollywood and Alaska to West Palm Beach, lights up the already warm south-Florida day.

Teresa launches into a tale of how, at age nineteen, she learned to fly — "It was a man, of course" — and laughs.

*I was never interested in flyin', but my brother Francis was.*

*He and two of his friends took off one Sunday from this field outside of Pittsburgh — it wasn't an airport, just a field surrounded by trees and wires. They were going to Detroit but only got as far as Cleveland. They ran into high winds, ran out of gas and crash landed. My brother's leg was broken, bad. They thought for awhile they'd have to amputate.*

*When he got out of hospital and was home, he couldn't drive, so he got me to drive him to the airport. I told him he was crazy, but I took him and he got me out there listening to these guys hangar flyin'. On Sunday, these guys' girlfriends would pack picnic baskets and they'd all fly off somewhere and have a picnic. They tried to get me to go along, but I wasn't havin' anything to do with flyin'.*

*Then, one day, this beautiful silver airplane lands and out steps this Greek god. Oh wow! I want to meet this guy bad. He says to me, "where you been hidin'?" Then he asks me to go flying with him the next weekend. I said no, and then I coulda killed myself. I was really nuts about that guy.*

His name was Bill and, two weeks later, Teresa did go flying with him.

*I sat stiff as a board, my feet tucked down by those rudders. It was a trainer airplane with an open cockpit, tandem — one seat behind the other — and I sat in front. I had a full set of controls in front of me just like he had in front of him. I was scared to death I'd move and accidentally touch one and throw the airplane into a spin and we'd both be killed. My ankles were frozen in one position, I could hardly walk when I got out of the plane when we got to the picnic spot. Oh, I had a good time while I was there, but all I could think about was when I had to climb back in the airplane again. Oh, God, I was terrified.*

Soon after that, Teresa learned that Bill had gone to Chicago to take an airline job. Love got put on hold for awhile.

Even though Bill was gone, Teresa continued to drive Francis to the Wilkinsburg Airport. But she refused any further offers of rides. Then Harry Fogle flew into her life.

"Harry was fresh out of Parks Air College in St. Louis. Francis kept needling me. 'Why not learn to fly and surprise Bill when he comes back,' he says. 'Get Harry to teach you.'"

So early one Sunday morning in July 1933, Teresa James took a deep breath, swallowed her terror, pulled a leather helmet over her protesting curls, secured the goggles, and stepped into the back seat of the Travel Air biplane for her first lesson.

Once in the air, Harry put the airplane in a shallow turn to the left. Teresa looked down, over the side of the plane, and quickly shut her eyes. "Oh, my God! I was so scared I reached forward and tapped him on the shoulder. When he turned around, I said 'please . . .' and motioned at the ground below. He says, through the gosport tube, "Put your feet on the rudders and your right hand on the stick. Feel what I'm doing.'

"All I felt was the wind on my face and that sinking feeling in the pit of my stomach."

But gradually, she began to follow his movements and, soon, she thought she was simply moving the stick and rudders in concert with him. They would be back on the ground before she learned that, by then, she was flying the airplane. Harry had taken his feet and hands completely off the controls.

"That airplane had no airspeed indicator — your own ears and the singing of the wind in the wires told you how fast you were going. There was an oil gauge and an altimeter on what passed for an instrument panel. The fuel gauge was a wire on a bobber. The Travel Air had no brakes — I found that out when he had me land it. And no tail wheel, just a skid, which was fine because we were landing on grass. You had to learn how to taxi."

She took a couple more lessons then, two weeks later, on August 3, Harry called her early.

"He said it was a good morning to fly, so come on out. I had a total of four hours and twenty minutes in the air when, after two practice landings, Harry got out of the airplane, picked up the tail, turned it around, and told me to take it up — solo!"

Teresa would remember the monumental implications of that moment ten years later when — once again — she sat, alone, on the runway, ready to make her first flight in the seven-ton, 2,800-horsepower single-seater, flying arsenal known as the P-47 Thunderbolt. But that's another story.

Without Harry's weight, the Travel Air literally jumped into the air as she ran it along the grass.

*By the first turn at Grand Boulevard, I was two hundred feet too high. By the second turn, over the house that was our landmark, I was four hundred feet too high. My legs were shakin' on the rudder bar and I'm really praying. I'm prayin' I'll get back on the ground safe. I hadn't been to Mass that mornin' because Harry called me so early and I'm thinking, Blessed Mother, don't desert me now. I'll go to Mass every mornin' I'm alive if you'll only help me land this thing.*

*When the wheels hit the grass, I tried to remember how Harry stopped the thing, but all I could remember was taxiing for a long time and then the tail skid settling into the grass and the airplane just kinda stoppin' of it's own accord. So that's what I did. I let it roll. I was shaking so bad, I swore I'd never get back in an airplane again. But, of course, I did.*

*A few weeks later, a flying circus came to town. And there was this stunt pilot who was trying to date me. He kept tellin' me he wanted to get me up in an airplane and teach me all these maneuvers. Yeah, what kind of maneuvers, I wondered.*

*"Teresa," he said, "we can make a stunt pilot out of you and you can make a lot of money." I liked the sound of that. And there was Francis, again, telling me how Bill would be so proud of me, learning how to fly, and how if I could do all these fancy maneuvers, he'd be even more impressed.*

*Remember, I was really in love with this guy Bill. But, of course, he had no idea I had this crush on him and he was off in Chicago. So I went up with this stunt flyer. We did a wing over and there I was hanging in my seatbelt in mid-air. The sky had disappeared and there was nothing but air between me and the ground. And I thought, stomach, stay with me now or somebody down below will get rained on.*

*Then we did a hammerhead stall, with the plane fallin' back on its tail, and a loop and, once again, I wanted to grab for the sissy bars on the side of the cockpit. But then he had me try it and I began to get the hang of it. Damn if I wasn't on my way to becoming a stunt pilot. I was already starting to add up all that money I was gonna make and we hadn't even landed.*

And the eighty-six-year-old sitting across from me who, but for the gravel in her voice, sounds like she's still nineteen, pauses and fixes me with those sprightly eyes of hers and laughs.

"Not long after that, we got word that Bill had gone and got married. I was devastated. He had no idea I had this crush on him. Breaks o' the game."

But by then, Teresa was doing stunts with the best of them — twenty-six tailspins followed by a series of loops in an OX-5 — though she claims that even when she had more than fifty hours in the air, she still was scared.

"That helped me later on when I began instructing 'cause I could relate to how the student felt, how scared he might be. I could always tell by their body language. I'd been there."

Teresa received Private License #31249 on October 12, 1934.

The world of flight was waiting for her on an 80-horsepower, single-engine platter. The war, the WAFS, and the events that would change her life were still eight years away.

# 4

The gods of aviation smiled the day in 1942 that Bob Love and Bill Tunner met over the water cooler at ATC headquarters. Colonel Bill Tunner — he would be Brigadier General Tunner a year later — was a bit of a dashing figure, young (only 36) and ruggedly handsome. A West Point graduate, Class of 1928, he had opted for the Air Corps on the basis of five flights in five different airplanes within the space of a week.

Tunner writes in his 1964 autobiography, *Over the Hump*, that during his senior year at the Academy, the cadets were given a week at Mitchel Field on Long Island in order to learn something about the Air Corps.

> Though I was never permitted to touch the controls, I still remember each flight as a thrilling experience. No tricks, no stunts, nothing but just straight flying, but that was enough for me. *Man could fly.* I was subjective proof of that electrifying statement.
>
> From there on, there was no question in my mind. Sure, the Air Corps was considered the lunatic fringe, but the extra pay and additional opportunities for travel more than made up for that. On the other hand, the washout rate was high: seven out of ten officers failed to make the grade.

Of the seventy-seven from the Class of '28 who opted for the Air Corps, fifty-five made the grade and went on to receive their wings. Bill Tunner was one of the fifty-five. His parents thought he had taken leave of his senses, but when he told them he had already been flying for a year and was, obviously, still alive, they gave tacit, if grudging, approval.

With his wings pinned to his khaki shirt and wearing cavalry breeches and riding boots, he reported to his first Army station, Rockwell Field near San Diego, California. "We didn't fly planes in those days, we rode them. We were supposed to get the feeling of the plane through the seat of our pants." Not long after, the Operations officer called him in and told him to take a three-engine Fokker to the Sacramento Depot.

He had never flown the sleek, powerful, Tri-motor Fokker before. It was, in fact, bigger than anything he had ever flown. When he climbed aboard, he found not just an airplane needing to be delivered but twelve somewhat gray-faced passengers as well. Tunner located a mechanic who could clue him into what some of the gauges, dials and switches were. Of particular importance were the switches that allowed the pilot to switch from one gas tank to another. In less time than he would have liked, he was checked out in a new airplane.

And, unlike flying today with detailed aeronautical charts, the only map available was a Rand McNally road map of California.

The short of it is, he relates in *Over the Hump*, he delivered both plane and passengers all in one piece — a trip of some 430 miles that took five hours. Mindful of a rule he had learned early — *know, every second, where you are going to land if you have to* — he kept a lookout ahead for any emergency landing places where he could set the plane down should, heaven forbid, he have to make a forced landing.

When they arrived, a sergeant, an old timer, thanked him for the ride. "Best one I ever had."

"Oh, have you flown much?" Tunner asked him.

"No, sir, Lieutenant, this was the first time I was ever in an airplane in my life."

Bob Love hadn't adequately prepared his boss for the lovely lady to whom he was married. Colonel Tunner found himself fixed in the gaze of a pair of cool, arresting hazel eyes. A maverick streak of premature gray swept back from her right temple, cut a swath through her brown hair, caught the light, and shown like a beacon leading an airplane home. Her practiced pilot's grip belied the slender, manicured, feminine hand he shook in greeting.

Here was a woman to be reckoned with. And what an ally she turned out to be for the beleaguered commander.

Yes, she told him, there were nearly a hundred proven, capable women pilots out there — probably more. Yes, she knew many of them personally, the ones on the East Coast. Then she and Tunner got down to business. Plans had to be drawn up.

Tunner recognized ability when he saw it. She had business experience from working with her husband at Inter City, organizational experience working with Phoebe Omlie on the airmarking project. Now she worked in the Central Office of the Northeast Sector, Domestic Wing, of what was about to become the Ferrying Division. Her job included mapping ferry flights and routes, learning military procedures, and helping find sources for pilots. Organization and administration came easily to her. And with nearly 1,100 hours in the cockpit, she could fly.

"Mrs. Love and I prepared a lengthy memorandum proposing a complete program for acquiring, training, and using women pilots." He adds that neither he nor Nancy knew, at that time, that Jacqueline Cochran also had proposed a program using women pilots.

As it turned out, Tunner said, "in hindsight, our plan was less grandiose than Miss Cochran's, and probably prepared in a simpler, more military manner."

He sent it off to his new commanding officer, General Harold L. George who, in April 1942, had replaced General Olds as commander of what was then known as the Air Corps Ferrying Command. In June of 1942, just as Tunner and Nancy Love were putting their plans together, the Ferrying Command was redesignted the Air Transport Command (ATC). Tunner's Ferrying Division then became the major component of the ATC. General George remained at the helm of the ATC throughout the war.

Tunner was so sure that their plan to use women as ferry pilots would be approved, he immediately went to New Castle Army Air

Base (NCAAB) in Wilmington, Delaware, where the 2nd Ferrying Group was stationed, to make arrangements for housing for the women pilots he expected to recruit. NCAAB was close to the Fairchild factory in Hagerstown, Maryland, where the primary trainers the women would be ferrying were built.

Of the birth of the WAFS, Delphine Bohn, a pilot from Amarillo, Texas, who became one of them, has this to say in her unpublished autobiography, *Catch a Shooting Star*:

> The well-established ability of women to man-handle airplanes was 'old hat.' Many military men had raced against women and had competed with them in air shows. They knew better than to denigrate the women's successes or their love of flying. These men liked most of these women. They had contributed greatly to a small aviation world.

In Bohn's opinion, General Robert Olds — to whom Nancy had gone in the first place — was an officer who held such an enlightened opinion of women's abilities. General Hap Arnold, she felt, was not.

General George did buy into the program and transferred Nancy Love to Wilmington to work with Colonel Robert Baker, base commander. The Tunner-Love connection was on its way even though General Arnold was dragging his feet in approving the idea.

Requirements the women pilots must meet were an early sticking point. Male ferry pilots could be between the ages of nineteen and forty-five. Because the Army didn't want to be "baby sitting" female minors, the age at which women would be accepted was set at twenty-one. Likewise, the men were leery of the dreaded "menopause" which they thought interfered with the ability of a woman past forty to think rationally and function properly. So thirty-five was set as the outside age for women. That way, even if the war lasted five years, the women would just be beginning to reach that "questionable" age.

The women needed five hundred hours, a commercial license, a 200-horsepower rating, and recent cross-country experience.

Women also needed a high school diploma. The men, on the other hand, were only required to have three years of secondary education and two hundred hours to qualify. Men were hired as civilians, trained for ninety days, then commissioned into the Air Forces. Why, then, couldn't the women be commissioned into the Women's Auxiliary Army Corps? But the WAAC had no provision for flying officers or for handling flight pay, so the women pilots could not be commissioned — yet. Changing those rules was up to Congress.

That alone should have been a clue that trouble lay ahead.

August 1942 was a frustrating month for Nancy Love as she awaited General Arnold's decision. He appeared to seek every possible way to avoid using women as ferry pilots. Finally, Arnold flew to England leaving the issue unresolved. In the meantime, characteristically, Nancy looked ahead, getting ready to resubmit the plan when he returned.

No one is exactly sure what happened. Upon Arnold's return, General George took something Arnold said or did as approval and, the first of September, the ATC moved quickly to activate the first women pilots' group to fly for the military, naming Nancy Love the commander. The day she got the word — September 5, 1942 — she and Colonel Baker sent the first telegrams. And with that, the Women's Auxiliary Ferrying Squadron, was on its way.

IWASM

**Nancy Love and Colonel Robert Baker
check out a wall chart for ferrying routes.**

# 5

***March 2, 2000, Lake Worth, Florida***

Teresa and I have been talking for more than an hour. The tape recorder is whirring away. In front of us are several scrapbooks. Teresa looks out from the pages — a comely young woman dressed one time in jodhpurs and a leather flying jacket, the next in a mid-calf white dress with high heels, elbow-length gloves and a white picture hat worn at a jaunty angle. Another shot shows her holding a bouquet of gladiolas in one hand and a mail sack in the other. Then there's the one with her decked out in a bulky winter flying suit. What the photos have in common, other than her image, is that there is always an airplane in the background.

"Did I tell ya about the time I popped the buttons off Giuseppe Faranessi's pants?" Teresa asks, turning to the page with the photocopy of her advanced instructor's license.

"No," I answer. "Who was Giuseppe Faranessi?"

*I had already gotten my Primary Instructor's Rating from Buffalo Aeronautical in New York, in August 1939, and was ready for my Secondary. By the winter of 1940-41, I had saved enough money to go for a course in Advanced Aerobatic and Inverted Flying. That's what I needed to teach in the Army Cadet program. There were rumors of the U.S. getting into the war. I would be teaching young men looking at flying combat.*

*I was told that Max Rappaport's Flying Service at Roosevelt Field on Long Island had the best flight instructors for aerobatics, so that's where I went. My instructor turned out to be Bill Pyhota. First I had to convince him that his efforts to scramble my brains in the air weren't going to send me packing. When we came to the understanding that I was sticking, we got down to business.*

*Finally, the day came for my flight test. I waited in the Pilot's Lounge and listened to three male pilots waiting for their tests, discussing how tough the CAA Flight Examiner, Giuseppe Faranessi, was. I was number four to fly.*

*His reputation was confirmed real fast! He flunked two guys before I got to fly. Then I overheard Bill telling the examiner there was a mechanical problem with the plane I had been flying. Faranessi's reply was "Let her fly the new one you got this morning. If she can fly one, she should be able to fly 'em all."*

*I started for the plane and got in the front seat — like I had been doing. He said "Get in the back, I'll fly the front seat." I'd never flown that plane from the back seat. The attitude [orientation of the aircraft in relation to the horizon] appears different. Anyway, we get up and in this commanding voice, he starts telling me what to do. "A slow roll to the left." I did it. Right on the money. Then he did a couple. I didn't think they were any great shakes. Then he said, "Your trouble is you're not exerting enough pressure on the stick."*

*I thought, OK, buster, this one you'll remember. I popped the control stick so fast he was straining against the belt. Then in a very calm voice he asked me to do a two and a half turn spin to the right. I was so intent on doing my best I didn't realize I was frantically chewing my gum. It's such a good tension reliever. Then I caught him looking in the rear view mirror, his jaw pumpin', mocking me chewing my gum.*

*When we got down, he didn't say a word, left me standing by the plane unbuckling my parachute harness. Bill asked how I did and I said, "I don't know. He didn't tell me."*

*Then Max appeared. He motioned me to come in. As I entered, there stood Giuseppe Faranessi holding up his pants with one hand and his suspenders with the other. "Young lady," he said, "Any woman who can pop the buttons off my pants at 7,000 feet deserves a ticket. You damn near catapulted me outta the plane."*

*I had passed!*

Teresa was now qualified to teach combat aerobatics to cadets headed for the war zone. She went home and landed a job at

Pittsburgh's Tomak Aviation Corporation. Having earned her Secondary rating, she could teach combat aerobatics to young men who wanted to fly fighters.

On September 6, 1942, Teresa, just like some eighty other experienced women pilots, received a telegram from Nancy Love and Colonel Robert Baker, U.S. Army Air Forces. Minus Western Union's standardized gibberish, here's what the telegram said:

> Ferrying Division Air Transport Command is establishing group of women pilots for domestic ferrying. Necessary qualifications are high school education, age between 21 and 35, commercial license, 500 hours, 200 horsepower rating. Advise commanding officer Second Ferrying Group, Ferrying Division Air Transport Command, Newcastle County Airport, Wilmington, Delaware, if you are immediately available and can report at once at Wilmington at your own expense for interview and flight check. Bring two letters recommendation, proof of education and flying time.

Three months earlier, in June 1942, Teresa had married her former flight student, George "Dink" Martin in a "secret" ceremony. His mother and her sister were present in Colorado Springs, Colorado, when Teresa — who had hoped to hold out for a big wedding — said "yes." The bride and her attendant, her sister Betty, wore their Civil Air Patrol uniforms for the ceremony. The "secret" was out the next day, however, when a newspaper carried the story as "Famous Stunt Pilot Married." Teresa's days on the barnstorming circuit and her famed twenty-six tailspins followed by a series of loops in the OX-5 had caught up with her.

"My mother picked up the paper back in Pittsburgh and damn near had a heart attack. She was hurt about it."

For several months after joining the WAFS, Teresa kept the fact that she was married a secret other than from her commanding officer Nancy Love and, later, Love's executive officer Betty Gillies. Several of the WAFS, in fact, were married, many of them being older than the required twenty-one and several of them very close already to the thirty-five mark. Teresa was twenty-eight.

Teresa wasn't sure what kind of ruling the military would make about married women serving and there was talk even then of commissioning them as officers — though they were recruited as civilians. Also, Dink was, at that point, an enlisted man and Teresa, as a WAFS, was treated as an officer. That meant she couldn't go out with or be seen socially with enlisted men. Imagine the fur that would fly if she showed up on the arm of an enlisted man, even if he was her husband! It wasn't until Dink entered flight training later in 1942 that he had officer status. Until then, he and Teresa had to be downright clandestine on the rare occasions that they saw each other.

Two weeks after the wedding, Dink Martin, who was with the 6th Photographic Squadron at Colorado Springs, was assigned to flight school and transferred to Santa Maria, California, for primary flight training. Teresa went back to teaching at Tomak Aviation.

It was there that the telegram from Nancy Love and Colonel Baker caught up with her. Teresa now had 2,254 hours flying time.

# 6

If Nancy Love ever felt lonely in her life, it was that August of 1942. New Castle Army Air Base was hardly more than a muddy hole in the ground.

This twenty-eight-year-old woman was accustomed to a comfortable life — she and her husband were considered well off and among the socially prominent in East Coast aviation circles. Now she was plopped down in the middle of an Army-base-under-construction with ten thousand men, all of them strangers. The handful of women, who only appeared during working hours, were civilian secretaries and administrative assistants, not pilots or women officers. There were, in fact, no women officers. The Women's Auxiliary Army Corps (WAAC) had just been established three months earlier (May, 1942) and it would be July 1, 1943 before it became the officially militarized Women's Army Corps. Nancy and Colonel Robert Baker began to get ready for what they both hoped would be the Army's first squadron of women pilots.

At first, Nancy stayed with friends who lived in Wilmington. Colonel Baker commandeered Bachelor Officers Quarters (BOQ) 14 to serve as housing for the women and proceeded to get it in readiness. First the men living there had to be moved out. Then it took forever to get Venetian blinds to cover the windows, a concession to the arrival of young women. The young men living on the up-until-now all-male army base apparently had no need for such privacy.

A ditch ran in front of BOQ 14. When Nancy saw it she realized that, in order to gain entrance, the women would have to leap over it. She suggested that wood planks be installed to allow them to walk across without tumbling into the muck below. More than one hopeful young officer, seeking a date with an attractive member of the WAFS, would come to regard that ditch as a moat not to be breached. The only males allowed inside BOQ 14 were officers on official inspections. To stand guard over the moat, and presumably the girls' honor, a housekeeper named Mrs. Anderson came to live in BOQ 14 the latter part of September 1942.

IWASM

The day the telegrams went out to eighty-three women pilots, the barracks still wasn't ready for them, but Nancy Love knew her idea's time had come and she moved forward.

First to arrive was Betty Huyler Gillies, age thirty-four, of Syosset, Long Island, New York.

Nancy and Betty already knew each other through the Ninety-Nines — Betty had just completed two years as president — and through mutual membership in the Aviation Country Club on Long Island. On receipt of the famous telegram, Betty asked her husband, Bud (B.A. Gillies), "What should I do?" And he answered, "Isn't this just what you have been preparing for and wanting to do? Go, of course."

Bud Gillies was a vice president and engineering test pilot for Grumman Aircraft. Betty was listed as "utility pilot," flying a Grumman Widgeon twin-engine airplane. Her job was to fly the engineers and the Navy inspectors to their urgent wartime meetings. She also ran flight errands, picked up needed parts from their satellite manufacturers and flew them back to Long Island. Throughout her term as president of the Ninety-Nines, Betty had urged the membership to think ahead to potential service to their country and to upgrade their skills should the war widen to include the United States. She spoke at luncheons, wrote articles, and served as a reliable source for the news media in its write-ups telling of the need for pilots in the coming hostilities. So Betty Gillies was not unprepared for her friend's telegram seeking a commitment, nor for the meaning behind it and the potential sacrifice.

Betty and Bud Gillies had two school-age children at home. Right before Christmas 1941, the Gillies' youngest child, a daughter, had died at age four of leukemia. Friends and family thought being part of the first all-woman ferrying squadron attached to the Army was a way for Betty to get her mind off the family tragedy by using her considerable aviation skills to help the war effort.

Patriotism and sacrifice were very much a part of the American landscape by mid 1942. Men and women alike sought ways to serve their country. Betty was no exception. She was anxious to do her part. Besides, Bud's position with Grumman was critical to the war effort and made him exempt from the draft. And, to further ease the decision, Bud's mother agreed to help care for the children, ages eight and nine, in Betty's absence.

"It really was hard to leave Bud and the kids, but we managed to keep in close touch and see each other from time to time. TDY [temporary duty] at Farmingdale [1943-44] was a joy to me because then I could RON [remain over night] at home. I loved flying and I was, and still am, very patriotic," she admitted fifty-five years later.

At that time, wartime flight regulations were in effect all along the coastal U.S. Pilots did not take off without a flight plan, and there had to be a reason given for the flight. The armed services could force an unidentified airplane to land.

The day after they received Nancy's telegram, Betty scheduled her flight plan to Wilmington as an Operational Instrument Training Flight. She planned to fly "under the hood" from Bethpage, Long Island, to DuPont Field, the airfield used by New Castle Army Air Base. Under the hood means to fly blind under a black cotton covering that obscures the world outside the cockpit. Pilots learn and practice instrument flying that way. Flying with Betty was Barbara Kibbee Jane, a co-worker for Grumman Aircraft's flight department. Barbara was a Ninety-Nine and she, too, had received a telegram. Barbara acted as safety, or lookout pilot on the trip down. On the trip back,

Barbara flew under the hood and Betty was the lookout.

Once they landed their Fairchild at DuPont Field, Betty and Barbara headed for Nancy's office to learn just what might be expected of them if they became pilots for the military.

"You don't have to stay for long," Nancy told them. "Just the first ninety days until we get started." For Betty, those ninety days turned into a twenty-eight-month commitment. Barbara, whose husband was a naval aviator, elected not to join the WAFS.

They flew home and Betty returned by train two days later to take her flight check. Betty faithfully kept a daily diary throughout the time she served. In her diary for those days in early September 1942, she noted:

> I told Nancy that I would be down again on Wednesday for a flight test. Wednesday, September 9 was pouring rain all day so I didn't get back to New Castle AAB until the tenth. I took the train down because the weather was lousy in the morning. But it cleared in time for me to get my check flight with Lt. Joe Tracy in a Fairchild trainer. Lt. Joe was a civilian pilot before they let him into the ATC, so his flight test didn't have any surprises. We were out about fifty minutes. Then after a bull session with Nancy Love, I caught the train for home.
>
> I guess I'm going to join the WAFS. Bud thinks it's very worthwhile trying out, and so do I. We have to sign up for three month stretches and duty begins on September 21.

Betty Gillies was the first woman, after Nancy Love, to sign up for a ninety-day appointment to the WAFS. She returned home to finish setting up arrangements for the children and reported for duty at 8 a.m. on September 21. By then, nine WAFS, counting Betty and Nancy, had survived their tests and moved into the newly opened BOQ 14.

Now, in the person of Betty Gillies, Nancy Love had a friend, a confidante and, as it turned out, an executive officer to act as second in command. She would not be lonely again for a long time.

Betty Huyler was born January 7, 1908 in New York. She was one of countless girls in her generation who were coming of age when Amelia Earhart began to capture the imaginations of all Americans, young and old, male and female.

On June 18, 1928, Amelia Earhart became the first woman to fly the Atlantic. She did not pilot the airplane, an orange pontooned Fokker; she was a passenger. Amelia vowed then and there that the next time she flew the Atlantic Ocean she would do it herself, alone. She made good on her vow on May 20, 1932, when her Vega monoplane took off from Harbour Grace, Newfoundland, and landed the following day in Londonderry, Ireland.

The fall of 1928, fresh from that first Atlantic flight and in the early stages of her fame that was to captivate America and the world for ten years, Amelia Earhart became the aviation editor of the popular women's magazine *Cosmopolitan*. And she began to set trends of independent thought and fashion for the impressionable young women of the late 1920s. Her first assignment was an article called "Try Flying Yourself." It was an invitation to young women to take to the cockpit and try their hand at the sport that seemed to be drawing the interest of a significant number of young men. This was the height of the Roaring Twenties. Young women had been emancipated from their stodgy Edwardian parents and Victorian grandparents. They could, so to speak, do anything they set their mind to.

Twenty-year-old Betty Huyler, a nursing student at Columbia Presbyterian Hospital in New York City, read the article and said, "Why not."

She knew very well the fascination flight had for young men of her generation. She was particularly mindful of the hold aviation had over a young naval aviator named Bud Gillies. Realizing that her competition was an airplane, not another woman, Betty decided to learn to

**Betty Huyler, age 21**

fly. She did so by signing up for half-hour flying lessons at Roosevelt Field on Long Island and making the long trek between classes at the hospital to the airport, via the Long Island motorway, and back. She soloed on December 23, 1928, in an OX-5 Travel Air and went on to earn her private pilot's license while continuing her nursing studies.

Soon after she obtained her license she was offered a job at the Curtiss Wright Corporation, also on Long Island. Her job was to demonstrate the new trainer airplane, the American Moth, to potential students and show them what they would be expected to learn if they took flying lessons.

With that, her nursing career ended and her flying career began.

On November 2, 1929, twenty-six licensed women pilots met at Curtiss Field on Long Island to discuss forming a woman pilot's organization. Betty was one of them. She was delighted to find her heroine, Amelia, there as well. At the time, the United States listed one hundred seventeen licensed women pilots. Ninety-nine of them responded either by attending the meeting or by letter. The group, unable to come to a decision over such names as Lady Birds or Homing Pigeons, decided on "Ninety-Nines" in recognition of their charter membership. Amelia Earhart was elected the first president.

Betty remained active with the Ninety-Nines the rest of her life. She also married her naval aviator.

It was Betty who, back in the 1930s, fought the Civil Aeronautics Administration (CAA) over the regulation that stated a pregnant woman couldn't pilot an airplane. It was a personal crusade as she was — during that decade — in the process of becoming the mother of three children while continuing to fly. Betty's contention was, if a woman can't fly while she's pregnant, she can't get in her required ten hours in six months to keep her hard-earned commercial license. If she lost her license on that kind of technicality, then she would have to take the test all over again after the baby came. It wasn't fair, she said. And it was potentially expensive.

She lost that round, but she showed her fighting spirit to be giant sized, in contrast to her actual physical stature. Betty was a petite five feet one.

The arrival of Betty Gillies on September 21 signaled a new era for Nancy Love. Nancy had been sweating out establishing a squadron of twenty-five women pilots. True, present strength now stood at eleven, but she and Colonel Baker had turned down several applicants for various reasons. Some washed out on their flight test. Some wanted to join, but could not leave their young families.

Still, she assured a nervous Colonel Baker that many of the younger, unmarried women on her list had not shown up yet because they were, for the moment, tied up with jobs as instructors with the Civilian Pilot Training (CPT) Program. These young, able, qualified women pilots had contracts to fulfill teaching basic flying skills to future fighter and bomber pilots. But they would come when they could get free.

Nancy also didn't want just anybody who could fly. She had an idea of a team approach and she wanted women with a sense of purpose who could work together. They would be in the tenuous position of women encroaching on a previously all male profession. On one side, they needed to be women about whom no potential scandal might swirl. And Nancy knew each woman must exhibit a special mix of flying skill, ability to adapt — take orders and let potential insults roll off their backs — and sheer determination. A tall order, but she knew there were

IWASM

**Nancy Love and Betty Gillies**

women out there who could do just that. She already had a few of them in her growing squadron.

The morning Betty Gillies reported at New Castle, she and the other early arrivals were sworn in as civilian pilots of the Air Transport Command. The women took the same oath men joining the Ferrying Division were required to take, except that the men would have a commission waiting for them at the end of ninety days if they fulfilled their contract and didn't screw up.

The WAFS would have officer privileges. They would also be expected to stand for roll call — in formation — at 8 a.m. Once their uniforms arrived, the WAFS would be required to march with the men in the Saturday morning air base parade.

The BOQ was declared "ready" on September 18. The women could move in. Up until then, the earliest arrivals had been staying at a guest house called Kent Manor.

BOQ 14 consisted of forty-four square-shaped rooms. Each had an iron cot, an iron chair, and a dresser. Clothes were hung from a pipe between a pair of two by fours. No door. The latrine and shower facilities were even worse.

Of her first impressions, Betty Gillies wrote in her diary:

> As I remember, my reaction to the physical properties of the base was mainly AWE! The huge airport with all the fantastic flying machines scattered about. Our quarters were rather drafty. My room was on the northwest corner and one could see daylight through several of the cracks. But I loved it! BOQ 14 was right in the center of the base and next to the Officers' Club, which we were privileged to enjoy.
>
> What we wore didn't concern me in the least. The "pinks" (standard Army-issue khaki) were fine. I guess I liked them better than the grays and blues that followed. We had the ATC insignia, the civilian pilot wings and patches, and could get any cold weather gear that the quartermaster had that would fit us.

The "choice" rooms on the second floor were grabbed by the

first WAFS to qualify — Nancy and Betty as well as Cornelia Fort, Aline (Pat) Rhonie, Teresa James, Del Scharr, Helen Mary Clark, Catherine Slocum, Esther Nelson, Helen Richards and Barbara Towne.

Barbara Poole and Alma Heflin had been sent back to get higher horsepower ratings. Poole did and eventually rejoined the squadron. Heflin, a test pilot at the Piper Cub factory in Lockhaven, Pennsylvania, didn't.

With the advent of Poole (age 25), Towne (age 26) and Richards (who had just turned 21), the younger women began to arrive, just as Nancy had predicted.

〜◎〜

The official announcement of the creation of the WAFS and Nancy's appointment as the head of the squadron was made on September 10 by Secretary of War Henry L. Stimson, in his office and in the presence of ATC commander General Harold George. That was a last minute change because General Hap Arnold had suddenly been called out of town. The following day, Arnold was back — and so was Jacqueline Cochran, fresh off the plane from England. She confronted Arnold with the newspaper article datelined September 10, 1942, announcing Nancy Love's appointment. Jackie was furious. In her eyes, Arnold had promised *her* command of a women's squadron of military flyers — if in fact one was to be organized. Arnold now had a real problem on his hands.

"I remember asking him point blank, 'What do I do now?' Cochran wrote in her second book.

"'You work directly out of my office, write down your directive, and let's train 5,000 women,' was his answer."

So a second woman pilot program was set in motion. The problem was Arnold also told General Harold George that his ATC had to find a way to work with Miss Cochran. There couldn't be two women's programs. George's solution: Nancy Love would command the women in the Ferrying Division of the ATC; Cochran would form and run a training facility for women pilots — to be known as the Women's Flying Training Detachment (WFTD). Pilots who graduated from that school would be destined to fly with Nancy Love's WAFS.

Cochran wrote:

> Between September 10 and 14, a two-pronged women's program became evident. The experimental squadron of experienced women pilots would remain part of the Air Transport Command under Nancy Love. Secondly, I would take charge of the women pilot training program and come under the direction of the Flying Training Command. I was to train five hundred women pilots, though that number was later increased to more than a thousand. I was pleased.

But Cochran later claimed the ATC "put one over" on General Arnold. Meanwhile, she was put in the hands of General Barton Yount at the Training Command in Fort Worth, Texas. Arnold told Yount to give her anything she wanted. Colonel Luke Smith, a general staff officer in Washington, D.C., to whom Cochran was briefly assigned, warned Yount that "a bundle of trouble" was headed in his direction.

"According to Smith, I was a very determined obstinate woman," Cochran says in her autobiography. "He was right about that but Barton and I usually agreed with each other. He's one of the loveliest men I've ever met."

What Cochran needed was an airfield, trainer airplanes, instructors, and facilities in which to feed and house several hundred young women. And, with Yount's help that is what she got. Initially, training was done at Howard Hughes Airport in Houston, next to Ellington Army Air Base. Aviation Enterprises, Ltd., was under a government contract that was about to expire. Yount hired them to train Jackie's girls, under Army supervision. Their original equipment was old and beat up, but newer, better equipment was coming.

The first class of twenty-five girls was scheduled to report in mid-November. On September 15, Colonel Tunner read in the news-papers that Jacqueline Cochran would be training five hundred women pilots for his Ferrying Division. Eventually Tunner expected to hire a few more women pilots — maybe one more squadron, which meant an additional twenty-five — but certainly not five hundred. And he was alarmed because the Ferrying Division's very exacting standards for the training and accepting of pilots were under fire.

Initially, Cochran agreed to consider only women with a minimum of two hundred hours and to provide them with a curriculum that, by graduation, would qualify them with 200-horsepower ratings and commercial licenses.

A couple of days later she told the press, "I've been called back by General Arnold to be head of a women's air corps in this country. Our goal is 1,500." Then she added that, as time went on, she would accept girls with lesser qualifications because, "I've had such success with my girls in England that I know this will work."

Tunner, now genuinely concerned about Cochran's interference in his command, set out to learn more about her role with the American women pilots who went to England to fly for the ATA. What he discovered was that she had a volunteer, administrative position with the ATA and held an honorary commission. But she had done no training herself, and very little flying. He also heard that Cochran had stirred up considerable resentment among the military over there, what with her flashy lifestyle and flamboyant ways.

He insisted on maintaining the Ferrying Division standards and rights of refusal of graduates of Cochran's school if they didn't measure up. At the same time, Cochran set out to make sure that her girls would be accepted by the Ferrying Division, no questions asked. General George knew, considering Cochran's clout, that Tunner was going to have to at least give them a chance.

By spring of 1943, Cochran had dropped the required hours for entrance into her school to seventy-five and then, by summer 1943, to thirty-five. She also tried to establish an additional women's ferrying squadron in Dallas to deliver the airplanes from the many aircraft factories nearby. She would be in command of that squadron, of course, but the ATC said no, it was a duplication of what the Wilmington WAFS were doing.

The battle lines were drawn and Jacqueline Cochran had only begun to fight.

In early October, Nancy Love received the following letter from her old friend Major General Robert Olds, giving a needed lift to her spirits.

October 2, 1942

Mrs. Nancy Love
Headquarters Second Ferrying Group
New Castle Army Air Base
Wilmington, Delaware

Dear Nancy,

I was terribly pleased to read of your appointment and appreciated your letter. I think one of the smartest things we ever did after the Jackie Cochran flare-up was to lay low, quietly, give you the opportunity to work into the system at Baltimore, keeping your eye on the situation at Hagerstown, and be in the most favorable and strategic position to take over when the higher-ups were finally forced to see the necessity for it. I know that you can handle the job and build it up far beyond the scope authorized at present. So, don't be surprised if I call on you unexpectedly sometime in the future for approximately 200 to 300 of your pilots to fly these tow target planes we have scattered all over the country.

I have the Civil Air Patrol under contract now, connecting many of the bases in the Second Air Force, running regular schedules, carrying mails, light parts, express and a few passengers. It is working out very satisfactorily while giving pilots in that category an opportunity to increase their piloting time and thus become eligible for service pilot ratings later on. I believe that some women could fit into this too, in the future.

Keep your chin up. Be firm and patient. Watch your weather like a hawk; and for heaven's sake bear down like a ton of bricks on the individuals who violate your regulations or make stupid mistakes. They will always repeat the same offenses if you let them off the first time.

As ever,
Bob
Robert Olds, Major General, U.S. Army

Olds' letter alludes to several things, but the "best-guess" translation is this: "The Jackie Cochran flare-up" would appear to be Cochran's letter to Hap Arnold in January that put the kibosh on Olds' plans to activate a squadron of women pilots early in 1942 following Pearl Harbor. The reference to Baltimore refers to Nancy's job with the former Ferrying Command. And Hagerstown was the home of Fairchild, the company that built the primary trainers, the open cockpit PT-19s that the WAFS initially were recruited to fly. Hagerstown's proximity to Wilmington, coupled with that of Lockhaven, Pennsylvania, where the Piper Cubs were built, were the prime factors in deciding to place the first women's ferrying squadron in Wilmington.

Towing targets for gunnery practice was one of the jobs Cochran later hit on for the graduates of her training school to perform — which shows several like minds were headed in that direction.

Apparently Olds was working with the Civil Air Patrol with an idea of using that organization as a potential supply line of ferry pilots, both male and female.

His comment on watching the weather would seem to refer to staying alert to Cochran and her plans.

The "bear down like a ton of bricks" is a warning from one experienced in command to one who isn't. The idea that the women chosen for the WAFS must be, and remain, above reproach was a strong one early on. It was very much on both Nancy Love's and Colonel Baker's minds as they sifted through the applicants. And it was a dictum that Cochran also applied to her girl trainees at her Texas flight school.

**Teresa James**

# 7

As she boarded the train for Wilmington, Teresa James began a journal that she kept until the women were deactivated in December 1944.

***September 17, 1942 — On the train en route from Pittsburgh, Pa., to Wilmington, Del.***

Here I am on my way and I still don't believe they will let us ferry airplanes for Uncle Sam! Could it be that I lack faith? Imagine it. The Spirited Women, Powder Puff Pilots, Bird Women, Sky Menaces trying to get in the Army.

Whereas, they have decided to let us try, be it resolved that come hell, high water and insulting criticism, we will not let Washington down. Amen!

***September 18, 1943, 5:45 a.m. — Hotel DuPont, Wilmington, Del.***

I cannot sleep. I don't know whether this is a normal situation or not, but I do know that I am not reacting normally to it. Am to meet two prospective WAFS in the Coffee Shop at 6:30. They can probably give me some pointers.

***September 18, 10 a.m. — Headquarters, New Castle Army Air Base***

I rode out to the Base with Aline Rhonie and Helen Mary Clark. Helen Mary was encouraging, said I had nothing at all to worry about but I find myself afraid I'll be afraid.

The cabby stopped at the guard gate for clearance to drive us to a building called BOQ 14. We drove up a three or four block long dirt road that had been graded but with no asphalt topping. The cabby stopped in front of a two-story building and the guard who had accompanied us said "this is it." And, my God, I just looked! How in the hell do you walk the planks where the steps should be? Well, we did. It's a good thing I had a little overnight bag. All I can remember was the miserable rain and mud, mud, mud!

Our new home was built from two by fours, planks and boards. One window per room, two if you had a corner room. I think at that moment I had to be crazy for leaving my comfortable home and lucrative job as flight instructor. I never expected to see such a barren structure, because I had been informed that the men who had occupied BOQ 14 had moved to another building. I was expecting furnishings. As I strode through the first floor, layered with mud, I passed the vacant rooms and was astonished at the sunlight peeking through the cracks in the walls.

I thought maybe the second floor might be better. I proceeded to the stairs in the rear of the building, climbing the 14 steps. I immediately picked out a room with the least daylight peeking through the cracks. Furnishings consisted of one sagging cot and one iron chair. I left my bag in the room and reported to Onas P. Matz at the Operations Building across the mud puddles from BOQ 14.

This is not at all what I had expected an Army Base to be. I don't know what I expected, probably old red brick buildings with ivy clinging all over.

Matz told me the reason everything was knee deep in mud and otherwise under construction was the base was new. He told me to report to Lt. Tracy for a flight check and he told me how to get to the flight line. God, I was dodging backhoes, scrapers, bulldozers and stares from civilian heavy-equipment operators and wondering how in the hell I was going to scrape off the mud from my shoes so I could work the rudder pedals.

My flight check is scheduled for 11. I hope, with fear and trembling, it will not be in that low-winged job I see in the distance. Don't know where the nose rides.

*Later — same day*

Well, the flight check was made in the low-winged job. Lt. Joe Tracy checked me out. We took off and climbed to 2500 feet. Did power stalls, 720-degree turns, lazy eights, chandelles, etc. Came back and landed and I began to wonder how everything had gone. The lieutenant didn't say a word. He didn't look encouraging or discouraging. I was told to go to Headquarters, which I did, sweating out a couple of eternities until Nancy came and told me I passed.

I feel very warm inside, but there's no use to relax, putting it pessimistically, because the Board has to pass me and I have to do the same thing at the physical.

Nancy Love is everything I thought and more! Beautiful, capable, charming. Wish she would show up right now. Twice already she has put me at ease, and I could stand it again.

*Even later — same day*

Things I Bet I Never Forget: The sensation of sitting on one side of a closed door while your destiny is being tossed about on the other side. Relief when Colonel Baker said I was accepted for training. The friendliness I saw registered in Adela Scharr's large eyes.

*Very late — same day*

I wallowed through the mud to the sub-depot to draw out flying jacket, helmet, goggles, boots, coveralls. I never was sure of my size. Now I never will be. If those coveralls are a 36, I am evidently size $13^{1/4}$.

I look forward to knowing these girls better. From all appearances and conversations, I do not have any doubts. Met Betty Gillies, a wee person with the merriest blue eyes; Esther Nelson, a tall pleasant girl who looked as if she had escaped from a page of Vogue; and Cornelia Fort. Cornelia was instructing in Honolulu that fateful day the Japs struck. After getting back on the ground with her student, they discovered a couple of bullet holes in the right wing.

What a day! Eleven years ago on this date a bomb exploded in Manchuria and gave the Japs an excuse to go a warring.— Regular school session begins tomorrow.

*September 19, 1942*

Except it didn't. We were photographed, interviewed, and measured for uniforms. 8:30 p.m. finds me dog tired.

I find I selected the wrong room. I'm across from the "bippy." Commodes flushing at all hours, singing in the shower. And speaking of the bath facilities! No doors on the stalls! No curtains on the showers! I thought I'd die of embarrassment. I have so many personal hangups to overcome! Sitting on the commode while everyone is showering and putting on their makeup in front of that mirrored wall was a bit much. Several of the girls didn't seem to mind it, but I found out later they were graduates of exclusive girls' schools. They were used to it.

*Several days later*

Our education broadens and lengthens. Meteorology. Navigation. Military Courtesy. Forward March! Lt. Jordan is a patient drill master. It looks as if the rains have come. For six days we haven't been able to fly.

New recruits from every section of the country. Helen Richards, Boise, Idaho; Barbara Poole, Detroit; Gertrude Meserve, Boston; Barbara Erickson, Seattle; Florene Miller and Delphine Bohn, Texas; and Phyllis Burchfield, Pennsylvania. They are all starting where we started.

*Late September*

Flying is flying, but Army flying is another story. Now and then in a moment of confusion, I am reminded of the old woman who didn't understand the pin because it was pointing one way and heading another.

We are used to the masculine attitude toward women and aviation, thank goodness! Funny about men. They even speculate when they see a woman back into a parking space in an automobile. If she does a good job, they swear it was luck or an accident. I wonder how they will eventually react to us. There is no such thing as flying day in and day out by luck or accident.

Mrs. Anderson came to live with us. She is official housekeeper of our BOQ. She likes girls and flying. Plenty of both here. We like her, too — so much that she has already been designated as "Andy."

Strange what a lamp or two will do to a room — even this room. My mother made sure I got my chaise lounge from home, some cotton sheets, a bedspread, curtains and a rug. And I've got my table RCA radio — birthday present from Dink.

Officers Club opened. It's nice. I know I'm going to like it. Things are going awfully fast around here. Houses, for instances. They are lines drawn in the mud at dawn and inhabited at sunset. Roads become paved thoroughfares in the twinkling of an eye. Everything seems to be mushrooming. The ugliness is being transformed from a mudhole to a busy, acceptable place.

*October 6 (Red Letter Day!)*

Gillies was made Nancy's executive officer. I was sworn into the WAFS.

*October 12*

Columbus Day. He discovered America in 1492. Again, we march. Poor Nancy! She is the one in line for sympathy, having to bear the brunt of our zigging when we should have been zagging.

We are standing on a newly paved runway watching the men pass in review this morning. They were just passing the stand when a B-24 and six P-38s took off for foreign territory and flew right over us. A goose pimple moment!

The mud doesn't matter. The continuous rain and cold don't matter. I'm just so proud to be here, to be a part of this Army. There's something a little difficult to describe about soloing a plane with a big star on it.

*October 19*

We were graduated today. Eight of us! Our cross country in PT-19s is finished. Can't wait for orders to deliver. Our uniforms are green-gray with both skirt and trousers and overseas cap. They were designed for utility and not glamour, I read somewhere, which reminds me that I certainly hated the snip, snip of the scissors that cut my long hair. Somebody told Nancy they didn't think it was very military looking. True, this is really no place for it but I hated to see my curls go. Faces are going to be lucky if they get any attention.

*October 20*

Slept swell last night. Dreamed I was ferrying a bomber. Well, they didn't say we could, but they didn't say we couldn't either.

**Nancy Batson**

# 8

The sun was just beginning to burn off the October morning fog when the taxicab pulled up at the guardhouse. The sharp smells of aviation fuel and metal, the musty odor of dampness, and the crisp, clean aroma of autumn competed for air space as the tall blonde climbed from the cab. She wore a stylish brown herringbone suit, small matching hat and brown leather high-heeled pumps.

Belying her slender build, hands capable of controlling a balky airplane in weather wrestled three suitcases out of the cab. After paying off the cabby, the young woman carried two of the bags to the guardhouse, deposited them at the door, returned to pick up the third and dropped it next to the other two.

The minute he saw her step from the cab, the MP on duty rang a familiar number down at the flight line. He spoke into the telephone. "Miz Love. I got another one."

The MP's call produced a Jeep driven by a young GI. Before he could set the brake and hop down from his perch, the young woman had hoisted her suitcases into the back seat. Then she climbed in beside him.

"Hey," she said, in a voice that carried a distinct southern drawl, "I'm Nancy Batson from Birmingham, Alabama, and I've come to join the WAFS." The word "hey," when spoken by a Southerner, translates the same as the more Yankee-fied "hi."

Until three days earlier, twenty-two-year-old Nancy Batson had been a flight instructor at Embry-Riddle Aeronautical Institute in Miami. She was about to become number twenty of a total of twenty-eight women — later known as The Originals — who would be accepted into the Women's Auxiliary Ferrying Squadron at New Castle Air Base, Wilmington, Delaware, between September 1942 and January 1943.

On October 12, 1942, Nancy Love was, by her own reckoning, behind in recruiting the first twenty-five of what was authorized to be a fifty-woman squadron. It had been over a month since she sent the telegram looking for willing recruits among America's elite professional or experienced amateur women pilots. Many of them had answered the call and already a dozen had qualified for the program. Getting wind of the search for women pilots, several not-so-qualified also had descended on New Castle. She and base commander Colonel Robert Baker already had turned down some of the more bizarre applicants.

Here, Nancy Love surely must have thought, was another one who had come without benefit of a summoning telegram.

But Nancy Batson had no idea of the consternation she might have created — if any — at Love's headquarters. This time the driver, an enlisted man but nevertheless a gentleman, was quicker on the uptake. Out of the Jeep in a flash, he grabbed and carried two of her bags inside the gray wood-siding building leaving the smallest, lightest one for the "looker" to carry herself.

In one glance, Nancy took in what would become her second home in the ensuing months — a drab military office complete with gray metal filing cabinet, folding chair and desk. But what really riveted her attention was the trim young woman, dressed in a fitted, gray-green gabardine, collared jacket and matching trousers, who sat behind the pockmarked desk. This was the other Nancy — Nancy Love herself. A startling streak of gray swept back through her otherwise brown hair. Her inquisitive eyes seemed to see through the younger woman who now stood, suddenly ill at ease, in front of her.

Nancy Love put out her manicured left hand and Nancy Batson handed over her precious log books, where a pilot's best and worst and every flight in between are recorded. That's when Nancy Batson was treated to a full glimpse of one of the biggest diamond engagement rings she had ever seen. A matching wedding ring completed the set. Later that evening over drinks and dinner, Miss Batson learned that Mrs. Love was wife of Major Robert Love of Colonel Tunner's staff. Wow, she's not only gorgeous and a crack pilot, young Batson thought, she's married as well and to a major. One side of what was to become a lasting mutual admiration society had begun.

"Sit down, Miss Batson." Nancy did as she was told and perched nervously on the edge of the uncomfortable metal folding chair.

Love glanced through the log books. Batson noted what appeared to be a satisfied smile when Love came to the total number of hours listed on the final page — 503. Just enough!

"And your other credentials?"

Nancy handed Mrs. Love her certificates and ratings, her high school and college diplomas, and two personal letters of recommendation.

"Excuse me a moment." Love got up from her desk, walked to an adjacent door and entered another office that bore the name Colonel Robert M. Baker. When the door swung open, Batson saw a man in uniform seated at the desk inside. He had dark hair and a black mustache.

While Batson waited, another tallish young woman strolled in. She was wearing zip-up khaki overalls.

There's one, Batson thought. She's one of them. And she watched as the black-haired girl casually picked up what was obviously her mail from the mail slots on the wall, glanced coolly in Nancy's direction and then strolled out.

Confidence, Batson thought, she exudes confidence. I'm going to be like that.

The belle from Birmingham had every reason to believe exactly that.

### June 23, 1999 — Birmingham, Alabama

*When I was seven years old, my mother took me by the hand to the municipal auditorium in Birmingham to see Charles Lindbergh. We stood there on the sidewalk outside — it was October 1927, just a few months after he flew the Atlantic solo, the first man to do that. We watched as he and some other men got out of a car and walked into the auditorium. That's all. But we saw him. He was so tall!*

*My mother knew then that I had a yen for anything related to airplanes. When I was little, my bicycle was my very own airplane and I pretended it had a double set of wings to match the biplanes I'd seen. I didn't want to be a ballerina in a poufy pink dress, I wanted to wear jodhpurs, jacket, boots and a white silk scarf. That's what all the flyers wore.*

*The first Saturday in June, the Birmingham municipal airport put on an air show. The year I started driving, I was taking my father out to play golf—he was letting me keep the car while he was on the course—and we passed by the airport. Near the fence was a silver biplane, a tail-dragger, and there was this girl standing by it. She was putting on a helmet and goggles and I thought, that girl is going to fly that airplane!*

*Well, a few years later, I was a sophomore at the University of Alabama, this boy I was dating said "Nancy, they're givin' rides in an airplane for $2 down at the Tuscaloosa airfield." He and I hopped in his open-air roadster, drove down there, and paid our $2 each.*

*The plane was a Ford tri-motor. We sat inside in wicker chairs and looked out this tiny window. But I remember watching the ground droppin' away as we took off and I thought, I'm flyin'! The flight was only ten minutes—five minutes over to Tuscaloosa and five minutes back, but I was hooked.*

That was in the fall of 1938. In 1939, General Hap Arnold authorized the Civilian Pilot Training (CPT) program and placed it on college campuses around the country. His idea was that young men, wanting to be pilots, would flock to the subsidized learn-to-fly program. Flying was expensive but that move put flight training within reach of anyone who could afford to go to college.

Hap was a cagey character. He sensed the larger war coming, though at that point, only Europe was in flames. Britain was threatened with potential invasion by German forces. An air war veteran of World War I, Arnold knew that World War II would be fought and won in the air. But in 1939, the Air Corps (as the Army's aviators were then known) only had about a thousand pilots, including the Reserve. He needed men.

The only snag he hit was the fact that his CPT program "smelled" of exactly what it was: preparation for war. However, at this time, the U.S. was a peace-seeking country that professed neutrality in the current exchanges of fire. So how could Hap Arnold make the program appear non-war related? Why, open it up to women, of course.

Nancy Batson continued her story:

*One day this girl came running into the dormitory dining room hollerin' that the Civilian Pilot Training Program was coming to the University of Alabama and they were going to take one woman for every ten men signed up to learn to fly.*

*I couldn't wait to get out of there. I ran across campus to find Professor Fred Maxwell who was the man I had to see to get admitted to the program. He told me I needed three things: permission from my parents since I wasn't twenty-one, forty dollars, and a physical examination.*

*Well, it just happened that my father came through Tuscaloosa that evening on his way home from a building job and stopped on campus to see me. My father was a contractor and he built roads and bridges. "Daddy, Daddy," I said, "they're starting a CPT program here and they'll take five girls along with fifty boys. I've gotta be in that program, Daddy. I want to learn to fly."*

*"Sis, you're crazy," he said, but the more I talked, the quieter he got. I finally ran out of talk, but by then, he could see I was enthusiastic. "Well, I'll talk to your mother," he said.*

*My younger sister, Amy, later told me what happened the next morning when Daddy told Mother. She just said to him, "Well, write out the check and give it to me. I'll get it in the mail this morning."*

*I had two things that are very important to flying — a sense of adventure and good coordination. My mother had a sense of adventure and she passed it on to me. I got my good coordination from my father, who played football for Auburn. My mother encouraged me. She never tried to stop me, never told me not to do something because I'd get hurt. Even when my only brother was killed in flight training in 1943, my parents never asked me to stop flying. My mother was proud of my flying 'til the day she died. She used to say, "She does it so well."*

*Thanks to Hap Arnold, for nearly two years, one college coed learned to fly for every ten college men. Then the program was closed to women in 1941 when war appeared so imminent that Congress finally was willing to finance it as a method of training pilots for combat. By then, I had my bachelor's degree from the University of Alabama and my private pilot's license and was moving toward a commercial license — which I got in the spring of 1942. So I went to Nashville and tried to join the Air Transport Command. I couldn't believe it when they told me they only took men.*

*Well, I went home and earned my instructor's rating in Birmingham and tried to land a job flight instructing with the school I had just gotten my ticket from. The embarrassed looks I got from the director of flying preceded the news that they weren't currently looking for flight instructors. What he didn't say was, they weren't looking for WOMEN flight instructors.*

*So then I went to Embry-Riddle Aeronautical Institute in Miami where I was hired to give primary instruction to Army cadets. Two weeks after I got there, I heard from home that two new instructors — male, of course — had just been hired at my old flying school.*

*I was one of three women flight instructors at Embry-Riddle — teaching men my age and younger to fly — when, in late September, a newspaper article caught my eye. The ATC — the ones who had turned me down in Nashville — was forming a woman's squadron to ferry airplanes.*

*I told my boss at Embry-Riddle, "That's where I belong."*

*But I had so recently acquired sufficient hours to qualify, my name didn't appear in Nancy Love's searches for qualified women pilots. Of course, the lack of that little piece of yellow paper from Western Union was no barrier to me. A few days later, I was on the train headed for Wilmington, Delaware, unannounced. It never occurred to me to wire ahead.*

All of that was running through Nancy's mind as she awaited Nancy Love's return from Colonel Baker's office. She didn't have to cool her heels long. Love was back quickly.

"You may spend the night in the BOQ where the other girls are staying. Tomorrow, we'll give you a flight test."

Another GI escorted Nancy to BOQ 14. As she recalls, wood planks stretched over a murky ditch that ran in front of the entrance. Carrying one of her bags while the GI carried the other two, Nancy — still dressed in her brown suit, hat and high heels — picked her way gingerly across the abyss to the other side and up the stairs to what would be her quarters on the second floor. A ten by ten cubicle with metal Army cot, dresser, mirror and a rod from which to hang her clothes greeted her. She sat down on the cot and surveyed the otherwise bare room.

This is the Army, Miss Batson, she thought to herself, paraphrasing a popular song of the day. What have you gotten yourself into?

**Lined up for inspection by Colonel Robert Baker and Nancy Love are
Betty Gillies, Esther Nelson, Cornelia Fort, Teresa James, Catherine
Slocum, Del Scharr, Helen Mary Clark and Aline Rhonie.**

## 9

"When we all assembled in Wilmington, it was like we spoke different languages" says Gertrude Meserve, who arrived September 30. "Florene with her Texas drawl, Nancy Batson and her even more leisurely Alabama drawl, Jamesy with her slangy Pittsburghese, me from Baahston."

Not only did their speaking styles vary, but their backgrounds were vastly different, too — from wealthy Southern socialite Cornelia Fort to Evelyn Sharp, who was raised by adoptive parents struggling through the Depression years in rural Nebraska. Four were from prominent East Coast families: Barbara Donahue (Woolworth), Betty Gillies (Huyler Candies), Catherine Slocum (Luden Cough Drops), and Helen Mary Clark, whose husband was from a well-known real estate family. Betsy Ferguson and Bernice Batten hailed from the wheat farming communities of eastern Kansas. Teresa James was the daughter of a Pittsburgh florist; Del Scharr, the daughter of a St. Louis police officer; and Nancy Batson, the daughter of a Birming-ham building contractor. And Aline "Pat" Rhonie was a divorcée who already had served with the British Red Cross Ambulance Corps in France before Dunkirk.

Most were employed in aviation as flight instructors. A couple were corporate or charter pilots or flight service owners like Dorothy Fulton and Esther Nelson. Esther was also a qualified interior decorator. Pat Rhonie was an artist who painted aviation murals. Del Scharr had her master's degree in psychology and had taught disadvantaged children in the St. Louis public schools until she married Harold Scharr. She was forced to quit because the schools wouldn't employ married women teachers. So she taught flying and ground school instead.

In age, they covered the allowed span — Helen Richards being the youngest at barely twenty-one; Betty Gillies, Pat Rhonie, and Del Scharr all thirty-five or close to it.

Admission to the squadron required that they be high school graduates. By today's standards, that carries little significance, since bachelor's degrees have become the basic qualification requirement and advanced degrees are more common place. Actually, finishing school and attendance at one of the exclusive eastern women's colleges was the norm among the earliest arrivals — with the exception of Teresa James and Del Scharr. As the younger women arrived, the mix became more diverse, more democratic, as Nancy Batson likes to characterize the group.

Teresa delights in telling the story of an early BOQ 14 bull session where the women bragged about their impressive alma maters. Nancy Love and Barbara Donahue both attended Vassar and Cornelia Fort had spent two years at Sarah Lawrence in Bronxville, New York. Then Betty and Cornelia — more than ten years apart in age — discovered that they both were graduates of The Ogontz School, a fashionable finishing school in Philadelphia that was also Amelia Earhart's prep school alma mater.

By then, Colonel Baker had announced that the women would be required to march just like the men on the base. Betty and Cornelia revealed — with some degree of pride — that they already knew how to march in formation. "I was a drill sergeant at Ogontz," petite Betty told the gathering. "We marched on the hockey field and carried heavy guns made of wood."

"We were the only girls' school I know of with military battalions — three of them," Cornelia chimed in.

"I should have been kicked out of that school for things I did," Betty admitted, laughing at her memories of a misspent youth. "The seniors at Ogontz got to have parties in the woods and we undergrads would slip out and heckle them. We climbed down the slate roof to where the garbage truck came in and slid down from there. One night we got caught. The headmistress threatened to stay in my room all night to keep me there 'unless you promise you won't go out again.' I said 'Miss Sutherland, I promise I won't go out.'"

"I once crawled out a window in a biology class to avoid having to dissect a frog," Cornelia added.

"Well," Teresa cleared her throat, "I always thought the education to be had at Thorne Hill was the absolute best money could buy."

That brought the conversation to a stand still. Then, slowly, a chorus of courteous nods went round the circle. No one was familiar with that particular school but, their social upbringing and impeccable manners showing, everyone was too polite to ask for clarification.

Quiet, shy Gertie Meserve sat looking intently at Jamesy, barely managing to hide her grin and smother her infectious giggle, but she didn't say a word. Only her raised eyebrows might have given her away. She had heard of Thorne Hill and knew Teresa was pulling their legs. But she didn't blow her cover.

The story came out years later when Teresa finally admitted, "Thorne Hill is a correctional school for boys in Pittsburgh. But I got tired of all the fancy talk about Wellesley, Vassar, and Smith. Then when Betty and Cornelia started exclaiming over this Ogontz School, I couldn't control myself." And she hoots with laughter at the memory.

"Only Jamesy with her raucous sense of humor could have pulled it off," says Gert.

Once the press got wind of the fact that women were being hired to fly airplanes for the Army, New Castle Army Air Base was deluged with reporters and photographers and requests for interviews. This, it seemed, was the story of the century. Strikingly beautiful Nancy Love was subjected to requests for "cheese-cake shots"— showing lots of leg or a bare shoulder. She endured commands like, "Give us a smile — a big one now. Show your teeth." She even made the list of Best Legs Among Women in Public Life in America in 1942 — in the company of movie star Dorothy Lamour and radio's Gracie Allen of "George Burns and Gracie Allen" fame. Nor were the other WAFS immune from this attention.

"No one had anticipated the heavy, widespread publicity," Delphine Bohn says. "The military was deeply affronted that this strange, multifaceted publicity could afflict them so. We were women looked upon as two-headed oddities. Everyone wished to examine each of us minutely. For some of us it was purely terrorizing."

Many of the stories written and disseminated were blatantly incorrect, grossly exaggerated, or just plain fabricated. The Army tried to protect the women from the spotlight, but they were under not only the bright glare of publicity, but the microscope of public opinion as well. To their credit, not a word of scandal was ever connected with one of The Originals during the time they served Uncle Sam.

In preparation for his newly coed base, Base Commander Colonel Robert H. Baker put out a memorandum on September 21, 1942. The WAFS would be designated Civilian Pilots. They would have all the privileges of officers including the use of the Officers Club and the Officers Mess. They would stand formation and roll call along with the men at 8 a.m. each morning. And they would live in BOQ 14 during their indoctrination period.

The indoctrination period consisted of thirty days, twenty-five hours of flight, and seventy-two hours of ground school made up of a review of communications, navigation, meteorology, power plants, military forms, military law, and military drill. Flight instruction consisted of re-familiarization with standard flight maneuvers and cross-country navigation. After that, ground school was continually in progress and when not out ferrying, pilots were expected to attend and keep updated on increasingly complex aircraft, advanced communications and instruments, and Link trainer (instrument training) time.

Then, when the women's uniforms arrived, Colonel Baker decided the WAFS needed to take part in the base's close order drill, as well. Nancy Love and her girls found themselves in for a challenge. Other than Betty and Cornelia, with their Ogontz School experiences, and Teresa who had been in the Civil Air Patrol, marching was a new experience.

"Nancy's inability to develop a loud-mouthed 'hup, two, three, four' Marine drill sergeant style was legend," says Delphine Bohn. "It caused her to develop occasional mental lapses when we were drilling."

"We were obliged, among other routine indoctrination courses, to learn close-order drill. As Commander, I had to lead the formation and give the commands, which, because I was very self-conscious, was not one of my strong points," Nancy Love said of her own self-admitted inadequacy. "In fact, I so hated having to roar out orders that I occasionally drew a blank on what command to give next. This happened to me one dreary morning when we were drilling on an inactive runway. The squadron was marching smartly down the paved runway toward its end, where there was a sharp drop-off of about ten feet. Panic struck me as we approached the precipice and I found myself incapable of giving the command, 'To the rear — march!'

"So off went twenty-four girls, still in close formation and roaring with laughter. Straight down the embankment they went and into the field, leaving me standing at the top, still speechless."

"When Delphine Bohn was writing her book back in the 1980s, she wrote to all of us asking what we thought was the single quality present in all of The Originals," B.J. Erickson says. "We were so very diverse. I don't think she ever came up with that single link."

The common thread that tied this group of otherwise "rugged individualists" together was that they flew airplanes and, in the late 1930s and early 1940s, women who flew airplanes were NOT the norm. However, the American public did hear a lot about the few women who flew, most notably Amelia Earhart and Jacqueline Cochran. The names Louise Thaden, Ruth Nichols, Elinor Smith, Phoebe Omlie, Bobbi Trout, Viola Gentry, Blanche Noyes, Helen McCloskey, and Helen Richey may not have been the household words Earhart and Cochran were, but their ventures into the male-dominated world of aviation were noteworthy. The press did pay attention and recorded their accomplishments and feats of daring.

Louise Thaden, a founding member of the Ninety-Nines along with Amelia Earhart and Betty Huyler Gillies, was considered by many to be a far more skilled pilot than either Amelia or Jackie. In 1979, looking back forty years for Claudia M. Oakes's book, *United States Women In Aviation 1930 to 1939*, Thaden described it "as the first time women began to be accepted on their own merits as pilots. It was a time of growth and exploration, when all 'firsts' were *really* firsts, a time when camaraderie existed because words were not always necessary between fellow pilots, a time of instant friends and a spirit of cooperation, and most of all, a sense of something shared."

Nancy Love became part of that select sorority when she joined Thaden and the others in the Airmarking project. She took those ideals and the camaraderie of the older women pilots with her into the WAFS several years later.

∾⊘⊚∿

When the Ninety-Nines were founded in 1929, one hundred seventeen American women held pilots' licenses. Twelve years later, when Nancy Love and Jacqueline Cochran went searching the Civil Aeronautics Administration records for licensed women pilots, the number had risen to 2,733. Cochran boasted to General Arnold that two thousand women were qualified to fly for the Army, but only one hundred fifty had more than two hundred hours flight time. And she had to work hard to gather twenty-three from that number to take to England in the spring of 1942.

Nancy worked equally hard to get her magic twenty-five a few months later to launch the WAFS. She had found only eighty-three women who met those qualifications the Ferrying Division set for women pilots: five hundred hours, 200-horsepower rating, recent cross-country experience, between the ages of twenty-one and thirty-five, and in possession of a high school diploma.

Thaden, Nichols, Omlie and Noyes could have qualified but for the age constraint. Many others, such as Ninety-Nine's founder, Nancy Hopkins Tier, couldn't see their way clear to leave their young families. Although a lot of men went off to war and left their wives and children home, not many wives went off to war and left their husbands home. Three WAFS were exceptions — Betty Gillies, Helen Mary Clark, and, briefly, Catherine Slocum, all with school-age children. Nancy Love, Teresa James (married name Martin), Del Scharr, Katherine Rawls Thompson, Phyllis Burchfield (married name Fulton), Helen McGilvery, Barbara Towne (married name Dickson), Esther Nelson, Dorothy Fulton, Lenore McElroy, and Esther Manning (married name Rathfelder) had husbands serving in the armed forces in some capacity.

On October 19, at the end of the first thirty-day training period, eight WAFS graduated and began ferrying airplanes: Nancy Love, Betty Gillies, Cornelia Fort, Pat Rhonie, Helen Mary Clark, Del Scharr, Teresa James and Esther Nelson. Catherine Slocum finished the training period but immediately resigned. Her husband needed her at home to help with their four children as the housekeeper had fallen and injured herself. By then, another dozen women pilots had been accepted for their thirty-day training and were living in the BOQ.

On October 22, 1942, six WAFS were assigned to deliver six L4-B's, or Cubs, from the Piper factory in Lockhaven, Pennsylvania, to Mitchel Field on Long Island. Nancy Love appointed Betty Gillies flight leader. With her would be Fort, Rhonie, Clark, Scharr and James.

Their new gray-green wool uniforms — fitted by a tailor in Wilmington — had arrived, just in time for them to wear on the trip. In 1942, the world was not used to seeing women in slacks. In fact, women in slacks were most often refused entrance into restaurants — something the WAFS contended with early on. The only answer to a snobbish maitre d' was for a WAFS attired in trousers to accept the snub, be turned away, and hope for a more liberal policy elsewhere. The WAFS were not out trying to prove they could wear pants. They only wanted to prove they could fly.

On this, their first official outing, they wore the slacks under their flight coveralls and packed their skirts, their proper brown medium heeled shoes, and brown leather handbags with shoulder straps in their B-4 bags.

"Those shapeless khaki B-4 bags are assigned to all ferry pilots," Teresa recalls. "They're made of canvas and are coat length when unzipped. They have huge patch pockets on each side. No matter how much is put in them, there is still room for one more coat and a medium-sized cook stove. I took four or five things I didn't need and left several I did, but that was no fault of the equipment. After all, foresightedness was not one of the items issued at the sub-depot."

The six ferry pilots, anxious to shake the down from their wings and fly for real, boarded a Boeing twin-engine transport, piloted by none other than Colonel Baker, for the short flight to Lockhaven. "Black Bob," as they called him because of his black mustache, had taken pity on them and decided to send them off for their first trip by air — far preferable to spending four hours in a Pullman car and rising at five in the morning to get off the train in Lockhaven.

Even though the Piper factory employed numerous women, the arrival of women ferry pilots was a big deal. According to Teresa, "necks stretched and eyes popped. They couldn't have stared any more had we been freaks from the circus side show."

The six inspected their ships, climbed in and prepared to take off. A twenty-five-mile-an-hour wind was blowing from the west, promising them a hefty tail wind all the way to Long Island.

"Those little four-cylinder go-carts actually leaped into the air," Teresa remembers. "Clark had never flown such a light ship and we laughed when she said later, 'Jeepers, I just couldn't keep the thing on the ground.'

"We RONed in a hotel in Allentown, Pennsylvania — two to a room. We had been thoroughly trained and familiarized with how to fill out the necessary RON (Remain Over Night) forms, but that's like making an *A* in geometry at school and trying to apply the knowledge when you need to build a fence later in life.

"Then we got a glimpse of ourselves in a full-length mirror for the first time. BOQ 14 had no such luxury. We were horrified. The pants bagged in the seat and the legs were big enough for two. The tailor, used to measuring male legs and rumps, had mis-configured the trousers meant for a female form!"

As per Betty's orders, they were up at sunrise the next morning. Nancy had already warned them not to fly in formation like the men. Her instructions were, "Stay at least five hundred feet away from each other and anything else as well — and that includes clouds — and high enough over towns that you can deadstick outside them in case of emergency."

Deadstick means no power. If the engine quits, the pilot hopes to be high enough to spot an open space in which to land the little ship and then establish a glide path to get her there.

The flight leader's job was to assign the navigator for each leg. The navigator led until she was about ten miles from the airport destination, at which time she was to throttle back so the flight leader could come forward to take them into the airport. "From then on you move in echelon formation," Del Scharr recalls Nancy telling them, "single file with each airplane a bit to the right of the one in front of it."

The night before, when Betty talked to her husband, Bud, he had warned her that bombing practice was planned the following day in the area where they would be flying. All flying was ordered grounded during the bombing. So Betty wired Mitchel Field operations to let them know the WAFS were coming in with deliveries that morning and to call off the guns until they could get the planes safely on the ground.

Cornelia navigated the first leg, but when they got to New Jersey, Betty, being familiar with the look of the greater New York area from the air, took the lead. "When we got over New York, I couldn't tell Brooklyn from Coney Island in all that mass of buildings," Teresa says.

"They were expecting us at the airport and every man who could leave his post was outside to watch us land. I can just imagine the remarks that flew right and left. 'Those dames! Why don't they get smart and let the men run this Army.' 'Steady, men, we'll probably see some high bouncing and modernized ground loops!' 'Line up, fellas, and protect the buildings.'

"Well, six little Cubs came in and made six perfect landings. We had made the trip in sixty-five minutes. Betty was so pleased!"

Flight leader Gillies then signed over the planes to a thunder-faced officer, who told her — in no uncertain terms — that he needed them two months ago, not now.

"That's not my problem," she said, sweetly. "I'm merely following orders. You may speak to my commanding officer, Colonel Robert Baker at New Castle Army Air Base, or call Colonel Tunner himself at Ferrying Division headquarters." She gave the man a big smile.

Considering the man's rudeness, and knowing Betty, the others knew that her smile was delivered around clenched teeth. About then the phone rang. It was the telegram Betty had sent asking them to call off the bombing until the Cubs were safely in. Only it was a couple of hours late being delivered.

"Betty paled when she heard the news," Teresa remembers. "But the Cubs were safely in, no thanks to either Western Union or Operations at Mitchel Field."

Nothing kept Betty down for long. With her airplanes safely delivered, she won over the other men in Operations — ignoring the one who told her he didn't want the planes anymore. She enlisted the help of someone else who succumbed more readily to her polite smile and cultured voice and asked him to call for ground transportation for six WAFS, to get them to the Aviation Country Club nearby. Betty and Pat Rhonie were members and, therefore, they would all be welcome.

"Betty's call to Nancy in Wilmington netted us the afternoon off," says Teresa, "so she called home. Her family seemed quite surprised to hear from her. This was when we realized that our families and friends expected us to fall off the face of the earth and never be heard from again. We all split up for the next few hours. Gillies went home. Clark dashed off for Jersey to see her husband and two children. Fort called some friends. She was like a sailor — friends in every port. Rhonie dashed off somewhere.

"It was Scharr's first time in New York, so she and I decided to see the city, including Radio City and the Rainbow Room. We marched right down Broadway in those strange-fitting trousers. Our uniforms got many stares, wild looks and questions. At least seventy-five people asked us what we were. They mistook us for everything from Red Cross Volunteers to Junior Commandos. We hereby stake our claim to being the first WAFS in New York City.

"Scharr was curious about slot-machine food, so we ate at the automat.

"Everybody met back at Pennsylvania Station at 6:30. Helen Mary brought her family to meet us. Her boys were ten and twelve, and certainly something for her to be proud of. And were they ever proud of their mother!

"Back at base, the others swore we had been gone a week. We'd only been gone two days. It was fun — in fact, so much fun that we were anxious to go right back out the next day."

IWASM

**Nancy Batson, Delphine Bohn,
Gertrude Meserve and Helen Mary Clark**

**Barbara Poole, Major Gibson, Esther Manning, B.J. Erickson, Evelyn Sharp and Barbara Donahue at an Army air base in North Carolina**

**Eight Wilmington WAFS in their Army overcoats, winter 1943. Helen Mary Clark, Nancy Batson, Helen McGilvery, Teresa James, Gertrude Meserve, Esther Nelson, Betty Gillies and Dorothy Fulton**

# 10

Ferrying began in earnest on November 1, when the squadron stood at twenty. By then, several more had passed their thirty-day trial period and had been added to the active list. At first, a few WAFS at a time were dispatched to Lockhaven to pick up Cubs. The women left Wilmington in small groups to deliver these airplanes to cadet flight training facilities located across the southern United States. The squadron was up and running.

Then on December 19, 1942, the list reached the magic number of twenty-five. In the order of their acceptance, they were:

1. Nancy Love
2. Betty Gillies
3. Cornelia Fort
4. Aline (Pat) Rhonie
5. Helen Mary Clark
6. Adela Scharr
7. Esther Nelson
8. Teresa James
9. Barbara Poole
10. Helen Richards
11. Barbara Towne
12. Gertrude Meserve
13. Florene Miller
14. Barbara Jane Erickson
15. Delphine Bohn
16. Barbara Donahue
17. Evelyn Sharp
18. Phyllis Burchfield
19. Esther Manning
20. Nancy Batson
21. Katherine Rawls Thompson
22. Dorothy Fulton
23. Opal (Betsy) Ferguson
24. Bernice Batten
25. Dorothy Scott

Two of the earliest women accepted — Alma Heflin and Catherine Slocum — never ferried. Heflin was listed briefly on the roster in September, but she never obtained the necessary horsepower rating to qualify for the thirty-day training. Betty Gillies commented on Heflin's departure in an entry in her diary dated October 1, 1942, "We lost one of our members today, Alma Heflin. She wasn't at NCAAB even ten days."

Alma Heflin McCormick — she had just married an RAF pilot bound for England — was a test pilot for Piper and also the author of several books about her adventures flying Cubs over some pretty unforgiving terrain in Canada and Alaska. She passed her initial flight test for the WAFS but was sent back to get the 200-horsepower rating she was missing. Apparently, she did not get it.

Betty also commented on Catherine Slocum. "She completed training at NCAAB and was ready for orders, but felt that the job would keep her too far away from home for too long. So she resigned to go home and take care of her four small children. Catherine left October 20, which was two days before we received our first orders. So Catherine didn't do any ferrying — to the best of my knowledge." Slocum was actually the sixth woman admitted to the squadron but is not counted in the final roster since she never ferried.

**Sis Bernheim**                    IWASM

Aline (Pat) Rhonie was the fourth woman to qualify for the squadron. She enlisted for the initial ninety-day period and made several ferrying trips between October 22 and late December. She resigned the end of December. Rhonie is always counted as one of the final number of "official" WAFS — twenty-eight — because she actually ferried airplanes for the Ferrying Division.

In January 1943, the following women were added to the list: Kathryn (Sis) Bernheim, Helen McGilvery and Lenore McElroy.

Bernheim and McGilvery got Nancy Love's approval and were accepted in Wilmington on January 3, 1943, after passing their flight checks. Later in the month, McElroy joined the 3rd Ferrying Group stationed in Romulus, Michigan. She never went through the training in Wilmington; instead she did her thirty-day orientation in Romulus.

With the acceptance of those final three, The Originals were in tact and ready to go into the history books as the first women to fly military airplanes for the U.S. Armed Forces. The squadron now officially numbered twenty-seven.

రుSo్కు

On November 10, Gillies, Fort, Richards, Erickson, Poole, Towne and James took seven Cubs south. Flying into Charlottesville, Virginia, both Poole and Fort nosed over, damaging the propellers of their airplanes. The field had been under water for three weeks and was a sea of mud, something they had no way of knowing. Richards landed safely, but went in up to her knees when she got out of her airplane. The others got down as best they could. The accidents were hardly the WAFS' fault.

Leaving the two with their damaged planes, the other five continued on south. Helen Richards delivered to Selma, Alabama, and Barbara Towne to Jackson, Mississippi. The other three headed for New Orleans where they managed dinner at the famed restaurant, Antoine's. Erickson went home the next morning and Gillies and James continued on to make their deliveries in Lake Charles. As was to be the custom for some time, each pilot caught an airliner back to Wilmington after making her delivery.

The Air Transport Command's tenet for delivering airplanes was "rapidly but with safety." Ferrying in late 1942 and early 1943 was not something that could be done swiftly. Cubs had a fuel capacity of twelve gallons, 65-horsepower engine, and averaged 75 miles per hour. They had to make frequent stops to refuel. The Cubs carried no radios and only rudimentary instrumentation, so they could not fly in anything but good visibility known as VFR (Visual Flight Rules). Consequently bad, even marginal, weather grounded plane and pilot indefinitely. Winter weather made day-to-day flying conditions for light aircraft highly unstable.

Even if the airplanes had been equipped with instruments, the WAFS, with one or two exceptions, were not instrument rated. That would come later. Besides, ferry pilots, male and female, were restricted to flying between the hours of a half an hour after sunrise and a half an hour before sunset. In wintertime, this didn't leave a lot of actual flying time, consequently trips cross country in Cubs took several days. Sometimes, going west, pilots encountered headwinds so strong that forward progress was severely impeded. One WAFS joked that while heading west across Ohio and Indiana, the cars going 60 miles an hour on U.S. 40 below were "passing" her.

On November 17, Gillies, Fort, Towne, Erickson and James were sent out again to pick up Cubs in Lockhaven and deliver them south. Weather delayed them in Lockhaven and they didn't get away until November 18.

RONing in Quantico with the Marines that night, the girls were invited out to dinner and then to the Officers Club. Teresa relates that the evening turned liquid on them — cocktails before dinner, wine with, Old Fashioneds after, followed by some celebratory champagne. The champagne was ordered by an officer in a particularly festive mood. Consequently, nearly everyone poured themselves into bed that night.

Of course, the inevitable happened. There was a mix up of beds.

The women had been given blocked-off quarters on one floor of the BOQ and the men who belonged on that corridor were asked to make other arrangements.

When Teresa made her way to the bed where she had carefully laid out her pajamas before leaving for dinner, she found a major, clad only in his shorts, snoring away. She sought out the corporal who had led the five women to those quarters in the first place and asked him to evict the major from her narrow cot.

"He's a major. I'm only a corporal," the man insisted, and backed out of the room refusing to have a part in this drama.

Teresa finally managed to snake her pajamas out from under the major — the movement did not disturb him in the least — and went with the corporal to find another room.

When the major awoke the following morning, he acted quite nonchalant, as if no mistake had been made. His quarters, Teresa learned, were actually one floor below — which accounted, belatedly, for the mix up.

Nor did Cornelia fare too well that evening. The beleaguered corporal, it turns out, deposited Teresa in Cornelia's room because it was empty at the time. Cornelia, suffering from the same indulgence as the major and several others, was in the shower trying to clear her head. When she got back to her room and found Teresa in her bed, Cornelia returned to the shower room and stretched out her five-foot ten-inch frame in the bathtub. A veteran of Eastern girls' school parties where the young ladies frequently stayed overnight in New York hotels, she knew that a bathtub was a useful, if not the most comfortable, substitute for a bed. Particularly if one had drunk too much and might, just might, need to use the facilities quickly. So — finding her bed occupied — she turned to the next best sleeping spot.

The WAFS love to tell the story on Cornelia, who paid dearly for the night before with a monumental hangover the following morning. When a plate of steaming fried eggs was placed before her at breakfast, she fled the table. Her friends swear that, even under normal circumstances, Cornelia couldn't "look a fried egg in the eye in the morning."

Mercifully, for them all, the weather on the morning of November 19 kept them grounded until noon. They took off for Winston Salem, North Carolina, and RONed there that night at the Robert E. Lee Hotel. The next day, Gillies, Towne and Fort went on to Greenville, South Carolina, and James and Erickson returned to base. Betty made a delivery to Greenville and returned to base, and Towne and Fort, who was feeling better, went on to Biloxi, Mississippi, with their aircraft.

⁓◌◌⁓

For the sake of individuals not even born in 1942, let alone old enough to remember any of that time in history, the social world was quite different from what it is today. Though a goodly portion of the U.S. population did not drink alcoholic beverages, an equally goodly portion did. The U.S., in 1942, was less than ten years out of Prohibition, when the sale of all alcohol was forbidden. The illicit thrill of "drinking" illegal booze in the Roaring Twenties had colored many minds as well and, to some degree, glamorized the practice of imbibing alcohol. Drinking and driving an automobile did not carry the stigma then that it does now and many couples in the wealthy and the upper-middle classes took it as their sacred right and privilege, in fact ritual, to have a "highball" or cocktail or two before dinner. According to *The Fine Art of Mixing Drinks*, a highball is a shot of whiskey (bourbon, rye, blended etc.) and a dash of carbonated beverage (or water) over ice and served in a tall glass. The proportion of water to ice to whiskey is according to the drinker's taste and constitution. A cocktail is defined as an "iced drink made of spirits, bitters, flavoring and sugar."

And certainly the penchant for men coming out of the factory at the end of a long day's work to congregate at the local bar for a quick beer or a shot 'n' a beer before going home was a practice enjoyed by another large segment of the population. Pilots, particularly the young men going off to war to fly airplanes, were inclined to "live on the edge" anyway and alcohol was a part of that existence. After-hours parties were the norm and usually the alcohol flowed. They knew better than to fly while intoxicated and did their drinking after a flight, not before. The dictum "eight hours from bottle to throttle" was the rule. But it was through alcohol that these men — and in some cases these women, too — unwound after a day of flying.

These people were young — mostly in their twenties — and were involved in a war that daily rained death and destruction on a part of the world where the men were ultimately headed. "Eat, drink and be merry for tomorrow you may die" was not just an idle saying. As for the women, even though they weren't headed for combat, some endured the loss of a husband, a fiancé, a brother, a cousin. Even more prevalent, the WAFS lost many good friends among the men who were their fellow pilots either in the Ferrying Division or in their civilian flying days. Unlike the women, the male ferry pilots were rotated overseas. Some went on to fly combat. It was not a pretty time and people were inclined to live life to the fullest extent their individual consciences allowed. It was part of the culture of the times.

As in any society, or group, no sweeping generalizations can be made. Some of the WAFS — particularly the older ones and the married ones — drank and smoked. Nancy Love and Betty Gillies had their rum and Coke in the BOQ before heading to the mess hall or the Officers' Club for dinner. Sis Bernheim is legendary with her love of rye and Coke. Some of the younger ones never did drink. Others learned to drink by watching and being associated with their "elders."

"Betty takes credit for giving me my first drink — a Cuba Libra or rum and Coke," says B.J. Erickson. "I was this naive little girl from the northwest. Betty and I were on a ferrying trip south and we got weathered in — for five days! We got to know each other pretty well and she taught me to drink rum and Coke. We became close friends on that trip and we remained close for the rest of her life.

"Of course, we had to wire the base every night and tell them where we were. And Betty always called or wired Bud to let him know as well. By the time the fourth day of bad weather rolled around, she was tired of spending a lot of money on long telegrams, so she came up with the idea of sending Bud a short cryptic message that would tell him everything he needed to know. It read 'Hebrews Thirteen-Eight.'

"Production at the Grumman factory on Long Island came to a halt while management scurried around trying to find a King James Bible so that they could decipher the message, which simply said, 'Jesus Christ the same yesterday, and today, and forever.'"

ϲꙠꙠꙠ

In some respects, the WAFS and later the Women Airforce Service Pilots (WASP) — the women who graduated from the Flying Training School in Texas and who were first known as WFTDs — were a microcosm of society-as-a-whole. The twenty-eight WAFS were a group unto themselves. Each WFTD/WASP class at Houston, and later Sweetwater, was a group unto itself. And those groupings still exist today, just as does any group of women — or men — who attend college together and belong to the same sorority or fraternity. This camaraderie among the WAFS, however, was much more apparent in those who arrived early.

"Those who arrived late were not known to those of us who were accepted in September and early October because, in January, we were split up into four squadrons and assigned to four different bases," B.J. explains. "The last few women to come in were just finishing their thirty-day orientation period when the squadron was broken up. I never knew Sis Bernheim and Helen McGilvery because they came as I was preparing to leave Wilmington, and I barely knew the late fall arrivals like Dorothy Scott, Betsy Ferguson, Dorothy Fulton, Phyllis Burchfield and Katherine Thompson."

The women known as The Originals never were all together in one place and though individuals retained lifelong friendships, the group has never held regular reunions like their sister pilots, the WASP. The WAFS reunion, held by Nancy Batson Crews in Birmingham, Alabama, in June 1999, was the first get-together in many years. According to Nancy, one was held in 1960, there was at least one other between 1945 and 1960, and Barbara Poole recalls one in Wilmington in the 1970s. The WASPs began holding informal reunions and actually put an organization together in the 1970s. Now they meet biannually and the women attending usually cluster according to their graduation class.

On November 22, Gillies, Clark, Miller, Erickson, Sharp, Batson, Nelson, Richards, Scharr, Burchfield and James were dispatched on their first PT-19 delivery. PT stands for primary trainer. The 175-horsepower Fairchild PT-19 was built in Hagerstown, Maryland. It had a greater fuel capacity than the Cub and therefore greater range. The PT-19 also sported an open cockpit.

By late November the weather along the eastern seaboard was getting cold on the ground and colder aloft. Not only did the WAFS have to lug parachutes, they also had to pack and carry bulky winter flying gear with them on the train to Baltimore and then the bus to the Fairchild factory in Hagerstown. They missed their bus in Baltimore by two minutes and, since there wasn't another one until seven in the morning, they had to sleep on benches in the station propped against parachutes and B-4 bags.

Their tardy arrival in Hagerstown brought the wrath of the Army down on them. "Where the hell have you been?" the captain in charge asked. "Everyone in the Army has been looking for you." Their

explanations fell on deaf ears. Betty wrote a letter of explanation and sent it to Colonel Baker back at Wilmington. The weather closed in and they couldn't leave anyway, so they spent that night and the next in a Hagerstown hotel. Del Scharr came down with something and had to be taken to the hospital.

Finally, on November 25 — the day before Thanksgiving — they took off. But the weather over Hagerstown was soupy and they couldn't see each other so Clark, Batson, Nelson, Sharp and James returned. Gillies,

**Phyllis Burchfield climbs into a PT-19**

Richards, Burchfield, Miller and Erickson went on through — eventual destination, Union City Tennessee.

On Thanksgiving Day, the other five got off and turned their noses south as well. They had their turkey dinner that night in Charlotte, North Carolina, where the men at Morris Field made them feel very welcome. They were lodged in the nurses' BOQ and some of the officers on base took them to the O-Club for drinks and dinner. The following day they flew on to Union City where they just missed the other five WAFS who had gotten off a day earlier than they did.

Back to base just after midnight on November 28. Then off again the next morning. Same crew — Clark, Gillies, Burchfield,

Nelson, Batson, Sharp, Miller, Erickson, Richards and James — but back to the Cubs that Teresa calls "those Lockhaven spitfires!"

Colonel Baker, again taking pity, flew them up to Lockhaven in the transport, but weather closed in on them enroute and he had to go on instruments. The rest of the way they flew looking out the window at soup. On the ground, it was snowing.

This time everybody was going in a different direction. "Jamesy" and "Burchie" — Phyllis Burchfield had acquired a nickname as well — headed for Vermont. It was November 30. They RONed that night in Albany where the ground was covered with snow. Fort Ethan Allen was their destination and they arrived on December 1. That night they read in a newspaper about a fire in a restaurant/night club in Boston. Several people were killed.

They caught an airliner headed for LaGuardia Field outside New York City and flew through a snowstorm to get there. "Couldn't even see the edge of the wings," Teresa relates.

Jamesy and Burchie got to spend four hours in New York, time enough for dinner and movie, before catching a late train out. They arrived back at the BOQ at five a.m. the morning of December 2 where they were told that Gertrude Meserve's brother had been a victim of that nightclub fire in Boston. A tragic wartime loss that occurred far from the battlefield.

"Seven of us were in the BOQ that night," Teresa says. "The wind was blowing and it really started to snow. Then Nancy called and said for us to pack, that we were on our way to Montana! Everyone went crazy with excitement."

# 11

**Teresa's journal . . .**

*December 3, 1942*

Something is cooking! And I don't mean the trip to Great Falls. Something else. Something big.

We all got up at six a.m. Everybody anxious and ready to travel. A mad house with all these females getting clothes ready with only one iron and three wash basins in the place. At two, Nancy called and told us we weren't going until tomorrow. She had to go to Washington.

Ah, hah!

*Look Magazine* was here. Took pictures of all seven of us doing our regular work back at the base. We never know what minute of the day or night we will be notified to leave. After eight hours of photographs, we were all ready for bed.

*December 4, 1942*

Same old story! We were up and ready to travel at seven a.m. We didn't leave until the day was almost over and after Nancy informed us that she wasn't going on the trip. She seemed very disappointed and we felt sorry for her. But like I said — something's going on.

She's named me flight leader in her place.

Thompson has been waiting for her husband — Captain Ted Thompson of the British Royal Air Force (RAF) — to get time enough off so she could see him. He called today and announced he would have four days. And we're getting ready to leave! Even though her time was limited, she had dinner with him in Philadelphia, then they rushed back to Wilmington where we were to meet at the station at nine p.m. Honest, she was beaming like a Fourth of July sun, and who could blame her. Is he a handsome fellow or not? He rode with us to Pittsburgh on the train.

Going away was madness. Twenty-four guys — all flying officers — are going with us, carrying the same cold-weather-flying baggage. Everybody rushed and shoved and fell against everybody else. We had just three minutes to change in Philadelphia's 30th Street Station to a shuttle train that took us to Broad Street Station, and a matter of about as many minutes to get on the train to Pittsburgh.

When it was all done, we were in a state of nervous collapse. Instead of the staterooms we had expected, we found that the six girls and twenty-four men were to occupy one Pullman car. The berths were made up, so the only thing to do was go to bed. A lot of wisecracking accompanied this — like, "don't walk in your sleep!" One girl had a fellow in the berth above her. I don't think she took her clothes off the entire night.

I wired my sister Betty to meet me in the station in Pittsburgh as we were to have a fifteen-minute stop there.

I met an Army cadet who had ridden home to Massachusetts with Gert Meserve. He found her crying in the dining car and asked her what was wrong. She was crying over her brother's death. The cadet, it turned out, was taking his buddy's body home. The boy had been killed in a plane crash. That must be the human side of the news.

*Early in the morning, December 5, 1942*

Nobody could sleep we were so cold. The train was stopped stone still, for the longest time. Turned out one of the steam lines had burst. Thus the reason for our frigid surroundings. The brakeman told us we were already four hours late. And I had told Betty to meet me.

We got rolling again and made up some of the time, but were still three hours late getting into Pittsburgh. I took an awful chance getting off. I couldn't find out if the train would be there ten minutes or not. My throat was dry from sheer fright that they would go off and leave me. Then, there she was. I dashed back with her in tow, found the car again and she stayed for about forty minutes. It was fun introducing her to everybody.

I might as well admit I had a little spell of homesickness right then and there. About the only thing I could think of that would help would be to stay right there in Pittsburgh.

That afternoon, most of the girls spent time catching up on the sleep they'd missed the night before. Miller addressed about two hundred Christmas cards. That evening the boys loosened up, told some jokes, and we did a bit of hangar flying. They really treated us swell, gave us credit for being capable, most of the time, so we can't complain. Went to bed about 1 in the morning.

### December 6, 1942

Got up around noon the next day. They left six of the berths made up at the end of the car and we took turns napping. Sang all the old songs we knew. There is much joy in mass singing. The fellows played every card game imaginable — from poker on down.

We pulled into Chicago at eight thirty p.m., three hours late, completely starved. Miller, Batson and I, and three of the guys decided to go have dinner. We crowded about four days into that four hours.

This job has been mostly hard work and waiting and wondering, but we have our moments of "goose pimple" thrills and going into the Pennsylvania Station in Chicago and looking at that collection of airplane models there was one of those. The ceiling is rather high. A model of every type of airplane was there on that wall, from P-38s, B-25s, B-24s on down to the training ships. An exhibition of U.S. flying strength. And somewhere, I'm not sure just where, I am part of it — and that moment was worth remembering.

We walked and it was snowing. Traffic was slowed by it and we could reach out and pick handfuls off the cars. Naturally, we had a snowball fight. And we heard Christmas carols. We were in uniform and caught the eyes of hundreds of passers-by. Ate dinner at the Panther Room in the Hotel Sherman. Everything covered with panther skins, really an exciting place. We went on to the famous Black Hawk where Chico Marx (of the famous Marx Brothers clan) and his band were holding sway. But we couldn't get a table.

Going home, we planned a little to-do because tomorrow is Miller's birthday. No shops open, so in the station we bought her a Santa Claus filled with Hershey's Kisses. At midnight we presented the card and gift and sang Happy Birthday. We had some grape juice and had planned to drink a toast but it had frozen. One of the fellows had a bottle of Sherbrook. He said, "Bet this will melt the ice." Which it did, very quickly! We stayed up until five in the morning, singing and having a merry time.

One of the lieutenants is falling in love with Miller. He follows her around the train with that look in his eyes.

### December 7, 1942

Nobody got up until late. We had nothing to do but sleep. We were getting pretty close to Great Falls, started getting ambitious and began digging out maps and talking business. We got in at noon.

Batson and I saw real live Indians for the first time.

The Army bus took us to the Hotel Rainbow. It was about five above zero and snow over everything. We had the rest of the day off to do as we pleased and that made us very happy. All of us felt a bit apprehensive of the rugged country and mountains all around.

We went out to the Officer's Club at Gore Field and it is really one of the most beautiful I have seen. Western in design and music every evening, which is rare. We had a couple of cocktails before I got called over to Base Operations. I found that instead of flying east and then south, because of the low temperatures predicted, we were to fly south and then east. The country looked rough and all the girls were upset about it. But we met this with an "if the fellows can do it, so can we!" attitude.

I was surprised to see so many young officers. The Operations captain couldn't be over twenty-five. He must be a darned good pilot and manager. Otherwise, he could never have become a captain. He really knows his business.

We went into town and had dinner. Met an officer who knew Del Scharr and another who knew Ev Sharp. "Hello's" to deliver. Burchfield and I had caught colds, so we decided to go back to the hotel and go to bed.

A year, to the day, since Pearl Harbor. Seems like ten, so much has happened. Got my secondary rating in February, married Dink in June, joined the WAFS in September, and here I am in Great Falls, Montana, in December, ready to lead a flight of six WAFS ferrying PT-17s south to Tennessee.

### December 8, 1942

Slept until noon. Might as well. The sun doesn't come up until after nine. Not even daylight until eight thirty. We had breakfast in bed for the first time and really enjoyed it. Bohn took a captain with her Christmas shopping, to carry the packages he discovered later. The society editor of the Great Falls newspaper came to the hotel with the Public Relations Officer and took pictures. Spent three or four hours with that, then we went ice skating at the Civic Center with some of the boys. None of the group, with the exception of Yours Truly, had ever been on ice skates before. After all, Batson, Bohn, Miller and Thompson all come from somewhere down in y'all land. But before the evening was over, they all had made solo flights.

Bohn's boyfriend got pretty jealous because she skated with a couple of the other fellows, so he went home. By that time, I knew old man flu was working on me 'cause I felt pretty sick.

*December 9, 1942*

I'm sick. Burchfield is sick. Miller's beginning to feel sick. But we had to go to the airport to get checked out in the PT-17. Most of us had never flown this particular primary trainer before, so we each made a couple of trips around the field.

Had dinner at the Officer's Club. Then one of the lieutenants took Miller and me back to town to see a doctor as we were feeling mighty low. The doc says stay in bed, that I have the flu. I don't dare see the Flight Surgeon for fear of being grounded for a week.

*December 10, 1942*

I did stay in bed. Drank three quarts of orange and grapefruit juice 'til it ran out my ears. And medicine galore! The lieutenant called to see how I was.

*December 11, 1942*

We got up at six a.m. Went to the airport and had to wait around. It was a swell day, clean and clear, and all prospects that it would be warm. I felt terrible. So did Burchfield, and Miller said she didn't think she could make it. The captain in Operations said if we didn't feel like it, not to go. I certainly felt as if pneumonia was about to make his bold appearance, so I decided to go back and go to bed. I was so sick, I didn't care if the whole Army threatened to be waiting at the next airport. I don't remember being that sick for a long time.

A major asked Miller to go as copilot on a C-84, the new Douglas, and sick as she was, she went. I went back to the hotel and went to bed and the others went ice skating. They seem to have caught that fever.

I stayed in bed until four that afternoon then went to the public stenographer to have my journal notes typed before I get too far behind. As I came back to the desk for my key, I heard someone call my name. When my fever-impaired vision finally focused in the right direction, who should I see standing before me but Nancy Love. And with her were a colonel and two captains.

There I was, fully dressed, and they had told her I was ill. I could have dropped through the floor. As flight leader, things didn't look very good for me.

I asked her what she was doing there and she replied that she was flying around the country. "Come up to my room while I get changed. I've got an hour and I want to talk to you," she says.

We had been feeling sorry for her not getting to make the trip with us and here she was flying around the country with three men! But I had a feeling I was about to find out what was going on. I was right!

As soon as I got to her room, I asked what was cooking. She was suave and subtle, but when she said we would probably have to start wearing ties, I figured we were in line for commissions. Boy!

She was on the trip to visit all the ferrying squadrons, of which there were only seven in the U.S. She is checking on possible quarters for women. We're going to be split up. Naturally, I asked for Long Beach. Dink is out there.

I got on the phone and attempted to round up the rest of the girls for Nancy and found them. I want things to go off nicely on this trip since she made me flight leader. An hour or so later we were assembled. One of the captains with Nancy was there too. He is perhaps the handsomest man living. We six reminded me of she-wolves sitting around Nancy's room staring at him.

Nancy had a nasty blister on her right hand. When we asked what caused it, she explained the trials of acting as a co-pilot on a Lockheed 13. The landing gear kept sticking and she kept knocking it out — thus the injury. She's co-piloting some big stuff.

When she had us all together, Nancy told us that the Ferrying Division was forming women's ferrying squadrons at other ferrying bases around the country and that some of us would be assigned to them. Some would remain in Wilmington. And she added that, eventually, girls who graduated from Jackie Cochran's flight school down in Texas — known as the Women's Flying Training Detachment — would be joining us at these bases and helping flesh out each of the women's squadrons

We had been together just over three months and, already, we were being split up. I'd grown to like these girls. On one side, I was sorry to hear the news. On the other side, things were starting to get exciting.

**In winter flying gear looking very much like penguins:
Betty Gillies, Nancy Batson, Esther Nelson,
Helen Mary Clark, Teresa James and Evelyn Sharp
(with an unidentified officer)**

# 12

The airplanes the six WAFS were scheduled to fly out of Great Falls were PT-17s — yellow bi-wing Stearmans with a single 225-horsepower radial engine. Nickname, "Yellow Peril." The airplanes had been used by the Canadian RAF for cadet flight training, but, like the PT-19s, they had open cockpits. The winter weather in Alberta was not conducive to open cockpit trainers so the Canadians were turning them back to Uncle Sam. They were now destined for a flight training school located in the warmer climate of Jackson, Tennessee.

The temperature the day the WAFS planned to depart in the Stearmans was hovering around zero. They eyed the open cockpits with considerable trepidation. Since they already had been flying open cockpit PT-19s out of Hagerstown, Maryland, in the damp cold November weather back east, they were no strangers to aerial discomfort. But this zero degrees Fahrenheit was compounded by the five thousand-foot altitude at Great Falls. To add to that, they were flying in mountainous country with sharp, rocky ridges and few hospitable places to put an airplane down in an emergency.

These primary trainers carried no radios. The pilots could not communicate with each other or call for help.

And the last problem they had to contend with — it was so cold the line crew had to heat the oil in order to get the engines started on the Stearmans.

As the WAFS waddled to the flight line, looking like giant overstuffed penguins in their winter flight gear, the six women were apprehensive. Even Texans Bohn and Miller, used to wide open spaces, were not accustomed to rugged high country like this. And the other four were strictly Easterners.

Army-issue bulky winter flying gear was a challenge. First layer consisted of long scratchy woolen underwear and layers of socks. Over the long johns, they pulled on high-waisted, fleece-lined leather pants. These zipped from the shinbone of one leg up to the sternum and were held in place by suspenders. They topped that with fleece-lined leather jackets.

Leather flying caps with chin straps and goggles, fleece-lined leather gloves and wool-lined boots completed their standard flying garb.

"We thought, surely, all this would be enough to keep the cold out, but it wasn't," Nancy Batson remembers. "To that, we added our parachute, with straps over the shoulders and around the thighs."

For the flight out of Great Falls, the girls also received chamois masks held in place by wide black elastic bands. The masks were to provide at least some semblance of protection against frostbite since they would be flying another few thousand feet above the earth where the air was even colder.

The WAFS already had learned that when flying in open cockpit trainers, a runny nose was a constant companion.

Finally, the morning of December 12, they took off from Great Falls and headed south.

### December 12, 1942, Teresa's journal

This was a morning I'll never forget. Snow covered everything. The world was white. We couldn't make out highways or railroads or rivers. Even though the airplanes were yellow, they were hard to see. You particularly couldn't see the airplane ahead of you if you were level with it.

Florene was navigating and, in accordance with the WAFS rules of group flying, leading the line of airplanes in a loose formation. Not far out of Great Falls, I noticed that the other aircraft were circling. I watched, then flew down and tried to straighten them out. Went back to my spot, but Florene kept circling, followed by the others. I don't think we flew ten miles straight. Finally, I had to find out what was going on.

I was sure there was no place to land, not in this country. Then, by some miracle, I noticed a small auxiliary airfield that had been plowed out. I knew we needed to land so I could find out what the trouble was. It isn't easy to put an airplane down in a furrow and I

# The Great Falls Six

Delphine Bohn, Nancy Batson, Katherine Rawls Thompson,
Florene Miller, Phyllis Burchfield and Teresa James

On the flight line: Thompson, Burchfield, Batson, Bohn, Miller and James

had visions of a crack-up, but I had to get to the bottom of this. I landed and the others followed. Even though it was icy, we all got down. We also had to leave our engines running 'cause they'd never have restarted in that cold.

I found out what the trouble was.

Florene lost her maps twenty miles out of Great Falls. The wind caught them and tore them right out of her hand and out into the frigid air. She gave her fishtail signal for someone else to take over, but nobody saw it, so she flew with only her compass and her watch until we finally landed on this remote field. We found out we were in a place called Lavinia and, in spite of the lost maps and circling, we were only ten miles off course! We took off out of there — everybody got out fine — and flew on to Billings.

We RONed in Billings. It gets dark early up here and there is no other place to stay within reaching distance. Batson won the toss and accompanied the airport manager on a coyote hunt, from an airplane cockpit, a popular sport in this part of the country, I am told.

Now I am beginning to realize the demands and the loneliness of command. I go to bed in a hand-wringing, hair-tearing mode while the other five go to a movie.

### December 13, 1942

Today we stay close together, determined not to have the same trouble. We flew at ten thousand feet. Snow still covered everything. Landed at Casper, Wyoming, at two p.m. and, stiff from the cold, continued on to Denver's Lowry Field to RON. Thompson navigated this leg. We all had a little trouble flying at such a high altitude.

Checked into the Cosmopolitan Hotel. I called Dink. Miller and Bohn called their mothers and told them to meet us at the airfield in Amarillo the next day.

### December 14, 1942

Bohn wants to leave early. She's going "home." So we're up at five a.m. But thanks to trouble getting breakfast and other delays, we don't get off until five minutes of nine. Landed at Pueblo, Colorado, at five minutes after ten. I did a bit of reminiscing as I flew over Colorado Springs and quaint Manitou Springs which is tucked up against Pikes Peak. Such memories. Dink and I, and the happy hours last June. "The little perching paradise that men call Manitou," with Williams Canyon, Cave of the Winds, Seven Falls. Flew over the Garden of the Gods at about eight hundred feet.

On to Amarillo by way of Las Vegas, New Mexico, which meant flying at ten thousand feet over Raton Pass, the nearly eight thousand foot route over the Colorado-New Mexico state line. The motors kept cutting out and we couldn't imagine what caused it. Believe me, if we'd been called on to make a forced landing, I'm not real sure where we could have put those ships down in that rugged terrain. We made it, though, on into Las Vegas, an old frontier town. They filled our tanks with the wrong octane gasoline, which we didn't know until the motors sputtered and stopped and gave us all kinds of trouble on the way to Amarillo.

As we approached, it was clear and I could see Amarillo for a long time before we got there. I thought about how happy Bohn and Miller were bound to be, getting so close to their families and home.

Bohn led us in and everyone followed. Miller's mother, brother and sister were there and Bohn's mother and stepfather. Bohn's folks gave us a reception and dinner at the Herring Hotel. The usual photographers were there. And a toastmaster. We were called on to tell something of our experiences and of our present duties.

The only nightclub in Amarillo was the Old Tascosa in the Herring Hotel. All Western with murals depicting pioneer days, chuck wagon and all, done by outstanding Western artist Harold Bugbee of Clarendon, Texas. The furniture is rustic and the atmosphere is enhanced by gourds, strings of hot red peppers, unborn calf skin, branding irons, even a corral fence with saddles on it. The bartenders wear red checked shirts and the waitresses really are cowgirls with boots, wrist guards, riding skirts, bright colored satin shirts with contrasting necker-chiefs knotted around their necks, and Stetson hats — a new world to us Easterners!

### December 15, 1942

Got up early and called the airport to see if the ships were ready. They were to drain the bad gas we got in Las Vegas, fix Batson's wheel, and repair the place in Burchfield's wing where the dopey mechanic stuck his foot through. But the planes weren't ready. Talked to Dink, thinking I would probably not be this close to him again before Christmas. Seems funny wishing somebody you love a Merry Christmas and Happy New Year on the 15th of December. But if you get down to stranger things — what about telling somebody you love you hope to see them sometime? The whole world is an abnormal place right now.

### December 16, 1942

Plans were to leave bright and early. Called the airport and they were vague about everything. I decided to go out and see what was wrong. Thompson, thinking we were not trying to get out of Amarillo because it was Bohn's home territory, took it upon herself to telephone the airport. She told them she was Squadron Leader Teresa James and demanded the ships to be ready in five minutes.

I can forgive her in a way when I realize that Captain Ted was waiting on her somewhere back east.

When I did get to the airport, the mechanics treated me like something akin to scum, and could you blame them? They are new and rushed, and certainly not the kind who take impossible commands from females!

Well, it was a terrible day. I spent hours out there. After getting the boys to work, assuring them that no one in authority had called them, they went ahead and fixed the ships. But it was too late to leave.

Turned out there was a big party that night. Bohn, Batson and I were invited. First time I really had fun since the trip started. Three hours of dancing and fun and talking to a bunch of really interesting guys.

### December 17, 1942

And paid for it the next morning. The others tried to wake me, unsuccessfully, until Batson tried a towel soaked in ice water. Oh my head. Reminded me vaguely of fog horns and fire bells and a bird singing somewhere. But it was worth it!

Had to wait for daylight and took off right into the sun. That's another of my firsts — never flew east into that blazing ball of fire before. Nearly blinded me. Then about five miles out, just as we were pulling into position with me at the rear, this Waco breezes by me. I figured it was one of Bohn's friends from her airport. Then I look back and here comes a Ryan S.T. and a Stinson. They flew right by me, being last, and got very close to the other girls. They heckled them for twenty minutes, then came back to give me the works.

I'll admit they gave me the jitters. Practically scared the pants off me! Fred Hall had the Ryan doing double snap rolls all around me. "Cookie" Cooke was on my left in the Waco. And Tom Reems was on my right in the Stinson. They pulled in so close I could see that Cookie didn't brush his teeth that morning.

The day was perfect. Air smooth as glass. Could see fifty miles. I like the west. It's difficult to believe the level plains would make such dazzling patterns from the air. The colors of rose, green, purple, blue and gold remind you of a patchwork quilt. The Red River was dry as a bone. Alene, a woman pilot I met in Amarillo, said that the first time she flew over the Red River at nine thousand feet at two hundred miles per hour, all she could remember was that just twenty-five years earlier, she had forded the Red River with her parents in a covered wagon.

Landed at Wichita Falls. Sheppard Field — forty thousand men. The hospital unit alone takes up four acres. Also, the most complete aircraft mechanical school in the Army. And a Service Club beautifully decorated for Christmas. Sorry to leave, but we were on our way to Love Field, Dallas. They say Dallas is the most cosmopolitan thing between New York and Frisco.

Had a tail wind, so breezed right in. Ran into Erickson, Poole, Manning and Donahue getting out of PT-19s. They were on their way to Ballinger, Texas. Nancy Love had been gone only two hours.

### December 18, 1942

The planes won't be ready until one p.m. Slept 'til noon then made a mad dash to the airfield. Met Esther Nelson's husband.

Flew at three thousand feet coming into Longview. I didn't know there were so many oil wells. From a distance they resemble tall silver poles. Just think of all the trouble Hitler is causing Russia just to get some of the stuff produced from the ground beneath those silver poles.

Arrived Shreveport at five thirty. Stayed at the Washington Youree Hotel. Batson and I both hit the sack. She had tonsillitis. I wasn't much better. I coughed away half a lung. Had trouble sleeping.

### December 19, 1942

Thompson has apologized and I really think she felt badly. We shook hands and everyone feels better. The girls had given her the cold shoulder and it really hit home.

Visibility was poor this morning, but we were ready to take off. Miller was fourth in line and pretty close when she hit a field marker with her prop. She didn't do any damage, but we had to have the prop balanced. By the time it was fixed, it was too late to leave.

### December 20-22, 1942

The weather closed in and we were stranded in Shreveport. Cash supply critical. Can't buy anything we need — let alone want. Batson and I decided to wash all our clothes. Then we improvised an ironing board from the glass top table padded with bath towels. Before we could finish, one of the lieutenants dropped by. When he knocked I said, "come in" without taking notice of the state of our room. Batson was on the bed convulsed with laughter. I wondered why her sudden glee when it dawned on me that my newly washed long underwear was hanging on a coat hanger from the chandelier.

He handled it well, though he finally remarked that he couldn't believe his eyes — the 1942 version of the modern miss.

### December 23, 1942

By noon the weather cleared. Side light to feminine allure. There were six mechanics helping Miller into her flying suit while the rest of us struggled into ours alone.

Landed in Little Rock.

Batson is excited because her boy friend — "the one" — is going to meet her in Nashville. Incidentally, the boys in Shreveport called her the Veronica Lake of Birmingham. [Veronica Lake was a 1940s movie star with long blond hair.]

### December 24, 1942

The day before Christmas and here we are. Everyone is so damned unhappy, it's a shame. We waited at the airport until eleven thirty for the soup to thin. Batson called home, but "he" had already left for Nashville.

We had all hoped to eat Christmas dinner at the base in Wilmington. At least we would have felt more at home. We are really down in the mouth. All of us are threatening to get pleasantly plastered. At three, we thought about going to a movie to break the dangerous mood, but think better of it and read magazines instead. All the guys heading west are trying to get home.

Funny how at Christmas your thoughts turn to home. I suppose that is the case with millions this year. You just don't take Christmas Eve like all the other days. We really don't have a thing to gripe about. After all, we are here in the good old U.S.A.

Miller called her boyfriend and he is on his way here. Batson contacted hers in Nashville and he is on his way here, too. Poor fellow, he will be worn out. We got dressed and went walking, looking for a nice place to eat. There are hundreds of enlisted men here. Many of them saluted us, and we gave them a snappy one back.

We grabbed a street car to the station to meet Miller's boy friend. The train was due at eleven, but it was two hours late. Took another car back to town. Went to midnight Mass at St. Andrew's. Despite the bright lights, holly and decorations, this was the first real spirit we had felt.

Had to leave at twelve forty-five to meet the train.

Back to the hotel and the party started in Miller's room and lasted until four a.m. The fog was terrible. You couldn't see across the street. Tried to call Nancy Love to wish her a Merry Christmas, but couldn't get the call through.

### Christmas Day, December 25, 1942

Batson's boy friend arrived at five thirty in the morning. I dragged out at 11. Miller is out with her honey somewhere. I'm glad someone is happy today.

Sat in the Hotel McGeehee Coffee Shop drinking egg nog and they informed us there was no more turkey or chicken. Who ever heard of a Christmas without turkey? We settled for pot roast.

It's eighty degrees here today. We went to see "The Palm Beach Story" then had a late dinner — found some turkey after all. In bed at ten o'clock. Have been thinking about everyone at home and wondering what they are doing. Can't forget the feeling I had during the Christmas sketch in the movie — a soldier on guard, marching up and down before a pine tree gaily decorated and beside it a cannon, this scene fading into a huge cross.

*December 26, 1942*

Got clearance about ten thirty in the morning and took a crack at getting to Memphis. Only had a thousand-foot ceiling. Had fun flying in and out of the clouds. Thompson was navigating.

Flying over Brinkley, Arkansas, I saw a lot of smoke and flames and dropped down pretty low to look. A house was a solid mass of flames and people dashing about. I was so sorry to see a home burn the day after Christmas. I kept circling until I lost the gang. They kept on going. I finally caught up to them.

We hit Memphis right on time, landed and went into Base Operations. Ran into an old friend from Johnston airport in Pittsburgh, Lt. Donald Whitelaw. As there were thunderstorms all around Memphis, we couldn't go on, so he took Thompson, Bohn and me home to his house for the day. Don is married to Anne, also a close friend of mine. Did a lot of socializing with their friends and I spent the night with them.

*December 27, 1942*

Rained all day. Anne, Don and I spent three hours cleaning, washing dishes, running the sweeper. Reminded me of home.

*December 28, 1942*

Couldn't sleep. Weather still bad. We called the girls at the hotel and invited them out for a spaghetti supper. Took the girls back to the hotel at two thirty a.m. after a midnight snack at a popular Memphis eating place, Donley's. Crawled in bed at 4 a.m.

*December 29, 1942*

This is really getting to be funny now. Everywhere we stop, we sit for at least three days. There hasn't been any flying at all out of Memphis except by the airlines. It's a good thing I have good friends here. I only had fifteen cents when I hit town. The other girls have been cashing checks and they are just about bankrupt, too. It looks like we will be going home on an airliner New Year's Eve — maybe. All we do is wonder from one day to the next.

Anne and I did positively nothing today but lay around and read and listen to the radio. Heard my favorites — Bob Hope and Red Skelton. Now Ted Lewis' band is now playing "When you are a long, long way from home." My heart sank to the bottom of my shoes. I'm just plain homesick tonight — for Dink, for my mother, for my sister Betty. I'm only one of the millions though.

Miller just called pretending she was Nancy Love calling from Wilmington. Scared my pants off. Thought someone was ill at home. Wait 'til I get her tomorrow. I'll ring her neck.

### December 30, 1942

Miller called again, this time to tell me that our commanding officer, Colonel Baker, called the commanding officer here to tell Miller to return to Wilmington immediately. She is being transferred to Love Field in Dallas. It's funny I wasn't called back too. We're probably fired. Everyone is in a dither wondering where they are going to wind up.

Put in a call to Nancy Love. Wanted to wish her a Happy New Year. She appreciated our call. I was disappointed when she told me I wasn't going to Long Beach. I'm to stay in Wilmington. The only way to find out where everyone is going is to wait until we get back to the base.

Don, Anne and I took Miller to the airport. She's leaving on an airliner tonight. I was a mite on the sad side when she left. Felt as if I were losing my best friend, but that's the Army. You meet people, become attached to them, and then the old stuff, you're transferred. Batson, Bohn, Miller and I had hoped that we would be together for awhile. Miller promised she'd write me. We came back to the house and I was feeling mighty low.

### December 31, 1942

Didn't get away from Memphis until one ten p.m. as the ceiling was low. Then, big sigh of relief, we got off and delivered the ships to Jackson, Tennessee, our final destination — where we were met with, "Well, did you finally get here?"

Turns out we beat *all* the men in. Yep. Out of twenty-four guys and six gals, we are the first ones to arrive out of that whole contingent that left Great Falls what seems like ten years ago. How 'bout these gals!

Don flew up to Jackson on the Hudson and flew us back to Memphis.

After an anniversary dinner for Don and Anne — their first — we said goodbye and left for the airport. We caught the American Airlines flight out of Memphis.

One of the loveliest scenes flying is skimming over the clouds with the moon shining on them. It's like looking at silver balls of cotton. It's an awesome sight regardless of how many times you see it. Happy New Year!

Then coming into Washington D.C., I watched the sun come up. It's one of those moments that make you feel it's great to be alive!

*January 1, 1943*

The train pulled into Philadelphia at ten a.m. Got careless with Bohn's money and took a cab from Philadelphia to the base — cost thirteen dollars — but we were so tired we were dragging.

Went galloping through the BOQ hollering Happy New Year. The gals and Mrs. Anderson gave us a royal welcome. Hugging, kissing, gee, it was just like coming home to your own family.

Gillies, Clark, Batson, Bohn and Thompson sat in my room and we talked about what all was going on. Clark and Gillies got to spend Christmas with their families close by.

Got all the dirt. The second women's squadron is being formed at Love Field in Dallas and Nancy Love, Helen Richards, Florene Miller, Dorothy Scott and Betsy Ferguson are going immediately. That's why Miller was called back. But she's still here going out of her mind checking in all her equipment, packing and so on.

More news! Betty Gillies is our new boss. Also, Pat Rhonie resigned today. We're sorry to see her go.

Finally got to open my mail and my Christmas packages. Dink's letters are piled high.

By ten p.m., that uncomfortable old cot looked mighty good. What a day! I just told Batson, I can't be this happy. Probably going to get hell somewhere along the line tomorrow. Hope not!

# 13

The reason for organizing the WAFS squadron at New Castle Army Air Base in Wilmington, Delaware, was that it was located close to the manufacturers of primary trainers (PT-19s) and liaison airplanes (L4-Bs), the two types of airplanes the women originally were recruited to fly.

By the end of November 1942, WAFS had ferried forty L-4Bs (Cubs) and ten Fairchild PT-19s to flight training facilities located mostly in the Southern states. In December, the women ferried twenty-four more L4-Bs, four PT-19s and six PT-17s — the latter on the trip from Great Falls to Jackson during which the six WAFS were off base for more than three weeks.

The women could handle these assignments. That was obvious.

But the war planes the Army needed delivered were getting bigger, faster, heavier — particularly single-engine, single-seater fighter planes like the P-47 and P-51 and twin-engine attack bombers like the A-20. Ferry pilots were needed who could fly these planes. Could the women do it? The factories producing these airplanes were scattered around the country, though the biggest concentration was in the Los Angeles Basin. The WAFS' potential for usefulness at other bases near these factories was up for discussion.

As the women's squadron neared the prescribed strength of twenty-five, and knowing that eventually the women graduating from Cochran's flight training school in Texas would be swelling their ranks, the Ferrying Division made plans to form other WAFS units at other bases.

The WAFS were itching to get their hands on the bigger stuff starting with the basic trainers (BT), advanced trainers (AT), and even twin-engine craft. They had seen the occasional P-47 on the flight line at Wilmington and watched the men take off in a roar, flying them into the wild blue yonder. They had listened to the tales of the big "Jug's" awesome might when the men, reluctantly, returned the 2,800-horsepower monster to earth. The girls lusted to get their hands on the controls of those brutes of the air.

During December 1942, Nancy Love traveled around the country to the other bases housing ferrying groups to determine where she could optimally place fledgling women's squadrons. She also checked out bases like the one in Great Falls, Montana, to which they eventually could be ferrying aircraft. Bed and board for the girls while on base was her major concern.

The decision was reached — WAFS units would be established with the 5th Ferrying Group at Love Field in Dallas; with the 3rd Ferrying Group at Wayne County Airport in Romulus, Michigan, near Detroit; and with the 6th Ferrying Group at Long Beach, California. The 6th, with a majority of the aircraft factories building war planes located nearby, was the largest with four male ferrying squadrons already stationed there.

Dallas offered eight, two-girl rooms in the nurses quarters, ready immediately, and a separate BOQ that would be ready in sixty to ninety days. At Dallas, the WAFS could transition into basic and advanced trainers and ferry PT-17s, AT-6s and AT-17s. They would service North American's plants in Dallas and Kansas City, Kansas, and the Cessna factory in Wichita, Kansas.

In Romulus, a barracks that had been built under the Federal program for civilian employees in Wayne County, Michigan, would be available for twenty-five WAFS. There, the women would ferry L2-Bs, PT-23s, PT-26s, AT-19s and AT-6s. Romulus ferry pilots also serviced the Bell Aircraft factory in Buffalo, New York, at the other end of Lake Erie, where the P-39s and P-63s were built.

In Long Beach, the women would have to live off base temporarily, but eventually would move into a traditional barracks where cots lined both walls with an aisle down the center. Initially, the women would ferry basic trainers, the Vultee BT-13. But with all those other aircraft factories so close at hand — Lockheed, North American, Douglas, Convair, Northrop, Ryan, as well as Vultee — it wouldn't be long before the Long Beach girls moved into much bigger, more complex aircraft.

No one knew yet when Cochran's flight school would turn out its first graduates, but when it did, they were destined to fly with the WAFS. This meant the number of women ferry pilots would grow. The Ferrying Division had to get ready for them.

By the end of December, Nancy had her four squadrons organized and her girls assigned. Colonel Baker, for all his support in the formation of the WAFS squadron, took a dim view of women flying aircraft heavier than the liaisons and trainers they now flew. Nancy, fed up with "flying a desk" and looking for more airtime as well as an opportunity to transition into more powerful aircraft, turned the Wilmington squadron over to her executive officer and friend, Betty Gillies, on December 30, 1942. On New Year's Day, she left for the warmer, friendlier skies of Dallas.

Nancy could see the handwriting on the wall. Jacqueline Cochran had succeeded in getting her flight training school and already nearly one hundred women pilots were in Houston learning to fly "the Army way" under her supervision. And more were on the way. Nancy didn't think Jackie would stop there and let something she had built slip easily away into another's — namely, Nancy's — hands. Nancy also knew that Jackie had Hap Arnold's ear, consequently, she was apt to get that which she asked for.

Remaining in Wilmington and running a small squadron of women ferry pilots who were limited to flying primary trainers and liaison planes while Cochran built her own air force was not Nancy's idea of the way to spend the rest of the war. So she took another tack. She had gotten into the Ferrying Division with the idea of flying airplanes for her country. She knew better than anyone the trend in war plane manufacture and what ferry pilots eventually would be asked to do. If the planes were there, they had to be ferried somewhere in order to be put to use. The pilots who took them to their destination would be the ones who had transitioned into those higher-powered airplanes and been checked out to fly them. Nancy intended to check out in everything she could handle, thereby proving women were capable of flying high-performance airplanes. In the process, she paved the way for her WAFS to fly them as well.

A few days after Nancy left, Florene Miller, Helen Richards,

Dorothy Scott and Betsy Ferguson followed her to Dallas. Because Nancy had bigger things on her mind, she appointed Florene squadron commander.

Florene Miller was a tall, black-haired Texas beauty from San Angelo. She learned to fly in the single-engine Luscombe that her father, who owned several jewelry stores in small Texas towns, bought in 1940. Her twenty-first birthday happened to be the day Pearl Harbor was bombed. By then, she was teaching men to fly through the War Training Program in Odessa and Lubbock. She learned about the WAFS from a friend, Don Teel, who was ferrying bombers to England in 1942, and immediately wrote to Nancy Love. Florene, who had 899 hours at the time, became WAFS number thirteen. By December 7, 1942, when she turned twenty-two, she was en route to Great Falls, Montana, for that ferrying trip with five other WAFS.

Helen Richards, the youngest of the WAFS at just twenty-one, was tall, had dark blonde hair, and was blessed with a slender, tomboy build. She was quiet and reserved, and though very confident, preferred not to call attention to herself. By 1942, she had earned a Liberal Arts Associate degree from Pasadena Junior College in California and, when word came of Nancy's Love's intention to form a women's squadron, she was teaching flying at the Floating Feather Airport just outside Boise, Idaho. With 975 hours to her credit, Helen was one of the first of the younger women to report to Wilmington.

Dorothy Scott and her twin brother, Edward, were born in Seattle, Washington, on February 16, 1920. She learned to fly while a student at the University of Washington and was a flight instructor in Pullman when she heard about the WAFS. Arriving in Wilmington two weeks before Thanksgiving, 1942, she had a bare minimum of 504 hours in her log books and was the twenty-fifth woman accepted into the WAFS. She wrote home to her mother describing BOQ 14: "aside from mice-walking noises and mud, it's fine. My room is Number Thirteen so I ought to be lucky."

Betsy Ferguson grew up on a farm near Coffeyville, Kansas. She and her sister Sally, dubbed "The Flying Sisters" by newspapers in their home state, got their private pilot's licenses the same day in

1937. Betsy went on to obtain her commercial license followed by her instructor's rating and taught Civilian Pilot Training (CPT) and War Pilot Training (WPT) to male student pilots before joining the WAFS with 873 hours.

"Vikings must have contributed to Betsy's gene bank," says Delphine Bohn. "She was a natural blonde, very pretty, very beguiling. The first Saturday night at the Officers' Club in Dallas [after the arrival of the WAFS at Love Field in January 1943], Betsy, the blonde, blue-eyed doll, and Florene, the tall, gorgeous, green-eyed brunette, nearly caused a stampede among the men in the 5th Ferrying Group."

Thus, the Women's Squadron of the 5th Ferrying Group at Love Field in Dallas was born.

By mid-January, the Romulus contingent also had left for their new posting. Del Scharr was named squadron leader. Unfortunately, Del and her girls — Barbara Poole, Barbara Donahue, Phyllis Burchfield and Katherine Rawls Thompson — encountered not only the ice, sleet, snow and gray overcast of a Michigan winter, but a professionally chilly reception as well. Apparently women pilots were not as acceptable to the men of Romulus as they were to other commands.

**Del Scharr**

Adela Riek "Del" Scharr, born in 1907 and therefore one of the oldest of The Originals, learned to fly in 1935 at Lambert Field in St. Louis, Missouri. In 1940, she became Lambert Field's first female commercial pilot, its first woman ground instructor and its first female flight instructor. Tall — five feet nine-plus inches — and slender, she was a tomboy growing up, but a tomboy who loved to dance. Del had 1,429 hours when she joined the WAFS as its sixth member.

IWASM

**Del autographed the photo: To Theresa "Jamesy" A real gal – fun to be with! Someday I'd like to race you across the continent. How about that? Love, Del**

Barbara Donahue was born in New York City on March 25, 1920. She attended Vassar for a year and learned to fly in 1939 — soloing in 1940 at Roosevelt Field on Long Island in a Stinson 105. She was teaching flying in Houston, Texas, when she heard about the WAFS. She did not receive a telegram from Nancy Love, but had received one from Jacqueline Cochran a few months earlier inquiring as to her possible interest in flying with the ATA in England. A young woman blessed with an incredibly rich sense of humor, she arrived at BOQ 14 in October 1942 carrying a leopard skin coat over her arm. She had something over five hundred hours of flight time.

Barbara Poole was born in West Virginia but grew up in New Jersey. She fell in love with airplanes at age three and a half when she saw a biplane make a forced landing in the field next to where her family was vacationing in New Jersey. She also learned to read that year. By age eight, she had read enough that she could talk airplanes knowledgeably with adults. She often knew more than they did. She soloed at fifteen, got her private pilot's license at seventeen, and her commercial license at eighteen. Before joining the WAFS she held a variety of flying jobs, from barnstorming to CPT instructing, even to jumping out of airplanes — which, she says, she didn't like at all. In September 1942, she became the ninth member of Nancy Love's squadron.

Phyllis Burchfield was born at Fieldmore, in Pennsylvania, in 1913. Her first love was horses and, an expert equestrienne, she showed them all over the state. But she learned to fly as well and, on May 28, 1938, she flew the first airmail out of Colonel Drake Field in Titusville to Pittsburgh for the special flight commemorating the tenth anniversary of airmail delivery. Fellow Pennsylvanian Teresa James took part in that same exercise. Tiny Phyllis, she's just a hair over five feet, was instructing in Memphis when she heard about the WAFS. She had 1,675 hours at that point in her flying career. "I was in the air when the tower called me and told me that the Air Corps had just opened up to women. I didn't get a telegram from Nancy Love, so I called her. I told my boss I had to do it, I had to go. He tried hard to get me to stay because there weren't enough instructors, and I was making twice as much money in Memphis, but I went to Wilmington anyway. I was like all the others, hopped up on the idea of winning the war."

Katherine Rawls Thompson was born in Nashville, Tennessee, in 1917, but the family moved to Florida in 1922. A champion swimmer coached first by her father and later by her husband, Kay earned thirty-three national swimming and diving championships in the 1930s, and was an Olympic Silver medalist for the United States in Berlin in 1936. She learned to fly at a flight school in Fort Lauderdale run by her husband Ted. When the Navy took over the airport, Ted joined the RAF as a ferry pilot. Kay followed suit and joined Nancy Love's squadron. She had 675 hours.

## *The Romulus Five*

IWASM

**Katherine Rawls Thompson, Lenore McElroy,
Barbara Poole, Barbara Donahue and Del Scharr**

Soon after arriving at Dallas, Nancy Love checked out in a 450-horsepower Vultee BT-13 (nicknamed the Vultee Vibrator) and the 650-horsepower retractable-gear North American AT-6 (advanced trainer). Then she saw to it that her girls there began transition into both. In mid January, Nancy ferried an AT-6 to Romulus. Her trip there also gave her a chance to check on the newly established squadron and help them get settled in and organized. What was planned to be a relatively short official visit turned into an enforced stay of several days, however, as she got weathered in with the rest of the 3rd Ferrying Group.

While she was there, Colonel Carlyle Nelson, the Romulus commander, convinced her to take a look at local flight instructor Lenore McElroy. The Ferrying Division had been told it could hire qualified women pilots until January 25, 1943, after which all additions to the squadrons would have to come through Cochran's training school.

Lenore McElroy, known as "Mac," was born February 18, 1907 in St. Paul, Minnesota, and began her flying career in 1930 with a ride in a Ford Tri-Motor that took her over Niagara Falls. She was too frightened to look out the window. Deciding that just wouldn't do, that she needed to overcome her fear, Lenore opted to learn to fly. She married fellow pilot/flight instructor Clarence McElroy in 1935. He was her second husband and she was, by then, the mother of three. During the war, the family was living in Ypsilanti, Michigan, a town just down the road from Romulus. Clarence was a ferry pilot for the 3rd Ferrying Group and Lenore was instructing. At that point she had 3,500 hours flight time.

She had not been willing to leave her children to go to Wilmington because her husband, as a ferry pilot, frequently had to be gone overnight. But now with the advent of the squadron in Romulus, she was anxious to join.

Nancy, herself, gave Lenore her flight check during a short break in the lowering Michigan cloud cover. McElroy passed with flying colors and the clouds rolled back in almost immediately, again grounding the squadron and Nancy. It was late January before the Romulus WAFS got off the ground for their first ferrying job. McElroy was still doing her orientation training when the five who came from Wilmington were sent to Buffalo to pick up PT-23s and ferry them to Montgomery, Alabama. Fighting bad weather all the way south, they didn't return to Romulus until February 5.

The same bad January weather system that hung over Romulus affected the rest of the eastern half of the country, including Wilmington. Betty Gillies, checking her log book for January and February of 1943, discovered that she had barely flown at all. Likewise, the remaining WAFS, and the men who flew with the 2nd Ferrying Group, were grounded more often than they flew.

Sis Bernheim and Helen McGilvery qualified for the WAFS squadron at Wilmington in January. Like Lenore McElroy, they made it in under the January 25 cut-off date and were immediately put into their thirty-day orientation.

Sis Bernheim learned to fly in a Taylor Cub the summer of 1934 at Roosevelt Field on Long Island. Her instructor eventually invited her to join him as a partner in his flying business, which they operated successfully until Pearl Harbor. After that, restrictions on coastal flying shut them down. Sis tried to join Jacqueline Cochran's group of women pilots bound for England to fly with the ATA, but she and the other five American women who were checked out that day were all flunked by a disgruntled RAF pilot who thought women had no business flying airplanes. She eventually joined Nancy Love's WAFS instead.

Helen McGilvery was known to one and all as "Little Mac." According to her closest friend in the WAFS, Nancy Batson, Little Mac was a petite woman, always immaculately dressed and well groomed. Very precise about all things, she possessed both a superior intelligence and a sharp tongue. "She was an excellent pilot," says Nancy, "but do you know how she got money to pay for her flying lessons? She went to the race track and bet and WON! She was married. Her husband was a ferry pilot, too, and they lived in town, in Wilmington. She didn't live in the BOQ with the rest of us."

One other incident occurred during the winter of 1943, somewhat shifting the makeup of the Wilmington-based squadron. Recently married Esther Manning turned up pregnant. Though some of her friends may have had their suspicions, nothing was said, even when the very attractive and usually well-dressed Esther began to wear

IWASM

**Four Wilmington WAFS, winter 1943:**
**Esther Nelson, Esther Manning, Helen Mary Clark and Delphine Bohn**

her gray wool WAFS topcoat everywhere.

Finally, Esther leveled with Betty Gillies. Betty, having flown through the early part of three pregnancies herself, let Esther fly until she got too big to be able to pull the stick back into her stomach, then addressed the situation with typical Gillies pragmatism and determination. Since the Army had no regulations for what to do with pregnant women pilots, Betty convinced Colonel Baker to keep Esther on the payroll and let her take over the paper work in the office, thus freeing both Betty and her new executive officer, Helen Mary Clark, for ferrying duty. Since both Betty and Helen Mary hated desk duty, much preferring to fly, the arrangement suited them both and Esther remained part of the squadron.

Delphine Bohn and Barbara Donahue were witnesses at Esther's wedding. Delphine has written this about the occasion:

> On a cold, wet Saturday evening, the four of us drove
> to a quiet parsonage an hour from the base. That is, it

would have been a run of approximately an hour if made by any other driver. On this trip, the driver was Donahue. It was her car. She drove with no respect for speed limits or speedometer readings. Once Donnie had decided it was impossible for her to survive in Wilmington without ground transportation, she had purchased the automobile from a soldier on his way overseas.

Immediately after we had recovered from the solemnity of the vows spoken by our lovely friend and had joined the good parson and his wife in their toast to the couple, we began the fingers-crossed trip back to base. Along the way we stopped at an elite restaurant in order that we might further toast the newlyweds and provide them with a wedding supper.

Then again crowded into the car, we took off, Donnie at the wheel. Within two or three miles, flashing lights pulled us over to the side of the highway. Two burly police officers opened the door on the driver's side. Their unfriendly eyes examined us thoroughly and lengthily. They asked, and certainly not politely, that Donnie furnish them with a driver's license.

It was not the most pleasant situation and this cowed Texan shivered with trepidation. I had a vision. It was a vision that the newly married pair would have their wedding night in jail, accompanied by their witnesses! You may take your choice as to whether our release was due to the fact we were highly publicized WAFS and possibly impressed them as such, whether it was that we could exhibit a brand new marriage license, or, so far, that night their tour of duty had been pleasant.

Years later, in a conversation with Betty Gillies, the subject of Esther Manning's wedding came up. I had begun with my wordy recollection of her wedding evening and my fear of the probability of a night spent in jail. Betty could not wait to inform me that surely I must be taking storyteller's license for it was SHE who had witnessed Esther's wedding in Wilmington.

Finally it dawned on both of us that we were talking about two different dates in two different years. There had been two perfectly legitimate weddings, with a lapse of time and a divorce in between . . . .

The squadron in Long Beach was the last of the three to be launched, but by early February, B.J. Erickson was on her way west to make the final arrangements. Their quarters would not be ready for a few more days, but not far behind her would be Cornelia Fort, Evelyn Sharp, Barbara Towne and Bernice Batten.

The smallest airplane the Long Beach WAFS would be ferrying was the BT-13. The five were quickly checked out in the basic trainer and, immediately, were sent out on ferry trips, mostly to Texas where many Army Air Forces' flight training bases were located.

And thus the lid had been lifted. The WAFS were transitioning into the more powerful trainer aircraft, like BT-13s and AT-6s, and were beginning to ferry them.

With the needs of the Ferrying Division changing, Nancy Love had tacit approval from Colonel Tunner to fly any airplane she was capable of handling. For a pilot as skilled and ambitious as she was, and since she had also learned which channels to tap and how to go about it without making waves, that amounted to carte blanche. Nancy made the most of it.

Several other factors contributed to Nancy being given the go-ahead for further transition. Going into the war, what was then known as the Air Corps was a small branch of the much larger U.S. Army and it was considered the stepchild of the older, more elite corps. What little was known about air war had come out of World War I. Since then, airplane design and capability had moved light years forward. How best to utilize this new might in warfare was pretty much unknown. World War II was the proving ground, the training ground, the time when the blueprints were drawn. There wasn't much to go on in the way of tradition, because little had been tried.

The war was now a year old. The Army had learned a lot — what worked, what didn't work and what needed to be altered to make it work better.

Some of the Reserve pilots the Air Corps began the war with were airline pilots. These men were masters at flying cross-country and with the safety of passengers uppermost in their minds. Consequently, they looked after their airplanes. Other Reserve officers, however, were barnstormers, stunt pilots, crop dusters — men who flew on the edge, took chances, showed off. If those men were going to deliver airplanes safely from one part of the country to another, they had to learn to look at flying differently. Some degree of retraining was definitely in order.

Early in 1942, a fledgling Air Transport Command began to discover how to train ferry pilots — that is, how to teach men who already knew how to fly the proper way to take an airplane across country safely and in optimum time; how to handle interim stops for fuel, weather, and overnights (RON); how to process the paper work; and how to get back to base quickly once they had delivered their airplane.

Tunner and his people realized that the best way to train men who eventually would ferry four-engine bombers and fly fully-loaded, four-engine cargo planes over oceans, deserts and mountains all over the world, was to start them flying cross country in little single-engine PTs and Cubs. Then, their instructors would let them transition up and deliver intermediate-sized planes and then larger planes. This way, they gradually would gain the confidence, experience, and skills necessary to be a ferry pilot.

Two things were obvious. One: what worked for the men surely could work for the women pilots as well. Two: if the Ferrying Division allowed the women ferry pilots to remain static, flying only the smallest airplanes at the bottom of the transition ladder, the men who needed to begin at that level in order to work their way up would be denied that valuable training.

Still, in mid-February 1943, only Nancy among the women had the go-ahead beyond the basic and advanced trainers they were just beginning to ferry. Most of the official restrictions on the women pilots lingered until spring 1943.

The final reason Nancy — and subsequently the other WAFS — got the go-ahead for transitions was that the WFTD trainees down in Houston were working their way up from primary trainers to basic trainers and soon would be moving into advanced trainers and eventually twin-engine aircraft. Tunner was not about to let his WAFS be bypassed by Jacqueline Cochran's flying school graduates-to-be.

By the end of January 1943, Nancy was ready for something even bigger.

IWASM

**Betty Gillies, Evelyn Sharp, B.J. Erickson, Helen Richards
December 2, 1942 — Camp Pickett, Blackstone, Virginia**

**Nancy Love and B.J. Erickson**
**outside the WAFS Operations Office, Long Beach, California**

# 14

Nancy Love went to Long Beach in February 1943 to oversee the transfer of the five WAFS to the 6th Ferrying Group. If she was going to lead the way for her WAFS to fly bigger, heavier, faster airplanes, Long Beach — with its accessibility to many types of aircraft — was the place to do it.

Officially, the WAFS were still restricted to trainer or light aircraft. But, already, they were beginning to ferry higher horsepower airplanes. The 450-horsepower BT-13 and the 650-horsepower AT-6 Texan were a far cry from the 65-horsepower Cubs and even the 175-horsepower PT-19s. Nancy's eyes were on even bigger game, specifically the hot new pursuit plane, the P-51 Mustang, being built at the North American plant near Long Beach. Quietly and with absolutely no fanfare — which, of course, was how Nancy preferred to do things — she began to work her way into its snug cockpit.

First step was to fly the now familiar AT-6 from the back seat. Nancy had flown the pug-nosed Texan with its A-shaped mullioned canopy from the front seat — as was customary — first with an instructor in the back seat and then solo. From the back seat, it was a completely different animal. The cant produced by the backward slope of the aircraft — from the bigger tires in the front to the pigmy-sized tail-wheel in the rear — put the pilot's view of the world at a decided angle. This made it difficult to see over the engine cowling, and that was the point. In the tail-dragger pursuit airplanes, because of the big engine, forward visibility was zero. So, the fledgling pursuit pilot had to deal with that by learning to look to the sides of the runway when landing and taking off and to execute a series of S-turns for visibility when negotiating the taxiway.

She spent her first flights looking around the instructor's broad back, taking off, landing, and taking off again. After a few back-seat encounters with the Texan, Nancy declared herself ready.

♻

The P-51 Mustang, when fully armed, was a compact war-making machine with six fifty-calibre machine guns. The wingspan of the sleek aircraft was thirty-seven feet. Its length was thirty-two feet and it was eight feet eight inches high. The Mustang was driven by an Allison, later a Rolls Royce Merlin 1650-horsepower engine. Speed — 425 miles per hour! The landing gear was a hydraulically-operated, retractable main gear and a tail-wheel. The propeller was a four-blade, hydraulic, constant-speed Hamilton Standard — eleven feet two inches. A forward-facing intake scoop on the underside of its belly served to catch cool air for both the oil and engine coolant radiators, even during taxiing or at slow engine speeds. Nothing obstructed the flow of air to keep the engine cool and running.

Production had begun in 1940. Each Mustang cost Uncle Sam approximately $90,000. North American built 15,586 of them between then and the end of the war. Their primary mission was to escort bombers deep into Germany. Because of the Mustang's efficient aerodynamics, it could out-climb the Luftwaffe's Focke-Wulfs and Messerschmitts. It made a name for itself by blasting trains, ships, and enemy installations in western Europe and by knocking out Axis defenses prior to the Allied invasion of Sicily and Italy. The Mustang also copped several firsts: first single-engine plane based in Britain to penetrate Germany; first to reach Berlin; first to go with the heavy bombers over the Ploesti oil fields; and first to make a major, all-fighter sweep to hunt down the dwindling Luftwaffe fleet. The Truman Senate War Investigating Committee in 1944 rated it "the most aerodynamically perfect pursuit plane in existence."

♻

First Nancy memorized the tech orders. Then, lugging her para-chute and with her instructor trailing behind, Nancy did a walk around, checking the condition of the tires, the landing gear, the tail-wheel. She inspected the propeller for nicks, checked the level of fuel in the gas tanks, and completed the myriad other life-saving checks necessary before climbing into the airplane.

She placed her parachute on the roof of the left wing, stepped up on the tire of the landing gear and onto the wing. Retrieving her chute, she carefully lowered it onto the bucket seat inside the cockpit. Leg over the side, she stepped down on her parachute, took the long step to the floor of the cockpit and sat down. First she tested the rudders, then the toe brakes on the tips of the rudder pedals. Next she tried the control stick, pushed it forward, brought it back, moved it to the right and then the left. With each hand movement, she checked the response of the airplane's controls to her bidding.

A radio check was next, followed by a mental check-off of the various dials and gauges.

Wedged down in the cockpit, with her instructor squatting on the wing beside her, Nancy thought fleetingly about Houghton, Michigan, and the old Fleet Biplane. Of Jimmy Hansen, her first instructor, and August 31, 1930, when she soloed at age sixteen. She wondered how she had ever got up the nerve to move from there to here. Just as Jimmy had grilled her on the Fleet's flight characteristics, this instructor had grilled her on the Mustang's, and now he waited for her to give the word that she was ready to try it. The difference was, Jimmy had flown with her until he was satisfied she could handle the airplane by herself. In the Mustang, her first flight would be solo. Whether she got off and landed safely was completely in her hands. Could she handle this airplane?

She looked up at her instructor and nodded. "I guess I'd better see if I can fly this thing."

He jumped off. Nancy cracked the throttle about an inch and moved the mixture control to "idle cut-off." A crewman turned the propeller several revolutions by hand, then stuck a battery charger into the side of the engine. Moments later, the engine roared to life. She pushed the button on the stick to activate her throat mike and called the tower. She was ready.

Gently working the rudders, she made her series of S-turns down the taxiway — the engine cowling blocking any view straight in front of her. When she reached the end, she ran the checklist once more — magnetos, manifold pressure, rpm's. When everything checked out, she sat for a few seconds, pressed the mike button on the throttle, called the tower, and was cleared for takeoff.

Nancy pushed the throttle all the way forward, felt the airplane surge and begin its takeoff roll as she watched the airspeed indicator climb. She could see nothing in front of her, only the little triangles of runway visible at either wingtip. Her body pressed back against the seat, then the tail came up and, before she knew it, she was off the ground and climbing. Soon, she was soaring over the Pacific Ocean at 10,000 feet, going 300 miles per hour. She moved the stick, very delicately, ever so slightly, and banked to the right. Then she moved it in the opposite direction and banked to the left. The response was immediate and sweet.

An hour later, after practicing maneuvers all over the sky, she began to prepare for her first landing.

The final approach in a pursuit was likened to a quick descent from the top of the Empire State Building in an express elevator. Nancy set up the continuous turn prescribed for landing pursuits and headed in. At just the right moment, she pulled back on the stick and set the airplane's wheels neatly on the runway. Moments later, she was streaking down the runway watching those two tiny triangles at the outer edge of the wingtips out of the corners of her eyes. She was down.

The date was February 27, 1943. Women had taken a giant step forward in the annals of aviation. A woman had just flown one of the fastest airplanes ever built.

From then on, Nancy took to pursuits like an eaglet to flight, executing the quick over and down movements with a delight but never abandon. She was too cautious for that. Nevertheless, she knew how to take charge of stick and rudder and what it meant to fly by the seat of her pants.

⌒⊚⌒

On March 8, 1943, Betty Gillies — who had been working her way into the cockpit of the P-47 — flew the mighty Thunderbolt.

And that occurred in the face of Colonel Baker's aversion to women flying heavy, high-horsepowered aircraft. In fact, he finally allowed Betty to fly the big pursuit because Nancy Love had told him, quite frankly, that his reluctance to let women transition was the reason she was transferring out of Wilmington and going to Dallas the first of the year.

IWASM

**Betty Gillies and a P- 47**

In preparation for her transition into the P-47, Betty got orders to go to Farmingdale, New York to the Republic Aviation factory on Long Island, and meet with the control officer.

"He had me play with the landing gear and other equipment on the P-47," she recalled. "And he answered every question I had."

Betty had only one problem with the P-47. At five feet one, she couldn't reach the rudder pedals of the monster pursuit and still see out of the cockpit. So she asked a pilot she knew who worked with her husband at Grumman Aircraft — a man not much taller than she — to make her a set of blocks to go over the rudder pedals so that she could reach and control them with her feet and still see out. He had done the same thing himself in order to be able to fly some of the bigger aircraft. With the blocks in place, Betty, with fifteen years flying experience and some 1,200 hours in the cockpit, began her quest.

Between January 12 and March 8, Betty Gillies had gone up the transition ladder to master the P-47. Years later, Del Scharr received the following letter from Betty, dated August 25, 1976:

It was mid-winter when I started and lots of time went by between flights. In between snowstorms and ferrying missions I got in about ten-plus hours in the AT-6. Transition consisted of about four hours, forty minutes of dual landings and takeoffs. The rest, solo practice. While I was getting the required time in the AT-6, I also checked out in the AT-9 (which had two 295 hp Lycoming engines in it), but I don't think that was the usual procedure. The AT-9 was used more for transition to the Martin B-26.

After my first solo flight in a P-47 on March 8, I put in about fourteen hours practicing landings at Newcastle and made a required cross-country with landings at two other airports. It was quite difficult getting those fourteen hours in as it was not very often that Transition School had a P-47 on the line and operating. Besides which, I was off on ferrying missions a good deal of the time. So it was May 4th before I made my first P-47 delivery.

It really was no problem fitting myself in the airplanes. I sat on a cushion which, with the parachute, put me up plenty high. And the only real long-legged airplanes were those for which I had the blocks. I could use a cushion behind me quite well in all but the P-38, the P-47 and the P-51. In those cockpits, the gunsights were too close to my face if I used a cushion behind me. The blocks Grumman made up gave my legs the length I needed. Grumman also made me a gadget to turn the fuel valve in the P-38.

I don't know why I happened to fly the 47 before Nancy. It just worked out that way. I don't suppose they had any 47s where she was. The 2nd Ferrying Group at Wilmington was responsible for the P-47 deliveries from Republic at Farmingdale, so I guess it was only a natural sequence of events that led to my getting the transition. Am sure that if Nancy had been at NCAAB she would have been the guinea pig!

As for the movement of women into the cockpits of pursuit planes, Scharr, the first woman to fly the P-39 (that story is coming later), said: "A small group of select women weren't intent on pulling male pursuit pilots off the pedestal upon which they had placed themselves. Instead, they were saying 'Move over, Buddy' and joined them on it."

Now the gates were wide open. On March 3, Nancy applied for a permanent change of station to Long Beach. On March 5, she made her first delivery of a C-47 — the twin-engine Army cargo plane that is better known to civilians as the DC-3 airliner. B.J. Erickson was Nancy's copilot on the trip from Long Beach to Memphis. By now, Nancy had checked out not only on the P-51 and C-47, but on the A-20 and fourteen other types of planes, mostly manufactured in the L.A. Basin. (The designation "A" is for Attack and denotes a single-seater, attack/bomber airplane.) Ferrying Division Headquarters approved her transfer on March 11, effective March 21.

By this time, B.J. Erickson had the WAFS' squadron of the 6th Ferrying Group up and running smoothly. B.J., born July 1, 1920, in Seattle, Washington, was a natural administrator and definitely cut out for command. Nancy must have recognized that capability early, because she didn't hesitate to put the twenty-two year old in the squadron leader's position.

Barbara Jane Erickson had entered the CPT program in 1939, during her sophomore year at the University of Washington, and soon soloed a Taylorcraft seaplane. After earning her commercial license and her instructor's rating, B.J. began instructing in that same program while she finished college. She was in the middle of teaching a class when she got word of Nancy Love's squadron being formed. Erickson knew that was where her destiny lay.

**B.J. Erickson, pilot in command**

"I was working for a guy who would let me go. In fact, he wrote me a beautiful letter of recommendation. 'What an opportunity for a kid,' he said. 'Go.'" She left immediately for Wilmington to join the WAFS.

With Nancy Love already in Long Beach, the squadron in Dallas was shorthanded. On March 4, 1943, Delphine Bohn was transferred from Wilmington to replace her.

Delphine was a native of Amarillo, Texas. When she joined the WAFS she had 815 hours — all of them flown "in the windshifts, duststorms, icestorms, and hailstorms of the Texas Panhandle."

Delphine was convinced that the best pilots earned their wings by learning to buck those capricious prairie winds. She soloed a Piper Cub in April 1940 at English Field in Amarillo, and thus began a lifelong career in aviation. By the time the WAFS came along, she was a primary CPT instructor on her home field for her original instructor and had to get her good friend to release her from her "war frozen" job in order to go to Wilmington.

"Rather than listen to me beg and cry, he released me."

∽⊙⊙∾

Back in Washington, things were heating up with Jacqueline Cochran as the arrival of the first Houston graduates at the four women's ferrying squadrons drew nearer. At first, they were expected around March 1, but that was quickly revised to May 1. Colonel Tunner wanted Nancy at Ferrying Division Headquarters which, as it so happened, was moving to Cincinnati, Ohio. He had no intention of dealing with an ever-increasing contingent of women pilots under his command without a woman he trusted — Nancy Love — to run interference for him. He did not trust Jacqueline Cochran. Another transfer went through and, in late March, Nancy was reassigned again — this time to Cincinnati.

Fearing she was heading back to flying a desk again, she stalled as long as she gracefully could — busily flying those big, beautiful West Coast airplanes — but finally, in June 1943, she acquiesced. On her way to take up residence in Cincinnati, she ferried a B-25 to Kansas City, thus adding the twin-engine Mitchell bomber feather to her flight cap.

**Teresa James**

# 15

A year later in February 1944, women would be ferrying pursuit airplanes from one coast to the other as a matter of course. In those lightning fast airplanes, equipped with instruments and radios, you could fly across the country in ten hours in good weather. But in the dreary, fog and ice-bound winter of 1943, the WAFS were barely able to get their putt-putt airplanes off the snow-covered ground. So on February 16, 1943, when Betty Gillies told Teresa James that she was going to ferry a PT-19 from Hagerstown, Maryland, to Burbank, California — all by herself — Teresa nearly came unglued.

First of all, Dink was out in Southern California so she would get to see him. Second, this was no ordinary ferrying job. Teresa would be delivering the plane to the famous flyer Major Paul Mantz who was doing the stunt work in the film *Ladies Courageous*, about the WAFS and starring Loretta Young as Nancy Love. Third, this was a very big first — the first time *a woman* ferry pilot had delivered an airplane from one coast to the other. And she was going alone. Teresa possessed a sharp sense of history. She knew this was important.

There had to be some wisdom, too, on Betty Gillies' part, assigning the Hollywood duty to Teresa. Jamesy was the ultimate extrovert — always friendly, never at a loss for words, she greeted life with a smile on her face, had a good time wherever she went, looked good in her uniform and was attractive even though her looks were not of movie star quality like raven-haired Florene Miller or blonde Nancy Batson. Besides, she was long on experience and she could fly anything!

So at 12:30 p.m. on February 18, 1943, Teresa James, dressed in winter flying gear with parachute bumping the backs of her legs, strode to the flight line amidst popping flash bulbs (the press quickly caught wind that she was headed for California), climbed into her PT-19 in Hagerstown and took off for the West Coast. Typically, the light, non-instrument-equipped, open-cockpit aircraft fell victim to fog and bad weather en route so her trip out to Burbank took eight days. By Ferry Division standards in early 1943, that wasn't at all bad for three thousand miles. And gregarious Jamesy had a ball in spite of delays. She met and talked with friendly male pilots all the way across the south to Dallas, flew with them when they were going her way, and left them in her dust when they weren't. She never lacked for dinner companions at the bases where she stopped — usually male, but sometimes female as she ran into some of her fellow WAFS en route.

### Teresa's journal (excerpted) . . .
### *February 18 to March 11, 1943*

I'm going part way with six lieutenants. Gassed up in Lynchburg then went on to Charlotte. Had a lot of fun trying to fly formation with the six Looies. They sure are good. My nerves got the best of me so I gave it up. They held the formation all the way to Charlotte, then peeled off into landing formation. Beautiful!

Fogged in early the next morning, but finally got off. Went to Atlanta where we landed to check the weather. It's very hazy. Could hardly see.

I'm really having fun flying formation with these former cadets.

We decided to go on to Birmingham. What a town! It's so smoky you can't see a half mile ahead of you. Talk about Pittsburgh. It can't hold a candle to Birmingham. We kept circling at four hundred feet. Finally found the airport. Another new army base. Stayed at the Nurses BOQ. Had dinner at the Officers' Mess with Helen Richards' boyfriend — the one who sent her roses. Not bad looking.

Next morning can't see the field for the smoke. Finally get out of there at 1:20.

We had ever so much fun flying to Jackson, Mississippi. Zoomed all the towns.

It's Saturday night! Even the YW and the YM are filled up. Finally got a room at the Nurses' Quarters on base. Went dancing.

The Royal Netherlands Army and Navy Air Force were training there. Danced with several of them. I got back to the Nurses' Quarters at 4 a.m.

Next morning, the airport was on instruments. Going nowhere today. Met some more of the Dutch boys and one of their American instructors who learned to fly with Batson. Another 'hello' to deliver.

Got out the next morning, headed for Shreveport. Two of the Looies dropped down to ten feet over the ground. One zoomed a train. That started me off. I flew about fifteen feet over the highway scaring the hell out of everyone. Then I followed the train track for fifty miles. Headed straight for a train, then hopped up over him. I expected the engineer and fireman to leap right out of the cab. Then I went and pestered the farmers. Scattered them in every direction. Boy, what a rip-roaring time I had. Good thing there are no numbers on the ships. After lunch, shoved off for Dallas where I left the boys.

Called the BOQ to see who was there. Nancy Love is in Washington. Florene Miller and Dorothy Scott left on a BT trip a few minutes before I landed. Richards and Ferguson were there. So spent hours chewing the rag with them. They have lovely quarters and raved about the base. I wish I were here.

Next morning left Dallas for Abilene. Saw nothing but cattle, sagebrush and waterholes. Gassed up and went on to Midland. Lots of oil wells. Met a friend of Delphine Bohn's. Another 'hello' to deliver. Flew over Miller's hometown, Odessa. I don't like the dust. The wind was blowing about thirty-five miles an hour and I really bounced around. On my way to Pecos, came across this big army base. Landed amidst a flock of B-17s. They asked me for my clearance. They didn't have a flight plan on me and no wonder. I wasn't in Pecos, I was in Pyote. Pecos is twenty miles west. I wasn't watching my time.

This is the base of the famous 19th Bombardment Squadron that blasted the Germans. Nearly everyone here has been across several times.

Left Pyote the next morning at 10:30. Had a heck of a time getting out. Everyone asking me questions. It was the first time a girl flyer had been on that base. My clothes were covered with dust, even my hair. Cleared to El Paso.

The sun shining on the Apache and Sierra Diablo Mountains is a beautiful sight. I feel so all alone up here. Nothing but vast space. I could see Guadalupe Pass for miles and miles. The mountains are several different colors — red, green, tan, brown and beige. I'm simply awed by the scenery. I flew the borderline of the United States and Mexico — separated by the Rio Grande River which looked like a narrow stream to me. Flew with one wing in Mexico and the other in the U.S. Crossed over the river at Fabens just to say I flew in Old Mexico.

Had dinner at the Officers' Mess with one of the captains. He showed me the base and took me to look at El Paso and Juarez.

Flying from El Paso to Columbus, New Mexico, is strictly desert for seventy miles. Then on to Tucson. Desolate country. Not a check point for miles. I'd hate like hell to have a forced landing here. Had trouble getting a room, but a colonel and his wife came to my rescue. He called the Nurses' BOQ, talked to the head nurse who gave me a room.

Had breakfast with the head nurse the next morning and then headed for Phoenix. From there to Blythe, California. That is by far the most desolate one hundred fifty miles I have flown. Nothing but airway light beacons for checkpoints. Left at 3:30 on my way to Riverside, California. More desert. Passed close to the Salton Sea, two hundred forty-five feet below sea level. Chocolate Mountains to my left and straight ahead, San Jacinto Peak. It's covered with snow although the sun is very hot now. I never knew there were so many mountains in California. I've never been this far west!

I'm going through San Gorgonio Pass and what a picture. When you start through it, you are about five hundred feet. Palm Springs is nestled at the foot of the San Gorgonio Mountains and the beginning of the pass. It gradually slopes upward to 1,963 feet. March Field is located at the top.

Landed. Recon car picked me up and took me into town. We stopped and picked some oranges and lemons off a tree. Called Dink that night. Was so excited, I couldn't sleep.

Next morning headed for Burbank. Flew over Esther Nelson's home at Ontario and over the Rose Bowl in Pasadena. I delivered the ship to Paul Mantz. Met Loretta Young. Snazzy looking dame. A real lady. Then got a C-78 ride over Hollywood, Los Angeles and Santa Barbara right up the coastline.

Spent February 27-28 with Dink in Santa Maria.

Next day, back to Burbank. Got the 2:40 a.m. train out. Major Paul Mantz wants to take me around to some of the studios. He gets me a room at the swankiest hotel on the West Coast. The manager is thrilled at having a girl flyer there.

March 2, met Ted Lewis. Walter Huston, Katie Hepburn, Spencer Tracy are staying here. Spencer Tracy came over to the table. Went to the set of the movie "Stormy Weather." Met Cab Calloway and Bill Robinson. Saw Jackie Cooper at the Brown Derby, then on to the Palladium where Benny Goodman was playing. Topped off the evening at Romanoffs'. Louella Parsons and Marlene Deitrich were there.

**Jamesy and Bob Hope**

March 3, had breakfast with Father Flannigan of Boys Town. Met the Baron von Rothschild. Went to Warner Brothers Studio and the set of *Saratoga Trunk*. Met Ingrid Bergman and Gary Cooper. Talked with Gary for an hour. Back to the Brown Derby for dinner. Was asked to join Bob Hope who was having dinner. I was thrilled to pieces. He invited me out to the Paramount Studio. Went on to the Coconut Grove at the Ambassador Hotel. Freddy Martin and his orchestra were playing. Met Freddy and, as usual, got questions about the uniform. I've caused no less than a sensation every place I've gone.

Met Jimmy McHugh, the famous song writer. He had just written "Coming In On a Wing and a Prayer." He's sending me a copy. Then he introduced me to Ginny Simms. Wow, was I ever taken off my feet. She asked me if I could get an extended leave so I could appear on her Philip Morris program as guest star. Back at the hotel, I sent a telegram to Betty asking for a four-day extension.

Telephone woke me from a sound sleep the next morning. It was the answer to my telegram granting leave permission.

They want a picture of me with Barney Ross, the lightweight boxing champion of the world. He's a Marine just back from Guadalcanal. He has over two hundred Japs to his credit. Had lunch with Ginny Simms and her mother, then dashed out to Paramount to meet Bob Hope. Went to the set of *Lady in the Dark* where I met Ginger Rodgers. She is one sweet girl. Met Warner Baxter, Veronica Lake, Paulette Goddard and George Reeves. Bob introduced me to everyone, calling me Jessie James, his little WAF. Met Eve Arden and dear sweet Zazu Pitts. Met Mary Astor that night.

Next morning tried to call Dink. He thinks I'm back in Wilmington. Finally reached him to tell him I'm coming up tomorrow.

Spent March 6 and 7 with Dink.

Back Monday morning, March 8. Had at least twenty-five phone messages. Had a date with Bob Hope to see his show last night and tossed it over to stay with Dink. Missed 'Meet the People' broadcast which I was to appear on. Ginny Simms called several times for a rehearsal. Everyone thought I had run out on them. I just wanted to spend some quality time with my husband — in the sack!

Had dinner at the Brown Derby with Ginny Simms and her mother.

Received a telegram from the girls back in Wilmington. It read:

ALL ELECTRICAL WIRING HAS BEEN CHECKED BY BASE ENGINEERING. NEW ANTENNAS ARE INSTALLED. AUDITO-RIUM ENLARGED. AWAITING THE HOUR. GIVE 'EM THE WORKS.

I thought it was funny. They were all gonna listen to the show.

Ginny took me to lunch and went over the script with me. We went on. That was, without a doubt, the longest five minutes I ever spent. Later, went back to the Brown Derby for dinner with the cast from the show, then they took me back to the studio for the big surprise. They had made a recording of the show and we sat there listening to ourselves. The evening wasn't over until I got back to the hotel at two in the morning. I met so many people, I couldn't begin to remember their names. Everyone was swell to me. But Little Cinderella goes back home tomorrow!

At the airport, people are staring at me like I'm a freak. This uniform attracts more attention. Major Mantz comes and keeps me company waiting for my airliner to leave.

Thursday, March 11, Cinderella arrived back at Wilmington aboard a pumpkin. Found a welcome home sign in my room and a pile of mail, but I was too tired to open any of it. All the gals went on a trip to Canada. So to bed I go. I'm weary —

*Editor's note:* Teresa's adventures in Hollywood certainly weren't the norm for the WAFS, but her own words written in her journal point up the hunger and willingness of celebrities and other civilians to treat the men and women in uniform well. March 11, 1943, marks the end of Teresa's surviving diary as all the rest was lost when the basement of her parents' home in Pittsburgh flooded several years later and Teresa's sister threw out the soggy mess because it was unrecognizable as anything worthwhile keeping.

## The 6<sup>th</sup> Ferrying Group

**Barbara Towne, Cornelia Fort, Evelyn Sharp,
B.J. Erickson, Bernice Batten
Vultee Factory, Long Beach, California**

# 16

*December 7, 1941, Honolulu, Hawaii*

Cornelia Fort, flying in a tiny two-seater Interstate Cadet with her student Suomala, a Honolulu-based defense worker, looked out in the distance into a gradually lightening blue sky and an even bluer Pacific Ocean. Not quite eight o'clock on a Sunday morning, it promised to be an exquisite day for flying.

Suomala was just entering the down wind leg in the traffic pattern to practice a touch-and-go landing at Honolulu's John Rodgers Airport when Cornelia spotted a military airplane coming in from the sea. Their plane was safely within the civilian zone, so she let her student continue his turn onto base leg. Then she noticed that the plane was headed straight toward them. They were, in fact, on a collision course.

In an article published in *Woman's Home Companion* in 1943, Cornelia wrote:

> I jerked the controls away from my student and jammed the throttle wide open to pull above the oncoming plane. I remember a distinct feeling of annoyance that the Army plane had disrupted our traffic pattern and violated our safety zone. He passed so close under us that our celluloid windows rattled violently, and I looked down to see what kind of plane it was.
>
> The painted red balls on the tops of the wings shone brightly in the sun I looked again with complete and utter unbelief. Honolulu was familiar with the emblem of the Rising Sun on passenger ships but not on airplanes.
>
> I looked quickly at Pearl Harbor, and my spine tingled when I saw billowing black smoke. Still, I thought hollowly,

it might be some kind of coincidence or maneuvers — it might be, it must be. For surely, dear God. Then I looked way up and saw formations of silver bombers riding in. I saw something detach itself from a plane and come glistening down. My eyes followed it down, down, down, and even with knowledge pounding in my mind, my heart turned over convulsively when the bomb exploded in the middle of the Harbor.

Suddenly that little wedge of sky above Hickam Field and Pearl Harbor was the busiest, fullest piece of sky I ever saw.

Most people wonder how they would react in a crisis; if the danger comes as suddenly as this did you don't have time to be frightened. I'm not brave, but I knew the air was not the place for our little baby airplane and I set about landing as quickly as ever I could. It was as if the attack was happening in a different time track, with no relation to me.

A burst of machine gun fire rattled in my ear. I headed for the runway, landed and taxied the plane toward the hangars.

That the attack did have relation to me was brought forcibly to my attention a few seconds later when I saw a shadow pass over me and simultaneously saw bullets spattering all around me.

We jumped from the airplane and ran for cover as a second volley of bullets ripped into the tiny plane behind us. We made it safely into the hangar.

We counted anxiously as our little civilian planes came flying home to roost. Two never came back. They were washing ashore weeks later on the windward side of the island, bullet-riddled. Not a pretty way for the brave little yellow Cubs and their pilots to go down to death.

Cornelia Fort survived the December 7, 1941 attack on Pearl Harbor, but some of her fellow pilots who worked at Andrew Flying Service did not. Airport manager Bob Tyce was killed by the burst of gun fire that Cornelia, upon reflection, thought was meant for her.

On March 1, 1942, the ship bringing Cornelia home steamed under the Golden Gate Bridge into San Francisco. She spent a few days there with friends and, her status as celebrity having preceded her back to the mainland, she was the subject of several newspaper stories. The same was true when she arrived home in Nashville, having driven across country from the West Coast. Immediately, the local heroine — a bona fide survivor of Pearl Harbor — was called on for newspaper and radio interviews and to speak at all sorts of functions, from selling War Bonds to addressing the local Civil Air Patrol meeting.

By summer, when the celebrity status began to wear thin, she signed up for a Link Trainer (instrument training) course in New York, hoping to get a chance to fly for Uncle Sam now that the war was on. Like most Americans, she wanted to get even for the attack on Pearl Harbor and to avenge the people, both military and civilian, who had died there. Several of them people she knew.

"Each of us had some individual score to settle with the Japanese who had brought murder and destruction to our islands," she related. That opportunity knocked at her door September 6, 1942, in the form of the telegram from Nancy Love and Colonel Robert Baker sent under the auspices of General George. She wired her mother in Nashville immediately:

> THE HEAVENS HAVE OPENED UP AND RAINED BLESSINGS
> ON ME. THE ARMY HAS DECIDED TO LET WOMEN FERRY
> SHIPS AND I'M GOING TO BE ONE OF THEM.

Cornelia was the third woman to make the WAFS roster, right behind Nancy Love and Betty Gillies.

ເອີຣ

Cornelia Clark Fort was the debutante daughter of a socially prominent Tennessee family in the aristocratic South. The family home, Fortland, was a twenty-four room mansion on the 365-acre estate, Fortland Farms, outside of Nashville. After two years at Sarah Lawrence College in New York, she hadn't really found herself. Then she took her first flying lesson. It was late winter, 1940. She was twenty-one and knew instantly that flying was her passion and her destiny. She soloed April 27, 1940 and earned her private pilot's license that June. Immediately, she put to use her new-found freedom by flying around the country to visit friends. A combination of fog and low fuel on one of those cross-country flights that summer frightened her enough to rethink her safety in the air. The next day she flew to Memphis for three weeks of advanced training.

She earned her commercial license and by March 1941 — a year after her first flying lesson — she had her instructor's rating. She was Nashville's first woman flight instructor and the only one in Tennessee at that time. Her ratings grew to include twin-engine and also sea planes.

The CAA's Civilian Pilot Training Program, designed to encourage and financially assist young collegians who wanted to learn to fly, gave Cornelia a chance to use that instructor's rating. She landed a job in Fort Collins, Colorado, teaching in the CPT program at Colorado A&M (now Colorado State). A few months later, she accepted a job teaching flying in Honolulu. And the rest of that adventure is in the history books.

She came to Wilmington immediately upon receipt of Nancy Love's telegram. As one of the first WAFS to sign on and pass both the flight and the physical exams, Cornelia was in at the beginning. News photographers captured her with Nancy Love and the other early arrivals, all wearing suits, high heels, hats and gloves, and carrying their suitcases, re-enacting their arrival at BOQ 14 at New Castle Army Air Base, September 1942.

Teresa James recalls Cornelia as "so regal looking. But I never really got to know her. When we first got to Wilmington, she and Rhonie, Gillies and Nancy Love stayed at the Dupont Hotel and the rest of us stayed at the Kent Manor Inn.

"Cornelia was a listener, whereas Rhonie was doing all the talking and telling about her trips and all the people she knew. I called the four of them — Gillies, Love, Rhonie and Fort — the upper crust."

Nancy Batson recalls the sweet sound of another Southern voice when she arrived to spend her first night at the BOQ.

"I was sitting there on the cot wondering what to do next, when this tall brunette stuck her head in the door and introduced herself.

She was Cornelia Fort from Nashville and would I like to come down to her room and have a cocktail and then go with her over to the Officers' Club for dinner. Well, I was so delighted to hear another Southern accent, I said yes, even though we didn't have cocktails in our home in Birmingham. Ladies in Birmingham didn't drink cocktails back then."

In Cornelia's room, just down the hall, Nancy was fascinated by the array of liquor bottles lined up on the dresser. "I felt quite sophisticated. When she asked me what I wanted, I said 'bourbon' like I had been drinking it for years."

What young, impressionable Nancy Batson really appreciated about Cornelia was her friendliness and the fact that she reached out to a newcomer. The two were casual friends during their three months together in Wilmington, but they never became particularly close. They were rarely assigned to the same ferrying flights — besides, Nancy was three weeks behind the first arrivals. She still had her thirty-day orientation period to go through and Cornelia and the others were nearly finished and ready to ferry. And then when the squadron was broken up in January, Nancy remained in Wilmington and Cornelia was sent to California.

Del Scharr, too, had a brief friendship with Cornelia. Because they were the two tallest WAFS — both were five feet ten — they became, in Del's words, "marching buddies" when the WAFS practiced formation marching drills in the fall of 1942 at Colonel Baker's order. They brought up the rear — or led when the order "to the rear, march" was given.

On the night of December 27, 1942, Del was in her room in BOQ 14, writing a letter to her husband, when she sensed someone there. She looked up and saw Cornelia standing in the open doorway looking like a ghost.

"Cornelia was holding onto the door jamb. As soon as I saw her, I realized that she was so stupefied that it was difficult for her to speak. She said 'I just had a telephone call from home — Fortland just burned to the ground.'

"Fortunately, no one was in residence at the time, therefore no one was injured. But the news stunned me. 'Oh, Cornelia!' was all I could say as tears came to my eyes.

"'Everything is gone,' she went on. 'All my diaries are gone. I sent them home rather than take them to Long Beach.'

"So I learned that from the day she began to fly, Cornelia had fashioned a chronicle of her life in aviation. Of the WAFS, she was certainly the one most qualified to write about us. She was an avid reader, she expressed herself well, and she had the patience to sit alone and write her thoughts while the rest of us either relaxed or ran about socially. No wonder Cornelia had not joined us at our end of the barracks — she had her work to do, a serious task for one so young in years.

"Cornelia showed some emotion to me, but she did not break down about her loss in front of the others. She had a certain nobility; she possessed quality and breeding. Now tragedy had threatened her life twice. First she escaped death at Pearl Harbor. Now, because she had not been home, she escaped fire at Fortland. But the hours and years of her career were only cinders. Pilots are superstitious. They believe that bad luck comes in threes. If there have been two accidents from one airport, for instance, everyone breathes easier once the third has happened."

෴

Cornelia left Wilmington for Long Beach in mid-February, 1943. Quickly she transitioned into the 450-horsepower, fixed-gear BT-13 and, along with the other WAFS and several male pilots, began ferrying the basic trainers to Dallas.

She wrote to a friend: "I know the route to Dallas so well now I've cut a groove in the sky."

To her mother she wrote: "I'm on my third BT-13 trip and writing this epistle two miles above the desert between Tucson and El Paso."

And to another friend she wrote: ". . .leaving El Paso for Dallas — had terrible carburetor ice over Guadelupe Pass — a very unhealthy place for ice. Limped into Midland, an army base."

***Editor's Note:*** 1) 5,420-foot-high Guadelupe Pass is in West Texas east of El Paso. 2) Carburetor icing is caused by humidity. A wet, cloudy day with a temperature of 50 to 70 degrees F. is the best condition for it to occur. If the situation gets bad enough, this can cause complete stoppage of the engine. If the pilot pulls the carburetor heat control knob, a butterfly valve opens and allows the pre-warmed air from around the exhaust to mix with the outside air coming into the carburetor. This prevents ice from forming or melts ice already formed.

Cornelia's biographer, Rob Simbeck, writes in *Daughter of the Air*:

Pilots from Long Beach kept a steady stream of BT-13s and BT-15s headed for Dallas early in 1943 for delivery to bases all over the South and Southwest. Men and women frequently flew joint missions, although they were never in the same planes. All flight orders were individual, but if several pilots had the same destination, they might well take off as a group. Even then, in many cases, the pilots would often lose sight of each other quickly and for the duration of the trip. Sometimes, though, they would fly in loose formation, keeping each other in sight as the WAFS had to do in Wilmington when they were flying tiny planes with no radios. Tight formation, however, with pilots sitting just off each other's wings, was forbidden for the WAFS had not been trained for it and had no experience.

There was another very practical reason for the ban on tight formation. A percentage of the men flying these missions were young, inexperienced, and sometimes reckless, and the presence of women could bring out the worst in them. All the WAFS experienced or heard of incidents in which male pilots, showing off or attempting to frighten the women, would play fighter pilot, rolling and weaving near them, buzzing them or coming suddenly alongside, so the women generally kept a wary eye on them. Still, the WAFS, especially as they grew more comfortable in their role, ignored the rule.

On Sunday, March 21, 1943, Cornelia and six male Long Beach

ferry pilots took off to deliver BT-13s once again to Dallas. Stories vary here. Rob Simbeck writes that Cornelia agreed, if somewhat reluctantly, to practice formation flying over sparsely inhabited West Texas between Midland and their destination in Dallas. The WAFS' instructions were, as in her Wilmington days, to stay five hundred feet away from any other airplane. But apparently, according to Simbeck's sources, Cornelia chose to ignore the order.

Approximately ten miles south of Merkel, Texas, the landing gear on flight officer Frank Stamme, Jr.'s BT struck the left wing of Cornelia's BT. The tip of the left wing of Cornelia's plane snapped off.

Cornelia's plane "suddenly broke off to the right as though on a snap roll," said one of the other flyers. Then it spun, rolled and went into an inverted dive, slamming vertically into the ground. The airplane was buried several feet into the ground and did not catch fire.

It is believed that the original impact involving Stamme's landing gear and her wing knocked Cornelia unconscious, therefore she was unable to try to come out of the spin, get the hatch open, and jump from the stricken plane. She died on impact.

Stamme, thinking she had pulled out of the spin, headed for Abilene where he made an emergency landing believing he had damaged his landing gear.

That is Simbeck's account of the accident that took Cornelia Fort's life. Published in 1999 in his biography of her, it is the most recently researched and written account.

Immediately after the accident, stories circulated and have continued to circulate over the years, that the young male flyers were horsing around and harassing Cornelia, who may have had more flying experience than they did, but did not have the formation flying or advanced aerobatic training they had.

B. J. Erickson, Cornelia's squadron commander at Long Beach, to this day believes the collision was an accident. "They were in two or three airplanes out there in the middle of nowhere trying to fly formation. I don't think there was anything malicious about it. I think it was a plain accident."

Whatever the cause, Cornelia Fort, one of Nancy Love's first recruits and an experienced woman pilot, was dead.

Nancy Love and B. J. Erickson flew a C-47 to Nashville for the funeral in Christ Episcopal Church. Because of the Fort family's standing in Nashville society, and because of Cornelia's popularity with a wide assortment of friends, the funeral was very nearly a state occasion. Cornelia was buried in Mount Olivet Cemetery next to her father. He had died on the same day — March 21 — three years earlier. The inscription on her footstone reads, "Killed in the Service of Her Country."

She was the first woman pilot to die on active military duty in U.S. history.

Nancy Batson, years later, said that she thought Nancy Love never truly recovered from Cornelia's death. The WAFS was Nancy's baby, her creation. She had hand picked her pilots. Now she had lost one of her Originals — a true friend — and she was devastated. Nancy didn't speak at the funeral, but she wrote this in a letter to Cornelia's mother: "My feeling about the loss of Cornelia is hard to put into words — I can only say that I miss her terribly, and loved her. She was a rare person. If there can be any comforting thought, it is that she died as she wanted to — in an Army airplane, and in the service of her country."

Rob Simbeck interviewed Cornelia's first flight instructor, Aubrey Blackburne, who commented on a letter Nancy Love wrote to him. The following is an excerpt:

> She said she felt she owed it to me to tell me that the military investigation following the mid-air collision completely exonerated Cornelia of any blame in any way. She also said, "If it'll be of any consolation, Cornelia was at least unconscious, if not dead, from the collision, because she was too good a pilot not to have cut the switch and turned off the gas before crashing." And I agreed with her because Cornelia — she wasn't afraid. If the last thing she was conscious of was that she was going in, she still was absolutely not afraid.

The conclusion of Cornelia's posthumously published article in the

July 1943 *Woman's Home Companion* reads:

Because there were and are so many disbelievers in women pilots, especially in their place in the military, officials wanted the best possible qualifications to go with the first experimental group. All of us realized what a spot we were on. We had to deliver the goods — or else — or else there wouldn't ever be another chance for women pilots in any part of the service.

We have no hopes of replacing men pilots. But we can each release a man to combat, to faster ships, to overseas work. Delivering a trainer to Texas may be as important as delivering a bomber to Africa, if you take the long view. We are beginning to prove that women can be trusted to deliver airplanes safely and, in the doing, serve the country which is our country, too.

I have yet to have a feeling which approaches in satisfaction that of having signed, sealed and delivered an airplane for the United States Army. The attitude that most nonfliers have about pilots is distressing and often acutely embarrassing. They chatter about the glamour of flying. Well, any pilot can tell you how glamorous it is. We get up in the cold dark in order to get to the airport by daylight. We wear heavy, cumbersome flying clothes and a thirty-pound parachute. We are either cold or hot. Lipstick wears off and hair gets straighter and straighter. We look forward all afternoon to a bath and steak; we get the bath, but seldom the steak. Sometimes we are too tired to eat and fall wearily into bed.

None of us can put into words why we fly. It is something different for each of us. I can't *say* exactly why I fly, but I *know* why as I've never known anything in my life.

For all the gals in the WAFS, I think the most concrete moment of happiness came at our first review. Suddenly and for the first time, we felt a part of something larger. Because of our uniforms, which we had earned, we were marching with the men, marching with all the freedom-loving people in the world.

I, for one, am profoundly grateful that my one talent, my only knowledge, flying, happens to be of use to my country when it is needed. That's all the luck I ever hope to have.

৵৩৩৶

# BT-13/BT-15/SNV VALIANT

The BT-13 came to be known as the Valiant and had the distinction of being produced in greater numbers than all other basic trainers produced in the USA in WWII. In fact, over 11,000 Valiants would be produced for the US Army Air Force and the US Navy in the period 1940-44. Initially referred to as the V-74, the first version for the USAAF was given the designation BT-13, while a later version with a different engine was referred to as the BT-15. The Valiants built for the US Navy were the equivalent of the BT-13, and were called SNV by the Navy.

The airplane carried the nickname Vultee Vibrator because it shuddered when approaching stall and the canopy rattled during aerobatic maneuvers. The BT-13 also provided student pilots with their first two-way radio for communication with the ground.

# PT-19

The PT-19 was an advanced primary trainer more like the fighter planes pilots would fly. It was the plane most ferried by the WAFS during the early part of 1943.

**A fellow WAFS "props" a Cub for B.J. Erickson
at the factory in Lockhaven, Pennsylvania**

# 17

March 1943 was a watershed month for the WAFS. The transitions of Nancy Love and Betty Gillies into pursuits and Nancy and B.J. Erickson into a twin-engine cargo plane — they ferried a C-47 from Long Beach to Memphis on March 5 — marked the high point. Cornelia's untimely death, the crowning tragedy of the Ferrying Division's fifteen-month existence, was the low. Surprisingly enough, in spite of the deep sorrow felt and expressed by all the WAFS over Cornelia's death, her accident did not bring about resignations nor did it affect the women's desire to ferry airplanes. That went on without a glitch. The women stuck to their ferrying schedules, which speaks highly of the calibre of women they were, to their deep commitment and dedication, and to the fact that they were a well-adjusted bunch.

Then on March 25, just when women were beginning to fly bigger airplanes, the women of the 3rd Ferrying Group at Romulus were blindsided. The Commander there put out a directive repeating the original restriction of WAFS to light trainer aircraft only. The women in Romulus were not to be assigned to transition on any high-powered, single-engine or twin-engine aircraft nor were they to fly as co-pilots on ferrying missions with a male pilot.

The directive went on to say that women were to be assigned deliveries on alternate days with the male pilots and, if at all possible, were to be sent in a different direction from any male flight. To that was added that no mixed flight or crew assignments would be tolerated. This meant women couldn't "build time" in different airplanes — work on transition — as co-pilots to male pilots other than instructors.

Nancy Love had not objected when the Air Transport Command forbid the women to "hitch" rides in other military aircraft cross country following a delivery. The men, of course, were encouraged to do this, but the women rode trains and flew on airliners to get back to base. The primary reason for this was the Army's fear of scandal. But it wasn't that they didn't trust the women in their employ. Who they didn't trust was the press that was already pursuing the "lady flyers" and publishing stories about them — many of them based on misinformation. The Army didn't want idle gossip to tarnish their WAFS' reputations. Nancy was in agreement there. But this from Romulus was too much.

Nancy objected strenuously to this directive. She felt it cast a slur on the morals of the WAFS. At that time there had been no gossip about any of the women. It was an insult, period.

And then came the ridiculous. Headquarters Staff issued a directive that came out of the blue and made no sense at all.

A letter went out on March 29 to all Group Commanders stating that no woman pilot was to be assigned any flying duties during pregnancy. That wasn't the bad part. At that point it only affected one of the WAFS, Esther Manning Rathfelder, and Betty Gillies had already addressed that dilemma. The rest of the directive was worse because it affected them all.

Women who had their menstrual periods were not to fly — including one day before and two days after, a real joke considering the vagaries of even the most normal woman's period. The restriction meant a wasteful eight or nine days of non-flying time a month per WAFS if adhered to strictly.

Nancy went over the heads of both Group and Ferrying Division Commanders and appealed the Romulus directive, and the one dealing with the menstrual periods, to ATC Headquarters. She risked Colonel Tunner's ire and was, in fact, not in his good graces for a period of time after that.

In addition to being in the beginning stages of transition to more powerful airplanes, the WAFS had an almost perfect accident record. Cornelia was exonerated of any blame in her fatal accident. There was no pilot error on her part. And the only other accidents at that point had been a couple of bent propellers following ground loops.

Consequently just when Nancy Love might have thought things were running smoothly, with the edicts of March 25 and 29, the turmoil returned as they moved into April.

But, once again, change was on the way.

Colonel Tunner had four PT-26s — PT-19s with canopies — that needed to be delivered to the Canadian RAF near Calgary, Alberta, before Easter. It was now the Friday afternoon before Palm Sunday. Knowing the importance of the assignment, Colonel Baker chose his squadron commander, Betty Gillies, to make this important mission happen. From her Wilmington cadre, she chose Nancy Batson and the two newcomers, Sis Bernheim and Helen McGilvery, both of whom she had known during her civilian flying days on Long Island before the war. She respected the flying abilities of both of them as well as those of young Nancy Batson.

Betty had, in fact, hand-picked Batson — along with Teresa James and Gert Meserve — to remain at Wilmington with her even though Nancy Love had originally assigned all three of them to go to the new squadrons.

⌖

"I developed an inferiority complex after Betty pulled me out of the Dallas squadron when I was supposed to go with them in January of '43," Nancy Batson related. "I thought I was being left in Wilmington because I wasn't any good. Betty never told us why the orders were changed. But when I mentioned it to her years later, she laughed and said 'oh, no, I kept the good ones on purpose.'"

Del Scharr concurs with Betty's comment. She says that Colonel Baker objected when Nancy Love "took all the cuties" for the newly formed squadrons and made her give up some of them — leave them in Wilmington. So Betty — by then in charge — sent three others out instead and kept Batson, Meserve, and a very unhappy Teresa James at Wilmington. Jamesy's husband was stationed in California, Nancy had promised her Long Beach, and she wanted to go in the worst way. But Teresa, characteristically, made the best of the situation. Ditto Nancy Batson, who may have felt the pull of disappointment and — in her words — "an inferiority complex" for a couple of days, but nothing kept resilient Nancy down for long. "Besides," she explained, "my older sister, Elinor, was living in

Baltimore, so I didn't have a problem with Wilmington."

As fate would have it, Batson, James and Meserve flew together almost daily for the next two years and became fast friends, a friendship that endured through the decades to come.

∽⊙⊙∾

PT-26s have a cruising speed of about one hundred miles per hour. When Betty told her crew where they were going and how long they had to get there, the three stared at her, total disbelief in their eyes.

"I know, that's more than 2,500 miles, but I promised Tunner and Baker we'd get them there before Easter," she said. Easter was only nine days away.

Batson let out a long, low whistle. "That doesn't allow for any weather along the route."

Betty nodded. "I know." What she didn't tell them was she had great faith in their abilities. Betty didn't say things like that, according to Batson. Neither she nor Nancy Love were loose with praise. The women under their command were professionals and were expected to perform at the top of their abilities. Consequently, praise for doing what was part of the job was not a side benefit.

Very early Palm Sunday morning, they were in Hagerstown checking out their aircraft.

"Eeeeyow!" Nancy let out a Rebel yell as she climbed into the cockpit of her PT-26. "We're goin' back to Montana and on to Calgary, Canada!" The other three laughed. They were used to Nancy's sudden outbursts of enthusiasm.

They left Hagerstown early, headed west across spring's shades-of-green patchwork quilt of Ohio, Indiana, and Illinois. They ran out of daylight in Joliet, Illinois, but not before they had flown an astounding 697 miles. Nancy noted that, thankfully, the weather was improving over what they had been having in Wilmington. It seemed, to her Alabama blood, like winter lasted forever in Delaware.

Spring definitely was on the way. Besides, these airplanes had canopies so they didn't have to contend with wind in their faces and icicles forming on their runny noses. Tomorrow morning, they would cross the Mighty Mississippi.

Batson recalled the trip in vivid detail:

*That night at the hotel, Betty informed us that we would be up at four in the morning. "We're going to get an early start," Betty says. "I want to be sitting in our cockpits with the engines running when the sun breaks the horizon. Now get some sleep. Tomorrow's a long day."*

*Well, Sis and Little Mac began to howl — "Today was a long day," said Sis. "We went seven hundred miles!" said Little Mac.*

*"Four a.m.," said Betty.*

*I was on my way to bed when I overheard Sis and Mac grumbling. They said there was no way in you-know-where that they were going to get up at four o'clock in the morning. Well, I listened to them bellyache for a few minutes and I got mad. Betty was putting her reputation on the line and here these two were saying they were too good and too tired to get up in the morning and get a move on and help get those planes out to Canada on time like Colonel Tunner wanted.*

*So I marched into their room and gave them what-for. Well, when I got through, they just stared at me. Then I turned on my heel and walked out and went to bed. The next morning, I was in the lobby at four a.m., dressed and ready to go. And, you know what, so were they!*

*We were sitting in our cockpits when dawn broke and we were off in a flash, headed due west again. This time our destination was North Platte, Nebraska, a six-hundred-mile flight. We crossed the Mississippi and pretty soon we were looking down on the cornfields of Iowa and later on the wheat fields of Nebraska. It was like I'd never seen corn and wheat fields before. We crossed the Missouri River below Omaha and kept on cruising until we hit North Platte.*

*We were beginning to enjoy ourselves by then. Here we were, three Easterners and a Southerner, and we were crossing this great big country of ours. This country we were fighting for. And, we were so proud of that fact.*

*And, by golly, we were headin' west in the cockpits of sleek new Army airplanes and somebody else was paying for the gas. We were up at four again the next day and, that night, made Great Falls, Montana, a whopping 850-mile flight from North Platte.*

*When we got there, Betty reminded us — rather proudly, I think — that we had just done it in airplanes that had an average ground speed of one hundred miles per hour.*

*"Did you see those mountains!" said Sis, thoroughly taken with the scenery.*

*Before finding a hotel, Betty got all the Customs forms filled out. We were tired.*

Great Falls, Montana, is only one hundred miles from the Canadian border. During the war, it was the home of Uncle Sam's ferry base where planes were processed for lend-lease delivery to Canada and for aircraft bound to Alaska and, eventually, Russia. The WAFS' four airplanes, however, were bound for a Canadian RAF pilot training facility somewhere in Alberta.

*The next day, up at four again, we flew along those majestic snow-capped Canadian Rockies. What we had seen the previous day was nothing compared to this.*

*The last leg was a shorty — only 275 miles from Great Falls to a town named DeWinton. We had delivered the planes from Hagerstown in a record four days — and four days before the Easter deadline. Betty had done her job — so had the rest of us. And done it well.*

*We talked a lot on the train ride back. I think we took apart the entire women's flying program and put it together again. Much of the conversation centered around the news that Cochran's first class was destined to swell our ranks early in May. Betty had heard that they were to graduate April 24 — only two days away. The twenty-three graduates would be divided among the four existing women's squadrons.*

*The four of us were back on base by Friday night, April 23 — Good Friday. And do you know what that sweet Colonel Baker did? He gave us all a Commendation — "for our efficient and prompt delivery which included not only flying of the planes but also the paper work involved in such deliveries, flight logs, gasoline reports,*

*RON messages, etc." I gotta tell you, I'm real proud of that!"*

What Betty and the others had proved was what Nancy Love already knew — that women made excellent ferry pilots. Now Nancy could point with pride to their accomplishment and tell the men to whom she answered that there was a lot more where that came from.

Women were much more likely than were men to take a plane directly to its delivery point. The men were apt to stop off en route — even go out of the way — to visit a girlfriend or two. As of April 24, 1943, the WAFS' stock was very high with the entire Ferrying Division — particularly the boss, Colonel Tunner.

And it paid off.

Unbeknownst to the four ferry pilots, just before they left for Canada, General C.R. Smith, former president of American Airlines, now Chief of Staff of the ATC, was in the process of addressing Nancy Love's appeal — the one in which she went over the heads of her commanding officers. He stated that certain flight limitations were being imposed on women pilots by the Ferrying Division without giving full consideration to the professional qualifications of the individual pilots; that the ferrying activities of women were being restricted to trainer aircraft only; that women were being prohibited from acting as co-pilots on ferrying missions; that they were being prohibited from transition training on single-engine aircraft of the high horsepower class or twin-engine aircraft.

General Smith concluded his letter of April 17, 1943, with the following statement: "It is the desire of this Command that all pilots, regardless of sex, be privileged to advance to the extent of their ability in keeping with the progress of aircraft development."

On April 26, a new directive was issued by the Ferrying Division Headquarters rescinding the letter of March 29 relative to WAFS not flying during periods of physical disability and the letter of March 25 forbidding the use of women as co-pilots with male pilots.

The WAFS would be transitioned on multi-engine and high-powered, single-engine aircraft under the same standards of individual experience and ability as any other pilot. However, still tiptoeing around the morals issue, the directive further stated that normally the WAFS would be given transition on cross-country checkouts by other fully qualified WAFS "when and if available."

Now nothing stood in the way of the WAFS moving up the transition ladder.

**Lenore McElroy**

**Barbara Poole**

**Gertrude Meserve**

**Katherine Rawls Thompson**

# 18

Approaching Kansas City from the west on June 23, 1943, Nancy Love was struck by the lush green of the Missouri River Valley. It was a different green from the dark primeval green of Michigan's Keweenau Peninsula where she grew up — and from the sea shore green of her more recent home, Massachusetts. Very different, she knew, from where she had just come — Southern California with its sage green patches surrounded by miles and miles of desert sand and mountain brown. Yes, the green of the Midwest was a verdant shade from which one could wring moisture — that commodity so lacking in the desert Southwest.

Well, she'd be in the thick of the humid Midwest now. After she delivered this airplane, she was on her way to Cincinnati, Ohio, that thriving "Porkopolis" on the Ohio River — overlooking Kentucky and upstream from Louisville. She wondered if it would be as uncomfortably sticky as Washington, D.C., and Wilmington had been the previous summer. She also knew, from communiqués from Colonel Tunner, that things were getting sticky between Army Air Forces Headquarters in Washington and Ferrying Division Headquarters in Cincinnati as well.

Nancy was aware of a memorandum that had come out of General Arnold's office the previous day that seemed to give Jacqueline Cochran some kind of vague authority over all women pilots in the Air Forces, whether they were assigned to the Flying Training Command, as were the girls now training in Sweetwater, Texas, or to the Ferrying Division, or to any other Army Air Forces organization.

Yes, she was convinced that it was going to be not just a sticky summer, but a turbulent one.

But right now, her job was to land this airplane. She and her co-pilot Barbara Towne were about to make their first delivery of a North American B-25 Mitchell bomber. In May, Nancy had checked out on the B-25 and logged more than five hours in five mid-month flights. Then, just the day before the flight from Long Beach to Kansas City, she had done a recheck in preparation for the ferrying flight.

Towne was a willing and able co-pilot who, like Nancy, had been steadily transitioning up through the airplanes available to the squadron based in Long Beach. As a teenager, Barbara had become infatuated with aviation. She began to take flying lessons on the sly and soloed in a Taylor Cub in 1936 in Santa Rosa, California. When her father learned what she was up to, he enrolled her in Ryan School of Aeronautics in San Diego. She went on to teach in their CPT program. Barbara, a tall, stunningly attractive strawberry blonde, newly married to USAAF pilot Robert Dickson, "decided not to spend the war in a community of women knitting." When she learned about the WAFS through an article in a San Francisco newspaper in fall 1942, she headed for Wilmington. She was the eleventh woman selected for the WAFS. In February 1943, Nancy sent her to Long Beach.

⌒⌒⌒⌒

Nancy set the wheels on the runway and let the twin-engine bomber run easily until they reached the optimum turnoff point. Then she taxied it to the parking area where she and Barbara shut everything down according to the checklist.

The B-25 already had gained wartime fame. It was the plane that General Jimmy Doolittle and his Raiders had flown off the deck of the USS Hornet to bomb Tokyo in April 1942, when U.S. military forces were in disarray and in need of the psychological lift such an heroic feat could offer.

The wing span of the bomber was sixty-seven feet seven inches and its overall length was fifty-two feet eleven inches. Like the C-47 she and B.J. Erickson delivered to Memphis in March, it was a lot of airplane, and she liked getting the feel of the twin-engine aircraft beneath her. And now, Nancy had her eyes on something even bigger.

**B-25 MITCHELL BOMBER**

Nancy knew her hard work and steady but rapid transition were beginning to pay off for the other WAFS. On May 4, 1943, Betty Gillies delivered her first P-47. Helen Mary Clark became the second woman to check out in the Thunderbolt, and by the end of June, the two of them had accounted for the delivery of seventeen P-47s. A few of those flights were to Republic Aviation's modification center in Evansville, Indiana, but most were to the docks at Newark, New Jersey. The latter was a short flight — less than fifty miles as the crow flies — from the Republic factory in Farmingdale to Newark. They flew due west over the Upper Bay below Manhattan Island, past the Statue of Liberty, over Jersey City, and across Newark Bay to the ships waiting in the docks.

Things, in fact, were running quite smoothly at Wilmington. Betty Gillies not only turned out to be a superb P-47 pilot, she also proved to be more adept at the job of squadron commander than was Nancy Love. That she was several years older and the mother of three children may have had something to do with that. From what the girls who served under her at Wilmington say, she was a good listener — a trait Nancy wasn't too well known for — but almost as stingy about handing out compliments as Nancy was.

"Helen Mary was the one you went to if you had a problem," says Teresa James. "She was more compassionate than Betty. But only to a point. Helen Mary's attitude was *take care of it and get back to flying*." But it was squadron leader Betty Gillies who — when Teresa's husband, Dink, landed in town with a twenty-four-hour pass just prior to heading for England with his bomber squadron — signed Teresa out illegally overnight so that they might spend those last hours together.

Helen Mary, also one of the over-thirty WAFS, and Betty Gillies were two who had left their children home with their draft-exempt husbands. Helen Mary's sons, Bill and Gerry, were ten and twelve at the time. Her husband, Gerould, was involved in government-related activities that assured he would stay where he was for the duration of the war, thereby leaving Helen Mary free to serve her country as a much needed ferry pilot. B.J. Erickson describes her as "a lady, a charmer, Miss Primrose. But she was very firm and a good leader, a good substitute for Nancy and Betty. In fact, she was a lot like Nancy. They were cut from the same cloth — that Eastern establishment education, able to lead with graciousness and finesse. She was from a very wealthy family and she was an excellent pilot." With her calm demeanor and no-nonsense attitude, Helen Mary was a natural to become Betty's executive officer.

That Betty and Helen Mary remained at Wilmington, within commuting distance of their families, would seem reasonable. In fact, wherever possible — at least initially — efforts were made to place women within some proximity of their families.

Betty had been the first to transition into flying the P-47. She was all for the other women at Wilmington following suit and encouraged Helen Mary Clark and then Teresa James to transition the summer of 1943. Gertrude Meserve was the fourth Original to get a chance to check out in the P-47.

Gertie's love of airplanes goes back to her childhood. "I made model airplanes, the ones of balsa wood, ten cents a kit and you got a lot for your money." She started flying during her final months in high school in 1938 — "Piper Cubs, forty and fifty horsepower." She knew Nancy Love from East Boston airport before the war and was ready to go when she received her telegram in September 1942. Gert had all but the 200-horsepower rating. By then she had her instructor's rating and was teaching CPT students at the various colleges around Boston. Immediately, she went to Concord to get her horsepower rating which she took in a Fairchild 24.

IWASM

**Gertrude Meserve in a P-47**

When the WAFS were split up in January 1943, Gert remained in Wilmington where, by summertime, she was right behind Teresa James for transition into the P-47. "The instructor told me to take it up and stall it. Well, there was a three-thousand-foot ceiling and we were supposed to stay five hundred feet away from clouds, so I only had twenty-five hundred feet of altitude. No way was I going to stall a P-47, the first time up, with only twenty-five hundred feet between me and the ground. So I did a partial stall and took it in. When I got down, he said, 'OK, now you're a pursuit pilot.'

"Well, when the men got to be pursuit pilots, they could wear the top button of their uniform blouse unbuttoned. A couple of us decided to try it. We walked into the mess hall with our top buttons unbuttoned and it got instantly quiet. Everybody stopped talking. We knew we had pushed it too far."

When Delphine Bohn was writing her book, she asked Betty how she felt the women P-47 pilots were accepted by the male pilots. In a letter back to Delphine dated January 8, 1984, Betty replied:

Not all of the male pilots were especially helpful to us, but most were and that was enough. I could easily understand how the young pilots felt. Here they were, just out of flight school and very proud of the fact that they were "fighter pilots" — flying the P-47s, the P-40s, the P-51s — and here the girls were starting to fly fighters, too. One day they were supermen and all of a sudden the next day the girls were doing it!

The boys usually had hair-raising tales to tell about their flights and they unloaded these over the dinner table in the mess, but the girls NEVER had any trouble — or if they did, no one ever heard about it.

I guess one could say that those pilots resented us — and I guess that I didn't blame them. But the older pilots, the more experienced pilots. No, I didn't feel any resentment on their part.

IWASM

**Esther Nelson**

Betty's squadron, in April 1943, consisted of herself, Helen Mary Clark, Esther Nelson, Teresa James, Nancy Batson, Sis Bernheim, Dorothy Fulton, Helen McGilvery and Gertrude Meserve. Esther Manning Rathfelder was now Betty's administrative assistant as she was several months pregnant.

Esther Nelson, another of the 'over-thirty' Originals, learned to fly in 1930 when she was twenty-one. Her husband, Arthur, taught her — in fact, that was how they met. They married in June 1936. Two years later they established a flying school in Ontario, California and Esther, too, became a flight instructor.

May 10, 1943 the first twenty-three graduates from Cochran's flight training school in Houston were dispatched. Six women each were assigned to Wilmington, Romulus and Dallas. Five went to Long Beach. These women were checked out at their respective bases and began to ferry airplanes. The newcomers also were considered WAFS because they had now joined the Ferrying Division and their job was to ferry airplanes. The WAFS' numbers were nearly doubled overnight, the first additions since January 25, 1943. And the expansion would continue for awhile as more graduates arrived roughly every five weeks from Texas to swell their ranks. The women from Houston's second class arrived on June 14.

The early graduates of the Women's Flying Training Detachment (WFTD) were, for the most part, women who had just missed out on joining the original WAFS. Many of them had the necessary five hundred hours and the other qualifications, but had been under contract somewhere else — usually flight instructing — and were not able to get away in the fall of 1942. Others were only a few hours short of qualifying and, by the time they had trained under the eyes of the instructors at Houston Municipal Airport, they met the qualifications laid down for the original squadron. That fall of 1942, Cochran had negotiated a requirement of only two hundred hours in order for these women pilots to be admitted for training at Houston. Their cockpit time during training would then be added to the amount of time they already had.

However, this relatively high standard of two hundred hours did not remain the case. By spring of 1943, Cochran had achieved two notable coups. She had moved the WFTD training school to Avenger Field near Sweetwater, Texas, and she had succeeded in lowering the entrance requirements for her school first to one hundred hours, then seventy-five, and in summer 1943 to thirty-five hours — the minimum required for a private pilot's license. The first class received one hundred fifteen hours flying time in twenty-three weeks of training. By the end of the program, flight trainees were getting two hundred ten hours in the air and the training period had been lengthened to thirty weeks. In August, 1943, the age requirement was dropped to eighteen and a half from twenty one and the height requirement raised to sixty-two and one-half inches, up from sixty inches (five feet). It was raised again to sixty-four inches in 1944.

After the first two classes, the newly graduated WFTDs no longer had to have the equivalent of the three hundred hours required of male ferry pilots entering the Ferrying Division, let alone the five hundred required of the original WAFS. Because of this, the Ferrying Division (FERD) did not want to accept these women carte blanche because they didn't meet FERD qualifications. FERD wanted rights of refusal. Cochran, however, insisted that the women be accepted under any circumstances.

The outcome of this wrestling match irrevocably changed the face of the women's organizations flying under the auspices of the Army Air Forces and it all happened between mid-June and mid-August 1943. This was the turbulent summer Nancy Love sensed was coming when she set the B-25 down on the runway in Kansas City.

# 19

"Miss Jacqueline Cochran has been named Director of Women Pilots within the Army Air Forces and Special Assistant to Major General Barney M. Giles, the Assistant Chief of Staff, Operations, Commitments and Requirements," said the formal announcement from the War Department on July 5, 1943. Miss Cochran's new office, it was revealed, was to be in the Pentagon Building. Previously, she had been in Fort Worth, Texas.

Also on July 5, the War Department announced the appointment of Mrs. Nancy Love as Executive for WAFS on the Staff of Colonel Tunner, Ferrying Division, Air Transport Command.

That was only the beginning.

The news media thought they had a hot story and played it for all it was worth.

"The media took the opportunity to exploit the tussle for supremacy between the two women and to toss off just enough half-truths to make their stories more saleable," says Del Scharr. "*Newsweek*'s article, which was headlined 'Coup for Cochran,' began, 'Last week came a shake up—' The implication was that Nancy Love had not been a satisfactory executive. There was no mention of Cochran's connection with AAF headquarters because of her school."

Marianne Verges writes in *On Silver Wings*, "The newspapers and magazines had a field day with the shake up in the women pilots' program, playing up the rivalry between Jackie and Nancy. They made Jackie's appointment seem like a victory in an ongoing war. Up until now this war had been undeclared, but from July 5, 1943, onward, the careful guarding of command prerogatives versus the aggressive attempts for headquarters-staff control often over-shadowed the accomplishments of the women pilots — and in the long run contributed to their doom."

On July 14, a memorandum further spelled out Nancy Love's duties as: advise the Ferrying Division (FERD) Headquarters Staff as to the best use of the WAFS; plan the allocation of the WAFS to the various Ferrying Groups; plan and supervise training standards and a progressive air training program. This program was designed to arouse interest among WAFS to fly the more advanced aircraft coming available for ferrying and "thus avoid stagnation on lighter types." Hardly needing a stimulant to transition, most of the WAFS — Originals and new squadron members alike — could hardly contain themselves in their enthusiasm. The bigger, the faster the aircraft, the better. Getting checked out in order to ferry them was, as of summer 1943, their primary aim in life.

Nancy's other assignment — obviously to relieve Tunner and the male officers on his staff from having to deal with such things — was to formulate "rules and regulations governing conduct, morale, and welfare of WAFS."

Now Nancy wasn't expected to do this alone. The wording was such that she was to coordinate with the appropriate FERD personnel in affecting each of these duties. And it was expected of her, in order to carry out these duties, to make necessary trips to the four squadrons for inspection purposes and to be the liaison between FERD and the Ferrying Groups, thus keeping the WAFS informed.

When the announcement was made that Cochran was now Director of Women Pilots, neither FERD nor the ATC was notified as to whether this meant the WAFS would now fall under her jurisdiction or not. Then FERD chose to reorganize itself that late July-early August. Just as the new organizational charts were approved, FERD learned that one new women pilots organization — Women Airforce Service Pilots (WASP) — would take the place of the two women pilots organizations, WAFS and WFTD, and that Jacqueline Cochran was the head of that newly formed organization. The official announcement was made August 20, 1943.

"We went to bed WAFS and woke up the next morning WASPs," Betty Gillies said.

To say that Cochran and Tunner interpreted this announcement differently is an understatement. Tunner considered Cochran to be an advisor to Air Staff. Her job was to recruit and train women pilots. Cochran took quite seriously her new position — director of women pilots. Coupling her new title and this new organization — the combined women pilots groups or WASPs — with the still vague authority her title gave her, Cochran assumed this was the next step on the way to a women's air corps under her leadership.

Now firmly entrenched in the Pentagon, Jackie had the opportunity to watch her mentor, Hap Arnold, in action. She liked what she saw. Their *modus operandi* were the same. He was in the habit of issuing verbal orders and going directly for his objectives. Steamroller might well be applied to the general when he made up his mind. If that was the way he did it, that's how she would do it, too, and the devil take the hindmost.

All this didn't add to Nancy Love's ease of mind. Brigadier General Tunner (he was officially promoted early in July) wanted her in Cincinnati to help him deal with his ever-increasing women's squadrons. By the end of June, eighty-eight women made up the Women's Auxiliary Ferrying Squadron and it was growing every few weeks. The last thing Nancy wanted was to be permanently stuck behind a desk where she couldn't fly, where her workday would consist merely of tedious administration and paper work and dealing with problems the squadron leaders couldn't handle.

Worse, here she was embroiled in what private Nancy Love had tried for nearly a year to avoid — a confrontation with Jacqueline Cochran that the press was blowing way out of proportion. How much of the controversy was press prattling and how much was based in fact is only partially known.

Nancy's daughter, Marky, thinks a letter from Bob Love to his wife, apparently written at the height of all this, points up that Nancy was stressed out over the turn of events and he was worried that she would say something she would regret. The letter is not dated, but appears to have been written in mid-August because of a post script (on a totally different subject) that will be shared in a later chapter where it has more meaning.

The Love's daughters have shared the original of the letter. Minus the post script but including his specific underlining, it reads:

Next morning

I felt like hell after that conversation last night as no doubt you did. What I really wanted to say wasn't gotten across at all and, sweetie, you must listen.

None of us here [ATC Headquarters] feel any differently about quote "that bitch" than you do. The thing that hits us, however, is that your background and her "grossness" are now <u>sharply</u> contrasted in everybody's mind. When you begin to rant and rave about her or lose your composure at all and admit that you can't deal with her you are playing into a neat trap that every tabloid, newsmagazine and cheap reporter has carefully set for you. Outside of the fact that I was really trying to be helpful on the uniforms, your attitude seemed to me to be dangerous at a time like this when an awful lot of people are soon to draw further comparisons. Keep analyzing this as you go along and make certain you don't lose anything by getting this far ahead. Every time I think of that woman I get mad. <u>I</u> know <u>you</u> won't change <u>but</u> other people <u>don't</u>. And count on the press and public to get you into fame and "bitchdom" simultaneously.

I know you know all this but I got the feeling last night that you were just too busy to think about it and your attitude seemed to be — 'Ah, the hell with her. I don't like her and I don't care who knows it!' I'm sure you see and will forgive my shortness.

All the love there is, RML

The remark about the uniform is in response to a letter from General Tunner to the secretary of war concerning a proper uniform for the newly arrived graduates of Sweetwater. He had written to the effect that the more than sixty new women pilots on the job in July were wearing attire dictated by individual tastes. He suggested that a uniform slightly different from that of the original WAFS would be appropriate and that the original WAFS then could continue to wear theirs.

Cochran didn't like the WAFS' uniform. Thought it was too

drab. So she hired a fashion designer from New York's Bergdorf Goodman to design a new one. The outcome was the now familiar uniform of what is known as Santiago blue — a sharp looking, light-weight wool jacket, skirt and slacks, accompanied by a matching beret and a pair of silver wings. Tunner didn't like the new uniform simply because his WAFS were being forced out of the uniform he knew they wore with pride. But Cochran won General Arnold's approval and Santiago blue carried the day.

Since the new uniforms wouldn't be ready for a few months, the new WAFS began to wear "pinks" — the khaki woolen shirts and pants worn by the male flyers that Betty Gillies had discovered and liked when she first arrived in Wilmington.

Cochran, with her new title and her "vaguely implied powers" in place, trod once again on General Tunner's toes. In mid-July, 1943, she ordered twenty-five of the newly graduated women from Sweetwater — destined for the Ferrying Division — on a secret mission without clearing the order with anyone. The Ferrying Division, now responsible for the women, was not told where they were going or for what reason, but was expected to pay their salaries, regardless.

Where they went was to Camp Davis in North Carolina to tow gunnery targets. It was Cochran's first move to place her Sweetwater graduates other than in the Ferrying Division. She had been getting flak from Tunner and the commanders of the four bases where the women's ferrying squadrons were located. The complaints about the first graduates were not about their flying but about their preparedness in processing Army paper work and in-flight procedures when ferrying in the loose formation employed by a group of WAFS delivering to the same destination. But as the graduates admitted to Cochran's school with low cockpit time began to show up, it was their flying skills that bothered Tunner and his commanders. FERD wanted refusal rights. Tunner tried to hold to the three-hundred-hour total flying hours required of male ferry pilots. He wanted to send some of the girls back to Avenger Field for further training. But Cochran, with Arnold's backing, over-rode that. Tunner didn't have to use the girls to ferry airplanes, but he had to take them and pay them, is what it amounted to.

Obviously Cochran was reading some handwriting on the wall and realized that she might have increasingly more trouble placing her graduates in the Ferrying Division because of its very high standards. So she began to shop around for potential commands in which to place her girls. She found them other flying jobs they could handle. Towing targets at Camp Davis was the first of many experiments to come — experiments, incidentally, that most of the future WASP graduates of Avenger were delighted to try. Most of them found their service experiences after Sweetwater to be exciting, rewarding, and something of which they could be quite proud. The later graduates from Sweetwater may not have had the total time in the cockpit the Originals and the early graduates did, but they weren't short on grit and determination and the ability to get the job done — whatever the job was.

While all this was going on in Washington, back at Wilmington, Teresa James had begun P-47 transition.

*I had just returned to the base, dog tired after a long flight in a PT-19. Betty Gillies, was sitting in the office. She handed me a copy of some tech orders. I was to check out in the P-47.*

*"Whenever there's a P-47 on the flight line, go sit in it and get familiar with the operating and emergency procedures," she said.*

*I got all palsy-jawed when I heard that! Most of my flying time was in smaller aircraft.*

*So for several days I warmed the cockpit seat and studied everything I could about the "Jug" as it is affectionately called. I was scared to death of flying it. This was no trainer. The cockpit had only enough room for a single pilot — me — so my first flight was a solo.*

*I'd heard the guys discussing the flight characteristics of this seven-ton flying arsenal. Twenty-eight hundred horsepower! I'd learned on something with about fifty. And the designer, something-or-other Kartvelli, armor plated the cockpit to protect the pilot from injury. I was happy to hear that — in case the engine quit on takeoff, you could plow through a building and only kill the people in front of you.*

*There was no forward visibility because of the huge engine.*

*One of the guys said the real sweat was trying to keep the plane in the middle of the runway while taking off and landing. You had to look out at a forty-five-degree angle to keep the same spacing between the wing and edge of the runway.*

*As it turned out my mother and sister, Betty, came down to visit on the Fourth of July weekend only to find I was scheduled to fly my first P-47 on July 5. They warned me the day before I was to fly it, so I had twenty-four hours to worry. And of course, Mom and Betty were there to see me being a total wreck. I later learned that while I was up, my mother disappeared to the base chapel to say the Rosary and beg God and the saints for her daughter's safe return to earth.*

*Anyway, the morning arrived too soon. I had butterflies in my stomach as I walked to Base Operations. I noticed a large crowd had gathered at the hangar near the P-47. There stood Captain Bing on the wing, waiting to give me a verbal checkout on pre-flight, cockpit and emergency procedures. Then, satisfied that I had done my homework, he wished me luck and told me to go up and practice stalls and spins.*

*His parting shot was "After takeoff, you'll be twenty miles out past New Castle before you get the gear up." What a confidence builder!*

*Well, my heart was in my mouth as I went through the thirty-two-item checklist before and after engine start. Satisfied that all the gauges were working, I closed the hatch, waved goodbye to Bing, released the brakes and slowly taxied — zig-zagging back and forth on the taxi strip until I reached the active runway.*

*I sat for several minutes until a couple of aircraft taxied up behind me. I finally got up enough courage to call the tower and say I was ready for takeoff— to which the operator replied, "Pull up into position and hold."*

*I pulled onto the runway, made sure I was lined up in the middle, and locked the tail-wheel. Then I heard the soft male voice from the tower, "P-47 cleared for takeoff."*

*I pushed the throttle to twenty-seven hundred RPM's. The sudden power pushed me back against the seat as I rolled down the runway. I was off in nothing flat. I had the flaps and gear retracted as I passed over the end of the runway. That engine was purring like a kitten as I climbed to altitude over the practice area at eight thousand feet. I flew some basic maneuvers, shallow, medium and steep turns. The stalls unnerved me, but I was amazed at the clean recovery.*

*My early flying instructor, Pete Goff, always told me to take an unfamiliar aircraft to high altitude and practice letdowns and landings at an imaginary airport in the sky. You can correct any mistake upstairs!*

*So I proceeded to land at Pete Goff's 'imaginary' airport in the sky, mentally contacting the tower, reporting positions throughout maneuvering up to landing. I slowed the plane to make a downwind entry into the traffic pattern — speed 170 miles per hour. I dropped the gear and, wow, what a thud! Rocked the wings back and forth to ascertain that the gear was down and locked.*

*I continued to the make-believe base leg, dropped two inches of flaps at 150 miles per hour, prop to 2,350, continued to final approach, dropped full flaps, cowl closed. Glide at 135 mph to landing.*

*OK, this works. Now all I had to do was get down all in one piece!*

*I started back toward the airport, called the tower when I was close, and was cleared downwind. I entered the traffic pattern just like I practiced upstairs, except this time was for real! Turning on base leg, my heart was racing while I kept my eyes focused on the landing area. Turning final, I got a 'cleared to land' from the tower.*

*As I crossed the threshold of the field, I shifted my gaze to a forty-five-degree angle to the runway to keep the plane in the middle of it. I made a beautiful three-point landing. I really greased it! The tower operator congratulated me as I rolled to the end of the runway and on to Base Ops to great cheers. All these people were applauding. They were thinking, "She didn't kill herself."*

*I did it! Thank you, Lord!*

*So, as it turns out, I found out the mystique was just a lot of male stories. The P-47 is a real pussycat, but with great claws and silky whiskers. What she's saying is, "Pet me gently!"*

# Republic P-47 THUNDERBOLT

Sis Bernheim, Nancy Batson and WASP Jane Straughan (43-W-1)<sup>IWASM</sup>

Gert Meserve, Dorothy Fulton, Betty Gillies, Nancy Batson and Esther Nelson (rear) study navigational chart in the Ready Room at New Castle AAB

# 20

After building up time in Wilmington's "Jugs" over the next month, on August 6, Teresa got orders to ferry her first P-47. She and Betty Gillies were sent to Republic Aircraft in Farmingdale, Long Island. Betty's destination was the 53rd Fighter Group at Paige Field in Fort Myers, Florida, and Teresa's was the 338th Fighter Group at Dale Mabry Field in Tallahassee, Florida.

With the WAFS flying the more advanced planes, ferrying was moving into a new phase. Up until then, standard operation was that several WAFS were sent at the same time to deliver several trainers to two or three fields down South. They flew in their loose formation — five hundred feet apart — on the way, had to stop and refuel frequently, and were at the mercy of the weather. Their light planes couldn't fly in high winds or questionable weather, they had no instruments by which they could fly blind, and they had no radios. The Ferrying Division said they could fly in daylight only. Their deliveries were figured in days and then, as per FERD's regulation, they had to make their way back to their home base by commercial rail or airline.

Emerging now in the summer of 1943 were the single trips, or maybe — like Betty's and Teresa's August 6 assignment — two WAFS were to pick up airplanes, like a pair of P-47s, at the same factory but deliver them to separate destinations. They might or might not fly "together" as far as the first delivery point. The pursuits and the twin-engine craft they now were ferrying were bigger, had radios and instruments, were capable of flying higher (often above the weather) and farther, and much faster. The trip from Farmingdale to Florida was made in a few hours, possibly with one refueling stop and, barring trouble with transportation, they were back in Wilmington overnight or, at worst, the following evening.

In late summer 1943 and all through 1944, as WAFS began to ferry P-51s from the West to the East Coast, things changed again. A P-51 could fly the 2,500-mile width of the country in a day. B.J. Erickson, who made many such trips, estimated approximately ten flying hours. Going east, she recalls stopping to refuel twice — usually in Albuquerque or El Paso and again in Indiana or Ohio — depending on the route. As the Ferrying Division "got smarter" it realized that instead of shipping that ferry pilot back to Long Beach via commercial airline, why not use her (or him) to ferry something west. So, more and more frequently, a ferry pilot was given an airplane going the other direction and they delivered it enroute home.

Teresa was one of the first WAFS to leave the light plane delivery business behind and move into something much bigger. She was about to become a fulltime pursuit ferry pilot with an occasional delivery of an attack bomber or cargo plane just to keep things interesting. And Betty Gillies was about to move on to something even bigger than that.

Wilmington wasn't the only base with women ferrying pursuit planes. B.J. and her girls in Long Beach, given the wealth of airplanes built by the many L.A. Basin factories, transitioned more quickly than anyone else. They flew the BT-13, BT-15, UC-78, A-24 Douglas Dauntless, C-47, and eventually the A-20. Then in June 1943, B.J. and Barbara Towne were sent to Palm Springs to learn to fly the P-51. Evelyn Sharp soon joined them. On July 27, B.J. became the second woman to check out in North American's swift Mustang. Towne and Evelyn Sharp were not far behind.

"This is when they were thinking of setting up a pursuit school there," B.J. says. "Barbara was four months pregnant at the time, but she got in it and she flew it. She could get the stick back. She flew 'til she couldn't, then went home. After she had the baby, she came back and ferried for us again for awhile. But she couldn't find a way to care for her son that satisfied her. She tried to stay, but her husband was gone quite a bit." Towne eventually left the squadron to go home to take care of her baby.

The women in Dallas ferried Beechcraft AT-10s, AT-6s, and Cessna C-78s from Wichita, Kansas; transport planes from the

Douglas factory at Tulsa, Oklahoma; and the B-25s at the North American factory in Kansas City.

Romulus was the most backward base as far as women transitioning into more powerful aircraft, which was well noted in the March 25, 1943 directive reiterating the original restriction of WAFS to light trainer aircraft only. That, of course, was turned around in late April thanks to Nancy Love's taking the initiative with the high command. With that, squadron leader Del Scharr went to work.

The women who graduated in Cochran's first and second classes had been trained at Houston Municipal Airport. Avenger Field at Sweetwater was not opened to women until spring 1943. By the time the twenty-three graduates arrived at their respective bases, they had received training in basic and advanced single-engine trainers and advanced multi-engine trainers. They also had had night flying, Link trainer time, and instrument flying. They were, in truth, now ahead of most of the WAFS in transition.

"A few WAFS felt cheated," Scharr says. "We had received cross-country time in puddle-jumpers in return for our patriotism. On the last day of April, Captain Hennessey said to me, 'We're going to give you girls some transition.' We'd been promised that since the middle of January."

The following day, Scharr, Barbara Poole and Barbara Donahue were invited to check out in an AT-9. "If you couldn't fly the AT-9, you'd never fly pursuit, especially not the P-39 Bell Airacobra," Scharr said. "The twin-engine AT-9 had no other role in the war effort than preparing pilots for pursuit. It climbed at 120 miles per hour, cruised at about 140, glided at 120, and landed at 110."

The high accident rate of ferry pilots flying the P-39s had been unacceptable in General Tunner's eyes. Too many pilots were being killed and even if the pilot got out alive, the airplane was a complete washout. "I put the cause down primarily as pilot failure. Sure the P-39 was a hot ship, but it was perfectly safe if it was flown according to specifications," General Tunner wrote in *Over the Hump*. "As a result of these accidents, we were getting a lot of static from pilots who claimed the P-39 was a flying coffin. Our women in the meantime had proved themselves as ferry pilots. They paid attention in class, and they read the characteristics and specifications of the plane they were to fly before they flew it. The solution of the P-39 problem was a natural one. I had a group of girls checked out on P-39s and assigned them to make P-39 deliveries."

Del Scharr and the others began to ferry the AT-9s immediately after transition. On their way to Dallas for their first delivery, Scharr, Poole and Donahue had their first opportunity to "fly the beam." Finally, they were flying aircraft equipped with instrumentation and radios. They learned to "bracket" the radio beam on a leg of the trip going toward it and how to bracket the beam flying away from it. Except for some Link training, they had never had the opportunity to fly the beam — or "by ear" — cross country until that trip.

The beam is a radio signal that produces a hum and pilots listened for it through their earphones. If you got off to one side you heard a *dit dah*. If you got off to the other side, you heard a *dah dit*. It told the pilot if he or she was to the right or the left of the directional beam.

On the way back from Dallas, the three of them were ordered to secure transportation only as far as Memphis. There, they were treated to a night flight back to Romulus in a B-17. Major Hennessey (he had been promoted) was the pilot and Romulus base commander Colonel Nelson the co-pilot. Colonel Tunner was flying with them. Tunner had called a meeting of all the group commanders in Memphis.

**P-39 Bell AIRACOBRA**

All three of the women had an opportunity to fly in the co-pilot's seat for a time while in the air.

With the AT-9 under her belt as of June 1, 1943, Del was on her way to flying the "big" plane available to Romulus ferry pilots, the P-39 Bell Airacobra.

This lightweight fighter airplane was slower and less maneuverable than the newer fighters that came along later, but, along with the P-40, it withstood the Japanese until better fighters arrived in late 1942. The Russians used it effectively as a ground-attack aircraft. The maximum speed on the P-39 is 376 mph. It is thirty feet two inches long and has a wingspan of thirty-four feet. The single engine is an Allison V-1710-85 — 1,325 horsepower inline. The P-39 also has a tricycle landing gear, which means the small wheel is in the nose of the plane, not the tail.

Since the pursuit was built in Buffalo, New York, the ferrying squadron at Romulus was the closest and therefore was called on most often to take the airplanes to their destination. However, as B.J. Erickson points out, later on she and several of the other Long Beach pursuit pilots were sent from Newark — where they had just delivered a P-51 — to Buffalo to pick up a P-39 or P-63. They made that delivery to Great Falls, Montana, on their way back home to California.

So many P-39s were destined for Russia, the base at Great Falls was the closest pickup point. From there, the male ferry pilots took them to Alaska for pick up by the Russian pilots. The WAFS were never allowed to ferry a P-39 all the way to Alaska.

The P-39 was known as a killer. Scharr points out that of thirty accidents in one month for which Romulus male pilots were responsible, fifteen were in P-39s and all were fatal. The P-39, it was said, was an airplane that did not forgive mistakes.

On June 24, Sharr was cleared for P-39 ground school. She was the only woman in the class. They were first treated to a film, but that was all the classroom time that day. Del, frustrated and wanting to know more, went looking for tech orders. She collected everything she could and retreated to her room to read, study and memorize.

Scharr was detail-oriented. She was methodical in her everyday life and methodical in her flying. She also notes in her book that, being a woman, she was not cursed with the need to be macho. She didn't have that never-admit-to-being-scared attitude most male pilots possess. She was careful, she was systematic, and she was proud of it. She was going to fly that airplane, and she wasn't going to let it kill her in the process.

Making the most of what she found in the various booklets the Bell people, on her request, had handed her, she made out her own checklist for the P-39. She reasoned that because the engine was not in the nose of the airplane but in the back of the fuselage, it didn't air cool like a nose engine did, therefore, it would have to be treated differently. She figured out that much of the checklist needed to be done while taxiing, not while standing still letting the engine heat up.

"The problem," she writes, "was to eliminate checking the aircraft when it was parked with the engine running, or during the taxiing, and never at takeoff."

Monday, June 28, she sat in the cockpit of a P-39 and did her blindfold test — locating every switch and dial from memory and feel. When she opened her eyes, Major Hennessey was standing beside the plane. He asked if she was ready. She was.

As with all pursuit aircraft start-ups, an enlisted man with the fire extinguisher stood by.

"Clear," she called. Followed by "switch on."

Moments later, the propeller turning, she began to taxi. Remaining alert to the gauges and dials, she worked her way through a couple of waiting periods while she allowed the engine coolant to drop below the red line. Finally, she and the airplane were ready. She pushed the throttle forward and the airplane surged forward.

"I felt the G's on my torso — my body was pressed back against the rear of the seat with great force. When the speedometer showed that the airplane was reaching ninety miles per hour, I eased the stick back exactly down the middle of my body toward my breastbone. I kept a steady pressure and felt the airplane lighten. The nose wheel had lifted and I was running on two wheels. Ahead was the metal fence at the end of the field, and it was getting closer and closer. Would the plane get off the ground before I reached the fence?

"I had flying speed now and I pressed back still more. The P-39 left the runway and immediately I flicked the landing gear switch up. I heard the thump of both gears entering the housing as we flew just a few feet above the fence. As I cleared it, I looked from one wingtip to the other, just checking that I was level. Aloud I said, 'Why, this is just another airplane!'"

Del Scharr had just entered the record books and the rarefied atmosphere of those who can be listed as "the first." She was the first woman to fly Bell Aircraft's P-39 Airacobra. She went on to ferry not only that pursuit, but the P-47 and P-51 as well.

"The women had no trouble, none at all. And I had no more complaints from the men," Tunner wrote in *Over the Hump*.

**Long Beach WAFS Barbara Towne and WASP Lovelle Richards march in review**

# B-17, THE FLYING FORTRESS

One of the most well-known bombers of all time, the B-17 Flying Fortress became famous in the long daylight bombing raids over Europe in WWII. While it lacked the range, bombload, and ceiling of its contemporary B-24 Liberator, the B-17 became the more famous of the two due to the many tales of B-17s bringing their crews back home despite heavy damage. With up to thirteen machine guns, the B-17 seemed to be a genuine "flying fortress in the sky."

# 21

The Boeing B-17 or Flying Fortress may be the most recognizable U.S. airplane used in World War II. It epitomized the Army Air Forces faith in long-range strategic bombing. It has been described as being rugged, stable and easy to fly. It helped Uncle Sam pierce the heart of Germany and was universally loved by its crews for taking extensive battle damage and still bringing them home.

The B-17 has a wingspan of 103 feet and is 74 feet long. Empty, it weighs 32,720 pounds. Loaded, it runs 55,500 pounds. The airplane is powered by four Wright 1,200-horsepower radial engines, has a maximum speed of 300 miles per hour at 30,000 feet, and its range is 1,850 miles.

Nobody really thought a woman could fly a B-17. Nobody, that is, but Nancy Love and a few of her more adventuresome WAFS. And, during the early months when they were flying PT-19s and Cubs, the thought of finding themselves in the pilot's seat of a B-17 was only a dream. But Nancy Love already had proved that she could stretch her limits and allow her imagination to roam free. She wasn't a dreamer, rather she was a doer who dreamed, who saw what was possible, then set out to accomplish it. After all, in the face of her mother's opposition, she had won her father's approval to take flying lessons.

Nancy's father, Dr. Robert Bruce Harkness, may have been a man of science and medicine, but he, too, had something of the dreamer in him, according to his granddaughter Marky Love. He made and lost a couple of fortunes. Why wouldn't he have risked a few dollars to indulge the apple of his eye — this beautiful daughter of his who perfectly personified the qualities of intelligence and grace he so much admired? Why not, as long as she kept her mother happy by following the path laid out for a proper young lady in the year 1930. That Nancy's father kept a detailed scrap-book containing the newspaper clippings and magazine articles about her and about her squadron, as well as a photo gallery of black and white glossy prints, is proof positive of his pride in his talented only daughter.

So, as 1942 drew to a close, Nancy once again dared to dream a little and she went to work to make that dream come true. Tired of sitting in an office while her squadron flew, she jumped at the opportunity in December to tour the bases where women's ferrying squadrons might be established. In the process, she began to position herself to fly any airplane she thought she could handle. The first such opportunity was to fly the B-25. The fact that she proved to herself that she was competent to fly this twin-engine, medium bomber was the beginning of a personal transition ladder that took her into the cockpits of nearly forty different kinds of military aircraft by December 20, 1944. The P-51 may have been the fastest thing she flew, but the biggest turned out to be the four-engine B-17. Her ferrying of the C-47s and the B-25s helped move her irrevocably toward this milestone.

On June 24, 1943 Nancy Love arrived to take up residence in Cincinnati. On June 28, Del Scharr made her P-39 flight. Within days, General Tunner called Nancy Love into his office and shut the door.

"You know the static we were getting from some of the men over flying the P-39 before one of your WAFS flew it?"

Nancy nodded, wondering where the conversation was going.

"We've been getting similar static from pilots objecting to ferrying B-17s over the North Atlantic to England." He stopped and cleared his throat. "Now these flights have become almost routine. There's no reason for this complaint."

Nancy held her breath and waited for what was to come next. Was he going where she hoped he was going with this?

"We've scheduled a blitz movement of two hundred B-17s to be delivered to the 8th Air Force in England in early September and I want you and Mrs. Gillies to fly one of them."

It took all of Nancy's legendary self-restraint to keep from leaping out of her chair and planting a big kiss on General Tunner's usually stern but now smiling face. She and Betty were about to make history. Two women were going to ferry a four-engine bomber across the Atlantic during war time. That would be a major first.

So, at General Tunner's direction, Nancy Love and Betty Gillies began what was probably the biggest transition of their aviation lives: to learn how to fly the up-to-now men-only, heavy bomber known as the Flying Fortress.

General Tunner was not out to make great heroines of his top two women pilots. That was the farthest thing from his mind. Rather, he was sensitive to the build-up of resistance from his male pilots over ferrying B-17s across "The Pond" to England. He also had noticed that every time a woman made something look easy by doing it well, the men thought twice about complaining over the difficulty or danger the next time they drew that assignment. He had his scheme and he thought he knew how he could turn it to his advantage again. And he had all the confidence in the world in his "number one and number two woman pilots."

"Nancy Love and Betty Gillies leaped at the chance to be the first women to ferry a plane overseas," Tunner boasted.

The route called Snowball, from Goose Bay, Labrador, to Prestwick, Scotland, was first used during Lend Lease to deliver goods and also airplanes to Great Britain. Now, in 1943, it was used to deliver Uncle Sam's own airplanes to the AAF squadrons stationed in England. The flight was dangerous not only because the pilot was flying over the cold, unfriendly North Atlantic much of the time; it was also dangerous because of the unpredictable weather — including wickedly capricious conditions of cold, snow, fog and bad visibility, icing, and something called white outs that were known as "flying in milk."

The pilot "flying in milk" sees the white snow beneath him, but the sky above him is also white. Tunner described it as, "no line of demarcation — no horizon. The eye alone cannot tell if the airplane is ten feet over the snow or ten thousand. This phenomenon is not fog. The wings of the airplane are clearly visible. Sometimes, the sun is even shining."

One pilot flying Snowball thought himself well beyond Greenland — out over the sea. He dropped down to five thousand feet and banked his transport to make a minor course correction. His left wing touched something solid. It was the top of the icecap that covers Greenland. Several weeks later, a large rescue team made its way to him and got him and the crew out. This adventure — or misadventure, depending on your viewpoint — greatly enhanced the Air Force's knowledge of the Arctic. After that, they maintained a full-scale rescue operation on the ready.

But still the men were leery. They smelled danger.

When Nancy told Betty, she said, "He was very pleased with your success with the Calgary delivery in April. We proved deliveries could be made on time if you stick to the schedule and the route and don't allow distractions to get in the way."

Just as Nancy had waited for Tunner to drop the other shoe, Betty waited, saying nothing.

"He's pleased with Del's flying the P-39."

Betty allowed herself a nod.

"Well, he's got the same idea here. The men can't stand being bested by women. He's banking on that. What he said to me was, and I quote, 'I've decided to let a couple of our girls show them just how easy it really is.'"

Nancy hesitated, letting the suspense build. "Guess who the 'girls' are?"

Betty's blue eyes sparkled. At five feet one inch, she was going to fly the B-17.

⮜◉◉⮞

In order to fly the B-17, Nancy and Betty first faced extensive preparation. Betty kept a daily diary throughout the war. Here are some of the notes she wrote in July and August 1943 about events leading up to their B-17 transition for a flight across the Atlantic.

*July 11* — Got number one typhoid shot and vaccinations.

*July 12* — [The following is underlined in red in her diary.] Received TWX from HQ: Commanding Officer, 2nd Ferrying Group, NCAAB — Commanding General desires that Mrs. Gillies be checked out in B-25, both day and night and that she be sent to instrument school at your group. Signed Tunner. — Began sand-bagging [building time] in a B-25 each day at Wilmington.

*July 19* — Received letter from Cincinnati HQ. Ordered to drop everything for instrument school. Began instrument school.

*August 3* — Received Army instrument rating. Got ninety percent on written. Did extremely well in flight check. B-25 transition follows.

*August 8* — Awaiting orders to head for Cincinnati HQ. Ordered to Fort Myers. P-47 delivery with Teresa James.

*August 9* — Arrived Cincinnati HQ. Met Nancy Love at the field. We sat in a B-17 and refreshed ourselves with systems and cockpit layout.

*August 10* — Nancy and I will be pilot and co-pilot with Captain Forman as our instructor, Lockbourne Field, Columbus, Ohio.

❧

Nancy and Betty were ready to begin cross-country training, including night flying, night landings, instrument operations and full operation of the B-17, all under the careful tutelage and watchful eye of their instructor, Captain Robert D. "Red" Forman.

Bill Tunner had met Red Forman when he was commanding the Memphis Air Corps Detachment back in 1939. Forman ran an ice skating rink and did a little flying on weekends. Tunner was recruiting Reserve pilots way back then, and Forman was one of the best. He got him in the Reserve and when war was declared, Forman went where Tunner went. He was, among other things, Tunner's copilot on The Hump in 1944-45. Forman eventually became Brigadier General Forman who commanded Military Air Transport in Europe in the 1960s. Bill Tunner trusted him implicitly, which is why he turned Nancy's and Betty's training over to him.

As it turned out, during their training period, Nancy, Betty, Red Forman and General Tunner had an unexpected adventure that probably all four could have done without.

Betty's diary entry for August 13 reads — "Tunner wanted to go to Ludington in B-17."

With Red Forman in the right seat as instructor, Nancy and Betty were taking turns flying the left seat, or that which is designated as Pilot-In-Command. They were beginning to build their time for their Atlantic flight under Forman's watchful eye. As it happened, that day they also were carrying their boss, General Tunner, and some of his staff officers on an administrative cross-country flight. Betty's diary does not say why.

They started to land at Ludington, Michigan. Realizing that the runway was too short to take the B-17, Forman shoved the throttles forward to full power and aborted the landing.

Betty writes: "Number four engine detonated on pull up. Capt. Forman feathered it."

Now what were they going to do? They had a cargo of VIP personnel aboard, one bad engine, and no place to land.

The closest alternate runway that would accommodate the B-17 was the runway located at the Traverse City, Michigan airport and that was the exclusive domain of the U.S. Navy. Surely the Navy would be hospitable to an AAF B-17 in distress.

They turned north.

As they approached the blue waters of Grand Traverse Bay and the airfield, Nancy took in the familiar beauty of Michigan's north woods. She hoped they would all have a brief R and R while the Navy mechanics hunted for the problem in Number Four. Lunch at a nice little restaurant on the bay would be nice. This was country like that around Houghton where she had grown up.

Forman set the big bomber down.

As they slowed, Nancy looked out her side window, already anticipating the sweet smell of pine. That was when she saw that a row of Jeeps was keeping pace with the gradually slowing airplane and the sailors riding in those Jeeps were armed.

"What the . . ." Nancy kept her eye on them.

"They're over here, too," Betty said, looking out the window on the right side from behind a frowning Red Forman.

The "Follow Me" Jeep led them onto the taxiway. The Jeep leading the left column pulled up to the left side of the airplane and motioned for Nancy to open her window.

She did.

What happened next is part of history, pieced together from Betty's journal, that indicated "the Navy was most inhospitable," and Nancy's log book.

The officer commanding the guard told Nancy she couldn't land there.

"We have General William H. Tunner, commanding officer of the Ferrying Division, Air Transport Command, U.S. Army Air Forces and his staff on board and we have lost number four engine. We need to deplane and make repairs."

The Navy would not budge.

General Tunner, who had seen the Jeeps, appeared behind them in the cockpit door. "What's going on?"

Nancy explained.

Tunner leaned down so the officer could see his brigadier's star. Still the young officer held his ground.

Nancy swore she could hear the general count ten, swallowing his anger.

Then Tunner turned to his three pilots. "Can we take off?"

Nancy stole a glance at Red Forman, caught his imperceptible nod. "Yes, Sir, we can take off."

"Then do it," Tunner said, turned on his heel and disappeared back into the bowels of the airplane.

"Betty," Nancy said, "start looking for the next nearest airfield that will take this airplane. Here's where we all earn these wings.

"Ensign," she said to the officer standing below her window, "I suggest you move your Jeeps out of this airplane's path, unless you want to go with us." She fixed him with the chilly half-smile she used when she was displeased with someone. Some of the WAFS said those hazel eyes of hers could turn as icy green as a tarn above timberline and the young ensign in command was now on the receiving end of that infamous look.

"Yes, Ma'am." This time, he saluted her.

"Prepare for takeoff," Forman said from her right.

Out of the corner of her eye, Nancy noticed that Forman wore a barely suppressed grin. Then he was all business again as she called out the checklist for him in preparation for takeoff.

The ATC base at Alpena, Michigan controlled the nearest runway that could handle a B-17. They flew across the upper part of the mitten that is the state of Michigan to Alpena on Lake Huron. From there, they flew back southwest, again across the state, to Muskegon which, like Ludington, is on Lake Michigan. Nancy's log book indicates that she landed the airplane in Muskegon, took off from there and landed that night in Nashville. Presumably the engine was checked and repaired in Alpena.

The reason for the Navy's paranoia had them totally puzzled. They finally agreed that some V.I.P. must have been due to land momentarily and they were in the way. That they were there on three engines and carrying the commander of the ATC's Ferrying Division made no difference at all to the Navy. In essence, General Tunner and his entourage were simply told to "git."

Long after the war, Delphine Bohn — who had pulled this story from the recesses of Betty Gillies' memory some forty years later — wrote in her memoir that the reason the Navy turned them away was because an airplane carrying President Roosevelt and Prime Minister Winston Churchill was due there momentarily. Up to now, no verification of that has been found. FDR's archivists tell us the two heads of state were at FDR's Hyde Park home in New York from August 12 to 14, 1943. We may never know if they took a secret flight to Traverse City to admire some of Michigan's loveliest scenery, but it was an auspicious beginning to Nancy and Betty's preparation for their flight to England.

∽⊙⊙⊙∾

On August 15, back at Lockbourne, Nancy and Betty qualified as pilots on the Flying Fortress, the first women to fly a B-17. They had hauled the big bomber around the sky using their hands and feet and refusing Red Forman's offer of help. "We have to be able to do it ourselves," Nancy told him, remembering Jackie Cochran's tainted delivery of the Lockheed Hudson to England two years earlier when she wasn't allowed to take off and land.

Nancy's log book says that on August 18 they delivered a B-17F from Cheyenne to Great Falls; on August 19/20, they delivered a B-17F from Seattle to Cheyenne via Pendleton, Oregon, and Ogden, Utah. They got weathered in in Seattle on August 21 and August 22-24 they spent delivering a B-17F from Seattle to Dallas via Sacramento, Long Beach, and El Paso.

On September 1, Nancy, the pilot, and Betty, the co-pilot, left Cincinnati in B-17F No. 42-30624 on their first leg of the trip that would take them across the cold, foreboding North Atlantic. With them were 1st Lt. R.O. "Pappy" Fraser, navigator; T/Sgt. Stover, radio operator; T/Sgt. Weintraub, aerial engineer; and T/Sgt. L.S. Hall, assistant aerial engineer. The plane was destined for the 8th Air Force in Great Britain. Flying along with them was B-17G No. 42-30541 piloted by Lt. Col. J.W. Chapman; co-pilot was Capt. Samuel Boykin; and Capt. Zych was navigator. Lt. Col. Coates, Director of Personnel at Ferrying Division Headquarters, went along as a passenger.

Nancy carried in her B-4 bag a letter of introduction to Major Roy Atwood, executive officer of the ATC European Wing in London written on official Air Transport Command letterhead. Following the salutation and a plea to receive and take care of the bearers of this letter, the writer stated:

> They should arrive in Prestwick presently and due to the shortness of time will bring this letter. I have known these people for a good while and they are thoroughly competent as pilots, as well as having a background in aviation activities. They are being sent to perform a certain amount of liaison with the ATA and other agencies interested in the ferrying of aircraft to the UK.
>
> I am sure you will find these two personalities pleasant,

if not unusual, in that they arrive as they did, and sincerely hope you will give them your highly accredited effort in showing them around.

> Very sincerely yours,
> Robert M. Love
> Colonel, G.S.C.
> Deputy Chief of Staff
> P.S. Incidentally one of them is my wife and the other a good friend.

They RONed in New Castle, where they picked up the fleece-lined flight suits and oxygen masks required for the North Atlantic air route. In the late summer heat that enveloped the Eastern seaboard that week, fleece-lined anything seemed a cruel joke. On September 2, they flew to New York's LaGuardia airport for an overnight briefing, proper clearance and the application of the appropriate and very popular aircraft nose art.

"WAFS" was painted in plain-jane block letters on the port side of their aircraft, right under the pilot's window. Then the name "Queen Bee" was added in flowery, feminine script.

From there, on September 3, 1943, the bombers flew to Presque Isle, Maine, to the staging point for the trans-Atlantic flight. They RONed there, received their briefing and clearance and left the following day for Goose Bay, Labrador, once a tiny Eskimo village on the tip of Lake Melville. Early in the war, the Canadian government had decided to build an air base there and invited the United States and the British to share the use of it. The base now served as air cover for transatlantic flights and as a staging field for ferrying bombers to Britain.

It was onto that cold, remote, wind-swept airfield that the two WAFS stepped the afternoon of September 4, 1943. Much of their trip had been under instrument conditions.

"When we leave for Prestwick, Scotland, tomorrow, do you realize we will be the first women to ferry aircraft over the Pond during actual wartime?" Nancy said, pulling her leather flight jacket close and zipping it up.

"I wonder if it's as cold there as it is here," Betty said.

The story that everyone would like to believe happened is that the two women pilots and their crew took off the following day and successfully crossed "the Pond" to Scotland and delivered B-17F No. 42-30624 to the 8th Air Force. That, of course, didn't happen. A telegram arrived at the eleventh hour from Hap Arnold ordering them to stand down and turn the airplane over to a male pilot and co-pilot.

**Nancy Love and Betty Gillies with crew and Queen Bee**       IWASM

The wave of disappointment that swept over Nancy was devastating. "It's midnight, Betty, and Cinderella's coach has turned into a pumpkin. We're not going to England."

As they sat in the mess hall, drinking coffee and waiting for their transportation back to New Castle, Betty finally broke the silence. "You don't suppose the indomitable Miss Cochran had something to do with this, do you?"

"She couldn't have known about it. Bill's kept a tight lid on," Nancy said.

No one knows for sure what the chain of events was that resulted in Nancy Love and Betty Gillies being denied their opportunity to fly the North Atlantic. If General Tunner had sent them from Gander, the jump-off point for the other bombers in the blitz, they would already have been out over the Atlantic. But he had tried to give them the optimum time over land, therefore had sent them from Goose Bay instead.

The official story is this: Tunner, thinking the two women and their crew were well on their way, sent a wire to England alerting commander of the ATC European Wing, Brigadier General Paul Burrows, that the plane flown by his two top women pilots was on its way. The telegram was delivered while Burrows was having dinner with his boss, Chief of the Army Air Forces General H.H. "Hap" Arnold. Burrows handed the telegram to Arnold who immediately ordered the flight stopped.

The word reached the two crews in Goose Bay as they sat in the mess hall finishing dinner.

Betty Gillies had this to say in an interview more than fifty years later: "What did I say? 'Damn!'

"Arnold didn't think about the personal disappointment. That wasn't his concern. His responsibility was for domestic flying. The B-17 was going to England. We were flying into war zone. He didn't want women flying into the war zone.

"We weren't taxiing out on the runway, though that is the story everyone tells. We were at supper the night before. We had plenty of time to go to the bar and drink our sorrows and get up with a hangover."

Nancy Love and Betty Gillies boarded a C-52A as passengers the morning of September 6, 1943. The flight was bound for Presque Isle. Two male pilots took their places and ferried B-17F No. 42-30624 on to Scotland.

# 22

Between July 29 and August 6, 1943, B.J. Erickson, squadron commander of the WAFS in Long Beach, made four, 2,000-mile deliveries in slightly more than five days of actual flying. B.J. held multi-engine ratings and therefore was at the top of the duty roster at each stop. In addition, she had perfect weather.

Her journey began when she delivered a P-51 from Long Beach to the modification center in Evansville, Indiana, on July 29. The following day, she took a modified P-47 from Evansville back to

**B.J. and the Mustang P-51**

San Pedro, California, RONing enroute, and delivering the aircraft on July 31. On August 2, she ferried a C-47 from Long Beach to Fort Wayne, Indiana. From there, she traveled approximately 250 miles to Ferrying Division (FERD) headquarters in Cincinnati where she was on duty for a couple of days. Then on August 6, she returned to California ferrying another P-47.

Such a series of deliveries in that short a time was unusual, even with all the elements in her favor. Word of her accomplishments was passed on in the Ferrying Division's weekly report to ATC. It captured sufficient attention and, eventually, B.J. was recommended for an Air Medal for her performance on duty.

**B.J. Erickson was awarded the Air Medal
in March 1944 by General Hap Arnold**

In truth, the award embarrassed B.J. as she felt she was merely doing her duty as any of the WAFS would have done under similar circumstances.

"The air medal was given to me to represent what all the girls do. I didn't accept it for what I did, but because it represented what women pilots were doing. The weather was good. You can make four quick trips across the country if the weather is good. I wasn't any better than anybody else. At the time, it was a tool to get our militarization through Congress. But by the time the bill got there, the war was winding down, we were winning. It was a year too late. Public sentiment had turned against us."

General Arnold himself pinned the medal on B.J.'s newly issued WASP uniform jacket of Santiago blue. The occasion was the graduation of 44-W-2 in Sweetwater, March 11, 1944, and both Nancy Love and Jacqueline Cochran were seated on the podium, there to witness the event.

By summer 1943, FERD was dealing with two distinct trends. One: manufacture of trainer-type aircraft was slowing. Fewer trainers being built meant fewer ferry pilots needed to fly them. Two: the manufacture of pursuit aircraft was on the rise. These new, high-performance, long-range airplanes, the P-47 and P-51, were capable of escorting the big bombers all the way to Berlin and protecting them on the trip home as well. And they could hunt and destroy enemy planes and installations in the process. In them lay the path to victory.

Factory assembly lines were becoming increasingly more efficient in turning out these warplanes. Delivery of those pursuits to modification centers or directly to the docks was now the Ferrying Division's primary job.

President Roosevelt had predicted that the U.S. aviation industry would eventually produce fifty thousand airplanes a year. In order to deliver the ever-increasing number of airplanes coming off assembly lines, Tunner sought to decentralize the Ferrying Division. No longer was it a simple matter of picking up a plane at the factory and flying it to its final destination, he pointed out. A plane destined for duty in one part of the world needed to be modified to meet both climate and combat conditions.

Already, Air Materiel Command had discovered that modifying an airplane at the factory was confusing. So the decision was made to set up modification centers. Then aircraft would be ferried from the factory to the center where the plane would be readied for overseas. Then the modified aircraft would be ferried to the docks. "Careful scheduling and supervision were required to keep both planes and pilots moving," Tunner said.

What FERD needed now, as quickly as it could get them, was a lot more pilots who were capable of ferrying the hot pursuits to and from the modification centers or from the factory direct to the port of debarkation. But first it had to train them. Creating yet another problem was the fact that the demand for pursuit aircraft was so great, the Ferrying Division was having trouble laying its hands on sufficient number of these planes in which to train new pursuit pilots.

In September 1943, General Tunner wrote:

> In view of the large number of tactical aircraft to be delivered and the decreasing proportion of trainers, it is essential that women pilots be trained to ferry other types [of airplanes] than trainers. The Ferrying Division can and will continue to train women as pursuit delivery pilots.

Tunner now had an added dilemma. He was getting more women pilots, but by now, the Flying Training Command graduates from Sweetwater did not possess the three hundred hours total flying time the Ferrying Division required. The accident rate among the newly arrived WASPs went up. In a letter dated August 28, General Tunner reported ". . . an excessive accident and mishap record . . . too many ground loops, examples of poor judgment in flying into thunder storms and bad weather, resulting in forced landings in unsuitable fields and cases of over or undershooting runways."

Between September and November 1943, the Ferrying Division fought to maintain its basic standard for ferry pilots — three hundred flight hours. FERD had learned, over nearly two years of experience, observation and documentation, that a minimum of three hundred hours was necessary for ferry pilots. Combat pilots, it was found, required fewer hours of training than did ferry pilots. This was because ferry pilots had to be able, potentially, to fly one hundred fifty different types or models of planes, from trainers all the way up to big bombers. The combat pilot was responsible for one type of airplane.

Finally, FERD asked that Air Transport Command send only the top fifteen WASP pilots per graduating class. In addition, as the using agency, FERD requested a beefed up curriculum at Avenger Field with additional flight time. This was done, beginning in 1944.

Lack of hours wasn't the only dilemma here. Simply put, the Ferrying Division no longer needed large numbers of pilots who could fly only light airplanes.

Ferry pilots — male or female — were not born to the job. Rather, they were made — groomed — produced by months and months of cross country flights in increasingly larger, more powerful, more complex aircraft. After primary trainers, the next step was to ferry larger training planes like the BT-13 and the AT-6 cross country, followed by the smaller twin-engine planes like the C-78 and the AT-9 and so on up the ladder.

The Ferrying Division now had two very distinct and separate needs. One was to train men who could ferry four-engine bombers or fly heavy transport planes across the oceans to foreign destinations — something that extensive cross-country flying in the U.S. prepared them for. Men were needed at the ATC's foreign bases. The other need was for pilots — male and female — who could handle pursuit planes and ferry them to the docks for shipment overseas. The former was a broad-based training. The latter was a specialized task. The men flying bombers and transports overseas — either ferrying them or in combat — did not need to know how to fly pursuits. Likewise, the ferry pilots who flew these single-engine fighters to the docks needed to know how to handle the powerful pursuit aircraft — but not B-17s.

If the women had — as originally planned — been kept on flying the smaller aircraft, they would have cluttered up the bottom rung of the ladder, creating a bottleneck, so that fewer men could go through the transition stages and arrive finally at the big multi-engine airplanes.

General Tunner and the Ferrying Division devised a classification system for rating pilots as to the types of airplanes they were qualified to fly, bearing in mind that women pilots did not ferry overseas. Pilots carried a card stating their classifications, which were:

**Class I** — qualified to fly low-powered, single-engine airplanes (PT-17, PT-19, PT-26, Cubs)

**Class II** — qualified to fly twin-engine trainers and utility planes (UC-78, AT-9)

**Class III** — qualified to fly twin-engine cargo/medium transport planes and on instruments (C-47, C-60)

**Class IV** — qualified to fly twin-engine planes in advanced categories, such as medium bombers and heavy transports (B-25, A-20, A-25)

**Class V** — qualified to fly the biggest airplanes, four-engine bombers and transports (examples B-17, B-24) and able to deliver them overseas

**III P** — qualified to fly single-engine, high-performance pursuits or fighters (P-39, P-40, P-47 and P-51)

**IV P** — qualified to fly twin-engine, high-performance pursuits or fighters (P-38, P-61)

Tunner adds, "[The P-class] was a special class because, although these fast and hard-to-handle planes certainly required more than average experience, the flying of fighters was not in itself of great experience value in working up to the big four-engine planes." And it was imperative that women not clog up the bottom of the delivery chain because the men who would be flying four-engine bombers overseas needed to learn cross-country skills in the smaller planes.

As of September 21, 1943, the Ferrying Division had 180 WASPs (the name change was official) within the ranks of its four squadrons. Twenty-two were original WAFS. The remaining 158 were graduates of the Flying Training Command school in Houston or Sweetwater.

To fly pursuit, a pilot had to be instrument rated. The Ferrying Division began to prepare its women pilots for the coming pursuit transition by sending them to instrument school.

Betty Gillies and Nancy Love already had their instrument cards as part of their B-17 transition in July and August 1943. B.J. Erickson received her white card (as it was called) on September 27, 1943, at Long Beach, her home base. She was the first 6th Ferrying Group woman pilot to earn one. Dorothy Scott got hers October 8 of that year at her home base, Dallas Love Field. The first female instrument-rated pilot there, she was scheduled immediately to begin instructing both male and female pilots in instrument flying. In fact, Dorothy gave fellow Original Bernice Batten her first instrument instruction on a flight on October 10 at Dallas. However, Scott was soon transferred to pursuit school.

Florene Miller also took her instrument instruction at her home base, Dallas Love Field. Her Link trainer instructor was none other than her mother, Flora Miller. After Florene's father and older brother were killed in a plane crash July 4, 1941, and Florene and her other brother volunteered to fly for the military, Flora and her younger daughter, Garnette, moved to Dallas and enrolled in Southern Methodist University. Flora learned how to teach the Link and landed a job at Love Field. "I probably had the best Link instruction of anyone because she tried her best to crash and burn me," Florene says.

Teresa James was sent to Dallas for her instrument instruction and Gert Meserve earned hers at her home base, New Castle Army Air Base in Wilmington.

Two others who received their instrument training at their home base were original Wilmington WAFS Helen McGilvery and Nancy Batson and, as it turned out, their instructor was destined to do more than teach aircraft instruments for a living.

As Nancy told the tale:

*Betty Gillies was trying to get us ready, I suppose, for pursuit training. In the summer of 1943, both Helen and I got twin-engine training in an AT-9 and the C-78, better known as the Bamboo Bomber. Then we got some night flying and also a lot of Link trainer time.*

*Now I liked to see where I was going. To me, that was flying — not instrument flying where you can't see the wonderful scenery and all the interesting things on the ground. But finally, in the fall of 1943, we started the real thing.*

*Helen McGilvery and I had the same instructor and we traded off. She flew with him in the morning and I flew in the afternoon. We'd get in the airplane — an AT-6 — and I'd be in the back seat and the instructor in the front. And he'd tell me to pull the hood up. The hood is this black cloth thing that you pull over your part of the cockpit so that you can't see anything but the instrument panel — nothing outside the cockpit.*

*The instructor taxied the airplane out and got it lined up on the runway, then he'd tell me to set my gyro at zero. I'd take off from a dead stop, blind, climb into that highway in the sky, and fly to Philadelphia watching the instruments and following the beam. The beam — a radio signal — is a hum and you listened through your earphones. If you got off to one side you heard a dit dah. If you got off to the other side, you heard a dah dit. It told you if you were to the right or the left of the directional beam.*

*Well, because I preferred flying VFR conditions — that means Visual Flight Rules — I guess I wasn't taking this instruction too seriously. One particular afternoon, I had been particularly bad. The next day, Helen McGilvery took me aside and told me that our instructor had told her I'd better "do better" or I was going to flunk this course.*

*Well, that afternoon, I was a different pilot! I loved flying those airplanes and I wasn't about to do anything to endanger my opportunity to fly them.*

*Finally, one afternoon, I guess I had done all right because the instructor told me he was taking the controls and for me to push the hood back. We flew out and swooped down over DelMarVa, where Delaware, Maryland and Virginia all meet. It was marshy, close to the coast. Turns out my instructor was a duck hunter and it was well into fall now — the colors were beautiful. He was thinking about getting in a little duck hunting and wanted to look over the territory.*

*I sighed with relief. I knew I had passed! I had straightened up in time. Both Little Mac and my instructor were looking out for me.*

*Well, in 1964, I was watching the Republican Convention on television and looked there on the screen and who did I see but my old instrument instructor from Wilmington. His name was Barry Goldwater. He was a senator from Arizona and he was about to be nominated to run for President of the United States!*

**Florene Miller**
5<sup>th</sup> Ferrying Group, Dallas

# 23

The hunt for pursuit pilots was on. The Ferrying Division needed to train as many pursuit-qualified pilots as it could in the shortest length of time because the factories were turning out pursuit planes as fast as the production lines could move them.

There was FERD with one hundred eighty women pilots. A handful were checked out in one or another of the pursuits. Among The Originals, Betty Gillies, Helen Mary Clark and Teresa James were now ferrying P-47s out of the Republic factory in Farmingdale, New York; Del Scharr and Barbara Donahue were flying P-39s out of Buffalo, New York; and B.J. Erickson, Evelyn Sharp and, until recently, Barbara Towne were ferrying P-51s from the North American factory in the L.A. Basin. Nancy Love, by then, was at Headquarters in Cincinnati and doing very little ferrying, but the others were all doing the job. Why, then, couldn't more women be trained to fly pursuit?

One problem was finding sufficient number of pursuit planes for training purposes. Every plane possible was being sent overseas. Why not put the pursuits used for training all in one spot, bring the trainees — male and female — into that location, and train them to fly all four single-engine pursuits in one intensive course in one place?

On December 1, 1943, pursuit transition school was born. The number of men in a class numbered anywhere from twenty to nearly fifty. The women in any one class numbered from two to twelve. At first, the facility was located in Palm Springs, California. There, pilots could learn to fly all of the pursuits in a focused, four-week training period. In spring 1944, the facility was moved to Brownsville, Texas.

According to Nancy Batson, "The rich retirees around Palm

Springs didn't like all the noise. That's why it eventually moved to Brownsville. But most of the people in Palm Springs loved us. We went into town at night and spent money."

When the first classes entered pursuit school in early and mid-December 1943, several of The Originals were among those sent to Palm Springs. They were joined by a far larger number of women who were the graduates of the earliest classes at the Flying Training Command flight school in Houston and Sweetwater — the WFTDs-now-WASPs who, by late 1943, were flying for the Ferrying Division under Nancy Love's command. In all, one hundred thirty-four women eventually flew pursuit — including sixteen Originals.

Up until late fall 1943, FERD had cautioned the base commanders to keep a lid on the transition of women into the pursuits. Consequently, only a few — those Originals mentioned above — were known to have had the opportunity. In fact, General Tunner asked Nancy Love to investigate rumors that the restrictions on women flying the P-47 were somewhat more relaxed at the 5th Ferrying Group in Dallas than at other bases. He wanted to know, had some of the women at Dallas been allowed to check out in the Thunderbolt even though they were scheduled to go to pursuit school within weeks?

Florene Miller, one of the Dallas WAFS, was scheduled to leave for pursuit school November 30. She had been reading tech orders and familiarizing herself with the P-47. On the flight line, she had received briefings by a P-47 instructor as to the cockpit and the flight characteristics of the "Jug."

The P-47 has a massive 2800-horsepower engine, a tremendously large, four-bladed propeller, and it's a tail-dragger — the back end of the airplane sits low on the runway on the little tail-wheel, with the rest of the airplane canted up at an angle. When you sit in the cockpit, you can't see over the engine and down the runway. You have to turn the plane side to side when taxiing — or "S" down the runway.

The day before she was to leave for Palm Springs, Florene took her first flight in one — with dramatic results.

It was late November, the sun was low on the horizon and setting early. On top of that, it was hazy. The active runway that afternoon was not the usual one. Instead, pilots were taking off and landing on the seldom-used, shorter, east-west runway. The more frequently used runway had brand new airplanes parked wingtip to wingtip on both sides — airplanes waiting to be delivered. Their presence made an already narrow landing strip appear even narrower.

Dallas Love Field, back in late 1943, still was girdled by a series of utility lines strung from steel poles. These lines transmitted power to the field and also to a large area of Dallas surrounding the field. Delphine Bohn said that the Civil Aeronautics Administration (CAA) and the military had tried to have the poles removed and the lines placed underground, but to no avail.

Florene took off, went aloft and did a few maneuvers to get the feel of the airplane. Then she came down and began a series of landings and takeoffs. The haze had gotten worse and it was late in the afternoon. The tower closed the field and she was told to come in. Her approach would be into the setting sun, her visibility hampered by the haze.

*As I came in, I knew exactly where I was except that I was about ten feet lower than I intended to be. I flew straight into a steel utility pole. It was strong enough that, as I found out later, I didn't knock it down but it made an awful, screaming metal-tearing-against-metal sound. The collision caused the airplane to shoot straight up and start to roll.*

*Fortunately, I had had aerobatic training before I joined the WAFS. When the plane started to roll on its back, I pulled up the gear, stomped on the rudder, jerked the ailerons, and poured on the power — all at once. I slammed everything so hard, I sprained my back and it hurt for days afterwards. I was doing acrobatics a few feet off the ground, but I managed to roll out. I held hard right stick and hard left rudder — cross control — sitting crooked in the seat and pushing down with one leg in order to keep it flying straight. The airplane was mushing along and vibrating something awful. I'm trying to keep the nose straight ahead.*

*Now I was off the runway and headed for a hangar. I knew that if I could get enough altitude to get over that hangar that I could get out of there in one piece. The instrument panel was vibrating so hard I couldn't read it, but I kept climbing. My first idea was to get enough altitude to jump.*

*I flew out north of Dallas where it was less populated. When I was high enough and flying level enough, I tried to assess the damage. I looked out the window and saw that part of the right wing was gone. I looked at the rear of the plane. The rudder and tail were messed up as well. And along with the vibration, there was a rhythmic clank of metal on metal beating on the side of the fuselage.*

Florene relates that as the sun sank below the horizon and first twilight and then night descended, she found a place to bail out, but finally realized that, in spite of the damage, she was able to fly the plane. She really didn't want to jump out into the darkness. Maybe, she thought, she could land it. But when she turned the plane around to return to the airport, she encountered total blackness. The airport wasn't there!

*All I could see was black night. No Love Field. What was wrong? I've always had a good sense of direction. Uncertainty, almost desperation set in. I had never flown at night. In the Ferrying Division, we did not fly at night.*

*Then in the distance, on my left, I saw a cluster of lights. Surely that was Dallas. If I could just find the red horse that rotated around the top of one of the buildings, I'd know it was Dallas. I flew toward the lights until I got close enough to make out the red horse. OK, I said to myself, if this is Dallas, the airport has to be right over there — in the middle of that big black hole. I knew the area. It had to be there.*

What had happened was that when she hit the utility pole, Florene had taken out the lights to Love Field and the surrounding community. The entire area was without power. The tower was out — the landing lights, everything — all the lights on the field were out. Radio contact from the tower also had been lost, but using the plane's radio Florene was able to make contact with a man working in one of the hangars. Through him, she and the tower relayed messages. In the meantime, she flew around burning up fuel. Finally, when she was ready to try to land, the airport lined up Jeeps on either side of the runway and turned on their lights, and that lighted up the runway for her.

Florene lined the stricken P-47 up and made her approach. In spite of the parked airplanes, she had asked for permission to land on the long runway to give herself more stopping distance.

*On my final approach, I knew I still had to clear those poles at the end of the runway. Suddenly, my landing lights showed one of those towers right in front of me. Since I was flying at full power, I had no extra power to 'jump' over the tower. I mushed over the top of it, then quickly put the nose down. I was on top of the sage brush as I came over the end of the runway. I pulled the throttle back and the plane sat down. They always said the Jug dropped like a rock.*

Florene taxied the battered airplane onto the taxi strip and in to the flight line, parked it and cut the switch. The first man to clamber up on the wing was her commanding officer. "I knew he was going to fire me or kill me or worse," she recalls. But he was so relieved that she was down safely that he congratulated her on landing at all.

Certainly, the ending could have been quite different. Florene could have lost her life and the stricken P-47 could have done considerable damage had it crashed in a populated area — with or without her still aboard. But the simple fact was, it hadn't. She had landed the airplane.

She saw all the people on the ground — and she had drawn quite a crowd. Several people were gesturing at different parts of the airplane. She deplaned, carefully as she feared her knees would buckle on her when she reached the ground, and looked first at the propeller. A large section of one of the prop blades was gone. "No wonder it vibrated. If I had known it was the prop, I would have gotten out. The engine should have fallen out of its mount."

Then she turned and looked at the rest of the airplane. From the engine nacelle to the tail-wheel, the P-47 was ripped open like somebody had taken a can opener to its belly. The tail-wheel was still in tact; otherwise, she would have lost control when she landed.

The final blow — a crewman climbed up on the wing and

jumped, rather cavalierly, Florene thought, down into the cockpit and promptly went through the floor. All that was left of the bottom of the airplane were the flimsy floorboards.

"If I had seen the ground between my feet, I wouldn't have stayed in that airplane."

The next day, somebody told her that when they checked the gas tanks, they discovered that she landed on vapor.

*Editor's note*: examination revealed part of one propeller blade sheared off; the right flap torn off and hanging by a ribbon of metal (the metallic clanking she heard); the right wing damaged; the right horizontal stabilizer damaged; the bottom of the fuselage from engine to tail-wheel slit open; the controls damaged and partially inoperative; a hole in the main gas tank (on rollout, fuel escaped); the hydraulic lines damaged.

Florene left for pursuit school as scheduled on November 30, 1943. Nancy Love met with her in Palm Springs a couple of days later. Then Nancy flew to Dallas on December 6 to check into the incident and to investigate those concerns originally expressed by Ferrying Division Headquarters staff that the women at Dallas' Love Field were being transitioned too fast.

Nancy Love is said to have been very unhappy with Florene for taking the P-47 up because the Ferrying Division commanders at the bases where WAFS were stationed had been instructed not to transition any more pilots into pursuit airplanes. They were to go, instead, to the newly established pursuit school in Palm Springs.

Nancy had a lot of pressures on her at that time. In the meantime, one of her Originals had been killed in an accident that happened the third day of pursuit school — less than a week after Florene's flight and while Nancy was in Palm Springs. In fact, Nancy and Florene were standing together on the flight line, talking, when it happened and saw the whole thing. (That story is in a subsequent chapter.) The woman pilot was exonerated of any blame in that accident.

Nancy was in a tough spot. She had the reputation of her women's Ferrying Division squadrons — by now better than two hundred strong — to uphold. If questions were raised about the women's fitness to fly pursuits, all of her hard work could come tumbling down around her. Florene was a good pilot. She had proved that in getting the airplane down safely. The less ruckus raised, the less attention called to the incident, the better.

By then, Nancy had established a reputation for coolness under pressure, of getting the job done without a lot of fanfare, and of keeping her mouth shut. With one of her pilots dead and another barely escaping with her life, she exercised the restraint for which she was famous, coped, and moved on. The WAFS squadrons continued to do their job — ferry airplanes — and the women pilots continued to be assigned to pursuit school. The last two women pilots to graduate — from Brownsville — did so October 15, 1944.

Nancy officially relieved Florene of her command in Dallas, put Delphine Bohn in charge of the 5th Ferrying Group's WASP squadron, and transferred Florene from Dallas to Long Beach. When Florene graduated from pursuit school, she reported for duty to squadron commander B.J. Erickson at the 6th Ferrying Group in Long Beach.

Other than a two-week stint flying a regular passenger and cargo run in a C-47 with B.J. Erickson out of Romulus in August 1944, Florene spent the rest of her WASP service in Long Beach ferrying mostly P-51s cross country to Newark and P-47s back to California. She resigned from the WASPs in the Fall of 1944 to get married.

# Evelyn Sharp

Evelyn entering the P-51 Mustang, considered one of the greatest single-seat fighters to be used in WWII. Its ability to fly long distances in the escort fighter role earned it fame during the long missions to Germany and over the expanses of the Pacific.

## 24

Following her investigation in Dallas, Nancy wrote the following recommendations to General Tunner on December 14 concerning transition of women pilots, particularly into pursuits:

That the transition department be much more thorough, first, in selecting suitable applicants for transitioning, and second, in instructing these students both on technical aspects of the airplane and on the proper flying of the ship. If a student does not display good judgment, thorough understanding of the airplane and good flying technique, she should be returned to her squadron for further time on less complicated aircraft.

That no quota for pursuit school be required of any WASP squadron. When a pilot is judged by transition to be superior, every effort should be made to give her an instrument course and to make her a thoroughly competent Class 3 pilot after which she should be sent to pursuit school. These pilots who are judged borderline cases should be given further ferrying duties until such time as their ability is considered sufficient to fly more complicated aircraft.

That investigation be made by this Headquarters of the transition policies and procedure at Dallas since the situation observed with regard to the WASP seems to be a general one which affects all the pilots at the Group.

General Tunner and FERD took immediate steps to improve WASP training. Ferrying Instruction 50-2 required that a student pilot needed a minimum of one and one-half hours in a C-47 in order to qualify for pursuit school — unless the student had fifteen hours co-pilot time. A few girls were sent to pursuit school without this requirement being met.

The problem was the old March 1943 restriction on women copilots flying ferrying missions with male pilots — the restriction intended to protect the WAFS' reputations. Times, and the needs of the Air Transport Command, had moved on. A limited number of women pilots were checked out in Class 3 — twin-engine cargo/ medium transport planes — so a bottleneck occurred at that point in WASP training. Women pilots destined for pursuit school were having trouble getting the proper transition to meet the requirements.

In a letter dated January 8, 1944, General Tunner reminded his Group commanders that delivery flights could be considered training flights.

> It is desired to progress qualified WASPs as rapidly as possible consistent with safe practice, so that they may be eligible for pursuit school. Copilot training will expedite transition on Class 3 and Class 4 aircraft. You are reminded that you are authorized to assign WASP copilots with male pilots on delivery flights. It is desired that this practice be instituted after careful consultation with your WASP Squadron Leader.

Not every WASP — not even every original WAFS — wanted to fly pursuits. Nancy Love did not think that a woman should be compelled to fly pursuit if she did not want to. But considering the ever and rapidly increasing need for pursuit pilots, in a letter to the Ferrying Group commanders dated January 10, 1944, Nancy eloquently pleaded to them to encourage their WASP ferry pilots to begin the transition. She wrote:

> This class of aircraft is ideal for capable women pilots, since it does not bottleneck the progressive training of male pilots for eventual four-engine overseas deliveries.
>
> It is felt that it is of the utmost importance that WASPs be made to understand the need for their services as

pursuit pilots. The Ferrying Division training plan is designed to progress male pilots toward four-engine overseas deliveries and transport flights. Pursuit training is not a necessary step in this progression. Thus, there is a genuine need for WASPS in both the single and twin-engine pursuit categories, and those WASPs who are capable of flying these types will be performing the greatest service for their country and for the Ferrying Division.

The duty of ferrying pursuits fell increasingly to the women pilots capable of handling such aircraft and as quickly as they were graduated from pursuit school — first in Palm Springs, California and later in Brownsville, Texas — they were put to work ferrying pursuits cross country in both directions.

Six of the original WAFS graduated in the first four Ferrying Division pursuit school classes at Palm Springs — Nancy Batson, Barbara Donahue, Gertrude Meserve, Helen McGilvery, Florene Miller, and Helen Richards.

Nancy Batson recalled:

*Gert and I shared a room in the barracks. Two iron cots and a partition for a wall. Donnie and Little Mac were roommates right next door.*

*Now I was this little Southern girl and I'd never been to Palm Springs — this glamorous vacation spot. Movie stars went there! And it was such a beautiful place in December. The San Jacinto Mountain was snow capped and the sun shown on it all day, from different angles — east, south, west — and it kept changing colors. At night, the sky was like black velvet sprinkled with millions of diamonds. We were in shirtsleeves during the day and at night we wore our uniforms into town.*

*It was beyond anything I thought I'd ever get myself into. Here we were flying these pursuit airplanes during the day and going into this glamorous town at night. A whole bunch of men pilots were taking pursuit transition the same time we were — we were all in ground school together — and then we'd go with them to the nightclubs at night and dance. Who-eee, we had a good time, but the next day it was all seriousness again. Flying those airplanes. Those wonderful airplanes. I tell you, I was gaa-gaa over the whole thing.*

*One day at lunch, Mac and I were talking about how short we could land the P-47 — that's the first pursuit plane we learned to fly. We had this one runway where if you did everything just right, you could take the first turn off to the taxiway.*

*When you're landing a pursuit, you're doing 120 miles per hour and you are making a continuous descending turn to the left. The reason is, if the engine quits at that point, you have the runway made. You planned ahead. As you came over the fence at the end of the runway, you couldn't see to the front because of the big engine, but peripherally you could see the white stripes on both sides and you knew you'd made it. You ease the stick back all the way and close the throttle and go to the flare landing and you set right down on the end of the runway. Then if you put on just a bit of brake — mind you, we didn't use the brakes much, just a touch, 'cause too much and the tail would come up — you could make that first turn off.*

*Mac and I wanted to see if we were good enough to do this. It was kind of a contest between the two of us and we were getting a big kick out of it.*

*Well, some guys at the next table overheard us and, not to be outdone by a couple of women, they decided to try it too. Well, these young guys, these cadets, didn't have the experience we did and one of 'em landed short, didn't make the runway. He hit the sand and the airplane flipped over on its back. Now he wasn't hurt, but right after that, the order came down. 'No more short turn offs.'*

*We were devils!*

*Now nobody ever said anything to us. Everything we did at the airfield was right out there in front of God and everybody. Our instructors were watching and so was the tower, we had no secrets, but after that incident, the order came down. But that P-47 was so easy to fly with that wide landing gear and all that power. It was a wonderful airplane.*

Sixteen of The Originals went on to fly pursuit. Of those, nine did not go to pursuit school: Nancy Love, Betty Gillies, Helen Mary Clark,

**Evelyn Sharp, Barbara Towne, Nancy Love, B.J. Erickson**

Teresa James, Delphine Bohn, Del Scharr, B.J. Erickson, Barbara Towne and Evelyn Sharp.

The other pursuit pilot who did not attend pursuit school was Helen Richey — the woman who had taken Nancy Love's place with the Airmarking Project back in 1935. She had worked for Pennsylvania Central Airlines before the war — the first woman pilot hired by the airlines. But she had not been accepted by the male pilots, was discriminated against by the pilots' union, and eventually left in search of flying jobs where her credentials would be better appreciated. She went to England to fly with the ATA in 1942. When she returned stateside, because of the January 25, 1943 cut-off date for qualifying for the WAFS, Richey — in spite of her hours and impressive flight record— had to attend the Flying Training Command school in Sweetwater in order to qualify. She graduated as part of 43-W-5 after which she was assigned to the 2nd Ferrying Group in Wilmington. Eventually she was appointed squadron leader for a group of Ferrying Division WASPs posted to the North American aircraft plant in Kansas City. They delivered the Mitchell bombers from the factory to AAF operational schools around the country.

Evelyn Sharp, B.J. Erickson and Barbara Towne, all original WAFS who had been assigned to the 6th Ferrying Group in Long Beach, California, already had taken their initial P-51 transition at Palm Springs Army Air Base in what B.J. characterizes as the beginning of pursuit school. When it looked like Palm Springs was going to be the site for a new women's ferrying squadron, they were sent back to Long Beach.

On August 3, 1943, Evelyn co-piloted a C-47 back east. She met with Nancy Love at Ferrying Division Headquarters in Cincinnati before returning west and wrote in her brown notebook: "Special Duty — Nancy Love. At ATC Headquarters RON." She wrote to her parents upon return to Long Beach: "Don't tell anyone, but perhaps there will be WAFS [WASPs] at Palm Springs and I'll be in charge. Maybe."

Immediately upon return from her meeting with Nancy Love, Evelyn went back to practicing takeoffs and landings in a P-51 — ten within two hours one day. On August 14, finally, she was assigned to deliver a P-51B to the docks at Newark. Having completed that job, she caught a westbound airliner from La Guardia and flew home.

By the end of August, she had nineteen hours in the P-51B — a new model with a Rolls Royce V-1650-3 twelve-cylinder, liquid-cooled engine. According to Evelyn, "It didn't get off as well as the A-model and landed a little slower." She also had logged nearly six additional hours in the C-47.

On September 20, 1943, Evelyn and several others reported to the 21st Ferrying Group, Army Air Field, Palm Springs, California. Five, like Evelyn, were from The Originals — Bernice Batten, Dorothy Fulton, Esther Nelson, Helen Richards, and Katherine Rawls Thompson — and the rest were graduates of the WASP Flying Training Command School. There, Evelyn mostly flew P-51s and C-47s, but in October ferried a twin-tailed, twin-engine Billy Mitchell B-25 to Indiana. Her copilot was Claire Callaghan (43-W-1) who had been at Romulus.

Rumors were that the new Palm Springs group — women pilots gathered from each of the other four squadrons — would be the first to attend the new pursuit school they were all hearing about. Actually, the intent was to use them to form a new women's squadron, but it didn't materialize. Few planes were available to the women in Palm Springs. "I think the Ferry Command forgot about us," Callaghan told Evelyn's biographer, Diane Ruth Armour Bartels, in an interview in 1992.

On November 17, 1943, Evelyn and the others received orders that they were being transferred to Long Beach. Palm Springs was to become the site of the new pursuit school beginning December 1. Of the six Originals, only Helen Richards (pictured here) eventually went to pursuit school.

Although Evelyn never was assigned to pursuit school, she continued to transition into more sophisticated aircraft and began instrument school after she returned to Long Beach. She wrote to Teresa James on November 29, 1943:

IWASM

*Dear Teresa,*

*How are you, you old slug. I am finally getting around to doing a little corresponding. Since that movement over Palm Springs and return, I haven't a chance to do any letter writing business. It seems all I get a chance to do any writing on is squadron papers. But now, I am back over here and I think I will have a little more time. I am in instru-ment school but I get a little tired of always studying about instruments so I will write a few letters.*

*Several of the girls on the post have gotten married. But not Sharpie. Guess I will have to be an old maid. Darn it*

*The kid I have been dating is from Stockton [California]. He is a Lt. on the field here. Very nice too. Ahem!*

*Well, I have to fly at three so I will get this off in the mail. Bye now and write soon.*

*Evelyn*

Early in December 1943, Nancy Love came to Long Beach to check out in the Lockheed P-38, the twin-engine fighter. This meant other WASPs could now transition into the distinct, twin-tailed fighter known as the "Lightning."

Evelyn kept at her instrument training, though she found it difficult. Much like Nancy Batson, she preferred to do her flying when she could see out and appreciate the beauty of nature below and around her. She kept busy ferrying mostly P-51s, and at least one P-47.

Finally in mid-January she began her three line checks required to get her instrument card. Her final one was on January 23 in, of all things, a B-17. She wrote to her parents: "No. 3. A B-17 from here to Oakland, California, and return. The trip back was at night. Boy, really wonderful. That is the first time I've been in a B-17. We had passengers — also cargo. More fun! That B-17 is a cinch to fly. Easier than a B-25. Darn thing takes off by itself."

In February, she checked out in an A-20 which she described as "almost as big as a B-25 and has two 1600 H.P. engines." She was one of three girls to be checked out on it at that point. So Evelyn, without benefit of pursuit school, had transitioned herself through most of "the big ones" and, with her instrument card now in her pocket, was looking to fly the awesome P-38.

*Palm Springs, 1943*

Standing: **Esther Nelson, Helen Richards, Zelda Lamer, Dorothy Fulton, Katherine Rawls Thompson, Ellen Gery and Claire Callaghan**
Kneeling: **Ruby Mullens, Evelyn Sharp, Mary Lou Colbert and Vega Johnson**

# 25

Dorothy Scott and her father arrived at New Castle Army Air Base, Saturday November 21, 1942. They had driven all the way from the state of Washington. Just days before leaving, Dorothy had taken her check ride to get her required 200-horsepower rating.

"What a ride! Dodging clouds, all aerobatics and hedge-hopping and *he* [the check pilot] did most of the flying — but I got the rating," she wrote to her mother.

She passed her flight check, her physical, and her board interview, and moved into BOQ 14 over the weekend. On the morning of November 23, she started attending classes and her father headed for home, leaving Dorothy's car with her in Wilmington. The twenty-fifth member of the squadron was now in residence.

Dorothy's first letter home to her mother, dated Thanksgiving 1942, told of the WAFS' everyday existence during training:

*We wear khaki coveralls and leather jackets mostly but are issued all flying equipment — which is some array (military secrets, etc.). We pay out about $150 for dress uniforms for after we graduate. Class consists of drill, meteorology and navigation and later to include military law and First Aid, etc. After lunch (we eat in the Officers' Mess) we report to the field for flying, weather permitting. After five is our own time. There is a post theater (15 cents) and Officers' Club (I haven't been there yet.)*

*The flying instructors and ground school officers are swell. All the girls are OK too. They are a little older mostly and many are famous. I am not worried about my ability in comparison though.*

On December 13, she wrote:

*You ask about my experiences, they really accumulate but seem even commonplace to me now. Saturday is parade day — the entire post marches out onto a runway and forms by squadrons with the WAFS last. If there are only four of us on the post we don't make a very large showing. We stand at attention and get inspected, then "at ease" while our leader calls down the line "present and accounted for, sir." Then we "right face, forward march" and go past the Colonel (commanding officer) and his staff doing "eyes right." Then we march back to the hangar, fall out, and dash for a radiator to warm up.*

*Ground school is really unique. With only four of us in class [Dorothy Scott, Dorothy Fulton, Betsy Ferguson, and Bernice Batten] we get in on any special lectures being given to officers so I've learned everything from tropical diseases to altitude flying. It's not that we are going to use all this, but it's available so we learn it — and do I like it! I can do a neat "present arms" or yank down a submachine gun using only a cartridge. I know sentry procedure and how the army is organized, and can put on a gas mask in about three seconds.*

*You want to know about the social life too. Well, mostly it's very casual and we "date in bunches."*

As one of the last WAFS accepted in 1942, and because she left for Dallas on January 1, 1943, Dorothy spent a mere six weeks at New Castle Army Air Base. She and Betsy Ferguson drove to Betsy's home in Coffeyville, Kansas, where Dorothy left her car to be picked up by her brother Ed, who was stationed in Colorado Springs. She and Betsy drove the rest of the way to Dallas in Betsy's car.

In mid-February 1943, Dorothy and Florene Miller ferried BT-13s to a base in Arkansas. She wrote home:

*Being the first girl pilots in there, we were mobbed and escorted to the Officers Club. During dinner, couldn't get a bite for being introduced. Two officers offered to fly us to Memphis to catch an earlier airliner back to Dallas.*

*Climbed into two different BTs — the major and Florene in one and the captain and I in the other. I'll never forget that ride. In the rapidly fading light, the field looked like a million small fires. It was a very clear night, but dark, so the stars above looked like the fall clearing fires below and I had to check the instruments to believe anything. I've never had such a ride. We made a formation takeoff and flew really close for quite a ways, guided by our wingtip lights only. All of a sudden our two planes separated and swish, we were in a snap roll. From there to Memphis we did all sorts of acrobatics and it was wonderful. Coming over Memphis at six thousand feet, the city's lights looked like a magic carpet.*

*We landed in Memphis and shocked the natives by walking into the terminal with flying suits on and with a couple of handsome officers. They stayed with us until plane time, when who should step out but Mrs. Love returning from Washington D.C.*

Stationed in Dallas together, Dorothy and Helen Richards — about the same age and both from the West Coast — formed a lasting friendship. In fact, at one point they considered renting a house together and, running with the same crowd of male officers, frequently double-dated.

Dorothy transitioned quickly through the airplanes available at Dallas, checking out in the BT-13, AT-6, C-78, AT-17, AT-9, C-47, A-24 and C-60. She took her instrument training right there at Love Field and got her "white card" on October 8 flying a C-60. She did so well, she was immediately assigned to teach instrument flying, but it didn't happen without a flap. She wrote home on October 10, 1943:

*Dear Family*

*Friday morning, October 8, 1943 (red-letter day) your esteemed relative became an army instrument pilot. Hurray! I'm the only Dallas girl with an instrument rating. [B.J.] Erickson is the only one in Long Beach. A few in Delaware have them.*

*With that behind me finally, the deal was for me to instruct it to the girls and some fellows perhaps. Well about that same time the C.O. hears about the deal of me teaching and says "no." His argument (though they don't argue) was that no new instrument pilot is qualified to teach. It goes round and round and still is no. That was surely too bad because the instrument school had made a new name plate for me and hung it with all due ceremony, and I had a plane, students, and was ready to go.*

*That was the situation last night. This morning we have a review and so get out before daylight and freeze to death before the head guys along with the rest of the post. And my last one was a few weeks ago in the afternoon where we all sweated it out — this Texas weather! Right after the review I go with Delphine and a check pilot on a C-47 and we spent the rest of the morning in the air. Back here instrument school calls up and says to hike right over with a student to fly instruments! I recover from a faint and do so. Somewhere the wires got twisted and up I go. It was quite a deal.*

*Teaching again is swell. I just love to talk anyway and to get a student in my power on the listening end is wonderful. The girl was Batten, the little short girl who joined when I did in Delaware. She sure tries hard and did OK too.*

*We landed after five p.m., so now I don't know whether I'm actually an instrument instructor or not (everyone quits here at five except pilots). But now it doesn't matter because something else has come up.*

*Nancy Love comes back on a one-day visit on another matter — I asked her — "what is the deal on pursuit school?" Now this has been my pet for a long time so I ask if I can get on and she says yes. It may mean a transfer to a training school and then to a pursuit base so that's one possibility. What else is up to the gods and the powers that be.*

In mid-November, Dorothy heard that she, Helen Richards and Florene all were on the list for pursuit school in Palm Springs. Starting date was December 1, 1943. By then, Betsy Ferguson had come down with appendicitis, had an emergency appendectomy, and been put on sick leave so she was behind the others on transition.

*Palm Springs, December 1, 1943*
*Helen and I are roommates, and there are eight of us girls with*

*thirty-five fellows. We spent today getting passes and entrance red-tape then went to town. I'm surely sold on Palm Springs for its warm sun, beautiful mountains and quaint shops in town. This is on my "post-war living" list.*

*Our barracks are two-by-four with outside plumbing (building adjoining though modern interior). No hot water and sand, sand everywhere.*

*Tomorrow we start flying. It will be dual in BC-1's (AT-6 type). Then in order, the P-47, 39, 40 and 51. We are divided in flights A and B, fly half day, school half day. I'm in A flight and must be on the line at 7:15 each a.m.*

*We have to wear skirts at evening mess — dern it.*

On December 3, 1943, Dorothy Scott, 23, was landing her BC-1 trainer when her airplane was overtaken by a P-39 also in the landing pattern. Because he was above her, the student pilot in the P-39 could not see her, and, of course, he was descending fast. They were on a collision course and if a warning came from the tower, it was too late. The two planes, both on final approach, collided in mid-air about two hundred feet above the ground.

Dorothy was killed, along with her instructor. The P-39 pilot died as well.

Nancy Love and Florene Miller, standing on the end of the flightline, witnessed the crash. There was no question of pilot error on Scott's part. The P-39 pilot and the tower were assigned the blame.

Nancy ordered Florene to accompany Dorothy's body home. And Florene vividly remembers the trip in the hearse from Palm Springs. "It was just me and the hearse driver and the casket. And because I had been Dorothy's squadron commander at Dallas — and she and I had gone up to Palm Springs together for pursuit school — I had to call her father and twin brother and tell them. I'll never forget that."

Dorothy's twin brother Ed wrote his thoughts to the rest of the family in a letter dated December 22, 1943:

I guess a lot of American families have to give. It must

be just an act of God. We have to pay, ever so dearly, for
what freedom we can get out of life. And my sister was
always one to be out in front and I guess she just was cut
out to lead the Scott family into eternity. God made her
that way and perhaps just for that reason. She'll be up
there waiting, just like we last saw her.

The other six Originals who attended pursuit school in Palm
Springs went on to prove their mettle. They all graduated — no
washouts. But their accomplishment was marred by the tragic death
of one of their own. Now two of Nancy Love's original WAFS
were dead — Cornelia Fort and Dorothy Scott — both in mid-air
collisions.

By the end of 1943, WASPs (the original WAFS and the Flying
Training Command graduates who joined their ranks beginning in
May 1943) had delivered a total of 3,372 planes. The largest number
— 700 — were delivered in November 1943 by 284 WASPs when
the average delivery was 1,500 miles and the average number of
planes delivered per WASP per month was just over two and one-half.

As 1944 dawned, the 2nd Ferrying Group in Wilmington boasted
68 WASPs; the 3rd in Romulus had 72; the 5th in Dallas listed 71;
and the 6th in Long Beach had 64. Total strength was 275 and they
were ferrying some 43 different types of airplanes — a far cry from
the low-horsepower, single-engine trainer and liaison aircraft The
Originals were restricted to delivering just a year earlier.

Of the 275, at that point Love and Gillies were Class V pilots;
two others were Class IV; eighteen were Class III; and twenty-two
had instrument cards.

The first pursuit school graduations were held on January 1
and January 10, 1944, and with that, the face of ferrying changed
forever as more and more women — as well as men — came out of
pursuit school with their Class P cards in hand.

Bernice Batten, the "little short girl" that Dorothy Scott gave
instrument instruction to in Dallas, was accepted as a member of
the original WAFS squadron in Wilmington on November 21, 1942.
Barely over five feet, petite Bernice had such an intense desire to

fly that she left college — Kansas State Teachers College — in order to take flight training at Atkinson Municipal Airport in Pittsburg, Kansas. She worked part-time to pay for flying lessons and soloed on September 29, 1933.

After Bernice qualified for the WAFS, Nancy Love assigned her to Long Beach when that squadron was formed in February 1943. But after ferrying BT-13s for several months, she was transferred to Dallas. There, she checked out in and ferried the PT-19, AT-6 and the A-24 — the single-engine dive bomber known as the Douglas Dauntless.

**A-24 BANSHEE, the Army version of the SBD DAUNTLESS**

One day in mid-November 1943, Bernice picked up an A-24 in Tulsa and headed for the docks at Newark. With bad weather ahead, she landed in Pittsburgh and tried waiting out the storm. Finally, she took off again, unaware of how bad the storm really was. The inadequate weather reports available back in 1943 failed to indicate the severity of the weather. Over the mountains of western Pennsylvania, she ran into carburetor ice problems and the engine of the Dauntless began to run rough. The mechanism that allowed warm air to reach the carburetor and melt the ice would not hold and she had to concoct a makeshift solution. All the while, she had her head down, intent on the work she was doing on the instrument panel. When she looked up again, she was lost.

The race was on to see whether she ran out of fuel or daylight first. The radio produced only static. That area of the Pocono Mountains is known to pilots as The Graveyard. Her stop-gap measure meant to prevent carburetor icing wouldn't hold as the plane was tossed on the winds of the storm. Finally, the engine quit.

"I cut the switches and climbed out on the wing. I didn't have to jump. I was blown off immediately. For once my lack of height was an advantage. It saved me from decapitation by the tail surfaces. Then, with a jerk, the chute opened."

As Bernice floated to the rapidly darkening earth, she watched her airplane plow into a mountain top and burst into flames.

Bernice rode her parachute down, buffeted by heavy rain. The chute, according to regulations, had been packed for an average-sized man — 170 pounds. Bernice barely weighed 100. She was at the mercy of the winds until the shroud lines became entangled in a tree, suspending her above the forest floor. As she swung there, she considered her options and finally used her small body to gradually increase the size of the arc on which she swung. Finally, she was able to grab the trunk of the tree, hold on and release her parachute harness, then shinny down the tree.

Some of the locals had seen the plane go down and spotted the parachute drifting to earth. The search for the downed pilot had already begun. Bernice, who had had some survival training during the ATC's thirty-day indoctrination course when she joined the WAFS, started downhill and eventually met up with her rescuers — farmers, State Forestry Service personnel, and inhabitants of a nearby religious sect.

Bernice was the only member of the original WAFS to join the Caterpillar Club — the club begun in 1922 by the Pioneer Parachute Company. Membership included any pilot, male or female, who bailed out of a disabled aircraft. Members wore a pin in the form of a caterpillar — shaped like the ring that the pilot pulled to activate the parachute.

"I later learned that a woman had packed my parachute."

ఴ⊚☖౨

In January 1944, the WASPs set a new record for monthly

deliveries: 840 planes of some 29 different models; 6,382 hours and covering approximately 600,000 miles. That averaged out to just over twenty-three ferrying hours during the month per WASP and slightly over three airplanes. The average distance delivered was 833 miles.

That is particularly interesting because, in July 1943, a question was raised as to a so-called "fatigue factor" among the women pilots. A few male members of the military establishment were concerned about women's ability to deliver over long distances, so a proposal was offered that women pilots should be restricted to 1,500 miles on a mission, "in view of the frailty of their sex and the fatigue involved on long ferrying missions."

Nancy Love got wind of this and, as it turned out, headed off trouble at the pass by suggesting to General Tunner that the Surgeon of the Ferrying Division check this "fatigue factor" out with the various Group Surgeons.

A Major Raymond J. Lipin, Base and Group Surgeon at the 2nd Ferrying Group, reported:

> There is no record at this station of the occurrence of flying fatigue in any WAFS. It is not the distance that has any profound effect on the physical or mental status of the individual pilot. It is felt that the number of hours flown daily or in any one day is far more important than the total distance of the trip.
>
> If WAFS are restricted it should only be in the number of hours flown in any one day. It is recommended that this should be less than six hours. If sufficient rest and relaxation is obtained between hops, distance should not be considered detrimental to the physical or mental condition of the pilot on domestic trips.

Colonel Baker, commanding officer at the 2nd Ferrying Group, was in agreement. He felt the Group would be inconvenienced and that it would be an inefficient way of handling deliveries if it became necessary to work the WAFS in relays — an idea once proposed by Jacqueline Cochran. In fact, there was some suspicion that this concern might have originated with Cochran as she was casting around for reasons to send additional women pilots to the Ferrying Groups.

Morale among the WAFS, as well as their general health, was excellent, the Flight Surgeons found. They made few visits to complain of fatigue or anything else. General Tunner was assured that the physical endurance of the women ferry pilots was excellent and on par with that of the male pilots and no recommendations were forwarded as to any restrictions upon length or duration of flights by WAFS pilots.

## 26

Militarization was something some of the WASPs wanted and others didn't. The original WAFS had been led to believe that they would be militarized when they joined in fall 1942, but it wasn't what really mattered to them. "We just wanted to fly those beautiful airplanes," said Nancy Batson Crews.

When the Ferrying Division first looked at taking on women ferry pilots in the summer of 1942, Nancy Love was slated to be commissioned a first lieutenant. So FERD consulted Colonel Oveta Culp Hobby about the possibility of the women ferry pilots becoming members of her Women's Auxiliary Army Corps or WAACs. However, legislative problems with assigning WAACs to flying status and to their receiving flight pay stood in the way. The WAACs still were not officially military. They were "with the Army" not "in the Army."

And as Jackie Cochran recruited girls for her flight training school during fall 1942, winter and spring 1943, she told them that they could expect to be militarized.

As far as the Ferrying Division was concerned, part of being military was wearing a uniform. Nancy Love selected the WAFS' uniform the fall of 1942 and, immediately, the women began to wear it with pride. That uniform consisted of a gray-green wool jacket (the military called it a blouse), slacks for flying, skirt for formal military and social occasions, khaki shirt and flight cap. The WAFS paid for their uniforms with their own money. Actually, they bought two of them, so that they could wear one and send the other to the cleaners.

FERD liked its WAFS in uniform, even though, officially, they were civilians. The WAFS were doing the work of officers. Ferrying operations were exacting. That they should be subject to a discipline and a control greater than ordinary ground employees was a given and the uniforms strengthened that image.

Colonel Tunner didn't want his WAFS in the WAACs because he would lose control over their selection and their discipline. After he learned that commissioning in the WAACs was not feasible, he submitted a formal proposal to commission women ferry pilots into the Army of the United States. In a letter dated November 30, 1942, he commended their work to date. "The women of the Ferrying Division have gone at their respective jobs with a zest and enthusiasm that is admirable and obviously inspired not by the financial remuneration, but by the desire to serve to the utmost of their abilities."

Nothing happened. Colonel Tunner's letter apparently was on the slow track up through channels. In the meantime, plans surfaced to offer Cochran a commission and to take the newly established WFTD training school — part of the Army Air Forces' Training Command — into the WAACs. Then on July 1, 1943, the Women's Army Corps was born. The WAAC had become the WAC. The anticipated militarization of that women's group was a *fait accompli*.

FERD then asked to have the WAFS (which by now included graduates of the Flying Training Command's first two classes) incorporated into the WACs. Jackie Cochran, who on June 28, 1943 had been appointed Director of Women Pilots under the Assistant Chief of the Air Staff for Operations, Commitments and Requirements (OCR), opposed this. She believed women pilots were entitled to a separate organization: "The Army had its WACs. The Navy had its WAVEs. The Marines had their women's group. I believed that there was a reason for the Army Air Forces to have a separate women's group. *Separate* [her italics] is the key word as far as I could see."

Also, Cochran didn't like WAC commander, Colonel Oveta Culp Hobby, and refused to take a commission that would put her under Mrs. Hobby's command. "Those girls [the graduates of her flight training school] will become a part of the Women's Army Corps over my dead body. No way . . . Hobby has bitched up her program and she's not going to bitch up mine."

Cochran also referred to Hobby as "the woman I loved to

hate." In fact, she gives her own account of the formation of both the WAFS and the WASPs in 1942 and of the subsequent militarization skirmishes she had with Colonel Hobby in two chapters in her autobiography.

On September 30, 1943, Congressman John Costello of California introduced a bill calling for the militarization of the WASPs. The bill went to the House Committee on Military Affairs for study and was subsequently amended to include the appointment of female trainees (the girls at Avenger Field in Sweetwater, Texas) as aviation cadets. It was reintroduced to Congress on February 17, 1944.

The Ferrying Division was not consulted and played no part in the sponsorship of this bill.

The women pilots of the Ferrying Division already had been incorporated into the WASP against their wishes. Now, they were concerned with the outcome of this bill. Generally, they were in favor of militarization but were skeptical of a militarized status that would place them directly under Cochran's control.

True, WACs answered to male superior officers, but the women in the Ferrying Division knew that the administration of the WASP was frequently handled directly by Cochran who never consulted with the male officers who used the women pilots' services. In their opinion, it was one thing to be militarized into the WAC with flying status, but quite another to be militarized into an organization commanded by Jacqueline Cochran.

In essence, what the Costello bill said was this: For the duration of the war, women would be commissioned as flight officers or aviation students in accordance with existing regulations; however, no woman would be appointed to a grade above colonel and there would be not more than one officer of that grade. Female flight cadets, upon successful completion of the prescribed course of training, would be commissioned as second lieutenants in the Army of the United States (AUS). All commissioned women would receive the same pay and allowances as male members of the AUS and they would be entitled to the same rights, privileges and benefits according to their rank, grade and length of service.

What really changed the complexion of the entire hearings was the fact that the Committee on the Civil Service of the House of Representatives proceeded to conduct a detailed and factual study of the whole situation and, in fact, of the whole question of WASP training and utilization. This committee was ever after known as the Ramspeck Committee, named for Robert J. Ramspeck, the Congressman from Georgia and a former deputy U.S. Marshal. His committee, on the urging of Congress, launched an investigation of the WASP program. The WASPs were under Civil Service, therefore public funds were being expended on their program — a program that Congress knew next to nothing about.

When the hearings before the Committee on Military Affairs commenced, only General Arnold was heard. No other witnesses were called.

Congress was not so much interested in the women pilots as it was in the male trainees and instructors who at this time were being released by the Army Air Forces. Pilot casualties on the battle fronts had been far less than anticipated. In the early days of the war in England, a novice RAF pilot was given, at best, three months to live. But American pilot casualties never were as high as anticipated. Early in 1944, the AAF began to cancel its civilian contracts for training flying personnel and cut back on its own pilot training program. Consequently, when the news of the WASP bill reached the streets through the nation's newspapers, Congressmen began to receive angry protests — from civilian flying instructors now out of jobs and threatened with the draft, from the American Legion and other veterans' organizations, and from mothers of boys who had been transferred from aviation cadet training to the infantry.

Up until this point, Congress had pretty much given Hap Arnold anything he asked for, but now things changed.

The short of it is, instead of quickly passing the bill that General Arnold personally asked for and fully supported — in fact, earnestly sought, the politicians in Congress listened to the outcries in the press and from pressure groups. The WASPs were portrayed as low-time, airport pilots out for a lark at the expense of the American taxpayers.

Arnold tried to explain the manpower shortage in the Army — thus the need for men, once destined to be pilots, to be transferred to the infantry — but the feeding frenzy was on. The press had a field day at the expense of a small band of loyal, patriotic women pilots, some of them already serving on active duty and some still in training.

The bill did not go to the floor of the House until June. In the meantime, charges of favoritism were leveled against the WASPs. Their detractors said that the women were given more opportunity to fly and that they were flying more frequently than the men and had better assignments. They alleged that men sat on the ground while the WASPs were kept busy.

ATC Commander General George asked General Tunner to compile a complete report concerning the WASPs performance on the job in the Ferrying Division. General Tunner sought input from the commanders of the 2nd, 3rd, 5th and 6th Ferrying Groups and of the Air Transport Command Pursuit School now located in Brownsville, Texas, all of whom had had daily dealings with the WASP ferry pilots. He knew he would get an accurate report from them.

Tunner's report, based on what his commanders told him, said that resentment did exist among a minority of the male pilots and that minority was quite outspoken. But the supervisory and operational personnel, whose sole interest was the efficient operation of the ferrying mission, did not share this resentment. "Those personnel are familiar with the pilot shortage in the Ferrying Division and appreciate the WASPs' contribution," stated the report.

General Tunner also addressed the charges of favoritism.

"The WASPs flying time has consistently averaged slightly less than the flying time of male pilots," he said. WASP pilots took their turn in frequency and type of assignment. Normally, any pilot in the Ferrying Division, including the WASPs, who has returned to his base was placed at the bottom of a roster consistent with the type of aircraft he was qualified to fly, and ferrying missions were assigned to the individual who had been on base the longest.

The Ferrying Division, it was pointed out, had been extremely busy with domestic operations and all pilots, regardless of sex, had been utilized without anyone waiting an undue length of time for assignment. Some pilots were qualified only on a few types of airplanes and had to sit on the ground while other pilots who were qualified on many types got to fly because of the kind of airplane that needed to be ferried. That was true among WASPs as well as male pilots.

"WASPs have assisted in the performance of the Ferrying Division's mission at a time when assistance was not available from any other source," Tunner concluded.

Interestingly enough, during the early months of 1944, when all this debate was going on and male pilots were ostensibly "sitting around" while the women did all the flying, the Ferrying Division had to cancel all pilot leaves due to a pilot shortage. It is doubtful that any qualified ferry pilot sat anywhere for very long under those circumstances.

General George submitted Tunner's report, but apparently, it was never presented to the members of Congress. The Ramspeck Committee made clear that the contemplated recruiting of inexperienced personnel was its greatest concern, not the use of women as pilots.

Of course, by then the pool of experienced women pilots in the United States was exhausted. In September 1942, Nancy Love had sent out only eighty-three telegrams — to women she found to be qualified for what became the WAFS. Twenty-eight of those women flew with the original WAFS. Several others simply couldn't get away from their jobs in time to come to Wilmington and apply. By the time they got free, the WAFS squadron had been closed — at Jackie Cochran's insistence. Most of these women pilots were then picked up by Cochran to be enrolled in her training school in Texas. When that supply was exhausted, she dropped the requirements for entrance to the school — in stages — eventually to thirty-five hours, the required cockpit hours for a private license.

The Ramspeck Committee contended that training women pilots — from scratch — cost too much. There were male pilots out there — including some returning combat veterans who had flown their maximum number of missions — who could be retrained to ferry much more quickly and cheaply than women who had just managed to fly the thirty-five hours necessary to get a private pilot's license.

The Ramspeck Committee also addressed the cost to the taxpayers of what they termed the "designer" uniforms now worn by the WASP personnel — a half-million dollars was spent to furnish these at government expense, for which the War Department was responsible, according to the House Report.

That the original WAFS *bought their own uniforms* in the fall of 1942 was long forgotten. [author's italics]

Finally, the Ramspeck Committee recommended that *the qualified WASPs continue to be used and that their salaries be adjusted in accordance with their experience and responsibilities, and that provision be made for them to obtain insurance and hospitalization* — one of the main reasons that militarization had been sought in the first place.

In keeping with the wish not to recruit inexperienced personnel and pay to train them, the conclusion of the committee was to shut down the training facility at Avenger Field. No new classes would be allowed to start after July 1, 1944. Those already in training would be allowed to finish and, upon graduation, would be assigned to duty commensurate with their abilities. *All WASPs already on active duty would continue to serve.* [author's italics]

Congressional debate continued and the press coverage, most of it against the WASP but some decidedly in their favor, continued to gather speed and unwanted dirt, rocks and other detritus, like a snowball rolling downhill. The wall against which that out-of-control ball would come to a splattering halt appeared on the day the bill finally came to a vote in the House — June 21, 1944.

## Bell P-39 AIRACOBRA

During the development of the Bell P-39 Airacobra it was decided that a more powerful version was needed for use in a close-support fighter-bomber role. The result was the P-63 Kingcobra, which was similar in layout but larger, with a more powerful engine and a different tail design.

## Bell P-63 KINGCOBRA

## 27

In all, 134 women flew pursuit aircraft for the Army in World War II — 16 of The Originals and 118 women who were graduates of the flight training school Jacqueline Cochran established in Texas. Others, both Originals and flight school graduates, flew for the Ferrying Division but did not fly pursuit for a variety of reasons — often because they chose not to do so. Flying pursuits was dangerous, required a particular level of skill, and was definitely not for everybody.

Some knowledge of mechanics was needed to fly pursuit. Because women usually had not had the mechanical training or opportunities as men, the Ferrying Division eventually solved this problem by sending women pilots to pursuit school classes a few days ahead of the regular male class so that they could receive some intensive training in the mechanics of pursuit planes before the course began.

Sis Bernheim was the last of The Originals to attend pursuit school, graduating July 15, 1944. She was the only one to go to Brownsville. None of the original WAFS who went to pursuit school washed out.

Kay Gott, a 43-W-2 graduate of Cochran's flight school in Houston, completed pursuit school in Palm Springs in March 1944, and eventually wrote *Women In Pursuit*. Published in 1993, it depicted the qualities of the women who flew pursuit airplanes for the Ferrying Division of the Air Transport Command:

> They were good-looking, interesting, highly competent, confident. They were assertive in that they were able to hold their own in a profession that was largely ruled by men. They were individualistic — no two alike. They

were loners in that they were able to function successfully alone, on their own resources. Mostly, they were fun-loving and they all proved dependable. They got the job done.

They were all proud of their flying ability, but tended to be overly modest in mixed company, and very casual about their accomplishments. One had to pry out of them what exactly they did. After all, they were "just moving airplanes" while men were facing, or about to face, the enemy, perhaps to be shot down and possibly killed in combat in these planes.

Some of the pursuit-qualified women pilots were called "Eager Beavers." The eager pilots had one thing in common — they loved to fly!

These women . . . felt as though they made a valuable contribution with their flying skills. Each job they did freed another man.

The women pilots who came through deaths of their comrades felt that accidents happened to someone else — never to them. Did they live with fear? No. Did they ever fear? Of course, all pilots do. These pilots were thorough, skilled in their flying, calm in emergencies: did the right thing and responded in time — almost automatically — to avert tragedy.

Once qualified, the women began to ferry pursuits immediately. Many of the Palm Springs graduates were taken to the North American factory near Long Beach and flew P-51s east from there to Newark on their way back to their home base after graduation. By this point in the war — late winter/early spring 1944 — ferrying pursuit aircraft to the docks for transport overseas to the war zone was the most important function of the Ferrying Division. And the need for qualified pursuit pilots became even more imperative as the war progressed throughout 1944.

As the number of women pursuit pilots grew — and given that the male ferry pilots did not need to fly pursuits in order to move up the transition ladder that would qualify them for overseas ferrying or combat duty — more and more of the ferrying of pursuit planes fell to the women. Consequently, by fall 1944, between sixty and sixty-five percent of *all* pursuit deliveries were being made by the one hundred thirty or so active WASPs qualified in those hot little airplanes. All of the P-47 deliveries were now made by women.

The P-39 Bell Airacobra and the P-63 Kingcobra were built in Niagara Falls, New York. The women from the 3rd Ferrying Group in Romulus, Michigan, ferried most of those airplanes, though many a Long Beach WASP picked up a P-39 or a P-63 after taking a P-51 to Newark. She then ferried the Bell-built aircraft to Great Falls, Montana, where it was destined eventually for Russia. From Great Falls, she either ferried something else back to Long Beach or caught an airliner home.

IWASM

**Dorothy Fulton, Sis Bernheim, Helen McGilvery,
Nancy Batson and Gert Meserve at Niagara Falls, February 1943**

Beginning in spring 1944 this pattern was also true of the women ferry pilots from the 21st Ferrying Group, newly established at Palm Springs. All thirteen of them were pursuit pilots.

Barbara Donahue of the 3rd Ferrying Group has never forgotten one particular P-39 delivery she made to Great Falls, Montana. She was flying the northern route when her aircraft developed a problem that could only be fixed on the ground. She checked out her surroundings, saw no optimum place to land so, since she was flying over a sparsely populated area, she set the airplane down on what appeared to be a deserted highway. However, as she made her final approach to touchdown, Donnie flew over a bus making its way along the highway.

Not only did the bus driver and his passengers look up to see a P-39 bearing down on them, they couldn't help but notice the very large red star insignia on the airplane, which denoted the Russians as its owners. Then, as if they hadn't seen enough already to tell their grandchildren about some day, out stepped a tall, willowy woman pilot.

The driver, according to Donnie, recovered his senses and possibly his sense of humor first.

"What's the matter, lady, get tired of flying?"

Since the bus and the P-39 were headed in the same direction, west, the driver had to wait until Donnie took off before he could get going again. Quickly, sensing that he wasn't too impressed with her dilemma and certainly not with being held up on his appointed schedule by an airplane, Donnie made her adjustment, climbed nimbly back into the single-seat cockpit, and took off down the highway in the legendary cloud of dust. Next stop, Great Falls.

The P-40 was built by the Curtiss factory in Buffalo, New York. Romulus pilots flew a lot of them, and West Coast ferry pilots, on their way back from a delivery in Newark, occasionally stopped in Buffalo to pick up a P-40 for delivery out west.

The P-47 was built at Republic Aviation in Farmingdale, Long Island. It was only a thirty-minute flight from there to the docks at Newark. WASPs from the 2nd Ferrying Squadron in Wilmington regularly rotated up there for four weeks temporary duty (TDY).

They were stationed at the Republic factory and lived in the Huntington Hotel in Farmingdale. All the pursuit ferry pilots stationed at Farmingdale were women. They did all the deliveries to Newark — sometimes five a day if the weather was good and air transportation back to Long Island was available. WASPs from the 3rd Ferrying Group in Romulus also pulled occasional TDY at the Republic factory.

"That was known as the 'gear up, gear down' flight," says Teresa James, who probably flew more such flights than anyone else. "Thirty minutes in the air, max, unless the fog came in. Then it was circle, circle, circle. There was always smoke and haze over the New York City area."

On one trip, Nancy Batson took her eight-millimeter movie camera in the cockpit with her. "Shooting back over my shoulder, I filmed the rest of the women flying their P-47s behind me. While I was up there, I also circled New York Harbor and shot some footage of Miss Liberty to show the folks at home when the war was over."

Once the airplanes were delivered to Newark, workmen removed the wings and "pickled" the aircraft to protect them from the salt spray on the ocean crossing.

Betty Gillies, women's squadron leader in Wilmington, early on convinced Colonel Baker, the base commander, to give the WASP contingent at Republic Aviation a C-60 transport in which to fly the ferry pilots from Newark back to Farmingdale. Nancy Batson, Teresa James and Gertrude Meserve checked out in that aircraft and traded off flying pilot and co-pilot duties. The C-60 followed each flight of the P-47s from Farmingdale over to Newark and returned all the pilots safely in the larger, twin-engine craft so they could repeat the process. Four or five trips were possible in a day, provided the P-47s were ready for delivery.

"It got boring sitting around the Alert Room sometimes," Nancy Batson says. "All we did was read and smoke. One day I said 'let's get a ball and bat and play outside.' Some of them thought I was crazy, but we did it." Nancy also took film footage of the girls pouring out of the Alert Room and heading for the airplanes, climbing into the cockpits and taking off for Newark.

By June 8, 1944, all the male pilots at Farmingdale had been replaced by WASPs. By the end of November 1944, the women had delivered a total of 1,987 P-47s to Newark. Kay Gott points out, "It was a very efficient operation, completely planned and run by women!"

The P-47 modification plant was located in Evansville, Indiana. Some of the P-47s from Farmingdale went there. Most of those had to be flown on to the West Coast. For a time, in late summer 1944, Nancy Batson was in command of a small squadron of WASPs in Evansville. Here, too, WASPs served a four-week TDY. Nancy Love rented a little house for them so that the squadron had living quarters near the plant.

"I really didn't like that duty," Batson admitted. "I just wanted to fly. I didn't want to be in command of anything and sitting behind a desk. I finally got Betty to transfer me back to Wilmington and up to Farmingdale, but I think she decided to punish me because for awhile all I did was deliver dogs — war-wearies — to the bone yard." Helen Mary Clark then took over the command of the Evansville squadron.

Now the P-38 was a different animal.

"The P-38 did have some unique flying problems, and was not regarded by some ferrying pilots as a desirable step up or upgrade," says Gott. "However, if you were a pursuit pilot and had the opportunity to check out and fly the B-25 Mitchell Bomber, the B-26 Martin Marauder (pictured below), A-20 or P-61 Northrop Nighthawk Black Widow, you were an eligible Class IV pilot and could be checked out in the P-38."

The P-38, like the other pursuit planes, had a single-seat cockpit. This meant that checkout included classroom study and passing tests on the aircraft's operation. Following that was a cockpit check. For this, the instructor stood on the wing and went over cockpit procedures with you. Then, on your very first flight, you took off — solo — practiced aloft and landed, all on your own. Ten of the original WAFS are thought to have qualified on the P-38: Nancy Batson, Delphine Bohn, Helen Mary Clark, B.J. Erickson, Betty Gillies, Nancy Love, Helen McGilvery, Florene Miller, Helen Richards and Evelyn Sharp.

"I received my Class IV rating, but did not check out in the P-38," says Gertrude Meserve. "I had no desire to fly war-weary P-38s that had come back from combat."

After Nancy Love checked out in the P-38 in December 1943, the others gradually did the same. Helen Mary Clark, one of only four Wilmington WASPs to fly the P-38, specifically recalls being sent to Long Beach for the purpose of P-38 transition training. None of the Romulus WASPs flew the twin-engined pursuit.

In all, twenty-five of the WASPs ferried the P-38.

Betty Gillies, B.J. Erickson, and Nancy Batson all had problems with P-38s along the way. But it is Evelyn Sharp's P-38 experience that everyone remembers.

**Nancy Batson with a P-38**

**Evelyn Sharp**

# 28

Evelyn Sharp and Nancy Batson roomed together on a trip to Hagerstown to pick up PT-19s. "It was early in February of 1943, and we were on our way to Toronto. I remember it was late and I was sleepy, but Evelyn wanted to talk. She told me that she had recently learned that the woman she had always known as Aunt Elsie was, in fact, her real mother."

When "Aunt Elsie" visited Evelyn at New Castle Army Air Base on November 20, 1942, several of the WAFS to whom Evelyn introduced the older woman said, "So, Evelyn, this is your mother?" and both Evelyn and Elsie laughed and said, "no, just an aunt." A photograph of them together, taken in January 1943, shows the striking resemblance of daughter to mother.

Finally, on January 23, 1943, at a restaurant across the street from Madison Square Garden in New York City, where Evelyn was enjoying a short furlough, Elsie revealed who she really was. Later, Evelyn wrote to her birth mother:

> I hardly know how to begin this letter as I've always known you as Aunt Elsie. You see, I've always thought that I was adopted but had never found out for sure. I figured it out that I resembled no one in our family and I could also never get Mother to say anything about my birth. Several people hinted it to me several times. So you see, I really wasn't surprised. What surprised me was who my real mother was. I never really bothered to ask what relation you were to us. I assumed that you were an aunt of some sort of Daddy's. It never occurred to me to ask.
>
> . . . I'm proud that you're my real Mother.

Not long after that, Evelyn revealed her new-found secret to Nancy Batson in their hotel room in Hagerstown. Then again, a week later, on an airliner to California, Evelyn told the same secret to Barbara Towne. Both were on their way to take up new ferrying assignments with the 6th Ferrying Group in Long Beach, California.

Evelyn Sharp was born October 20, 1919, in Melstone, Montana, to Elsie Haeske Crouse and Miles (Orla) Crouse. At twenty-one, Orla was six years younger than Elsie and not ready to settle down. Married in haste with the bride four months pregnant, the couple already had three strikes against them. The marriage ended in divorce. Orla's father, Dr. Sheridan Crouse, knew of a couple who desperately wanted a child — John and Mary Sharp, then of Kinsey, Montana.

On December 22, 1919, the little girl who had been named Lois Genevie Crouse became Evelyn Genevieve Sharp. The Sharps moved several times around Montana and Nebraska but, when Evelyn was ten, they settled in Ord, Nebraska, where she grew up and became the town's favorite daughter. Evelyn was a popular girl with lots of friends, both male and female. She truly was an all-American 1930s girl — in addition to sewing her own clothes, she was an all-around athlete (she earned letters all four years at Ord High School), a good student, a member of the girls' glee club and a Methodist Church youth group stalwart.

The chance to take flying lessons was an accident of fate. In 1935, Jack Jefford, of Jefford's Aviation Services in Broken Bow, flew to Ord to offer flight instruction twice a week. While there, he opted for room and board at John's Cafe, owned and run by John and Mary Sharp. When Jack later owed the Sharps money for that room and board, he convinced John to let Evelyn take it out in flying lessons.

Fifteen-year-old Evelyn — who, after watching barnstormers in Hastings at age five, had informed her family that she wanted "to drive an airplane" — had been listening with rapt attention when Jack did his hangar flyin' in the cafe for the benefit of anyone within ear shot. On Monday, February 4, 1935, she took her first lesson in a three-cylinder Curtiss Robin Alexander Flyabout.

"Learned to fly while in the air. I was up one half hour," she wrote as the beginning entry in her flight journal.

On March 4, 1936 — thirteen months and "Lesson 25" in her flight journal later — sixteen-year-old Evelyn soloed in Jack Jefford's new, yellow Aeronca C-3. On November 9, 1936, Evelyn earned her private pilot's license. She had fifty hours of solo flight time.

The eight-year-old organization for licensed women pilots, the Ninety-Nines, invited Evelyn to an organizational meeting in Omaha in January 1937. John — always looking out for his daughter's best interests — accompanied Evelyn, looked the ladies over, and gave her the nod. On January 30, 1937, she became a charter member of the Missouri Valley Chapter. There were, as of that date, 444 licensed women pilots in the United States. Eight were from Nebraska and Evelyn, who by then had sixty-two hours, was the youngest.

Following her graduation from Ord High School on May 28, 1937, Evelyn looked ahead. How could she make aviation her career? Her father knew he couldn't afford to buy Evelyn an airplane. He mentioned this fact to a friend who, in turn, suggested that John talk to the civic-minded optometrist, Dr. Glen Auble, one of Ord's leading citizens. Would he help her get the backing of the town's businessmen to finance the down payment?

The answer was yes. The community responded and, with the help of the people of Ord, on August 17, 1937, Evelyn bought a Taylor Cub. She was off and flying, hopping passengers around the nearby counties.

"She is quite a girl," her father told the *Omaha World Herald* reporter in a story that appeared August 19. "Never gets excited. Got her career cut out for her, now she has this plane. Doesn't care much about school or housework. Just interested in flying."

Evelyn hoped to become the country's youngest female transport pilot, but in November 1937, she flunked the written exam for that license. She could try again in three months. "I didn't have enough instruction, I guess. But, I'll get more," she told the *Ord Quiz* reporter. But how? She needed aviation school instruction, but that cost money.

The Ord community came to her aid again. Dr. Auble and her many other friends in Ord organized a benefit at the local dance hall. On Thursday evening, January 20, 1938, young and old couples in

Depression-weary Ord danced the night away for Evelyn. The event raised nearly one hundred dollars. The following Monday, Evelyn enrolled in the Lincoln School of Aviation. While in Lincoln, she lived with Herman and Winifred Mattley and their twenty-year-old daughter, Chelys, who became a close friend.

This time, Evelyn passed with "flying" colors and earned her transport license. Evelyn and her aviation exploits were big news in Nebraska and getting bigger all the time. She was heralded as the state's, and possibly the country's, youngest licensed transport pilot. Her name and photo frequently graced the front page of local newspapers around the state. The news was carried to other states as well.

In an interview with an *Ord Quiz* reporter, on February 4, 1939 — the occasion of her fourth anniversary since her first flight, Evelyn said that she had landed in thirty-one different towns, her barnstorming tours numbered twenty-three, and she had carried over one thousand passengers since August 1 of the previous year. "Stunt flying is much more fascinating than safe flying. But, if you once get started stunt flying, you can't stop. And then, you're very like to get your neck broken."

On a 1939 trip to Texas for the Southwest Aviation Conference (Evelyn attended as a Ninety-Nine) she rated a front page photo along with the story about the Ninety-Nines in the *Fort Worth Star-Telegram*. "Instead of spring clothes, the up hair do, or the servant problem, these women talk of hammerhead stalls, overcast fogs, and instrument boards. They're a tough group to glamorize because each presents herself as a normal woman who uses red fingernail polish, plays bridge, or makes her own clothes."

Mail began to arrive addressed simply to "Evelyn Sharp, Ord, Nebraska." One letter that came was from Eleanor Roosevelt, who had been a personal friend of Evelyn's heroine, Amelia Earhart.

Evelyn wrote to a friend later in 1939:

> I have 600 hours now and have carried over 3,500 passengers — am supporting myself and my mother and dad and have one fellow working for me. The last three days have been my worst. The most I've taken in one day has been $90.

We have had some tricky weather the last few days. Dust storms and what not but mostly hot weather. If my plane will just hold out it will be OK. But, if it doesn't I just don't know what I'll do. I'd like to get a job flying, and get a straight salary. This worry of hit or miss gets me. You got to just keep plugging along, I guess. I am planning to start south in the late fall and barnstorm my way into Texas.

Barnstorming was a tough way to make a living, as Evelyn and John discovered. They simply could not afford the up-keep and required maintenance on the airplane. After two years of barely making ends meet, they finally had to give up her airplane in December 1939. By now, she had "hopped" more than five thousand people. On June 9, 1940, Evelyn passed her instructor's re-rating test.

It was the Civilian Pilot Training program (CPT) that gave Evelyn the last big break she needed. A job as a temporary flight instructor teaching a primary flight training class in Mitchell, South Dakota, was the beginning. The newspapers trumpeted, "Evelyn Sharp is believed to be the youngest woman flying instructor in the country." She was twenty.

Two years later, in September 1942, the telegram from Nancy Love and Colonel Baker caught up with her at Lone Pine, California, where she was working for Roy Pemberton, teaching Navy cadets in the CPT program. That telegram completely altered her life, as it did the others who responded and joined the original WAFS. Evelyn and friend and fellow pilot Pat Thomas both received telegrams.

"I was the flight examiner and we felt it would leave [Roy] in the lurch if we both pulled out at the same time," Pat said. "We decided Evelyn should go and then let me know if it were for real or not."

So Evelyn, who now had 2,968 hours, went east. Of course, it was "for real." But by the time Evelyn could determine that and wire Pat back in California, the CAA had frozen jobs. Pat was ordered to Phoenix to teach instrument flying. Evelyn became Nancy Love's seventeenth member of the WAFS and went on to be part of the 6th Ferrying Group stationed in Long Beach.

Evelyn always had been a quick study when it came to airplanes. She moved through transitions rapidly — keeping pace with B.J. Erickson and Barbara Towne. She ferried her first P-51 to Newark on August 14, 1943. After she received her instrument white card in January 1944, Evelyn became the third woman in the United States to check out in the A-20, a twin-engine attack fighter-bomber also known as a DB-7 or The Havoc. She began to fly that airplane to and from Daggett, California, for modification — a forty-five minute delivery each way.

"Now this is an airplane! — really wonderful. And this coming week, I'll get my P-38 check," she wrote to a friend.

The P-38 Lightning was built with a tricycle landing gear. Unlike the tail-dragger pursuits, the P-38 gave the pilot great visibility because she sat in the single seat between and slightly above the twin-engine nacelles. Evelyn was delighted to discover that it handled easily on the ground. "No danger of nose-over or ground loop in this plane should it become necessary to turn sharply or apply full brakes," according to the pilot manual she carefully read and absorbed.

Delphine Bohn, one of the other Originals to ferry the P-38, describes it as the goddess Athena or a malevolent genie with supernatural powers, depending on her mood. "Flying the P-38, I was one of God's favorites. I was enchanted. I was made gloriously beautiful and all the world's riches were mine. In my P-38, whether silver or camouflage, this entire planet became my celestial kingdom. But the Lockheed P-38 was another United States aircraft put into the war theater before it was ready. It did, however, give many indications of its magnificent possibilities. It was another aircraft — with the long undefended tag 'extremely dangerous.' There were legitimate and illegitimate reasons for this characterization."

On March 26, 1944, Evelyn Sharp made her first flight in the P-38. "Long Beach Tower, this is Army 43-28721 ready to take off," she radioed. The power of the two 1,425-horsepower Allison inline engines pressed her body back against the seat — a heady sensation for a little girl from Ord, Nebraska, who had learned to fly in a three-cylinder Curtiss Robin.

She spent the next three days building time in her remarkable new aircraft, getting the feel of it. With three hours and twenty minutes logged, she felt qualified to fly the airplane and signed off on the Army's familiarization form. The following day, she received orders to fly a P-38-J to Newark. On her return trip, she was scheduled to fly an A-20 into Great Falls, Montana, where she planned to meet Orla Crouse, her birth father, for the first time. He was driving over from Missoula.

The Lightning had its good and its bad points. The tricycle gear made it easy to land on airstrips carved out of the jungle in the South Pacific. The counter-rotating propellers did away with the torque (pulling) problem of the powerful single-engine airplanes like the P-51 and P-47. However, the engines were known to quit on occasion. The nightmare of any pilot who flew the P-38 was losing an engine on takeoff.

The first leg of Evelyn's ferrying flight east took her to Palm Springs the afternoon of March 30. Long Beach ferry pilots frequently left there in the afternoon and flew inland to Palm Springs where they RONed, choosing to take off soon after daylight the next morning, something that was impossible from Long Beach because of the coastal fog that usually socked in the area until early afternoon.

She left Palm Springs the morning of March 31 headed for Albuquerque. There, the maintenance crew put six quarts of oil in the No.1 engine. She RONed that night in Amarillo, Texas. On April 1, she flew to Tulsa with a full load of fuel and forty quarts of oil in each tank, then on to Scott Field in Illinois, outside St. Louis. The oil level was holding at forty in each tank. She wanted to make Cincinnati that night — possibly to spend an evening with her commanding officer, Nancy Love.

She departed Lunken Field, Cincinnati, the morning of April 2, with her oil still registering forty quarts in each tank, and landed at Lockbourne Army Air Base in nearby Columbus, Ohio. There the service crew brought each oil tank up to capacity, fifty-two quarts. The number two engine had lost eight quarts. Number one was holding steady.

Weather wasn't looking good ahead in Pennsylvania, so Evelyn waited awhile, then took off, still hoping to make her delivery in

Newark that afternoon. She passed Pittsburgh, then saw the bad weather ahead over the Allegheny Mountains. Writing to a friend that night, she described "running into a snow, rain, and sleet storm," and so she executed a 180-degree turn and went back to the nearest airport in New Cumberland, Pennsylvania, right outside Harrisburg. It was only 12:55 p.m., but she knew she was going no further that day. She wired Long Beach that she would RON there.

The morning of April 3, 1944, dawned cold — thirty-one degrees with an eleven-mile-an-hour wind blowing from the north-north-west. Evelyn did her customary pre-flight inspection of the airplane and climbed into the cockpit. A few minutes later, the tower cleared her for takeoff. She advanced the throttles and watched the rpm's climb — her feet on the brakes holding the airplane that sat straining, ready to fly. She released the brakes and began the power-packed takeoff roll. The aircraft cleared the runway at 10:29 a.m.

Evelyn had to know she didn't have full power. The grounds crew saw the black smoke pouring from the left engine. They watched as the pilot and the airplane tried to fly. If she turned right into the good engine, she would be headed over Harrisburg and a potentially deadly, destructive crash in a populated area. Straight ahead was Beacon Hill, one hundred fifty feet higher than the airport. To the left, but uphill, were only a few farmhouses. She must have made an instantaneous assessment and a split-second decision. Even though the rule when flying a twin-engine airplane is never to turn into a dead engine, Evelyn began a shallow, climbing bank to the left — as seen clearly by the men on the ground.

"Keeping the towers on top of Beacon Hill in her view, she pushed the right throttle forward and increased the pressure on the right rudder. The crippled P-38 yawed and skidded to the left. Watchmen on duty at the Radio Range Station watched her plane go by, barely missing the tops of the 150-foot towers," the Harrisburg *Telegraph* reported on April 4, 1944. The P-38 stalled, hung for a moment in the air, caught a cluster of trees with the left wing tip and hit the ground in a flat position. It skidded broadside about ten feet. When it stopped, the Plexiglas canopy lay upside down a few feet ahead of the right prop. The clock on the instrument panel had stopped at 10:30.

Nothing moved.

# 29

"I was at the Republic factory in Farmingdale waiting to take a P-47 over to Newark when Helen Mary Clark came up to me in the Alert Room and told me Evelyn had been killed," Nancy Batson remembered. "I was stunned. Evelyn was such a good pilot. Of course, later we heard what happened to her.

"Then Helen Mary said, 'You have orders from Nancy Love to return to Wilmington, immediately. You are to go to Harrisburg to pick up Evelyn's body from the undertaker and accompany her home on the train to Ord, Nebraska.'

"I stared at her. I couldn't believe it."

Fifty-six years later, Nancy Batson furrowed her brow and searched the distant past. "Nancy Love never attended a funeral after Cornelia's. We think she was so broken up over Cornelia, that she couldn't face another one. Remember, she sent Florene home with Dorothy Scott. And she sent me with Evelyn."

Dressed in a Santiago blue WASP uniform — the new uniforms, by then, had been issued to the original WAFS as well as to the Sweetwater graduates — Nancy left Wilmington with $200 collected from the WASPs who were members of the 2nd Ferrying Group. Her instructions were to give it to Evelyn's parents when she arrived in Ord. By the time she got to Ord, she also carried the unanswered letters that Evelyn had in her purse.

"That was a long, lonely train ride," Nancy recalled. "Oh, it was crowded all right. Lots of people around. There always were lots of people around on the trains and planes during the war. But all I could think of was Evelyn lying in that wooden casket in the baggage car."

Nancy Batson never thought she'd live out the war. Her only brother had died in an airplane crash during Army cadet training at

Ellington Field in Houston and she was convinced she would go the same way. Unlike fellow Southerner Cornelia Fort, who had constantly written letters to friends, Nancy hadn't written a single letter to her friends and very few to her family. She preferred to drop in while on her way through Birmingham on a ferrying trip. Nancy had no sense of the future beyond the war. If her number came up, it came up — just as Evelyn Sharp's number had come up on April 3, 1944.

Nancy shed no tears during the trip west. All she could think of was the waste of a good friend, a good pilot, a young woman who had such a bright future ahead of her.

Ord and the surrounding communities turned out *en masse* for Evelyn. The Eastern Star, of which Mary Sharp was a member, officiated at the funeral at the Ord Methodist Church — the church in which Evelyn had grown up. The American Legion conducted the graveside service. Men who also had been Jack Jefford's flight students served as pallbearers.

One man asked Nancy Batson if he could drape Evelyn's casket with an American flag.

The WASPs, of course, had not been militarized. Right then, the heated debate was raging in Congress and all the brave young women like Evelyn and Nancy, who flew airplanes for their country because they wanted to, had become a political football that was being kicked from one end of America to the other. Nancy also knew that the WASPs carried no insurance, had no government benefits, no burial subsidy, and certainly were not in line for official military honors even though they died serving their country. That had become painfully clear with the deaths of Cornelia and Dorothy, as well as the deaths of several WASP student trainees in Texas and some on active duty. The classmates at Avenger and the women in the various ferrying squadrons or other duty posts kicked in whatever money they could to send their friends home in wooden coffins.

But, thought Nancy Batson, this wonderful, thoughtful, grieving man wanted to put the American flag on her friend's coffin and, personally, she couldn't think of anything more appropriate. "Of course you can," she said, her warm Southern voice positive and reassuring as she smiled through the tears she still managed to hold back.

Hundreds came to pay final tribute that Easter Sunday morning, April 9, 1944. The love of the citizens of Ord for Evelyn was painfully obvious to Nancy. She saw it in their red-rimmed eyes and heard it in their grief-stricken voices when they spoke to her. And she felt it in the appreciative looks she received when these people saw her, a young woman in uniform. They straightened their backs, held their heads a little higher, and offered their hands with a grip that showed respect, pride and gratitude.

∽⊙☉∾

Three years earlier, Evelyn had been interviewed by the Bakersfield *Californian*, and the reporter had asked if she would volunteer for service if the United States ended up in the war.

"Certainly," said Evelyn. "There's plenty of things a woman flier can do to help aviation branches of the service. I'll do everything I can."

And so she had. Now, she could do no more.

∽⊙☉∾

"Nancy Love was waiting for me at BOQ 14 in Wilmington when I got back," Nancy Batson related. "'How did it go?' was all she said, and I told her."

Both Nancys did their crying in private.

"Years later, Betty Gillies told me that she also lost an engine in a P-38, in the very same place as Evelyn," Nancy Batson Crews continued. "But the wind was blowing the other way, so she was taking off on the opposite runway. Going that direction, the ground sloped downwards and she flew out over the river. She was able to get her plane up enough to go around, come back, and land safely."

Evelyn had been in line to take over as commander of the about-to-be-established 21st Ferrying Squadron at Palm Springs. What had not come about in the fall of 1943 did come about in the spring of 1944. In her stead, Byrd Granger (43-W-1) took command of the new women's squadron. When Granger injured her leg, she was replaced by Mary Lou Colbert (43-W-1). It was the first time a woman's ferrying squadron was not headed by one of the original WAFS.

c๛๛

In order to prepare her WASPs for the militarization she expected to occur, Jacqueline Cochran had opted for officer training for her girls. General Barney Giles, Army Air Forces chief of staff, had it all arranged. Women pilots already on active duty were to attend officer training school (OTS) at Orlando, Florida.

The course was four weeks and the women selected had to have been on active duty at least ninety days. A new class would begin every first and third Wednesday of the month, each with fifty students. A total of 460 women pilots graduated from OTS before the school was closed to women in the fall of 1944.

The first class reported April 19, 1944. It was made up of squadron leaders and the women pilots who had been on duty the longest and included many of The Originals — Nancy Love, Betty Gillies, Barbara Donahue, Del Scharr, B.J. Erickson, Delphine Bohn, Florene Miller, and Nancy Batson, just back from Evelyn's funeral. Most of the other Originals attended one of the subsequent classes. Cochran did not have to attend. Competitive Nancy Love, with her executive title, set out to be the best in the class. By the time she reached Orlando, she had already studied all the class material.

Nancy Batson described that time spent in Orlando:

*We attended class six days a week, studying military discipline, courtesy and customs. We also learned about the organization of the army and staff procedures. Like they said, we were learning how to be officers. Oh, and another fun part was memorizing aircraft silhouettes. Every kid in America was doing the same thing by then. And we had to practice air-sea rescue and jungle survival, which meant catching, cooking, and eating of whole bunch of creepy crawly things. Yuk!*

*It was the first time some of us original WAFS had been together in more than a year. I had hardly seen B.J. or Florene since they left for their new assignments back in the winter of 1943.*

## *Orlando OTS*

Men and women attending OTS were treated very well. They were, after all, officers in the Army Air Forces or, ostensibly, about to be. Maids kept the barracks, did their laundry and polished their shoes. The women had never been treated so well.

Consequently, the WAFS — who hadn't had much in the way of leave time over the course of twenty months of active service and busy ferrying schedules — and their fellow WASPs set out, in their off time, to enjoy themselves on Florida's beaches, in the warm Florida sunshine.

The timing couldn't have been worse, of course, public relations-wise. The Congressional hearings were still on and the fate of women pilots was being debated far and wide. Now here were those very women being treated to a four-week training session to make them officers when their militarization was greatly in question. To add to that, this was exactly when the Ferrying Division desperately needed every pursuit ferry pilot it could lay its hands on and could ill afford the loss of several of them for four weeks. Though it wasn't publicly known then, D-Day was just over a month away.

A few more vocal individuals thought Jacqueline Cochran had lost her mind! But once the Army's organizational wheels began turning, they were almost impossible to stop.

The WASPs had many visitors while they were in Orlando — columnists from most of the east coast newspapers among them, asking all sorts of prying questions. They also received a visit from Jacqueline Cochran herself and one from Chairman of the House Civil Service Committee, Representative Robert Ramspeck.

In *Catch a Shooting Star*, Delphine Bohn describes Ramspeck's visit to the WASPs in Orlando:

> He invited Nancy Love and three or four of us to have dinner with him, all the while he queried us as to the WASPs. He was manifestly experienced as to this type research, too. He brought from Washington, newspapers which included many columnists' opinions as to the WASPs' programs. One which included the column of Major Al Williams is excerpted as follows:
>
> > The bill proposed to expand the WASPs from about 1,000 to 5,000 and to commission WASPs as officers of the Air Corps.
> > It was claimed there was a shortage of pilots.

This claim was discredited by the fact that the Army presently released 36,000 carefully selected combat flight candidates to the infantry and turned loose many thousands of CAA-CPT and WTS seasoned pilots who had "done the bulk of the work giving flight training to approximately 300,000 airmen of the Army and Navy."

The whole thing was unfortunate because it brought undeserved discredit upon the little band of gallant, able women pilots who stepped into the breech when there was a shortage of men pilots and ferried thousands of trainers as WAFS, respected by all flying people and deserving of the gratitude of the nation.

When the situation became really sticky — like the Florida humidity — and we were undecided whether we were supposed to be honorable or dishonorable, serving our country honorably or dishonorably, we would wait until after midnight and go skinny dipping in the lake. Sometimes we would pretend we were Loreleis drawing all males to crash on the rocks. With this formula, we could work off any resentment.

To be perfectly honest, the Originals weren't too keen on being militarized under "Colonel" Jacqueline Cochran. Already, they were quite upset at having to give up their familiar gray-green uniforms for the newly-arrived Santiago blue uniforms now worn with such pride by the WASPs who had graduated from Houston or Avenger.

Bear in mind that these were two distinct and very different groups. Both had reason to be proud of what they had done. But an artificial and unwanted merger had put the original WAFS in a situation not to their liking — under Jackie Cochran's thumb.

Nancy Batson, however, remembers an outstanding side benefit to her officer training assignment.

*I was scheduled to go home to Birmingham for a few days R&R at the end of OTS when Nancy Love took B.J. Erickson, Barbara Donahue and me aside and told us there were three DB-7s, also known as A-20s, there in Orlando that needed to be delivered to the West Coast. Would we three like to ferry them?*

*You know what the answer was. I was thrilled! A big twin-engine, single seater attack bomber! So I called Mother and Daddy and told them I wasn't comin' home after all.*

*That afternoon, after graduation, Nancy took the three of us out to the base. It was warm, and on the way out I fell asleep in the car. I think that impressed Nancy because I wasn't nervous. She gave us each a cockpit check and we took off and went upstairs to fly around and practice. Well, I was right at home. By that time I had had a lot of twin-engine time and I had already checked out in a P-38. Anyway, I loved it! I think I was the last one to come in. And there was Nancy waiting for us with a big smile on her face.*

*The next morning, right after sun up, we took off for California. I can't tell you how good it felt. Biggest thing I had ever flown.*

*To this day, I think Nancy Love was saying to me 'you've done a good job.' That was her way of patting you on the back and saying thanks for all your hard work and dedication. Because, you see, Nancy Love didn't say things like that to you in person. She expected you to do your job — the job we were hired to do, fly airplanes — and to do it right, no questions asked. She was a wonderful person to work and fly for.*

*Anyway, that's how I flew my first DB-7/A-20. Then when we got to Long Beach after making our delivery, B.J. gave me a brand new A-20 to take back east to Savannah, Georgia. I flew that one into Birmingham overnight so my parents could see it.*

*It was such a powerful, wonderful machine. I loved it. Twin engine. Single cockpit. It was like the wings came right out from my shoulders. It was mine, all mine. I was alone in it and it felt like a flying Cadillac. See, I get the feel of an airplane. My god, it was something. I knew that I could have gone to war in the A-20. When I flew that A-20, that was the first time I realized that I could have been a combat pilot and strafed railroads and dropped bombs.*

B.J. Erickson tells a slightly different story of that DB-7 flight.

*Nancy had these three bullet-ridden DB-7s that needed to be flown to Salinas, California. She picked Nancy Batson, Barbara Donahue and me to take them. We left at dawn and raced like fury to get them out there in one day. We landed just before dark, but we made it in record time. Well, the guy in Operations at Salinas wrote 'Class 26' on them.*

*"What does 'Class 26' mean," I asked.*

*"We're junking them" he said.*

*I asked him why, if they were junking them, didn't we just leave them in Florida? Why fly them all the way across the country? "What are you going to do with them?"*

*"Push them off the end of the runway into a parking area for junk," he told me.*

*"We beat our brains out, set a new flight record to get them out here, and you're going to junk them?" I said. I couldn't believe it!*

And Barbara Donahue adds, "That was a lovely aircraft. Such fun! I didn't get to ferry another one until later in Romulus when I made three A-20 deliveries to Montreal."

Nancy Batson tells one more A-20 story with great relish.

*En route to Savannah, I landed that A-20 in Meridian, Mississippi, stepped on the brakes and, whomp, they caught and pulled to the left. I tried again, same thing. By the time I got that thing stopped, I had burned out the brakes. Well, I started looking for help. I ran into Joe Shannon, an old friend from Birmingham, in the chow line. I asked him if he could help me get the brakes fixed on that A-20.*

*Joe said he was acting maintenance officer now that the former maintenance officer was on a ship heading overseas. He called the superintendent on the line and told him, "This young lady is an old friend of mine from Birmingham and she wants to know if we can help her get her airplane fixed."*

*You know what the guy said to him? "How long do you want to keep her here?"*

As the women were being trained to be officers, everything else was rapidly going sour. First the WASP bill went down to defeat in Congress on June 21, then Cochran told Arnold she would not let her girls go into the WACs under Colonel Hobby's command. Nancy Love, against her better judgment, had backed Jackie's play thinking her rival had the clout to pull it off. When the militarization failed to materialize from Congress, Nancy quickly wrote to General George and asked him to seek militarization for the women pilots in the Ferrying Division as soon as possible. It was a prescient move on her part, but it was too late.

In April 1944, the number of women pilots on duty with the Ferrying Division had reached its high point — 303. Now, with the crunch on to deliver pursuits, General Tunner wanted to transfer out those who were not pursuit material.

Nancy Love gave *any* woman ferry pilot who wished to fly pursuit the opportunity to do so. Her aim was to make her women pilots as essential to the Army as possible. Those who could not qualify would be transferred to the Training Command with the WASPs who were not serving as ferry pilots. By August, 125 women pilots had been released by FERD. A few were moved into administrative positions and a few continued to fly the lower-horsepower and some twin-engine aircraft that the Army still needed ferried.

From there on in, 132 women pilots flew a steady stream of pursuit aircraft to the docks for shipment overseas.

Sixteen Originals were still flying.

Jackie Cochran had managed to make an enemy of controversial newspaper columnist, Drew Pearson. He visited the WASPs in Orlando, talked to several of them, and, in early August 1944, wrote a scathing commentary about Cochran, General Arnold and the WASPs.

Air Force commander General "Hap" Arnold may not know it, but he is facing a regular cloudburst from Capitol Hill as soon as Congress gets back to a full-time job. The Congressman are up in arms over Arnold's effort to side-track the law by continuing to use the WASPs . . . the government has spent more than $21,000,000 training lady flyers, primarily at the behest of vivacious aviatrix Jacqueline Cochran, wife of financial magnate Floyd Odlum. Magnetic Miss Cochran seems to have quite a drag with the brass hats and has even persuaded air forces' smiling commander to make several secret trips to Capitol Hill to lobby for continuation of her pets, the WASPs — it was arranged to sign the WASPs up as WACs, then have them reassigned to the Air Forces, this despite Congress' clear ruling that the WASPs should not be taken into the regular Army. When Colonel Oveta Culp Hobby, head of the WACs got wind of this deal, she sent emissaries to Capitol Hill to have her rank raised from Colonel to Brigadier General. Oveta was afraid that Jacqueline Cochran would be made a colonel in the WACs and wanted to outrank her.

Cochran responded with her own eleven-page, single-spaced report to General Arnold. She outlined the WASP's accomplishments and history and her recommendations for the future. She also released the report to the public at the same time it went to Arnold, which was probably a big mistake.

Legislative action identical to the Costello Bill was currently in the Senate and she wanted the Army Air Forces to press for passage. She requested "simple justice" for the WASP, who got "none of the rights of military status, not even a military funeral." She demanded that Arnold put the women pilots into the Army with commissions or junk their organization completely.

It was ultimatum time. The gauntlet was down. Now the final chapters of the WAFS/WASP story were ready to be played out.

Standing: **Barbara Towne, Helen Richards, B.J. Erickson**
kneeling: **Teresa James and Betty Gillies**

# 30

The summer sun, not long past the solstice, sat like a ghost disk behind the murky haze that often obscured the skies in the vicinity of New York City. It would be a warm day and the humidity was up, but it promised to be even stickier inland fifty miles at Newark Airport, next to the docks where the ship sat awaiting its cargo of P-47s.

Three WASPs sat at the round wooden game table in the middle of the Alert Room, cinder block on three sides and wood paneling at the far end behind the pot-bellied heater that kept them warm in wintertime. The women pilots on duty didn't need heat today. They had enough — both literally, what with the summer weather, and figuratively. The WASP militarization bill had been defeated in Congress a few days earlier and they were left wondering what was coming next. In the meantime, they continued to do what they had been hired to do twenty-one months earlier — ferry airplanes for Uncle Sam.

Gertrude Meserve Tubbs was writing a letter — probably to new husband, Charlie, stationed back in Wilmington. They had been married all of two months and both continued to serve as ferry pilots for the 2nd Ferrying Group stationed at New Castle Army Air Base. Gertrude, like the rest of the WASPs in the Alert Room that day, was on TDY (a four-week, temporary duty assignment ) at the Republic Aviation factory in Farmingdale, New York. The women of the 2nd Ferrying Group rotated in and out of Farmingdale on a regular basis and by now, late June 1944, were doing all the ferrying of P-47s out of the Republic factory.

Helen Richey sat across from Gertie, reading a newspaper. Between them sat Teresa James, also writing but in her daily journal. She was catching up, doing yesterday's log. Nancy Batson was snoozing on one of the couches along the wall, and the rest of the on-duty WASPs were scattered around the room reading, talking and smoking. Basically, they were waiting to fly. The P-47s they were to take to Newark that day were undergoing final inspections and tests prior to being flown to the docks for shipment abroad. Somewhere across the ocean, in Italy or England, a fighter pilot anxiously awaited each and every airplane the women could deliver to the docks.

IWASM

D-Day was a mere three weeks behind them and, already, the P-47s and P-51s were making their presence felt over France and Germany, just as the P-47s already had made a difference in the Italian campaign.

The door behind Gert opened and Teresa looked up, anticipating the call that the planes were ready and the WASP must get a move on, slip on their parachutes and head for the flight line. The man who entered the room was in uniform, but he was not the all-too-familiar Operations Officer. He looked around the room, his eyebrows furrowing as he squinted at each of the women there, as if searching. Teresa had a sudden lurch in the pit of her stomach. In the man's hand was an envelope — the size, shape and yellow color of a Western Union telegram.

She scanned the room quickly for someone else who might be a next-of-kin or spouse. Gertie — but Charlie was flying stateside. Richey and Batson were unattached, though both had a lot of friends overseas. The rest were unmarried as well.

"Excuse me, I'm looking for Mrs. George Martin," the man said. It was like the voice of doom.

"Oh my God," said Teresa.

Every eye in the room was on her. Out of the corner of her own eye, she saw Helen stir and slide quietly from her chair. A fraction of a second later, Teresa felt Helen's hand on her shoulder.

"This is Mrs. Martin," Helen said in a low voice. "What has happened?"

The man came forward, his hand outstretched, holding the telegram where Teresa could see it. "I'm very sorry, ma'am, but this is for you, for Mrs. George Martin. From the War Department."

Teresa, her mind whirling now, realized the man was staring at her nametag. It read T. James. She had joined the WAFS as Teresa James, even though she and Dink were already married. She had never bothered to change it. She was used to being Teresa James. She had lived with that name for thirty years now.

"Yes." She finally managed to get her tongue around words again. "I'm Mrs. George Martin." And she reached for the telegram.

"Do you want me to read it to you," Helen said, her hand never leaving Teresa's shoulder and now gripping it very hard.

"N-no." Teresa caught herself before the stammering got any worse. "I'm OK, I can do it." And she took the offensive yellow envelope, opened it and pulled the message from inside. "We regret to inform you that Lt. George L. Martin 0-753906, 337th Bomb Squadron, 96th Bomb Group, is MISSING IN ACTION.

∽⊙⊙∾

Dink, a B-17 pilot, was stationed in Snetterton Heath, England, assigned to the 337th Bombardment Squadron, 96th Bombardment Group, which had been activated on July 15, 1942. For awhile, after graduation from B-17 school in Stockton, California, Dink had been an instructor at Roswell, New Mexico. But he had volunteered for overseas duty and was shipped out in the spring of 1944, to England. Dink and Teresa had seen little of each other since their wedding in June 1942. Mostly stolen interludes when she ferried a plane west and could arrange a RON enroute or a couple of days after delivery of one plane before she picked up yet another one to take back east.

When Dink got to New Jersey to ship out, he was issued a forty-eight hour pass. He went immediately to Wilmington where Teresa was on duty at NCAAB. She was on orders and wasn't supposed to leave the base. A sympathetic Betty Gillies, as squadron commander, risked court martial to give Teresa permission to leave with her husband, otherwise the two would not have seen each other before he left for England.

On June 22, sixteen days after D-Day, Dink's squadron took off on an offensive over northern France. His plane was hit and had not returned to base, but nothing else was known. He was classified as missing on an operational mission.

After the officer left, the women all clustered around Teresa. Helen asked her what she wanted to do.

"Go home — to Pittsburgh," a tearful Teresa finally managed to say.

Helen told the others to stay with her while she went and phoned Betty Gillies in Wilmington to get permission. She was back in no time, helped Teresa out of her chair and moved her toward the door.

"I've told Operations. Two of those Jugs will have to wait until you girls get back here, then somebody else can take them over," she told the other WASPs. I'm going to take Teresa back to the Huntington to pack and help her get transportation to Pittsburgh. Then I'll be back. Gert, Nancy, you two can handle the C-60 and see that everybody gets back?"

Both nodded solemnly and watched the pair of uniformed women exit, the taller one leaning slightly on the smaller one for moral if not physical support.

Teresa went home to Pittsburgh, but within two days, she received a call from Betty Gillies. "We need you, Teresa. You know we're desperate for every pilot we can get."

Never one to hide and lick her wounds, and knowing that she

had, by now, had more than her fill of family sympathy, and itching to get her hands back on the stick and throttle of a P-47, Teresa quickly acquiesced. "I'm better off flying and being with the girls," Teresa said. "I'll be back tomorrow." And so Teresa returned the following day to Farmingdale.

A week later, Teresa received Dink's last letter — written on June 21, postmarked June 22, the day his plane was shot down.

*Dear Butch,*

*How are you getting along, honey? Are you still working hard and doing a lot of flying?*

*We're really keeping busy over here and I'm not fooling. I'm tuckered out. If these jerks would quit shooting at us, it wouldn't be bad. I think they're mad at us though.*

*I had a close one on takeoff yesterday morn. I was loaded to gross and we had a 400-foot ceiling. It was still dark yet and the place was really closed in. I just got into the murk and good and solid in a climbing turn on the gauges when the horizon went out. I rolled right out of the turn and went on needle, ball and airspeed and stayed on them till I broke out on top. Whew! what a sweat. Bill, my co-driver turned about 40 colors when it went out, some fun. This place is just like a place I was instructing at.*

*How are you getting along with the gauges, honey. Are you driving on them yet or not. Learn all you can about them, honey, they're the best insurance in the world, next to a flak suit.*

*I still haven't received any mail at all, it has been $2^{1/2}$ months since I've had any. It's plenty lonesome — not getting any mail when we get home. I'd sure appreciate a letter about now. I don't know what's holding it up. I feel like a stinker, all I do is eat, sleep and fly. I haven't even had time to take a bath for a couple of days.*

*Enough griping now. I'm tired now. Still love me as much as ever, honey? I love you more than anything in the world honey and I always will. I miss you more every day and can't wait till this mess is over and I can get to see you again.*

*I'm going to grab some rest now, write soon.*

*Forever, "Pop"*

Teresa heard nothing more. It was like Dink had dropped off the face of the earth, and, in some respects, he had. When Teresa still hadn't heard anything further four months later, Helen Richey offered to write to her old and dear friend, General Jimmy Doolittle, at the Headquarters of the 8th Air Force, to see if he could learn anything more. Helen shared General Doolittle's letter dated 28 November 1944 with Teresa:

*Dear Helen,*

*Thanks for your note of 30 October received the other day. It was good to hear from you and learn that you are well. Sorry to hear that your little flock is being disbanded. What have you in mind now?*

*We have very little information on Lt. George L. Martin. Here's what we have. He was listed as missing in action on a bombing mission 22 June. His plane was hit and No. 3 engine caught fire. Immediately after the ship was hit it went out of control and three chutes were seen by crew members of other planes to open. Shortly thereafter, the airplane leveled off and four more chutes were observed to come out. It is impossible to say whether the last three got out or not as the ship went out of sight soon after this. While we have heard nothing further, you can see from the above that there is a good chance that George got out and is now a prisoner of war. Should we receive any more dope I will pass it on at once. Mrs. Martin will get some measure of comfort from the knowledge that George was very well liked by his associates, was doing a swell job and had made substantial contribution to the cause for which we are all fighting. Please extend to her my sympathy and I hope that George may yet show up.*

*Had Ernie Pyle out to the house for supper a short time before he went home. He is a great little guy and did a magnificent job over here. Should you see him give him my kindest regards and tell him we are all looking forward to the time his health will let him come back.*

*Sincere best,*
*As ever,*
*J.H. Doolittle, Lieut. General, USA*

In the meantime, Teresa had seen a photo in the New York *Daily News*. It bore the caption, "American Airmen Captured by Nazis." A side view of one of the men in the picture looked like Dink, with two of his crew members whom she had met prior to his volunteering for overseas duty.

"I figured he was a POW and would come home after the war was over," she said, fifty-five years later.

Unfortunately, this turned out not to be the case. On July 26, 1945 — a full year after Dink's disappearance — Teresa was notified by the Army that "an official determination has been made of the death of your husband, Second Lieutenant George Louis Martin, who has been missing in action since June 22, 1944, in the European Area." However, in answer to her inquiry, a letter from the European Theater Graves Registration Service dated August 30, 1945, stated that: "At the present time we have no record of the death or burial of Lt. Martin."

Dink's death remained shrouded in mystery and Teresa could not bring herself to believe he was dead until finally, on March 29, 1949, she was notified that his remains — which apparently had been buried with those of his comrades at Solers, France — were to be transferred to Jefferson Barracks National Cemetery in St. Louis, Missouri. Teresa received a second letter informing her that Dink's B-17 had crashed in Joinville-le-Pont, France, after being hit by anti-aircraft fire on a mission to Paris.

In 1950, Teresa was working in her parents' flower shop in Pittsburgh when a man came in and asked for Teresa James Martin. He had been the waist gunner on Dink's plane. He told her that he remembered the hit that blew off the whole front end of the airplane. He said that her husband, his co-pilot and the navigator never knew what hit them. His last memory, he said, was jumping out of the wounded bomber and his parachute opening.

"He said that he had to find me and tell me the story. Then he said he was going on to New York, but he would return so we could talk some more."

But the man never came back.

**Dorothy Fulton**

# 31

Instrument school, like pursuit school, was a child of the times. Both were established when the need arose. In late 1943, when the push was on to train more pilots capable of flying pursuit, the simultaneous need surfaced to get those pilots instrument rated. Rosecrans Field, outside St. Joseph, Missouri, was the site of the ATC's Operational Training School (OTS) No. 1 for pilots seeking an Instrument White Card.

Up until then the original WAFS who had obtained their white cards, took their training at their home base — Betty Gillies, Nancy Batson, Helen McGilvery, Gertrude Meserve, B.J. Erickson, Evelyn Sharp, Dorothy Scott and Florene Miller. Teresa James was sent to Love Field in Dallas to earn hers.

With the opening of OTS No. 1, Nancy Love decided to send some of her WAFS there. The first to go was the new Dallas squadron leader, Delphine Bohn, in February 1944, followed by Del Scharr, and later Sis Bernheim. Delphine, the Texas Panhandle native who had found the weather in Wilmington, Delaware, almost more than she could bear, observed the following Weather Bureau stats for her month in St. Joe: mean temperature, 33.7 degrees F.; average monthly precipitation, 5.10 inches.

Here's how she described her experience:

*Fog existed from September through April, engendered by the bends of the Missouri River that encircled the land abused by Rosecrans Field. There had been and were continuous severe thunderstorms and storms of hail, sleet, snow and freezing rain.*

*Continuous induction and airframe ice terrorized the airplanes. Broomsticks, ordinarily identified with housewives or witches, were applied to loosen the ice from the control surfaces of airplanes, once the runway ice had been safely negotiated to the ramp. Mostly, throughout the winter months, a tight, ugly layer of coal smoke crouched over the field. It smelled of cremated minerals. The landscape snow and ice were in shades of spook gray, rusty black and dirty white. Even as it fell, the snow was desecrated.*

*Rosecrans Field was fueled by hundreds of coal-burning stoves that, at that time of the year, had to be kept burning day and night to prevent frozen pipes and frozen personnel. Just call me lucky, I was their first, and, at the time, only WAFS student. Upon arrival from Dallas — where the winter sky had been blue and the temperature mild — I was informed I would have my first instrument instruction that very night. I was to be their guinea pig. I was to furnish them a scale of all future mistakes they might expect.*

*With Captain Harry Munson as my instructor, I was placed in the lefthand seat of a North American B-25 bomber. Imagine how sharply that contrasted the Douglas C-47, the fastest, most sophisticated, twin engine equipment I'd yet ferried. My ground check was thorough. Captain Munson was the officer in charge of the school and, of course, was super-excellent.*

*In the night's murkiness with many lights reflected by the thick cloud layer of coal smoke and pollution, we (he, actually) taxied to the run-up area and took off. At about 15,000 feet, I became aware of numerous lights, but was never certain which were the lights of planet Earth and which were the lights of the many stars. In fact, I was never certain which was 'up' and which was 'down.' Happily for me, my instruction was divided between the B-25 and the much more familiar C-47 throughout my instrument schooling.*

*Thirty days later, I took the test for my White Card.*

*The weather that day was made up of heavy sleet, freezing rain and ice — rime and glaze in all supposed degrees. We shot an approach at Scott's Bluff, Nebraska, landed and, before takeoff an hour later, had to borrow their broomsticks. It was lethal flying weather and composed of everything to persuade a new ticketholder to remember the fun to be had on the ground under those conditions.*

The women of the 2nd Ferrying Group, when assigned to the Republic Aviation factory, were always happy when Sis Bernheim was part of the flight team. Sis had a house on Long Island, not far from Farmingdale, and frequently played hostess to her fellow pilots.

Nancy Batson recalled many a delightful evening cooking their own dinner and spending the night. It was a chance to get away from Spartan hotel living at the Huntington.

*Sis had a car— a yellow Buick convertible, she loved Buick convertibles — and she would drive Gertrude, Helen McGilvery and me out to her house and we'd stay there instead of in town at the hotel.*

*She had this cute little bar with an airplane theme. I was so impressed that someone had a bar right there in their house. Sis loved her rye whiskey, which she drank with Coke. I had never had rye whiskey before, but I tried it. Sis was such a good friend and we all had such a good time together. She really was a good ole gal, a lot of fun with a great sense of humor.*

Sis, who had been flying since 1934, heard about the WAFS late in the fall of 1942, but didn't get in her first try. By the time she got to Wilmington, they had their full quota. She returned to her flight instructing job at Lyme Ridge near Pawling, New York. But not long after, Barbara Poole notified her that there was an opening in the squadron and, if she hurried, she might still get in.

"This time I was accepted," Sis said. "Who needed wings! I was a member of the Women's Auxiliary Ferrying Squadron. For a few days thereafter, I was on Cloud Nine. Actually I had a ninety-day contract to prove I was a good pilot. Fortunately, with a lot of hard work, I was able to prove myself and become a full-fledged member."

Sis remained in Wilmington with Betty Gillies' squadron her entire two years with the WAFS, other than her trips to instrument school and pursuit school. And once she began flying pursuits, she frequently rotated to Evansville or Farmingdale and, because Long Island was home, she was particularly partial to the Farmingdale assignments.

"The bus would take the WASPs back and forth from the Huntington Hotel to the Republic factory every day. But I still had my house there, so four or five of us lived there instead of the Huntington. We would get up early, drive to Republic, work flying all day, and return home at dark. It was lots of fun for all of us."

Sis, according to Delphine Bohn, disliked ground school — in fact school of any kind. She quickly found that the way to avoid attending compulsory ground school for those on base was to be out ferrying airplanes. Still, with good humor and a certain amount of relish, she followed Delphine to St. Joe for instrument training in May 1944, then took her pursuit training in Brownsville June/July of 1944.

"Joy with life and joy with flight were two of Sis' greatest assets," recalled Delphine. Once, on takeoff from Atlanta in a P-47, Sis discovered that she was getting red lights on the instrument panel telling her that neither the wheels nor the flaps would retract. She "positively reveled" in an authorized opportunity to buzz the tower in Atlanta while they checked to see if the gear was, in fact, down like the warning light said or up and stowed, and if the flaps had or had not returned to flight position.

New York born and raised, Sis was not afraid to take on anyone — including two high-ranking generals whom she and another WAFS bumped from an airliner in order to return to base as they were supposed to do after delivering their airplanes. However, Sis was terrified of lightning and thunder storms and was apt to be found hiding in a closet during one.

Delphine says she also threatened to buzz every bull, cow or steer she saw in Kansas after finding that the famed Kansas City steak she had been led to believe rivaled her favorite two-inch-thick New York T-bone turned out to be a disappointment. Her description was, "When it arrived, it was as flat and as big as the State of Texas and as thick as a piece of paper. And it was tough!" A telephone call from squadron commander Betty Gillies convinced her that discretion — regarding Kansas beef on the hoof — was the better part of valor, steak or no steak.

Helen McGilvery, like Sis, spent her entire WAFS service with the 2nd Ferrying Group and, like Sis and the others, did TDY in Farmingdale flying the P-47s. But her closest friend in the WAFS, Nancy Batson, remembers very well a PT-19 trip early in 1943 when

Little Mac, who was an excellent pilot and as exacting about her navigation as she was about her personal appearance, got lost — temporarily.

*Helen Mary was the flight leader and Little Mac and, I think, Gert and Delphine and I picked up our planes in Hagerstown. We were planning to RON in Chattanooga. Well, when we got in that afternoon, everybody landed but Little Mac. It was kind of hazy, you know how it gets down in the mountains in the south in the late afternoon. And it was still winter and getting dark.*

*Well, we realized she was past due. We waited and waited. Helen Mary was really getting concerned and we didn't know what to do when, suddenly, here came the PT-19. She landed and we ran over to find out what happened.*

*Turned out, they had given her an old chart in Wilmington that didn't have the new airport on it. The rest of us had new ones. So when she got to where she thought the airport was, it wasn't there. And she knew she had to find it because it was getting late. So she devised a way of searching. She flew out straight in one direction and then flew back to a point on the original line and then flew out on a line the other way. She kept flying out and back covering the territory and finally found the new airport.*

*She said the only thing that kept going through her mind as she was flying back and forth was the song "Chattanooga Choo Choo." She said she kept singing it, "Chattanooga Choo Choo won't you choo choo me home."*

*Well, when we RONed at the hotel that night, who should appear but her husband, Mac. That's why we called her Little Mac. He was a ferry pilot out of Wilmington too and he and a bunch of fellows flew in that afternoon and ended up at the same hotel.*

Dorothy Fulton brought with her to the WAFS more than 3,000 hours, which translated into a tremendous amount of experience. None of the other Originals exceeded her in cockpit time in the fall of 1942.

Dorothy did not fly pursuit, but she became a specialist at ferrying twin-engine airplanes from coast to coast.

Delphine Bohn tells this tale on her:

*On a very hot August afternoon, flying a very heavily overloaded Douglas C-47, Dorothy and her WASP co-pilot landed at Love Field to refuel. She made practically a turnaround takeoff on which she lost an engine too far down the runway to abort.*

*She was cleared to stay in the pattern for an immediate landing, but then she lost the hydraulic pump which necessitated that she and her co-pilot crank down*

**Dorothy Fulton with her own plane "Aeronca" in New Jersey, 1940**

*the gear by hand. Neither of them was a female Atlas. It took time. Finally, with everything down and done that was supposed to be down and done, she made a beautiful three-point landing. And this was a situation where any landing that continued upright would have been a good landing!*

*One member of an instantly convened safety board was waiting*

*for her at the flight line. Once she had her co-pilot placed on an airliner for Philadelphia, she underwent several hours of querying. In the process, the board also helped her fill out the requisite forms. Turns out it was the fact that the plane was overloaded that almost did her in. They didn't know whether to commend her for the excellent job she had done in getting the airplane back on the ground undamaged, or to chastise her because she ignored Weight and Balance.*

*When she appeared at our BOQ to await transportation back*

*to Philadelphia, she carried two paper sacks. The Red Cross ladies had come to her aid and packed her great quantities of their food to see her safely home. They had also produced for her one of those very small individual bottles of bourbon popular on airlines today.*

But it was Teresa again — "happy-go-lucky Teresa" in Nancy Batson's words — who tells the tale that sounds like a whopper and is probably the topper when it comes to adventures in ferrying aircraft across the United States during World War II. It seems that one warm spring day in 1944, she picked up a P-47 in Farmingdale bound for Evansville . . .

*I thought I'd be back by nightfall — they promised me a P-47 back to Farmingdale. So, dumb me, I didn't bother to take an overnight bag. All I had was, literally, the clothes on my back — my uniform trousers (it was too warm to need a jacket), khaki shirt, underwear, shoes, socks and parachute. I did have the foresight to put a lipstick in my shirt pocket.*

*Wouldn't ya know, at Evansville, they handed me orders to take another P-47 to Long Beach the following day. I didn't dare tell him I had no change of clothes with me. That I couldn't go because I only had one shirt. So I did the next best thing, I went to the PX and bought a toothbrush, toothpaste and a tube of cold cream.*

*Next morning, they told me the airplane needed repairs. By the time they were done, the weather had closed in. I sat for nine days in Evansville. Then finally, off I went in my latest P-47 — a trip of 1800 miles in the opposite direction of home. Well, I get out there and I see my airplane and the operations officer behind the desk says, "Ever flown a P-51?"*

*I shook my head. Not having been to pursuit school, I had missed out on that particular pleasure. In fact, I was wondering when I was going to get to fly that peashooter.*

*"That one over there has to go to Fort Myers, Florida," he says. "Here are the tech orders. Sit in the cockpit and get familiar, then check yourself out."*

*I spent that evening in the BOQ with the girls at Long Beach. I washed out my underwear and my shirt, borrowed an iron from one of the other WAFS, and studied the tech orders. Next day, I headed east along the southern route. I got into Texas and ran into a summer storm. Rain from the Gulf of Mexico all across Louisiana and half of Texas. I started puddle jumping, literally, my way across Texas, short hops from one base to another.*

*Several days later, my shoes are unrecognizable they are so badly caked with mud. The humidity is so high, my socks and underwear won't dry over night and I have to put them back on wet every morning. Worst of all, I didn't have my uniform jacket, so they wouldn't let me in the Officers' Clubs to eat. I had to be content with sandwiches and stuff from the Operation's canteens.*

*When I finally make Fort Myers and hand over the P-51 — I had gotten quite attached to it, actually — I prayed I'd get a plane to take to New Castle. But they gave me a P-47 to take to Oklahoma.*

*There, I was fortunate enough to run into B.J. Erickson, who had just delivered a plane on the East Coast and was on her way back to Long Beach. Since she was on her way home, when she left, she offered me her jacket. Boy, was that a lifesaver! I was really salivating for some real meals in the O-Club.*

*Two days later, instead of sending me home, Operations gave me a AT-6 to deliver to Great Falls, Montana. So off I go again, in the wrong direction — 1,200 miles north. I couldn't believe it!*

*In Great Falls, when I got my next set of orders, I was afraid to open them. I said "I gotta get a cup of coffee first." Then I sat down and began to read. I had to take a BT-13 to Idaho! Wrong direction again. Finally, in Idaho they gave me an AT-9 to take back to New Castle!*

Twenty-four hours later, Teresa entered BOQ 14. The other women couldn't believe their eyes. She looked awful. Her uniform trousers were rump sprung and knee sprung — "looked like I'd had a pair of cantaloupes in the legs. Those pants never really recovered, even after a couple of trips to the dry cleaners."

Teresa had covered 11,000 miles in seven airplanes. She had been gone for four weeks and covered seventeen states. It was a record for ferrying deliveries that no one equaled.

But Sis Bernheim tried — albeit unintentionally. As she revealed to Sam Parker for an article in 1995:

*I enjoyed flying most of the planes. My special favorite was the P-47 Jug. I used to love to fly that sweetheart of a plane. But the two that I hated were the Bell P-39 Airacobra and the Bell P-63 Kingcobra. Standard preflight procedure required the pilot to always check the engine magnetos just before takeoff. To do this, the wheels would be locked and the engine revved up. Everytime I attempted this safety check on the Cobras, the engine temperature gauge would indicate the damn engine was overheating. So, to avoid this, I had to check the mags on the takeoff run. This really wasn't a good idea.*

*I also remember the P-63s required constant fuel management to maintain flight trim. Another worry, another headache.*

*As luck would have it, I was assigned to an air base in Seattle after ferrying a new Bell P-63 out to Great Falls, Montana. That assignment required me to pilot worn out P-39s being returned to the United States from the Russians. In my opinion, the P-39s were no good when new. I sure as hell didn't like flying the worn-out Cobras one bit.*

*I pleaded with the CO in Seattle to please send me back to my base as I had left Farmingdale on a short hop to Newark in a P-47 and wound up in Great Falls by way of a P-63 out of Niagara, New York. I had been away over three weeks with only one uniform. I was gone so long, nobody would remember me. The CO in Seattle felt sorry for me and gave me a flight back as copilot in a B-17. Wow, what a great airplane. Almost as much fun to fly as a Jug.*

Betty Gillies' first P-38 trip turned out to be an aesthetic experience she never forgot. Here's her recollection about it fifty-five years later:

*The morning I took off in my first P-38 to ferry it back East, Long Beach was almost closed. We had an eight hundred to thousand-foot scud ceiling — wind driven clouds and mist. The tower said 'go' and I did. Really, they gave me clearance before they should have.*

*I plowed right up through it, though, and fast — this was a P-38*

*—and when I got on top of it, the plane burst out into this beauty. I was headed right for the San Jacinto Mountains. Two snow-capped mountains and the sun coming through the pass between them. Down below it was black fog. But the sun was coming up and it caught my silver wings and turned them to gold. It was the most beautiful thing I had ever seen. Suddenly I was flying on golden wings.*

As squadron commander at Long Beach, B. J. Erickson had her own fair share of vivid memories. Especially this one involving a P-38:

*I was very lucky, but I lost six of my girls during my time at Long Beach.*

*I wrote to my mother and father every week I was in the service. I wrote to them after Nancy and I flew to Cornelia's funeral in Nashville. We took a C-47 and I was her co-pilot. I tried to tell them not to worry. Then again after Evelyn died. I tried to reassure them. Evelyn was my best friend. But I only had one close call. Just like several of the others, it was in a P-38.*

*One of the advantages of being in Long Beach was we had all these factories close by and all these planes that we could fly. Well, one night I got a call. "Look kid, I've got some P-38s down here. Do any of you girls want to check out in one at night?" Well, down I went. I had flown the P-38 in daylight by then. No problem. I took it up and flew around for an hour. But when it came time to land, I couldn't get the gear down.*

*Well, I called the tower and they called Jack.*

[Jack London was head of flight transition for the entire base at Long Beach. He and B.J. already were dating and would end up getting married in the spring of 1945.]

*They told him, "We've got one of your airplanes."*

*Well, he drove over to the tower, got on the radio, and gave me instructions out of the manual. I had to pump the gear down. I had no hydraulics. So I went out over the ocean and flew around for an hour and pumped. Then I flew by the tower for them to see if the gear was down.*

*I was cleared to land, but because I had no hydraulics, I also had no flaps and no brakes. I was going to have to land without* brakes. *So they told me to land on the longest runway, 25 Right. Now Long Beach had five runways and there were one hundred airplanes parked in the area in the center and those airplanes were guarded by armed sentries with dogs.*

*Well, Jack got in his Jeep and came racing out to the runways to meet me. I landed and rolled all the way to the end of the runway. Then I had to find a place to park it.*

*The guard, with his dog, sees this airplane coming down the runway from one direction and a Jeep racing in from the other. He didn't know what was going on and raised his gun. I was watching all this from the cockpit and I just knew he was going to shoot Jack. But Jack stopped the Jeep, hollered to the guard, threw his ID on the ground, and got out with his hands in the air. Fortunately, the guard didn't shoot him, but I know for a minute there, he thought he had nabbed a saboteur red handed.*

*After Jack convinced the guard that we weren't there to blow up airplanes, Jack helped me park the P-38 and drove me back to Operations.*

*Like I said, that was my only close call in all my time in the WAFS. Those Rosie the Riveters built good airplanes!*

*You know, if anybody had the best job in the whole of the women in the Ferrying Division, it was me. Of all the WASPs and WAFS. I was one of the youngest girls, and yet I was the squadron commander at the best base. I was better off than Betty because I had so many more planes to fly — and a better location. We flew every day. They sat on the ground back east. I was better off than Nancy because she had so many other jobs she had to do.*

*I got everything first — the best location, I ran the squadron, I had the airplanes. Everything was built in the LA Basin. They all fought to get a P-47 to bring out here so they could come get checked out in the other airplanes. I was the luckiest of all and I'm the first one to admit it.*

*It was a fantastic time in our lives. We were lucky to be alive then and equipped to do the job. It all depends on where you are and when. Timing is everything.*

**War-weary, battered B-17**

**Nancy Batson climbing into a P-47**

Photo autographed: **To my chum Jamesie**
**Good Luck — Nancy Batson**
**August 30, 1944**

# 32

One of the least publicized facets of the work all the pilots did for the Ferrying Division in the second half of 1944 was to move war-weary airplanes. These planes had either been manhandled by students at training bases or had actually been flown back from overseas where they had been shot at. Mostly, these sad ships were destined either for "the bone yard" or to be used for ground instruction or target practice. These were the airplanes referred to as "Class 26."

"The Air Transport Command in its resolve to be primary movers of any and all airplanes, took over this chore," says Delphine Bohn. "We, the Ferrying Division females, were given our share of the orders covering these movements. They were, however, never publicized."

Nancy Love and B.J. Erickson once moved a Class 26 B-17 — a very tired, hard-ridden lady named Genevieve — from Patterson Field in Ohio to Amarillo, Texas. The third member of the crew on the lady's last flight was her equally war-weary crew chief.

"The propellers took turns running away, the superchargers malfunctioned, and we couldn't retract the gear," Nancy related. "So there we were staggering along toward Scott Field, when here comes a flight of P-47s alongside us. All the pilots were grinning derisively and pointing to our landing gear, making 'up' signals. We could just hear them saying 'women drivers.'"

Teresa James claims, "Flying war-weary junk airplanes gave me more than a few gray hairs." Here's one harrowing experience she's never forgotten:

*I picked up an A-25 out West, late in 1944. I nursed that baby all the way to the east coast. It took several days to make the trip. First, I couldn't get the gear up, so I had to stop and have that fixed. Then the radios went out and I stopped at another base. Next, I couldn't get the bomb-bay doors closed.*

*On the final leg of the flight, as I was approaching Aberdeen, Maryland — my final destination — exhaust fumes poured into the cockpit and I had to request a straight-in approach. They cleared me and I had to land with the canopy open and the wind blowing in my face. It was hard to see the exact height above the ground.*

*As my wheels touched the runway, the control tower operator said, "That was a beautiful landing."*

*I replied, "You ought to see me grease them in when I'm not applying my lipstick."*

*I walked into Operations to get my Memorandum Receipt signed for the aircraft and told them how much trouble I had getting there in one piece.*

*The officer said, "Well, no wonder. It's a Class 26 airplane."*

*"What does that mean?" I ask.*

*"They'll taxi it out to the Aberdeen Proving Ground and use it for bombing practice. The pilots will bomb the hell out of it to find out how accurate their air strikes are."*

The P-38 Betty Gillies flew out of Harrisburg that quit on her on takeoff was one of many war-weary Lightnings she flew in the latter part of 1944. "These were airplanes that had been sent back from the European war zones, and they were very, very tired," said Betty. Back stateside, the engines of some of the P-38s were reconditioned and modified to use automobile fuel rather than the standard aviation fuel.

As Nancy Batson recalled:

*There were six of us that went over to Baltimore to pick up these worn-out trainers. "Jill McCormick was one of 'em. I don't remember who else. We were to take those planes up to Reading, Pennsylvania, to the bone yard — a field where they parked the war-wearies.*

*I was the flight leader so I took off first — right out over the water — and the others were supposed to follow me. We were going to circle until everybody got off and then fly up there in loose formation. Well, I take off and I'm looking behind me, counting one, two, three, four, five. Then, out of the corner of my eye, here comes a boat tearing along the shore. I looked down and there was*

*Jill McCormick, perched on the wing of her airplane, which is siting in the water off the runway. Her engine quit on takeoff and she couldn't get it stopped in time. She went right off the end of the runway into the water.*

*Well, I kept on flyin'. The rest of us went on to Reading. And it turns out my compass didn't work. Amazing what you can do when you look at the ground and watch the section lines. I had my good ol' trusty chart. I set up a course and flew by the seat of my pants and I found it. You get pretty damn good navigating like that when you do it every day. If it's a matter of life and death, you get real good at it.*

Delphine Bohn and a WASP copilot named Ann took a beat-up B-25 from Brooks Field to Kelly Field, a short hop across San Antonio. She writes:

> Personal discomfort began when we were placed aboard a Brooks' Operations Jeep and carried to the area that served as a morgue for student-harassed aircraft. They groaned and clattered and, in that intense heat, smelled strongly of defeated, decayed metal. All that highly heat-retentive metal took the one hundred degree-plus heat and made it soar past all red lines.
>
> This massacred B-25 was in a shocking condition. It was coated with thick, red rust. It was without a canopy. And it obviously had been through a series of winter and spring storms. The cowling for one engine flapped noisily. The tires — the rubber rapidly disintegrating — were soft and flat. Heavy stains on the concrete under the airplane made it known that the craft was without life-giving fluids.
>
> Mechanics readied the airplane for flight. From them we learned part of the airplane's morbid history. The engines periodically fell out of their nacelles.
>
> By now, we were soaked with sweat. The heat was merciless, the sunlight, blinding.
>
> Our reluctance to climb aboard was real. Contact between bare hands, bare arms, even pants-covered

derrieres with blistering metal was something out of hell.

Aboard and with engines started, we were able to keep them running. The tower gave us clearance and we taxied to the take-off point. Heat waves distorted our long taxi. We considered shutting down and departing, afoot, that field of unhappy, ghost aircraft.

The airplane's history intimidated us. But then pride, a downfall in too many instances, took over and we rolled into our takeoff run. We managed gear up. But when we started a left turn at pattern altitude, we were thwarted. All efforts to make a left turn were useless. Our controls to the left were frozen. We and the tower concurred that we make only right turns in our traffic pattern.

On our final approach for our landing runway at Kelly, our speed was excessive. We flew the airplane onto the airport. Ann called out the airspeed in increments of five miles per hour or less. We had decided that if an engine fell out of its nacelle, it wasn't going to be the result of insufficient speed.

Coming over the fence, we saw that airport traffic was at a stand still. A mass of waiting humanity — students, mechanics, instructors, office personnel — were gathered for a grandstand view awaiting the probable disintegration of a dishonored airplane, or the pilots' courage, or both.

And then we were down. One more Class 26 delivered!

As the summer of 1944 wore on and the news out of Washington as to their status grew ever more dismal, the description "war weary" began to apply to more than the hapless airplanes The Originals flew. Their ranks had begun to shrink.

Betsy Ferguson, sent to Dallas in January 1943, had surgery and was put on sick leave. By fall 1943, Barbara Towne Dickson was several months pregnant — to the point where she could no longer get the stick back or easily climb in and out of the P-51s she had just begun to ferry out of Long Beach. She left the squadron, had a baby boy in December, and early in 1944 resumed ferrying. But as mentioned earlier, Barbara was not satisfied with the arrangements she had made for her son's care. She finally left the squadron later in 1944, to take care of him, after trying very hard to stay and do the job she wanted to do and for which she had trained.

By late summer of 1944, Del Scharr was grounded with apparent anemia. Helen McGilvery had a bout with pneumonia, as did Delphine Bohn, Dorothy Fulton, and Esther Manning. Several others were fighting one illness or other, probably brought on by lack of proper rest and the stress of an uncertain future.

Barbara Poole, Phyllis Burchfield, and Katherine Rawls Thompson all had left in the latter half of 1943. Esther Manning, after giving birth to her son in August 1943, had rejoined the 2nd Ferrying Group as Betty Gillies' administrative assistant and took an occasional flight. However, she was not checked out in pursuit aircraft. Illness finally forced both her and Dorothy Fulton out in 1944. That fall, Florene Miller left to get married, and Bernice Batten resigned and joined the Women Marines.

Cornelia Fort, Dorothy Scott and Evelyn Sharp were dead. And Teresa, since the news of Dink's disappearance, was a shadow of her former fun-loving self.

On September 4, 1944, Nancy Love wrote a letter to 5th Ferrying Group women's squadron leader Delphine Bohn who was, at that point, grounded and recuperating from pneumonia. Part of that letter is included in *Catch a Shooting Star*:

> The WASP situation remains in its usual SNAFU state, but I've acquired a new slant on it, and have tried to transmit same to the gals, i.e., we are now the long-sought-for, small select group. We've got a heck of a good record behind us and an even rosier one ahead, or should have with this bunch of good pilots. So forget the newspapers, the Training Command, J.C., WTS/CAA and the whole damned mess — and fly!
>
> If the WASPs are abolished, we're still civilian pilots, and darned good ones, and though I've outgrown optimism in the last two years, I have it on pretty good authority that we who are left in the Ferrying Division are not to worry, but to keep mouths shut, eyes on the ball, stop

arguing and fly the pants off any and all airplanes assigned to us — from L2s . . . to A-20s or B-17s.

I haven't seen J.C. in months, and have assiduously avoided her: our airplanes were both on Long Beach at the same time, but there's no use arguing with her — she only twists statements.

So that's the deal and I still have hopes — wouldn't it be nice not to be anything but c/ps (civilian pilots) again, no WASP or even WAFS?

. Anyhow, there's no use in getting het up and having a nervous breakdown over the deal. When you get back, you'll find your squadron small and self-sufficient, and there's no reason squadron leaders can't get out and have fun — only one responsible person need be there. We've all gotten so violent about this that I think its broken down our health — you and Esther Manning with pneumonia, I've had flu and now have trench mouth, of all things. And Erickson looks like a ghost. So let's stop worrying and have fun — and see what happens.

Nancy — you know, POLLYANNA — Love

Of course, it didn't turn out as Nancy Love had hoped. Hap Arnold picked up Jacqueline Cochran's gauntlet, thrown down in early August, and on October 3, 1944, announced that with the graduation of the class of women at Sweetwater on December 7, the Women Airforce Service Pilots — WASPs — would be deactivated. December 20 would be the WASP termination date. No one was exempt. Approximately 130 women ferry pilots now serving the Ferrying Division so well and with such dedication — ferrying two-thirds of all pursuit aircraft manufactured in the United States and so desperately needed to keep those aircraft moving to embarkation points for overseas — were being released as well. Nancy Love and her remaining WAFS were not spared.

The letters notifying them of deactivation were delivered on October 8 to all active WASPs — those with the Training Command and those on duty with the ATC's Ferrying Groups.

A little more than two weeks prior to that, however, the women ferry pilots had one more magnificent hurrah to their credit, and, once again, it was Teresa James who led the way — by the luck of the draw.

By mid-September 1944, Republic Aviation had put out word that it was nearing production of its 10,000th P-47 Thunderbolt.

The first P-47 had rolled off the line and been delivered to the Army on March 18, 1943. The Republic workforce, at that point, was 5,000 strong. Now, eighteen months later, 24,450 individuals — more than half of whom were women — were working at the Farmingdale plant. Production efficiency had improved as Republic worked to meet the Army's increased demands.

The first 773 Thunderbolts produced took 22,927 man/woman hours per ship. When that P-47 — known forever after as "Ten Grand" — rolled off the line in September 1944, total time was down to only 6,290 hours per aircraft. "The Racers," as the workers at the Farmingdale factory were called, were ready for the milestone. They had earned it.

Not counting government-furnished equipment such as engines, guns, radios, etc., by the time the 10,000th was produced, the initial cost of $68,750 (in 1942 dollars) per airplane had been reduced to $45,000. Republic Aviation Farmingdale Division earned the War Department's Army/Navy Production Award for the third time.

Teresa describes her unique relationship with Ten Grand:

*On September 22, 1944, they rolled Ten Grand through a paper curtain and out of the hangar door for delivery to the Army.*

*Everybody was there. Nancy Love, Betty Gillies, Gertrude Meserve, Helen Richey, all the other Farmingdale WASPs, and Lt. Joe Tracy who checked most of us WAFS out at Wilmington back in '42. And, of course, Jackie Cochran was there along with The Brass — President of Republic Aviation, Mr. Alfred Marchev, the Under Secretary of War Robert P. Patterson and a bunch of other uniforms. And the entire Thunderbolt workforce. They were a big part of the festivities.*

*I remember the Mitchel Field band led a march around the buildings and everybody applauded like crazy. There were a bunch of speeches, then they started to pull the aircraft up to the stand and the rope broke. They ended up having to push Ten Grand up to where Jackie stood, holding a bottle of champagne.*

*She was up on a lift-truck platform and she smashed the champagne bottle over the propeller hub. Then they moved the plane back and beckoned me to come on. I was the next pilot up to fly that morning. That's how I happened to be the one who took Ten Grand on its flight to Newark.*

*I stood around for awhile posing for pictures. Got tired of that pretty fast. Then I climbed up and they took a whole lot more pictures of me in the cockpit. Finally, they signaled me that I was clear to take off. I taxied that big beauty over to the duty runway and — off we go into the wild blue yonder — I was on my way to Newark. It was a very big day.*

IWASM

Ten Grand's first assignment was to the 79th Fighter Group of the 12th U.S. Army Air Force on the Italian Front, where it was first flown by the Group Commander, Colonel Gladwyn E. Pinkston.

**B.J. Erickson signs an autograph for a worker at the ceremony for the 10,000th Vultee BT-13.**

# WASP Squadron, 2nd Ferrying Group

**Front row, center: Betty Gillies and Nancy Love
(Housekeeper Mrs. Anderson appears on the right)
December 19, 1944**

# 33

Before General Tunner resigned his command of the Ferrying Division on July 31, 1944, to take over of the Hump Operation on the China/Burma/India front, he arranged to have two of the original WAFS test the feasibility of using women pilots on regularly scheduled cargo runs.

Nancy Love knew that a lot of the male ferry pilots wanted one of these Military Air Transport (MAT) runs and would be jealous of the women pilots getting such a plum assignment. She could smell trouble. But General Tunner stood by his decision. He wanted to prove that women could do this job. And the women chosen proved him to be correct in his assumption.

The "experiment" only lasted two weeks — August 2-16, 1944 — but that was long enough. B.J. Erickson and Florene Miller, both from the 6th Ferrying Group at Long Beach, were assigned to make daily runs in a C-47 from Romulus (Detroit) to Chicago. The military transport run by the Ferrying Division to move passengers around was referred to as SNAFU Airlines (Situation Normal All Fouled Up). This one carried passengers and cargo.

Both women had to qualify as first pilots for MAT. They had to meet strict requirements and pass a rigorous check flight. Two of the more experienced women pilots, they easily passed all checks and "got the job."

The flight regularly left Romulus in the morning at 0700, which necessitated their reporting for duty at 0530. They were never late.

"We were treated like any other airline," says B.J. "We landed and taxied up to the parking place and lined up along with all the other DC-3s loading and unloading. We wanted to put our wheel on our SPOT and be as professional as the regular airlines.

"There were some people who didn't like flying with girls up front, but we just closed the cockpit door and went about our business."

In fact, according to Florene, they were usually in their seats with the cockpit door closed before the passengers began to board. That way, nobody knew that two women were flying the airplane. But they did delight, upon landing, in exiting down the aisle of the airplane while the passengers were still getting their gear together. Watching the double takes and dropped jaws was great fun.

∽⟨◉⟩∾

As deactivation drew nearer, some rules that had been in place were eased or outright abandoned. One such instance came out of normally by-the-book, give-the-girls-no-quarter Romulus. The command staff of the 3rd Ferrying Group decided to let *Detroit News* reporter Gay Bartlett "take a ride" with WASP Lenore McElroy (one of the original WAFS) on a ferrying mission. "I'll give you a couple hours notice if I can," Major Francis Tilden, Public Relations Officer at Romulus Army Air Field, told Bartlett, "and we'll try to get you on one of the big amphibians."

This was definitely a first — a reporter riding along with a WASP on a delivery. The three-part story Bartlett wrote is dated November 2-5, 1944, and includes the following:

*The call came early Tuesday morning. "Probably be back tomorrow," the Major said. "Be out here by 8:30, to take off at 9." I tumbled into my clothes, stuck an extra shirt and a toothbrush into my bag, and whizzed out in a Detroit News chauffeur-driven car.*

*"You're going to Cheyenne in an OA-10," the Major said. It was a big white seagull of a plane, amphibious, and as queer looking as a Buck Rogers flying ship with its boat-shaped hull and pontooned wings.*

*Things were humming at WASP headquarters when we walked in. Our pilot was to be Lenore McElroy, one of the best of them all. Little — only about five feet two — keen eyes and dark curly hair, friendly but poised and sure. Mrs. McElroy is Operations Officer of the detachment of WASPs at the 3rd Ferrying Group and when not delivering planes herself, assigns other WASPs to ferrying missions. Two went out while I was waiting. The WASPs stationed here are always going or coming, rarely home longer than overnight.*

*Gracie Clark, from Wichita Falls, Texas, was to be the WASP co-pilot. It was her first trip in this type of ship. Cpl. Lawrence Suiter, just back from a ferrying mission to England, and Staff Sgt. Harold W. Smith, with eleven trips abroad to his credit, were radioman and engineer respectively. Gracie handed me my parachute. Everyone who rides in an Army plane has to wear one. I slung it over my shoulder the way they did, but it was bigger and heavier than I expected.*

*Pilot and co-pilot went into a huddle over a map of the airways, planning their course, noting the distances to be traveled and filling out busy-looking forms. Then to the weather room. "Kansas City, one mile of smoke; Moline, two miles of haze."*

*"OK, let's go," said Mac, as she picked up her chute, briefcase and overnight bag.*

*Everything was set for the cross country flight. We climbed aboard, dragging those parachutes behind us up the ladder and over the side. Cpl. Suiter took his place at the radio controls; Sgt. Smith disappeared into the top of the ship with only his feet visible at the upper part of the doorway. I perched on a high stool opposite the radioman and tried to watch everything at once.*

*Mac climbed up into the nose of the ship and slipped in, with Grace beside her, behind the huge instrument panel polka-dotted with intricate dials. The engines roared, first one then the other. The ship fairly danced with impatience to be off. Then as easily as though it were a light plane, Mac guided it smoothly and with assurance around the field to the runway. We stopped for a minute, waited for the go-sign radioed to the plane from the control tower, then zoomed down the runway, lifted into the air, and soared out into the blue.*

*I was fascinated with the ease with which Mac and Gracie controlled this impressive amphibian and was torn between a desire to watch over their shoulders and to look through the glass "blisters" at each side of the ship at the great panorama of smooth country below. Somewhere over the great patchwork of Indiana farms, Cpl. Suiter told me that the radio had gone dead. They said it wasn't anything to worry about, and before we reached Lincoln, Nebraska, our destination for that day, it was working again.*

*Mac rolled smoothly onto the airfield at Lincoln at 6 o'clock. Our amphibious ship was a novelty at this air base in arid Nebraska, but the eyes of the gallery that greeted us really widened when they saw the diminutive pilots.*

*"Did a girl fly this ship in," said the awe-struck gas-truck man. "Well, I'll be darned." I strutted around trying hard to look like a WASP too.*

*The blow came when someone called up to Mac before we left the plane. "Are you Mrs. McElroy? There's a message here for you." The base at Romulus had been trying to contact us to tell us that orders had been changed and the ship was to be delivered to Biloxi, Mississippi. That was when our radio had been out of commission.*

*The next day we flew southeast to Memphis, then on to Jackson.*

*Thursday morning an early start got us to Keesler Army Air Base at Biloxi, Mississippi, before noon where Mac "sold" our ship. The "selling" is figurative, involving only handing over the papers. One more ferrying job completed, the crew made plans for the home trip. I was their chief concern. Being a civilian, it meant that commercial airliners were probably impossible for me, while all but the President must make way for a WASP [any ferry pilot].*

*All was well after Lt. Charles Armbruster, Assistant Operations Officer at Keesler Field, said he could take us to Mobile in a B-25. The pilot had been on combat duty for a year overseas and could really "rack that plane around," as Gracie put it.*

*From Mobile, a C-46 was leaving at 10 p.m. for Fort Wayne and we could catch a ride on that. That was fine. From Fort Wayne we could go directly to Romulus by way of Military Air Transport (called the "MAT" or "SNAFU" airline) which takes crews back home after they've delivered their planes.*

*But the trick was to find the plane in the inky darkness. It was somewhere out on the field in the midst of scores of others. However, we had the number and a flashlight. We piled our chutes, brief cases and baggage on the back of a tiny Jeep and seven of us — our own five, the driver and another passenger, a soldier headed for Fort Wayne — climbed on top of the load and hung on as the little wagon went bumping and hopping over the field, sneaking in and out among planes, searching each ship for the right number.*

*We had hardly climbed aboard when the crew arrived and we took off for Fort Wayne. But we never arrived there. About a half an hour out of Mobile the ship gave a lurch. The radioman dashed out of the cockpit, literally ran through the plane, and spotted his flashlight on the port engine. We were losing altitude. That engine was out.*

*Will we crash land? Or is it serious at all? I didn't know. But when Mac started buckling her chute on, I wasted no more time. I thought I'd never get mine adjusted. Gracie said, "You'll go out that window and just slide off the wing, head first. Don't worry, the wind will push you. Then count ten."*

*"That long," I objected.*

*"Well, if you don't want to wait, just look back and make sure you've cleared the plane."*

*Imagine having presence of mind to do that while hurtling earthward in the middle of the night. Anyway I wanted to know what I was jumping into down there.*

*It was almost a letdown when we were told to sit down and buckle our safety belts around us. We were going to make it to Key Field at Meridian before too much altitude had been lost. The landing was without an extra bump, the taxiing in perfect, and the ambulances and fire trucks left the runway we'd come in on. Another false alarm.*

*We waited until 2:30 for the plane to be put in commission, then gave up and went to bed, once again finding refuge with the Army nurses.*

*Friday morning, the C-46 had been repaired and gone on to Fort Wayne without us. My heart sank when commercial airliners were mentioned. Sure enough, when the airliner landed at Meridian, room was made for the crew. From there, Mac said, I could go on by Military Air Transport, which was leaving sometime in the evening for Romulus. They went up the ramp leaving me with anxious thoughts about my return and last minute directions about getting to Birmingham.*

As duty required, the WASP crew went home without Bartlett. After a five and a half-hour bus ride to Birmingham, she caught a MAT plane home, arriving at Romulus around four in the morning.

Mac, Gracie and the guys were in their own beds by the time Bartlett's feet touched down on Michigan soil. But she had her story.

⊷⊙⊕⊶

One thing the women ferry pilots always are asked is how did they cope with the lack of toilet facilities on Army airplanes on long, cross-country trips — particularly in the single-seaters with the tight cockpits.

"There's no good way," says B.J. Erickson. "The relief tubes provided for the men were of little use to the women, though some of them tried them if they were desperate. Don't drink a lot of coffee in the mornings, was the best rule. Nowadays, you can take along a three pound coffee can with a tight lid. Back then, we were strapped into a parachute."

Lodging could vary considerably on ferrying trips, from nice hotels to not-so-desirable hotels, to the Nurses Quarters' on some bases, to sleeping on a hotel lobby couch, which Betty Gillies did one time in one of Dallas' better hotels. "The man vacuuming the lobby actually apologized when he woke me up."

"I took an A-20 from Douglas to Daggett," says B.J. "The only thing there was a weather station. No hotel. No place to sleep. No place to eat. We biked around the airport for exercise and slept under the wing of an airplane. We were young and pliable."

"It was fun," Betty Gillies adds. "I never had so much fun in my life. Here I am, a mother leaving all my responsibilities to my darling husband and my mother-in-law and they did fine! You had the attitude that no matter what happened, you could do it. You had no fear, no worry. You coped with the situation. You went ahead and did it. We were professionals."

# 34

Ferry pilots were only half joking when they said that the work they did involved hours of boredom interspersed with moments of sheer terror. Most of the stories that rate telling are of the flights where something went drastically wrong because they usually involved the drama of a life-threatening crisis. Obviously, most of the flights flown by WWII ferry pilots were without incident because of the incredible safety and on-time delivery record established by both the male and female pilots. But it is Murphy's law that if anything can go wrong, it will, and, like it or not, it is those instances that make for far more riveting reading. History is history, but certainly it can be enhanced by drama — particularly when the dramatic actually did take place.

Such is the story of Nancy Batson's harrowing P-38 flight over Pittsburgh.

Yes, the P-38 again. A new P-38 Lightning killed Evelyn Sharp. A war-weary Lightning tried to kill Betty Gillies — on the same field where Evelyn died. And B.J. Erickson had experienced nose-wheel problems with a P-38 at Long Beach. Now, here was yet another of the original WAFS wrestling with the vagaries of this sleek, powerful machine of death and destruction that Delphine Bohn called, alternately, Athena (the goddess of war) and a malevolent genie.

The same Tuesday in November 1944 that Franklin Delano Roosevelt won his unprecedented fourth term as President of the United States, Nancy Batson tried to crowd FDR off the front page of the Pittsburgh daily newspapers. She would just as soon have skipped the whole affair, would have much preferred a quiet uneventful delivery of her airplane to Newark without all the fuss.

*I picked up this brand new P-38 in California with orders to deliver it to Newark, New Jersey. I took off cross-country and made my last stop in Pittsburgh to refuel. When I left from there, I was headed directly for Newark. About twenty minutes out of Pittsburgh, I noticed that the two engine coolant needles were moving back and forth erratically instead of holding steady.*

*Already too many P-38s — including Evelyn Sharp's — had lost engines. So I turned back to Pittsburgh, called the tower to get permission to land, and was cleared for a straight in approach. I reached down and activated the gear handle and listened for the hum of the wheels descending into the down and locked position. But the lights on the instrument panel showed that the nose-wheel was not down and locked. The lights are in a triangle. The two at the bottom showed green, meaning that the main gear was down, but the nose-wheel light was red, meaning it wasn't down and locked.*

*Now the P-38 has these shiny aluminum reflectors on the sides of each of the engine nacelles that acted as mirrors — so the pilot can check and see if the nose-wheel is in the down and locked position. Well, the nose-wheel was just hanging there.*

Though Nancy didn't know it, she was having the same kind of problem B.J. Erickson had experienced only two months earlier with that night check-out flight out of Long Beach.

*I called the tower and advised them of my situation. Well, they wanted me to do a fly-by, low, and raise my left wing so that they could see for sure that the nose-wheel wasn't in the landing position.*

*I did the fly-by and they determined that, no, it wasn't locked in place. By then the coolant needles seemed to have stabilized. So I flew out away from the airport, away from traffic. I was going to try to pump the wheel down manually. The hydraulic pump, called a wobble pump, was there for the pilot to use to do exactly what I had to do, pump a faulty nose gear down by hand.*

*Well, I started pumping. Then I stopped and looked out at the mirrors and that wheel hadn't moved. So I pumped some more. Nothing!*

*The tower called periodically and asked how I was doing. I told them, "I'm still flyin' over Pittsburgh and still pumpin' and I still have a red light."*

Every airplane within earshot of the Pittsburgh radio frequency heard the exchanges between Nancy and the tower. A woman — particularly one with a Southern accent — flying around in a P-38 wasn't exactly an everyday occurrence.

*Well, finally I could see that what I was doing wasn't working. By now, the needle on the fuel gauge was telling me that I was getting low on gas. I was going to have to do something else.*

*There was also a $CO_2$ cartridge there that a pursuit pilot in combat could use to blow the nose-wheel down as a last resort. But at the factory, they told us very emphatically not to use the $CO_2$ cartridge because it might damage the landing gear — that it was there to save some combat pilot's life. About that time, it looked like the pilot whose life might need saving was mine!*

*I was in an emergency situation. I was going to have to do what I call creative flying. So I did. I horsed back on the wheel and at the same time reached down and pulled the $CO_2$ cartridge to see if that would sling it out.*

*Guess what? The green light came on. Was I relieved to see it! Then I looked down at that aluminum mirror on the nacelle and the nose-wheel was down and locked, just like it was supposed to be!*

Unbeknownst to Nancy, while she was flying around away from the airport pumping the wobble pump, someone in the tower called Nancy Love in Cincinnati to tell her that one of her WASPs was in trouble.

"Who is it?" Nancy Love asked.

"Nancy Batson," the man in the tower told her.

"Oh, don't worry about her. She'll be fine," Nancy Love told him.

It was years later before Nancy Batson learned the kind of confidence her commander, fellow pilot and friend had in her.

"She never said a thing to me. Never called me or asked about the problem I had. I was a trained, professional ferry pilot, doing my job. She expected us to handle situations as they came up. That's what ferry pilots do. We never knew what kind of plane we would be flying. All we knew was, they told us to take care of those planes so that they'd be in good shape for those boys to fly in overseas."

By then someone else knew about Nancy and her problem with the nose-wheel.

Fellow ferry pilot Helen Richey was inbound to Pittsburgh, also en route on a delivery to Newark. She heard the exchanges between the tower at the Pittsburgh airport and the woman in the balky P-38 who spoke with a decidedly Southern accent. She recognized Nancy's voice immediately.

By then it was getting late in the afternoon so when Helen landed, instead of refueling and going on, she called her home base and told them that she was going to RON in Pittsburgh that night. She had decided to wait out her friend's safe return. Besides, Helen was from Pittsburgh. She was going to spend that night with her sister and take Nancy with her. Helen figured it would take awhile for the mechanics to check over the airplane and her friend would be in need of a good night's sleep.

*I called the tower and told them the nose-wheel was locked in place, but they said they wanted me to slow-fly by the tower so that they could see for sure if it was down.*

*Shoot, by that time, I'd had enough of that P-38. Besides, by now I was really low on fuel! I told them I was coming in. They gave me permission to land.*

*I decided right then and there that I was going to make this the best landing of my life. And I did.*

*I was cleared for a straight in approach and I greased it. I put that sick airplane in the proper landing attitude and touched down on the main wheels. Then I held that back pressure on the stick — back, back all the way into my stomach — and kept that nose wheel up as long as possible. Then finally I let it touch down and did the roll out.*

*As I was rolling down the runway, out of the corner of my eye on my left I noticed this Jeep running alongside, signaling me to stop. So I did. And this guy jumps up on my wing and he says, "Get out, I'll taxi it in."*

*He was kind of nervous. So I looked back at him and said, "No, I'll do it."*

*Well, he got off the wing and I looked over my left shoulder and — much to my surprise — here came a couple of fire engines, an ambulance, several cars — a whole line of vehicles behind me. I taxied on in and stopped. And now here was a line of people waiting for me — photographers, Red Cross ladies who told me, "We've been prayin' for you, honey," airport officials, and lots of other people.*

*That's when they took that picture that ran on the front page of the Pittsburgh paper the next morning — along with the news that Roosevelt had been reelected. Then I turned the airplane over to the mechanics and told them what the problem was and they told me it would take a couple of days to check it out.*

*Helen Richey was waiting for me. She took me to her sister's to spend the night.*

*I woke up in the middle of the night with this awful throbbing, aching pain in my right shoulder and upper arm. I had to wake Helen up and ask her if her sister had any aspirin. She found me some. I was OK the next morning.*

*When the airplane was ready two days later, I flew it out of Pittsburgh and on into Newark. Coming in, I got my clearance from the tower to land, reached down and put the gear handle in the down position. Same damn thing! Two green lights and one red one.*

*I didn't think twice about it this time. I reached down and pulled that $CO_2$ cartridge and that nose-wheel locked into position. Thank heavens they had fixed that!*

*I landed and taxied it up to the guys waiting and said, "Boys, I've brought you a real lemon."*

The women pilots of the Ferrying Division continued to fly until as close to December 20 as possible. They were still needed. Pursuit airplanes were coming off the production lines faster than the ferrying squadrons could deliver them. And every pursuit was vitally needed overseas to win what was then a very hot war. In Europe, the Battle of the Bulge was about to begin.

"On December 15, a Saturday, the officers stationed at the New

Castle Army Air Field passed in review to honor the WASP for our service in the cause of victory," Sis Bernheim says. "My last ferry flight, a P-47 to Newark, was December 17, 1944. A few short days thereafter was the end."

"My last trip was in a P-61 to Sacramento on December 19," B.J. Erickson remembers. "We were picked up by military transport (SNAFU airlines) and brought back to Long Beach. I left for home the following day."

"My last two ferry flights," recalls Gertrude Meserve Tubbs LeValley, "were in P-47 Thunderbolts whose numbers were

IWASM

44-20940 and 44-20946, from Farmingdale to Newark on December 14, 1944. From there, we were flown to our home base in Wilmington in the C-60 Lockheed Lodestar, which I had flown any number of times myself, taking the other women pilots back to Farmingdale. That flight to Wilmington was my last one in a military aircraft and it was a very sad day, to say the least. The following week was used to turn in all of my military equipment in preparation to checking out of the 2nd Ferrying Group and off the base on December 20th. *Another sad day!*"

"Batson and I closed up the operation at Republic Aviation, December 19," says Teresa James. "We flew P-47s over to Newark that morning, and when we left Farmingdale, there was still a whole bunch of them sitting there and nobody to fly them. We were heart broken. Remember, it was all women in that ferrying squadron. No men."

"On Tuesday, December 19, I flew my last P-47 over the Empire State Building and on into Newark," Nancy Batson remembers. "As I flew, and felt all that power, that big engine, the speed, I knew I would never in my life again fly anything like that airplane.

"I spent that last afternoon in Wilmington turning in my flying gear, my parachute, the fleece-lined jacket, my gun — we actually had to carry a gun on some of those pursuit flights. If it looked like the airplane might fall into enemy hands we were supposed to shoot it — not the enemy — destroy the top-secret equipment in the airplane so it wouldn't fall into enemy hands.

"When I was all finished, I was crushed."

Banquets honoring the WASPs were held by each of the Ferrying Groups the evening of December 19. B.J. Erickson, Helen Richards (pictured below) and Del Scharr were the only Originals left in Long

Beach, and Del had already been given permission to leave the base with a medical discharge. Florene Miller had left that fall to get married. B.J. had served as leader for the entire twenty-three months of the 6th Ferrying Group women's squadron's existence.

Down at Dallas' Love Field, Delphine Bohn, squadron leader since December 1943, and Esther Nelson, a late transfer from

Wilmington and other duty bases, were the only Originals among the attendees at that banquet. Betsy Ferguson was serving with the WASPs in the Training Command at Walker Field in Kansas. Bernice Batten had already left to join the Women Marines.

Up in Romulus, squadron leader Barbara Donahue — the only Original left from Wilmington — was joined by Lenore McElroy, the only Original who did not start off in Wilmington. Lenore was second in command at Romulus throughout Donnie's tenure as leader, which began summer 1943 when Nancy Love transferred Del Scharr back to Wilmington and subsequently to Long Beach.

But in Wilmington, the eight Originals still actively flying gathered along with the rest of the squadron on December 19 at the NCAAB Officers' Club for what that group termed "The Last Supper." Dressed in their WASP uniform jackets, skirts and wings, the eight sat — Last Supper style — at the head table with Betty Gillies, squadron commander, and Nancy Love in the center. To Nancy's right were Nancy Batson, Helen McGilvery, and Gertrude Meserve Tubbs. To Betty's left were her assistant squadron leader, Helen Mary Clark, Teresa James, and Sis Bernheim. The rest of the squadron, thirty graduates of Houston or Sweetwater, sat at tables down each side of the head table, making a U.

The dinner was chicken à la king, sweet potato croquets, fresh fruit, chocolate eclairs and rare French wine to help with the toasts, which were sometimes long and often teary. Finally, the thirty-eight weary WASPs — including eight stalwart original WAFS — found the exhaustion of emotion to be too much. They said goodnight for the last time and went back to BOQ 14 to finish packing.

Not long after that, a male voice outside shouted, "Fire!"

Out they went, some clad in bathrobes, others in coats, some in both, into the cold December night. The women joined the crowd of male officers outside the Officers' Club that had been their haven for twenty-seven months and where they had just eaten their last dinner as active duty ferry pilots.

Nancy Batson looked at the building as it went down in flames. "Let it burn!" she hollered, and added a Rebel yell. "Let it burn!"

Teresa's recollection of December 20, 1944 is this:

*I remember it like it was yesterday when I walked out that gate. I stood there with the same emotion I felt later when they found Dink. Something died right there. After flying for twenty-seven months with the women like you were sisters, flying around the country and then coming back and chatting about it — just like a big family, and then all of a sudden you lose that.*

*How could we go home to people who didn't understand? We became part of each other because we could talk about what happened, the scary moments, and bolster each other. We became very close, and all of a sudden this association has ended. A letdown like this is bound to create a problem for a lot of people. There was a great deal of alcoholism afterwards — we had to get lost in something.*

*Fortunately for me, my parents had the family flower business, so I got lost in work. I felt sorry for the girls who didn't have families to go back to.*

*I was devastated when we were disbanded. I tried to get into the Chinese Air Force. They wrote me a nice letter saying they didn't need pilots. I tried the airlines and they all told me public opinion wouldn't permit a female pilot in the cockpit, even if she had a four-engine rating. So I went back to flight instruction, but there were very few students after the war. Private aviation was at a low ebb.*

എᏜᎶᏜᴗ

Nancy Love left on December 20 to ferry a C-54 (four-engine transport) to California.

"I'm going to fly all night and think about what has happened to me . . . and to us . . . . "

# EPILOGUE

When the WASPs of the 6th Ferrying Group, Long Beach, left for good on December 20, 1944, according to B.J. Erickson, there were sixty-six P-51s sitting on the runway at North American Aviation in the LA Basin — undeliverable because there weren't enough qualified pursuit ferry pilots to take them to Newark. The women who had been delivering them daily were gone. A similar dilemma existed at Farmingdale, Buffalo, Niagara, and Evansville.

Aviation expert Captain Gill Robb Wilson of the staff of the New York *Herald Tribune*, wrote:

> Training of men to take their [the WASP ferry pilots] places will require a million dollars, from four to six months' time, and even then will not replace the broad experience which the women have built up on pursuit-type aircraft. I just do not think the United States is rich enough to throw away two-hundred expert pilots, regardless of who they are.

Actually, the number of women pilots in the Ferrying Division as deactivation neared was one hundred thirty-six, of which one hundred seventeen were Class P or qualified pursuit pilots.

When General William H. Tunner left at the end of July 1944 to take command of The Hump, as the China-Burma-India Theater of War was known, General Robert E. Nowland replaced him as commander of the Ferrying Division. On November 1, 1944, Nowland wrote:

> [The WASP's] replacements must be chosen from the ranks of our more experienced personnel, since it has been demonstrated that a minimum of 400 hours and an instrument card are necessary prerequisites for pursuit training and subsequent safe delivery of fighters. The 117 WASPS we have been using on pursuit deliveries are already experienced in this specialized type of flying and have established a remarkable low accident record. There have been only two fatalities in their eighteen months of pursuit deliveries,

and both of these were due to mechanical failure.

The cost of training a fighter pilot at the 4th OTU [Brownsville Pursuit School] is approximately $9336 or $1,085,312 for the 117 replacements required upon the discharge of the WASPs . . . This same sum has, of course, already been spent on the trained WASPs and will represent an additional loss.

ATC Headquarters suggested that if the women could be kept on temporarily, no additional women pilots would be employed and that the 117 women pursuit pilots would be discharged gradually as qualified male pilots became available to replace them. As deactivation neared, most of the women of the Ferrying Division offered to fly for free in order to stay on and get the job done.

All of this, of course, went for naught. A Congress and military establishment so concerned about the expenditure of money on the training of women pilots, had no qualms whatsoever about spending an equal amount on the training of male pilots to replace female pilots already trained to do the same job.

Whatever the reasoning, the women felt betrayed. They had given their all. They knew they were still needed and yet they were dismissed. The Originals were, and still are, understandably bitter over Jacqueline Cochran's interference with Nancy Love's program and with her heavy-handed tactics which, ultimately, led to the deactivation of all women pilots flying for the Army in December 1944. For all she may have done to offer more than a thousand other women a chance to fly, the WAFS generally feel Cochran tainted — with her meddling — what they originally were recruited and hired to do. She and Nancy Love had different goals.

Nancy Love's intent from the very beginning was to recruit approximately fifty experienced women pilots to fly for their country in time of war and release male pilots for more hazardous duty. She had no aspirations to be a commander of anything. This is borne out in her lack of interest in later life of pursuing a career, or even a philanthropic or community activist role where her organizational and managerial skills would have been an asset. Her motivation had been simply to fly airplanes for her country.

Jackie Cochran wanted to train a corps of women pilots over whom she would have command authority — or as some called it, her own personal female Air Force. Cochran sought the affirmation of being "number one." She went on, after the war, to chase aviation records and "firsts" and to carve for herself a place in aviation history second, at least in her eyes and in the eyes of many others as well, to no woman.

There was merit in both their approaches given the fluctuating needs of a nation at war. In a perfect world, both programs would have been allowed to prosper. That was not to be.

&#8272;&#8272;&#8272;

Being sent home created a huge void in the women pilots' lives. Doing what one could to help win the war was on every American's mind back in those days from 1942 to 1945. Patriotism was at an all-time high. Once an integral part of a mighty war machine, overnight the WASPs were nothing — cast aside and forgotten like yesterday's garbage. They were devastated.

For women like Nancy Batson, B.J. Erickson, Teresa James, Gertrude Meserve, and one hundred thirteen other pursuit ferry pilots, deactivation meant stepping out of the cockpit of a hot P-47 or P-51 or P-38 for the LAST time — ever — and walking away. They knew they would never again fly anything remotely as fast, as powerful, as prestigious, as exciting as those "peashooters." And they had to walk away knowing that their job wasn't finished.

What now?

It is interesting to note that what happened to the WASPs was happening to all women in the United States on a much larger scale. It wasn't just a result of out-of-work flight instructors or a balky, conservative Congress — a not-so-subtle propaganda campaign had begun designed to get women out of those wartime jobs and back into the kitchen.

In *No Ordinary Time — Franklin and Eleanor Roosevelt: The Home Front in World War II*, Doris Kearns Goodwin points out that in the summer of 1944, the War Department published a pamphlet entitled "Do You Want Your Wife to Work After the War?"

As demobilization loomed on the horizon, the image of women as comrades-in-arms was replaced by the image of women as competitors for men. And with this shift came a shift in public opinion. Enthusiastic admiration for Rosie the Riveter was replaced by the prevailing idea that "Women ought to be delighted to give up any job and return to their proper sphere — the kitchen." All of a sudden, in every medium of popular culture, women were barraged with propaganda on the value of domesticity.

Nearly all the originals had been CPT or War Training Program flight instructors — sought-after and highly paid professional pilots — before the telegram came from Nancy Love. Those jobs had evaporated a year earlier, in January 1944, when Hap Arnold ordered the flight schools closed based on lack of need. And those women who had run flight services had closed down their businesses in 1942. So returning to pre-war flying jobs was not an option.

A couple of them did some limited ferrying for the government. At least three went into the airplane sales and brokering business after the war. A few did find instructor's jobs.

As the years went by, those who could continued to fly but on a more limited basis. Flying was expensive and only the well-to-do could afford it as a pastime and even then, they often had a business connected to their flying. And, of course, the women did their flying in airplanes that more resembled what they flew in their early days in the WAFS, not the power planes they had flown throughout 1944.

Nine of the sixteen original WAFS remaining at deactivation were married. Helen Mary Clark and Betty Gillies — now totally different people after their twenty-seven months of service — went home to their husbands and children. Nancy Love's husband was serving overseas, as was Del Scharr's. The husbands of Gertrude Meserve, Helen McGilvery, Lenore McElroy, Esther Nelson were in the Ferrying Division. And Teresa's beloved Dink was missing in action.

Delphine Bohn, Helen Richards, Barbara Donahue, Nancy Batson, B.J. Erickson and Betsy Ferguson were single, though

Helen was married Christmas day to her sweetheart from CPT days and B.J. got married in April 1945 to a Ferrying Division officer she met at Long Beach. All but Delphine were married by the end of 1946. Sis Bernheim, a widow when she joined the WAFS, remarried in 1947 and had two children.

They went home and picked up the pieces of their lives, but they never forgot those years. And though they moved beyond it, always there was the knowledge that they had been, forever, changed by the experience.

ొ∞๑๑

The Army, it turns out, did not completely forget the WASPs. After the new United States Air Force was formed in 1948, it offered the WASPs Reserve commissions — non-flying commissions, but commissions nevertheless.

According to the Official WASP Roster, several of the original WAFS took them. Nancy Love — lieutenant colonel; Betty Gillies, Helen Mary Clark, Teresa James, B.J. Erickson, Sis Bernheim, Del Scharr and Lenore McElroy — all majors; and Esther Nelson, captain. Bernice Batten rose to the rank of E-3 in the U.S. Marine Corps. Nancy Love's letter, dated August 9, 1948, reads, in part:

> In recognition of the outstanding service rendered by women pilots, the Air Force will offer United States Air Force Reserve commissions to those members of the Women's Auxiliary Service Pilots [sic] desiring and qualifying for such status. The Air Force is pleased to offer you a commission as lieutenant colonel in the Reserve.

A side note, also according to the Official WASP Roster: "In subsequent years a number of the volunteers faced discriminatory action and were released from the Reserve because they had minor children." This caused both Nancy Love (who by 1952 had three young daughters ) and Betty Gillies to give up their commissions. By that time, Helen Mary Clark's children were no longer minors, nor were Lenore McElroy's. Since Sis Bernheim (Fine) also had two children between 1948 and 1952, one may assume that the discriminatory action caught up with her as well. However, B. J. Erickson (London) had a child when she was offered her commission. She fought the Air Force, successfully, and stayed in the Reserve with twenty years of service. Her contention is, she had a child when the Air Force offered her the commission and they didn't ask her.

Most of the WAFS settled into the family-raising mode of the rest of the country from 1946 through the 1960s. Then, in the 1960s, Teresa James began a one-woman crusade to get veteran's benefits for all the WASPs. By 1972, she had persuaded Congresswoman Patsy Mink of Hawaii to introduce a WASP bill to the House Veterans' Affairs Committee. The committee chairman, however, would not allow the measure on the House floor for a vote.

In the '70s, with their children grown, the WASPs began to seek each other out. In 1972, the women who had graduated from the Training Command's flight school returned to Sweetwater for a Thirtieth Anniversary reunion and marched down the main street with the sons, daughters and grandchildren of the town. That truly marked the beginning of the re-birth of the WASP as an organization.

But the best was yet to come. . .

In the mid-1970s, the U.S. service academies began to admit women. In September 1976, ten women began flight training for the U.S. Air Force. A Pentagon press release heralded them as "the first women military pilots."

The WASPs were incensed! The recognition that should have been theirs had been lost in the mists of thirty passing years. No one remembered them. Well, almost no one.

Six weeks before the WASP biannual reunion in 1976, the U.S. Senate — led by Barry Goldwater — voted on an amendment to make the WASPs official World War II veterans. "These women are U.S. citizens who served with our Army Air Corps [sic] during World War II. This group of women was shunted aside by the country they served; and it is better that we should correct a past wrong now, rather than leave the record blemished." Most of the Senators were surprised to learn that women had actually flown for the United States Army in World War II.

Four days later, the House rejected the amendment. This un-
leashed a fight that painfully resembled the one back in spring 1944.

No wartime civilians have ever been allowed veterans status in
America, loudly proclaimed the veterans' organizations of the United
States. The cry had a familiar ring, but this time it was an insult to
the women who had served their country faithfully during wartime.
The men contended that this was a raid on their benefits. If the
women were allowed veteran status, all the other civilian groups
would come to Washington — hat in hand — looking for money.

It seemed as if the issue had come down not to honor, duty,
patriotism, service, and love of country but to the almighty dollar.

By now, the Women's Movement had made women more aware
of their abilities to fight for what they believed to be rightfully theirs.
The WASPs enlisted the help of Hap Arnold's son W. Bruce Arnold,
now a retired Air Force colonel. Hap, who had suffered a heart
attack during the war, had died in 1950.

In spring 1977, Goldwater introduced S.247 — "to provide
recognition to the Women's Airforce Service Pilots for their service
to their country during World War II by deeming such service to
have been active duty in the Armed Forces of the United States for
purpose of laws administered by the Veterans Administration" —
to the Senate. Congresswoman Lindy Boggs of Louisiana introduced
a bill — identical to Goldwater's — in the House.

"Bruce Arnold and Lindy Boggs had one ray of hope to
penetrate the House Veterans' Affairs Committee," writes Sally
Van Wagenen Keil in *Those Wonderful Women in Their Flying
Machines*. "The second-ranking minority member was the
committee's only woman, Margaret Heckler of Massachusetts. A
Republican, Heckler was co-chair — with Democrat Elizabeth
Holzman of New York — of the newly formed Congressional
Women's Caucus. On March 15, 1977, through Margaret
Heckler's efforts, the WASP bill, H.R. 3277, became the only piece
of legislation in history to be co-sponsored by every woman
member of Congress."

The veterans organizations continued to bring in the biggest
guns they could find to fight it. The WASPs countered. In September,
General William H. Tunner, now retired and accompanied by his

wife, WASP Margaret Ann Hamilton Tunner (43-W-2), appeared as witnesses seeking passage of the bill.

"Certainly someone today can partially correct the unfairness we showed by making veterans of these women who served so faithfully and well, and with little complaint," the General said.

Elegant, soft-spoken Mrs. Tunner — who had been a pursuit pilot stationed in Romulus — said simply, "I feel that those few of us still alive should be here in Washington to receive national recognition, instead of this humble plea for positive identification as a veteran."

Originals Nancy Batson Crews and Teresa James narrated a documentary film about the WASPs entitled *Silver Wings and Santiago Blue*.

"Jackie Cochran was notably absent from the hearings," writes Marianne Verges in *On Silver Wings*. "She had a bad heart and perhaps an attack of old resentments. In 1975, she had testified before a military inquiry board about training women as pilots, particularly at the United States Air Force Academy. She had said that, based on her experiences, women would be unlikely to make careers in aviation. They would leave the service after their initial commitment was over for personal reasons, and the expensive education would be wasted. Contradicting what she had written in her final report [1944/1945] and in her book, Cochran told the officers how disappointed she was because the women she taught to fly during the war, for the most part, simply went home, married, and settled down."

One might reflect that after she and the Army succeeded in shutting down the WASP program and sending the women home in December 1944 with little hope of finding jobs similar to those they were now trained for, Cochran might well have helped pave the way for a self-fulfilling prophecy. As history bears out, the entire war generation did go home, settle down and raise families. But by 1975, the women's movement was in full force and things already were changing.

"Assistant Secretary of the Air Force Antonia Handler Chayes decided to support the Women's Airforce Service Pilots," Verges continues. "The armed services had to continue enlisting women in sizable numbers or abandon the idea of an all-volunteer force. The Defense Department was spending hundred of thousands of dollars in advertising trying to convince women of the opportunities available and that they could expect to get a fair shake from the military. 'Be all you can be,' promised the Army. What would a public defeat for the WASP do for recruiting?"

In October, Goldwater introduced the WASP legislation as an amendment to the GI Bill Improvement Act, something the Veterans' Affairs Committee wanted passed.

Still, it appeared that a small group of diehard Congressmen — with the backing of the veterans' groups — was going to thwart the WASPs' right to this recognition. In a last ditch effort, Bruce Arnold put together a packet of documents and delivered copies to the entire Veterans' Affairs Committee. Among several far more impressive documents, he inserted at the last minute a rather humble afterthought — a copy of a WASP's service discharge.

Sally Van Wagenen Keil writes that when Congressman Olin E. "Tiger" Teague of Texas — former chair of the Veteran's Committee and still its most powerful member — read the WASP's discharge and compared it with his own from the service thirty years earlier, he saw that they were identical. Following some minor alterations in the bill's wording, he changed his vote and took others with him.

On November 3, 1977, the House passed the WASP amendment. The following day, the Senate gave its stamp of approval. On Thanksgiving Day, November 23, 1977, President Jimmy Carter signed the veterans status for the WASPs of World War II. The women had won veterans' benefits, which meant that they were entitled to a flag-draped coffin and burial benefits for their families. The GI Bill had long since passed them by.

In 1984, each woman pilot was awarded the Victory medal and those who had been on duty for more than a year also received the American Theater medal.

# AFTERWORD

The women who graduated from the flight training school —
particularly those who trained at Avenger Field in Sweetwater — have
a close-knit organization, The Order of Fifinella, named for the winged,
booted gremlin mascot Walt Disney created for the WASPs in 1943.
The WASPs meet for a reunion every other year. Their bylaws were
formulated by none other than Nancy Batson Crews when she served
as president of the WASP organization from 1972 to 1975. The WASPs
have become a much admired force for women in aviation and
women's accomplishments in general. Each graduating class has found
within itself the glue to be a thriving group unto themselves.

The Originals have not — with a couple of exceptions including
Nancy Batson Crews' brief involvement in the early 1970s and Florene
Miller Watson's continuing devoted duty as WASP Chaplain — taken
part in the WASP activities. Their service experiences were far different.
They don't feel at home with, or part of, the larger group.

The WAFS did not spend six months together in Texas in
intensive training and living in close quarters as did the WASPs.
With their thirty-day indoctrination under their belts, the WAFS
immediately were sent out on ferrying jobs that kept them away from
base for several days at a time. They got acquainted as they flew
together with the different members of the squadron. However, they
did have — in their beginnings at Wilmington in 1942 — feelings of
togetherness, of camaraderie. That is their "group," their "class," their
identity. To the Houston and Sweetwater graduates, they are known
not by a class designation, but as The Originals.

But once scattered in January 1943, The Originals rarely saw
each other. They crossed paths at an occasional airfield Operations
office or RONed together in the nurses' quarters at some base while
ferrying an airplane from one place to another. Maybe they had
dinner together when chance permitted.

The truth is, The Originals were *never* all together in one place.

The surviving WAFS remember a couple of informal reunions
being held after the war — one back in Wilmington and another at
Helen Mary Clark's.

Then in June 1999, when the youngest among them were
approaching their 80th birthdays, Nancy Batson Crews hosted a

reunion for the surviving WAFS in her hometown of Birmingham, Alabama. Her co-host was the Southern Museum of Flight located near the Birmingham airport. A press conference and a reception were held at the museum. The Irondale Cafe — made famous by Birmingham author Fannie Flagg in her 1987 book, *Fried Green Tomatoes at the Whistle Stop Café* — hosted the group for lunch.

Six of the nine living WAFS attended the reunion and appear in the picture below: B.J. Erickson London, Barbara Poole Shoemaker,Teresa James Martin, Florene Miller Watson, Gertrude Meserve Tubbs LeValley and Nancy herself.

The reunion was an unqualified success. The entire aviation community of Birmingham, including the membership of the Birmingham Aero Club, paid homage to one of their own — Nancy Batson Crews — and turned out for the reception.

Unable to attend were: Phyllis Burchfield Fulton, Barbara Donahue Ross, and Bernice Batten.

This book had its genesis in that Birmingham reunion.

In September 2002, the surviving WAFS will celebrate the 60th anniversary of their founding. This book is for and about them — and for and about their sisters of the sky who have "flown west."

# Nancy Elizabeth Batson Crews

**February 1, 1920 - January 14, 2001**

# DEDICATION

*January 15, 2001*

We lost Nancy as this project neared completion, but she lived long enough to read the manuscript, put her stamp of approval on it, and help launch it toward publication.

Nancy liked to point out that the WAFS was the most purely democratic organization she ever belonged to. "It didn't matter who your mama's family was or how much money your daddy made or what part of town you came from. All that mattered was that you could fly those airplanes." Being accepted in the WAFS was the defining moment of her life.

And so, with deep love and admiration, this book is dedicated to Nancy Elizabeth Batson Crews— pursuit pilot *extraordinaire* — without whom it would not have been written and who so very much wanted this story told.

# BIOGRAPHIES

## *Nancy Batson (Crews)*

At age 79, Nancy Batson Crews got a call from a pilot friend, Chris Beal-Kaplan, corporate pilot for American Equity Insurance Company out of Des Moines. The company's twin-engine, turbo-prop King Air was hangared at St. Clair County airport in Alabama, where Nancy kept her J-3 Cub. Chris needed a co-pilot and Nancy — if she was current in all her ratings — fit the bill. Nancy *was* current and she passed her simulator test and everything else they threw at her even though there was dead silence at the other end of the phone line when Chris told her boss that Nancy flew in World War II. In November 1999, Nancy became a part-time corporate co-pilot. The two flew several trips together until cancer grounded Nancy in May 2000.

Nancy Elizabeth Batson, born February 1, 1920 in Birmingham, Alabama, was the third of four children born to Stephen Radford and Ruth Philips Batson. She learned to fly in the CPT program at the University of Alabama, soloing a Piper J-3 Cub in March 1940 and earning her private pilot's license on June 15, 1940. Nancy was a flight instructor at Embry Riddle Aeronautical Institute in Miami, Florida in September 1942 when she heard about the WAFS and left to go to Wilmington, becoming number twenty of Nancy Love's "squadron of elite guinea pigs."

During much of 1944, she was stationed in Farmingdale, Long Island where she ferried P-47s from the Republic Aviation factory to the docks in Newark, New Jersey, 50 miles away. In mid-September Nancy Love placed her in command of the newly established 16-woman squadron at Republic's modification center in Evansville, Indiana. Nancy Batson did not like being grounded by the duties of command — "I just wanted to fly those airplanes" — and requested a transfer. Soon she was back in Farmingdale ferrying P-47s. "But Betty Gillies was mad at me for awhile. After that, I got my share of war wearies to take to the bone yard."

After deactivation, Nancy returned to Birmingham, worked with her father in his construction business, and on February 1, 1946 — her 26th birthday — she married her college sweetheart Paul Crews, then a lieutenant colonel in the Army Air Forces. They lived for several years in Washington D.C., then the Air Force transferred Paul to California in 1955. He retired from service as a full colonel in 1957 and went to work as director of personnel for the Northrop Corporation. Nancy and Paul raised their three children, Paul Jr., Radford and Jane, in California. Son Radford inherited his mother's love of flying and is now a captain with Sky West Airlines.

Nancy did not fly while her children were young, but returned to flying in the early 1960s as a flight instructor in Hawthorne, California. She also towed gliders, became a glider pilot and, subsequently, an instructor at Pearblossom Gliding School near Palmdale. Nancy flew in three Powder Puff Derbies, two as a copilot and one solo in which she piloted her Super Cub — the only tail-dragger in the race. In the mid-1970s, Nancy moved to California City — glider country. Paul Sr., ill with diabetes, died in 1978. Rekindling an interest in politics that stemmed from her days as president of the Women's Student Government Association at the University of Alabama, she served briefly as mayor of California City.

Nancy returned to Alabama in 1981 to become a real estate developer in St. Clair County northeast of Birmingham. She also served a term on the St. Clair County Airport Commission.

Nancy was inducted into the Alabama Aviation Hall of Fame in 1989 and the Forest of Friendship at Amelia Earhart's birthplace in Atchison, Kansas, in 1997. She donated her 1949 Mooney Mite and much of her aviation memorabilia over to the Southern Museum of Flight near the Birmingham Municipal Airport.

In recent years, she bought and restored a 1940 J-3 Cub and was still flying it when she reached her 80th birthday in 2000. Nancy served as president of the WASP organization from 1972-1975, during which time she established the bylaws and procedures still in use by that organization today.

Nancy died January 14, 2001, after battling cancer for eight months.

### *Bernice Batten*

Bernice Batten was born April 14, 1913, in Scammon, Kansas. She dreamed of flying while still in high school and finally got her chance in May 1928. "A barnstormer flying an Eaglerock landed near our town of Pittsburg. My dad and I were among the first passengers. Another ride soon followed, and that did it. I was hooked."

She left Kansas State Teachers College after two years to take flight training at Pittsburg's Atkinson Municipal Airport, working part-time to pay for her flying lessons. On September 29, 1933, she soloed a 65-horsepower Monoprop with a Velie engine — NC119K. She earned her private license on August 22, 1934; her limited commercial on September 19, 1934; and her transport license on March 5, 1936. "At the time, dual instruction cost $8 an hour and solo, $6."

Bernice and two other WAFS-to-be, Barbara Donahue and Esther Manning, were flight instructors for the Civilian Pilot Training program for Air Activities, Houston, Texas, in September 1942 when they heard about the WAFS. Manning and Donahue went to Wilmington, were accepted, and telegraphed Bernice to come join them. She did and was accepted on November 21, 1942, becoming number twenty-four on the roster.

"My first ferrying trip was in a Fairchild PT-19, with Del Scharr, Dorothy Fulton, and Nancy Batson. We delivered to Charlotte, North Carolina." Then in February, 1943, Bernice was assigned to the 6th Ferrying Group in Long Beach, California. "We checked out in the BT-13 and started ferrying them from the factory at Downey to various training bases. Later, I was sent to Love Field in Dallas, Texas, and ferried the PT-19, AT-6 and the A-24."

In 1944, Bernice was transferred to McClellan Air Field in Merced, California, where she served in Flight Operations. She resigned from what became known as the WASPs before the women flyers were deactivated on December 20, 1944, and joined the U.S. Marine Corps. She served at Air Base Group 2 in El Toro, California, in Flight Operations. Officially, her military flying days were over, but "sometimes the Marine pilots let me fly with them."

After the service, Bernice worked as a clerk for the U.S. Forest Service and eventually for the Publishing Department of the Seventh-day Adventist Conference, in San Jose, California. She is now retired and living in Pacific City, Oregon.

✍

### Kathryn "Sis" Bernheim
### (Fine)

Kathryn "Sis" Bernheim was one of three WAFS accepted after December 1942. She and fellow New Yorker, Helen McGilvery, were given flight tests on January 3, 1943.

Sis was born Kathryn L. Strouse on February 1, 1911, in Rockaway, New York. She was a graduate of Woodmere Academy in Woodmere, New York.

"Within a short span of years in the early 1930s, my mother, father, first husband Maurice Bernheim, and my grandmother all died," Sis told aviation author Sam Parker, for an article that appeared in the *American Aviation Historical Society Journal*, summer 1995. "I was really down in the dumps when, unexpectedly, something positive happened that changed my life forever.

"When I was a teenager I had had a few pleasant aviation adventures. I often talked about them, and my brother-in-law remembered. Trying to help me recover to my old cheerful self, he encouraged me to take flying lessons at Roosevelt Field on Long Island. It was summer 1934. His advice turned out to be some of the best I ever received."

At Roosevelt she was taught by Sig Uyldert and soloed on November 14, 1934 in a Taylor Cub, obtaining her private pilot's license shortly after that. In 1938, Sig invited her to join him as a partner in his flying business. They rented an office and storage space at Hangar 9 for their three aircraft: a Travel Air 16K, a Piper J-2 and a Piper J-3C-50.

Sis knew Jacqueline Cochran casually because Jackie flew in and out of Roosevelt Field before the war. Through Jackie, Sis had the opportunity in January 1942 to qualify to fly with the Air Transport Auxiliary in England. She went to Dorval Airport in Montreal, Canada, to take the compulsory flight test. She and another Original, Barbara Poole, were there at the same time. They and four other American women pilots were flunked by the check pilot, a regular RAF officer who made no secret of his belief that women were lousy pilots.

On January 6, 1943, Sis became number twenty-six accepted into the WAFS squadron and remained with Betty Gillies and the 2nd Ferrying Group in Wilmington her entire two years of active duty. She was given temporary duty assignments to instrument school at St. Joseph, Missouri, May 7, 1944, and to pursuit school in Brownsville, Texas, June 16, 1944. After pursuit school, from July 24 to September 12, 1944 — still as part of Betty Gillies' squadron — she was stationed in Farmingdale, Long Island ferrying P-47s from the Republic factory. She was then sent to Evansville, Indiana, for temporary duty at the modification center there, ferrying P-47s and P-51s. Sis also flew the P-39, P-40 and P-63 and was a co-pilot on a B-17.

After deactivation on December 20, Sis remained on Long Island and looked around for another job in aviation. In May 1945, she returned to the Republic factory and was hired as a flight instructor, teaching members of the Republic Aviation Company Flying Club to fly. She also worked as a flight instructor for the Lyon Flight School at Zahn Airport in Amityville.

In 1947, Sis married C. Robert Fine, a sound recording engineer who had served as a Marine in World War II, and they had two children: Dugie Fine Standeford and Robert B. Fine. Sis continued to fly until her husband's death in 1952, when she considered the risk factor too great while raising two children alone and quit flying.

Sis Bernheim Fine died June 24, 1996, at home. She was eighty-five.

⁓ঃ

## *Delphine Bohn*

During the 1980s, Delphine Bohn decided to write her remembrances of the WAFS. She wrote to the others seeking answers to a rather extensive set of questions. "Delphine also asked all of us what we thought was the single quality present in all of The Originals," B.J. Erickson says. "We were so very diverse, I don't think she ever came up with that single link."

But she did try. And she did write a memoir, *Catch a Shooting Star*, which remains unpublished. A few manuscript copies exist, including one at Texas Woman's University and one at the International Women's Air and Space Museum in Cleveland, Ohio. It provides an invaluable resource.

Delphine Bohn was born July 5, 1913, in Foss, Oklahoma to Marion Grover and Lenore Bohn. She graduated from Amarillo High School and attended Amarillo Junior College. But once she tried flying, it completely captivated her. She soloed in a Piper Cub in 1940 and eventually went on to fly pursuits, multi-engine bombers and cargo planes while serving as the fifteenth member of the WAFS. On March 4, 1943, Delphine was transferred from the 2nd Ferrying Group in Wilmington to the 5th at Dallas Love Field and was placed in command of the women's squadron in December of that year, serving in that capacity until deactivation.

After the war, Delphine and a partner established a Beechcraft dealership with two locations in Dallas and Fort Worth. In the late 1960s, they moved the business to Los Angeles. Eventually Delphine left aviation, moved to San Francisco and became a legal secretary. Then in the late 1970s, she moved back to Amarillo to care for her dying mother.

Delphine died January 18, 1992 of cancer.

≈§

### *Phyllis Burchfield*
### *(Fulton)*

Phyllis Burchfield was born to Dr. Samuel N. and Isabelle Campbell Burchfield on June 15, 1912 in Fieldmore, Pennsylvania. While in the oil business at the turn of the century, her father struck a flowing well of mineral water and built Fieldmore, a resort hotel and spa.

Phyllis grew up with an abiding love for horses, competing in shows in Pennsylvania as a teenager. Later, she attended San Mateo Junior College in California. "Mill's Field, now the San Francisco Airport, was close by. At that time, the southeast runway ended in tideland and mud flats. Landings and takeoffs were usually in a cloud of seagulls."

Learning to fly "was something I had to do," says Phyllis.

She soloed an Aeronca Chief on December 4, 1934, with Moreau Flight Service at the Oakland Municipal Airport, earning her private pilot's license flying a Great Lakes biplane in 1937, and went on to get her limited commercial license within a week.

"During that time, Amelia was preparing for her world flight. As we were both living at the Oakland Airport Inn, I saw and spoke with her frequently. Her Lockheed was in the Navy hangar next to Moreau. She made it a point to know and encourage all the girls currently learning to fly." Phyllis became one of the original members of the Ninety-Nines' Bay Cities Chapter founded by Amelia Earhart.

In fall 1942, Phyllis was instructing a Civilian Pilot Training class for Midsouth Airways in Memphis. "Nancy Love called me and said there was an opening — was I interested? I was. I was in the middle of a class and flight instructors were scarce, but I went up to New Castle anyway and took my flight test on October 9 in a Stearman. I passed with no problems. My flight time in the Great Lakes was a big help. A lot of the girls hadn't flown anything bigger than Cubs and the Stearman was more than some of them could handle. But then they said I was too short to qualify. I'm only five feet tall."

Back she went to Memphis, but not without stopping enroute at Petersburg, West Virginia, to see her fiancé, Army 2nd Lieutenant George Fulton. They decided to get married that Sunday in Baltimore — October 11, 1942. "Then I went back to Memphis and picked up my class. Ten days later, I got a wire saying report back to New Castle immediately. I had been granted a waiver on my height."

Phyllis became number eighteen on the active roster. In January 1943, she was transferred, along with Del Scharr, Barbara Poole, Barbara Donahue and Katherine Rawls Thompson, to the 3rd Ferrying Group in Romulus, Michigan. Then on August 24, 1943, Phyllis took emergency leave from the WAFS when George was seriously injured when he flipped a Jeep and badly mangled his left arm. She went to California to help him recuperate and applied for transfer to Long Beach to be near him until he was out of danger, but Commander deArcy at Romulus told her no. Phyllis finally had to resign. After that, she followed George on whatever assignment he was given and eventually the Army sent him to Triest, Italy where they spent more than three years, returning to the U.S. in December 1951.

"When I went overseas, I had multiple flight ratings. When I came back, I had none. They had expired." She never flew after that. However, she had gotten interested in German Shepherds and began breeding and showing them. Today, she lives with her four German Shepherds in the home she and George bought in 1963 — "a mountain top sanctuary" in eastern Ohio.

A widow since 1991, Phyllis has become an accomplished published poet. She is now the oldest of the surviving WAFS.

### Helen Mary Clark

Not many boys growing up in the midst of World War II could boast that their mother was a fighter pilot, but 12-year-old Gerry and 10-year-old Bill Clark could and did — and are still proud of it!

Born December 27, 1909, Helen Mary (Goodman) Clark began flying in 1934, owned her own plane — a Monocoupe— and had logged 629 hours when she reported to New Castle, Delaware on September 12, 1942 and became the fifth Original. When Betty Gillies took over as squadron C.O. on January 1, 1943, Helen Mary became her executive officer because of her superb people and management skills.

The wife of W. Gerould Clark Jr., a well known polo player and real estate broker, Helen Mary was a slender, attractive blonde with delicate features. She had known Nancy Love before the war and helped her search the C.A.A. files for women pilots holding commercial licenses. In order to join the WAFS, Helen Mary negotiated a release from the Civil Air Patrol, for whom she had been flying coastal patrol in the early days of the war. C.A.P pilots donated their time and their airplanes to help protect the American shoreline.

In May 1943, Helen Mary became the second woman to check out in the P-47 Thunderbolt and by July 28 she had logged 21.5 hours in the big pursuit. From then on she ferried them regularly from the Republic Aviation factory in Farmingdale, New York. She eventually spent time in spring 1944 in Kansas City ferrying B-25s and, like all the New Castle WASPs, did regular TDY at the Republic factory. Then in September 1944, she was sent to command the small detachment of WASPs stationed at Republic's modification center in Evansville, Indiana. She served there until deactivation in December.

Helen Mary did not go to pursuit school, but was sent to Long Beach in order to check out in both the P-51 and the P-38. In her WAFS/WASP career, she ferried pursuits, medium attack bombers, and heavy transports. She also attended Officer Training School in Orlando. When the war was over, Helen Mary did not just go home and settle back into domestic life as she had known it. When the new Air Force offered Reserve commissions to the WASPs in 1948, she accepted and was assigned the rank of Major. The September 1954 issue of *Air Reservist* magazine featured "Hold In Reserve," an article by Staff Sergeant M. L. Prosser that was all about Major Helen Mary Clark, "M-day chief of the Military Air Transport Service's Ferrying Division." Once a month, the piece pointed out, Major Clark "dons her smart Reserve WAF major's uniform and treks south from her Englewood, New Jersey home to MATS Headquarters at Andrews Air Force Base in Maryland. For a full day, she tackles man-sized tasks of the important Ferrying Division. As a mobilization assignee, Major Clark is tabbed for an important role should war be forced upon us."

Both W. Gerould Clark III and William Goodman Clark learned to fly after the war, taught by AF Reservist 2nd Lieutenant and former WASP (44-6) Carolyn Cullen, who managed the FBO operation at the air strip that was part of the Clarks' proprety in Martha's Vineyard. The Clarks owned what Gerry terms a "cow-to-the-customer farm" on the Vineyard. In fact, he recalls delivering milk to earn money for his flying lessons. Gerry and Bill went on to graduate from Cornell University and the Air Force ROTC program there and then became Air Force pilots in the 1950s. Helen Mary got to fly with Gerry once when she visited him in Japan. "I was stationed at Osaka. Mom flew over and back with me on a short weather mission. She rode in the jump seat of the B-26 I was flying."

The Clarks' Vineyard home, next door to the Loves' property, was a summertime reunion haven for the WAFS. "We never knew who would pop in," says Gerry.

Sadly, fire destroyed the Clarks' home in Tuxedo Park, New Jersey and, with it, most of Helen Mary's WAFS memorabilia. She died of congestive heart failure on April 22, 1979 — Gerry's 49th birthday.

### *Barbara Donahue (Ross)*

Several of the original WAFS had the misfortune of having their homes destroyed by fire: specifically Cornelia Fort, Helen Mary Clark and Barbara Donahue Ross. Barbara writes that her log books, along with much of her WAFS memorabilia, were lost in a fire that destroyed her home near Warrenton, Virginia.

Barbara Donahue, born March 25, 1920, in New York City, to Charles and Mattie Donahue, spent a year at Vassar. At age nineteen, realizing she wanted to learn to fly, she began lessons at nearby Roosevelt Field and soloed in a Stinson 105 early in 1940. The loss of the log books obscures some of her flying milestones but, possessing her instructor's rating, she went to Houston, Texas to teach flying through the CPT program there. Future WAFS Esther Manning and Bernice Batten were teaching there as well.

She went to New Castle AAB to meet with Nancy Love and Colonel Robert Baker and passed her test flight, becoming number sixteen on the WAFS roster. In January 1943, Barbara was transferred to the 3rd Ferrying Group in Romulus, Michigan, along with Del Scharr, Barbara Poole, Katherine Rawls Thompson and Phyllis Burchfield. She served for more than six months under Del's leadership, ferrying trainer airplanes. In mid-summer, when Nancy Love relieved Del of her command, she placed Barbara in charge of the squadron. Barbara served the remainder of her active service in that position with Lenore McElroy as her executive officer.

Barbara was the second woman to check out in the 1,325-horsepower P-39 Airacobra, soon after Del's historic flight on June 28, 1943. Then it was on to pursuit school in Palm Springs in December 1943. She graduated in Class 44-4 in early February. "After that, I flew mostly P-39s and P-63s." In April 1944, she was a member of the first Officer Training School class in Orlando, Florida.

After deactivation, Barbara went home to New York City and on November 11, 1946, she married Howard Clyde Ross — a fellow pilot whom she met while stationed in Romulus. They eventually bought a farm in central Virginia and had four children. Barbara still lives on that farm.

*Barbara Jane "B.J." Erickson (London)*

Barbara Jane Erickson, known as B.J. to the other Originals and to the WASPs under her command in the squadron at Long Beach, was born July 1, 1920 in Seattle, Washington. She learned to fly floatplanes through the CPT program at the University of Washington where she was a student in 1939. She soloed in a Taylorcraft Seaplane at Lake Union, Seattle, that year and earned her private pilot's license in 1940.

"I wangled my way into all four CPT classes. Girls weren't supposed to get secondary, cross country and commercial."

After receiving her commercial pilot's license and her instructor rating, B.J. went to work instructing in the same CPT program from which she had gotten her training. She was teaching there early in 1942 when she received a letter from Jacqueline Cochran about going to England. She opted not to go. Then later she heard about Nancy Love's WAFS program, decided that was for her, was released from her job, and left immediately for Wilmington. B.J. was number fourteen in the final squadron listing.

Stories about B.J.'s Air Medal and other events in her two-year career at Long Beach are told in various chapters in this book. In spring 1945, B.J. was on her way from Seattle to San Diego where Betty and Bud Gillies had settled and were working for Ryan Aviation. Ryan had offered B.J. a job. "I was supposed to come down in March or April to meet Betty and fly for Ryan. I stopped in Long Beach on the way and Jack convinced me to get married instead. We were married April 9, 1945."

Jack London Jr. was a service pilot with the Air Transport Command and head of flight transition for the Army Air Base in Long Beach. He was a captain when B.J. met him in 1943. Then in 1948, when the new Air

Force offered Reserve commissions to the WASPs, B.J. was commissioned a major — the same rank her husband also held in the Reserves. "We could reserve an airplane, an A-26 or a twin Beech, and go flying, but technically I couldn't log any flying time." They served as Reservists together and retired twenty years later. By then, Jack was a full colonel.

After the war, Jack and B.J. London went in business with Bud and Betty Gillies when they purchased Acme Industrial Supply. "Bud was an adviser because he still worked for Ryan. Jack ran the company until he died."

In the 1960s, B.J. went into aircraft sales — Barney Frazier Aircraft at Long Beach Airport. Though she now has sold her company, she still buys and sells aircraft on a limited scale. She has sold airplanes to and for fellow WAFS including Nancy Batson Crews, Betty Gillies, and Barbara Towne Fasken. B.J. also worked on the Powder Puff Derby (All-Woman Transcontinental Air Race or AWTAR) for twenty years with her close friend Betty Gillies and served as executive secretary of the organization for fifteen years.

B.J. has two daughters — both employed in aviation. Terry London Rinehart was the first woman hired by Western Airlines in 1975 and is now a Captain for Delta Airlines. Kristy London Ardizzone helped run Frazier Aircraft for several years, but now has her own public relations business — still in the same office. Both their husbands are pilots.

One of the few WASPs who held the 5-P classification (qualified to fly four-engine heavy aircraft like the B-17 as well as pursuits), B.J. has many fond memories of her WAFS/WASP service. And she still lives in Long Beach: "I went there in 1943 and never left."

≈§

## Opal "Betsy" Ferguson (Woodward)

Petite, blonde, blue-eyed Opal "Betsy" Ferguson grew up on a farm near Coffeyville, Kansas. She and her sister Sally, dubbed "The Flying Sisters" by newspapers in their home state, got their private pilot's licenses the same day in 1937. Betsy went on to obtain her commercial license, followed by her instructor's rating, and taught Civilian Pilot Training (CPT) and War Pilot Training (WPT) to male student pilots before joining the WAFS with 873 hours. She was number twenty-three of The Originals.

Betsy was transferred to Dallas Love Field and the 5th Ferrying Group on January 1, 1943. In September 1944, she was sent to Alamagordo AAB in New Mexico. Five WASPs were then assigned to Walker AAB in

Victoria, Kansas after October 7, 1944, including Betsy. Their duties are listed as: engineering/test; administrative; co-pilot. They flew the L-5, C-47 and B-17.

Both Dorothy Scott and Delphine Bohn write of Betsy's emergency appendectomy in late summer/early fall of 1943 and her possible leave of absence. Betsy's transfer out of the Ferrying Division and into the Training Command in mid-1944 is in line with the wholesale transfer of WASPs not ferrying pursuit aircraft out of the ATC and into other areas of the AAF beginning in August 1944.

Betsy is listed in Jacqueline Cochran's final report as having served until deactivation. No other information is currently known other than she married a man named Woodward. Information on her activities after World War II would be most appreciated by the author as well as the International Women's Air and Space Museum and Texas Woman's University.

᪐

## Cornelia Fort

Had she lived, it is the opinion of the WAFS who knew her that Cornelia Fort would have written a definitive history of the group, of the women themselves, and of what they did in the service of their country, 1942-1944. Instead, she was the first of three original WAFS to die on active service to their country.

Cornelia Clark Fort was born on February 5, 1919, in Nashville, Tennessee, the fourth child of Dr. Rufus E. and Louise Clark Fort. Dr. Fort was a physician and one of the founders, vice president, and medical director of the National Life and Accident Insurance Company of Nashville.

Cornelia graduated from Ward-Belmont, an exclusive girls school in Nashville. She badly wanted to attend Sarah Lawrence College in Bronxville, New York, but her father had in mind The Ogontz School and Junior College in Philadelphia where she would — in addition to a finishing school curriculum — learn military discipline. The young women of Ogontz regularly took part in close-order military drills carrying wooden dummy rifles. Amelia Earhart and Betty Huyler Gillies were alumnae. Cornelia bowed to her father's wishes, enrolling at Ogontz the academic year of 1936-37. The following year, however, she did convince her father to send her to Sarah Lawrence.

An early penchant for writing marked Cornelia's academic life and she was an insatiable reader. At Sarah Lawrence, she became chief editorial writer for *The Campus*, the college newspaper. On November 21, 1938, not long after Kristallnacht when the Nazis looted and burned synagogues and Jewish houses and businesses in Germany and Austria, she wrote an impassioned piece titled "Barbarism à la Hitler."

Still a child of her upbringing and a dutiful daughter, on December 29, 1938, nineteen-year-old Cornelia made her debut at the Belle Meade Country Club in Nashville. Then on June 10, 1939 she graduated from Sarah Lawrence's two-year program and would have been a junior if she had opted to return to Sarah Lawrence that fall. She did not.

A friend of Cornelia's was dating a young man who owned a flying service at Nashville's Berry Field. Early in 1940, the girls decided to take an airplane ride. Cornelia's biographer Rob Simbeck writes the following in *Daughter of the Air*: "At the moment the air caught the plane's wings and lifted it from the runway, she was transformed. The ground fell away, and she experienced a sense of freedom and exhilaration unlike any she had ever known."

Cornelia loved flying and her passion for it colored and directed her life thereafter until it ended abruptly in a field in West Texas.

She took her first lesson from flight instructor Aubrey Blackburne in a Luscombe 50, an airplane with a 35-foot wingspan, a 50-horsepower engine and a cruising speed of 95 miles per hour. On April 27, 1940, Cornelia soloed and by June, she earned her private pilot's license, followed by her commercial license and instructor's rating. In March 1941, a year after she started flying, she was Nashville's first woman flight instructor and the only one in Tennessee at that time. Her ratings grew to include twin-engine aircraft weighing up to 4,000 pounds and also sea planes.

She landed a job in Fort Collins, Colorado, teaching in the CPT program at Colorado A&M (now Colorado State). In October 1941, she accepted a job teaching flying in Honolulu on the island of Oahu. Young defense workers, soldiers and sailors wanted to learn to fly and that created a demand for instructors. And, of course, she was in the air the morning of December 7 when Pearl Harbor was bombed. (See Chapter 16)

Cornelia received a telegram on January 24, 1942, from Jacqueline Cochran asking if she was interested in becoming part of a group of

American women headed for England to fly with the ATA. Since the departure date for England was to be early March 1942 and Cornelia was still in Honolulu awaiting transport back to the mainland, she was unable to accept. She finally arrived back in San Francisco on March 1.

On September 6 of that year, she received her telegram from Nancy Love and left immediately for Wilmington to join the WAFS. With 845 hours of qualifying time, she was the third woman accepted into the squadron.

Though the WAFS were not ferrying pursuit aircraft in mid-March 1943 — Nancy Love had only just checked out in the P-51 and Betty Gillies in the P-47 — it would seem a certainty that Cornelia, with her experience and ability, would have gone on to fly pursuit had she lived. As it turned out, the 450-horsepower, single-engine BT-13 basic trainer was the biggest thing she flew in the service.

Cornelia died on March 21, 1943, as the result of a mid-air collision with another BT-13 near Merkel, Texas.

As a war hero, a survivor of Pearl Harbor, Cornelia was asked to retell her story many times — on the radio, at War Bond rallies, and through newspaper interviews. She wrote an article about it for *Woman's Home Companion* magazine that was published posthumously in July 1943.

&#x2767;

### *Dorothy Fulton (Slinn)*

Dorothy Johanna Fulton was — like so many young women of her day — enthralled with Amelia Earhart. Like her heroine, aviation became Dorothy's passion. This, says her sister Honey Fulton Parker, caused their parents some concern. But Harry LeRoy and Johanna Crystal (Jensen) Fulton — descendants of steamboat inventor Robert Fulton and a Danish shipmaster from Copenhagen respectively — didn't stand in their oldest daughter's way, opting instead to help her pave the road to aviation history for women pilots.

Born October 14, 1918 in Ridgefield Park, New Jersey, Dorothy began flying at fifteen. Then nearby Teaneck High School did something absolutely revolutionary — it became the first high school in the country to offer a two-year flying course that allowed students to work toward a pilot's license. Dorothy was the first girl in the class. She soloed March 27, 1936, was granted her amateur license a few months later, and earned her regular private pilot's license on August 5, 1937. After graduation, she went on to earn her commercial, multi-engine and instructor's ratings and taught flying and ground school at Bendix Airport, which is now Teterboro.

Flying and instructing on the side, Dorothy attended New York University as an aviation major and then went into the business, buying her own airplanes, and running a flying school at several New Jersey airports. "She did everything — ground school, flight instructing. Way back in the thirties, she was trying to prove that women could fly as well as men," says Honey.

When she joined the WAFS in October 1942 with 3,269 hours in her log books, Dorothy was number twenty-three to be accepted, but became number twenty-two on the final squadron list. She was posted in Wilmington for a year, then was part of the first group sent to Palm Springs in October 1943, where she served until November 18. From there she was sent to Long Beach where she received multi-engine checkout on December 2 and was then checked out on a BT-13, January 13, 1944.

On March 18 of that year, Dorothy was transferred to the $3^{rd}$ Ferrying Group in Romulus. There, she came down with a severe case of pneumonia — brought on, according to Honey, by ferrying open cockpit trainers. Hospitalized for two months with complications, she was released for ground duty and advised by her physician not to fly. Finally, she resigned from the WASPs summer 1944.

Among the planes Dorothy ferried in World War II were the PT-19, PT-26, L4-B (Cub) and several other liaison planes, BT-13, UC-61, and the C-47. The C-47 became her specialty.

Delphine Bohn says of Dorothy: "Over and above her normal piloting and her military-group chores, Dorothy must have made between forty and fifty twin-engine flights coast-to-coast. The woman was a patriot and a real worker, along with her many other attributes."

After the war, Dorothy went back to instructing and continued to teach in New York and New Jersey. She married, had one son, and was eventually divorced. She was a breast cancer survivor, but died of pneumonia and complications on February 11, 1985, in North Miami, Florida.

For Women's History Month in 2000, the public library in Teaneck showcased Dorothy Fulton and her aviation career — with information and photos compiled by her sister. Honey also sponsored Dorothy's inclusion in the Women In Military Service for America Memorial

(WIMSA), located at the gateway to Arlington National Cemetery and dedicated in October 1997. The purpose of the WIMSA Memorial is to recognize all women who have served in the armed forces — past, present and future; to document the experiences of women and tell their stories of service, sacrifice and achievement; to make their contributions a visible part of our history; to illustrate their partnership with men in the defense of our nation; and to inspire others as role models.

❧

### Betty Huyler Gillies

Betty Huyler Gillies, born January 7, 1908, was one of the older members of the WAFS. She was the second woman to join the squadron in September 1942. On January 1, 1943, Betty was named commanding officer of the WAFS squadron that was part of the 2nd Ferrying Group stationed at New Castle Army Air Base in Wilmington, Delaware. Nancy Love had left to begin establishing the new women's squadrons at Dallas, Romulus, and Long Beach, and to begin checking out in bigger, more powerful airplanes.

Betty was enrolled in nursing school at Columbia Presbyterian Hospital in New York City when she decided to learn to fly — an endeavor inspired somewhat by Amelia Earhart's article, "Try Flying Yourself," in *Cosmopolitan* and most certainly by her interest in a young Navy pilot, B. Allison (Bud) Gillies.

Her first half-hour lesson was on November 10, 1928, in an OX-5 Travelair at Roosevelt Field on Long Island. After seven hours and thirty-five minutes, she soloed on December 23, 1928 and was issued a private license on May 6, 1929. She then bought a used DH-60X Moth "to build up my time for my commercial and transport licenses." On November 2, 1929 twenty-one-year-old Betty attended the organizational meeting of what became the Ninety-Nines and became a charter member. She later served as president from 1939 to 1941.

Betty and Bud were married in 1930. When World War II came, Bud was a vice president and engineering test pilot for Grumman Aircraft located on Long Island. The couple lived with their two young children in nearby Syosset. Betty was a utility pilot for the company, flying a twin-engine Grumman Widgeon. She flew the engineers and the Navy inspectors to their urgent wartime meetings, ran flight errands, and picked up needed parts from their satellite manufacturers. At that point, she was one of the few women pilots to hold a multi-engine rating — she had 180 hours in the Widgeon and 1,261 flying hours overall. As a member of the WAFS, she became the first woman pilot to fly the P-47 — on March 8, 1943. Betty was also one of thirty-one women ferry pilots to fly the twin-engine P-38 Lightning. "Here's the book, go sit in it," the Operations officer told her when she was ready to get checked out in the single-seat P-38.

The engineers at Grumman were a big help to Betty who, at five feet one, was one of the smallest of the women pilots. In the larger airplanes, like the P-47 and the B-17, her feet couldn't reach the rudder pedals, so a male test pilot at Grumman with a similar height problem made a set of wooden blocks for her, like the ones he used. She put them over the rudders and thus extended her reach. "Grumman also made me a gadget to turn the fuel valve in the P-38."

After deactivation, December 20, 1944, Betty went home to Long Island, packed up the children and her mother-in-law who was taking care of them, and drove to California to join Bud. He was now vice president at Ryan Aviation. In May 1945, she, too, went to work for Ryan teaching instrument flying to its test pilots. She also test flew the Ryan Fireball, a Navy FR-1 fighter. "V-J Day occurred just after my fourth flight and the project was cancelled. And so ended my military flying!"

After the war, Betty and Bud along with B.J. Erickson and her husband, Jack London, bought Acme Industrial Supply in Los Angeles. Bud worked in an advisory capacity as he remained vice president at Ryan Aviation and Jack ran the business. Then, according to B.J., Betty had an automobile accident in the latter part of 1945 that "broke nearly every bone in her body. She was in a body cast, walked with first a walker and then a cane. It took her two years to get back to moving around." But in 1948, Betty became active with the All-Woman Transcontinental Air Race, or Powder Puff Derby, and served as its chair for nearly twenty years.

Betty continued to fly until she was in her eighties. B.J. sold her last airplane — a Baron — for her. Grandchildren and eventually great-grandchildren received much of Betty's attention in her later years. For most of her life, Betty was interested in Ham radio operations. The Navy gave her a special commendation for her Ham radio work in the Antarctic.

While in her eighties, Betty's eyesight and then her general health began to fail. A fall in August 1998 left her with a broken shoulder and hip. She died October 13, 1998.

## *Teresa James (Martin)*

For one who has lived life with such *joie de vivre*, Teresa James has known her share of tragedy. Like many women of her era, she married in wartime haste, spent precious little time with her bomber-pilot husband before he was sent overseas, and then learned that he was missing in action. After a given amount of time, the Army declared him dead, but his disappearance was cloaked for several years in mystery. Some of that has already been related in these pages. Here's the rest of the story Teresa calls "D-Day Plus Forty."

In 1984, the P-47 Thunderbolt Pilots' reunion was to be held in Paris, France. Teresa, a member and planning to attend, began to search through some of her old correspondence from the war. She found the name of the mayor of Joinville-le-Pont, where Dink's plane went down, and wrote to him. Monsieur le Maire Guy Gibout (now the former mayor), in turn, wrote to Roger Belbeoch, the President of the Veterans Association in that area, and both men asked her to visit when she came to Paris for the reunion. She also wrote to Levon Agha-Zarian, a former RAF pilot who flew the P-47, was now the president of the P-47 Thunderbolt Association and living in France. He also corresponded with Mayor Gibout and made a discovery.

He wrote to Teresa that, "there are people in Joinville-le-Pont who saw your husband George crash. Have spoken with the authorities — they await your visit." She also heard from Roger Belbeoch who wrote: "I can already tell you that I have found people who witnessed what happened."

On Sunday, May 27, 1984 — the French Mother's Day, Belbeoch, his wife, and an interpreter picked Teresa up at her hotel in Paris and they all drove to Joinville-le-Pont, some 45 minutes from Paris. They were met by the current mayor, Pierre Aubry, and a crowd of people.

*I saw a plaque that said, 'In Memory of George L. Martin.' And there was a piece of B-17 landing gear in the niche. After a welcoming speech, a caravan of cars drove out Avenue de Lille to the crash site.*

*We pulled up in front of the house that the wing had hit. The woman who was living there during the war still lived there. She was in her 80s. Through an interpreter I talked to this dear lady who said she was in her house when the plane crashed. She described to me her feelings about the crash and how it was a miracle that the plane stayed in the middle of the narrow street.*

A memorial plaque on the wrought-iron fence out front said "In Honor of the Nine American Airmen Who Gave Their Lives for Freedom, June 22, 1944."

*I was overcome with sadness. All I could think of was Dink's last letter, which bore the same date. Then we walked over to the garage where two 17-year-old boys hid when they heard the air raid siren back in 1944. They heard the crash moments later, and when they peeked out the door, they saw the smoking wreckage and a body lying between two trees. The body was intact. They rushed him to the hospital, but he was already dead. The man was my husband. The neighbors ran into the street and gathered pieces of bodies before the Germans arrived. They were later taken to Church for blessing, and then buried together.*

Then Teresa was introduced to the two "boys." They were, in 1984, fifty-seven years old, but they still lived in Joinville-le-Pont. Teresa asked how come everything and everyone was still there forty years later. She was told, "People in France don't move, they don't change, they just stay in the same place." Even the trees were still there where the boys had picked up the body. Teresa later found out that all the activity involved with Dink's crash had saved the Joinville-le-Pont bridge from being blown up.

*I just stood there and cried and cried. I felt like such a dope. But I could visualize Dink trying to get the B-17 down that narrow street between the houses, averting real tragedy as far as the townspeople were concerned.*

Finally — after a seven-course dinner in a posh restaurant — emotionally drained, Teresa was delivered back to Paris. *At last, I knew what really happened to my husband. May 27, 1984 was a day to remember, an incredible event that ended forty years of uncertainty.*

Teresa James was born on January 27, 1914, in Pittsburgh, Pennsylvania. Her parents, Herbert and Catherine Agnes (Ryan) James owned the James Floral Shoppes in Pittsburgh and Wilkinsburg. She became the eighth of The Originals.

From the day of her solo flight in 1933 until she stopped flying in the late 1980s, Teresa flew a total of 54 types of military and civilian airplanes — from the OX-5 Travelair to the twin-engine C-47 and C-60 and the powerful pursuits, P-47 and P-51. She checked herself out in the latter a few minutes before taking off on a cross-country delivery.

She was commissioned a major in the U.S. Air Force in 1950, based on her 27 months of WAFS/WASP service, and served until her retirement in 1976. Most of her Air Force work was done in and around her native Pittsburgh, but from 1961 to 1965, she was assigned to 5040th Air Base Group, Elmendorf AFB, Alaskan Air Command, Anchorage. She worked on casualty assistance and received two commendations. While living in Alaska, she gained experience in bush flying on skis and floats.

Teresa initiated the fight for veteran status recognition for the WAFS and WASPs in the early 1960s. "It was through my contact with Congresswoman Patsy Mink, of Hawaii, that she introduced the bill for legislation to gain recognition and Veterans Benefits for the WASPs. I spent a lot of my own money trying to get us recognized before anyone else ever got into it."

The WASPs finally gained their recognition as Veterans when President Carter signed a bill into law in 1977. (See Epilogue)

In 1979, Teresa was awarded the Pancho Barnes [pioneer woman flyer] trophy for active participation in promoting activities in Silver Wings. On July 20, 1986, she was honored with a plaque and a tree planted in her name at aviation's International Forest of Friendship in Atchison, Kansas — birthplace of Amelia Earhart. In 1993, she was inducted into the OX-5 Hall of Fame. On October 15, 2000, she was inducted into the Hall of Valor — New Women's Hall of Tribute in Pittsburgh. Her WAFS uniform is on exhibit in the Smithsonian.

Teresa has been featured on several video productions about the WASPs. She resides in Lake Worth, Florida.

### Esther Manning
### (Rathsfelder, Shively, Westervelt)

Esther Manning, Barbara Donahue and Bernice Batten were instructors for the CPT program for Air Activities, Houston, Texas, in September 1942. Manning and Donahue got telegrams from Nancy Love, went to Wilmington in early October, were accepted, and wired back to Bernice to come join them.

Esther had learned to fly in 1941 and soloed a Stinson Voyager in July of that year at Roosevelt Field on Long Island. A year later, not only had she earned sufficient ratings to be a certified instructor, she also had the 200-horsepower rating, commercial license and minimum 500 hours required to join the WAFS. Her date of acceptance was October 22, 1942; she was number nineteen.

Soon after joining the WAFS, Esther got married (see Chapter 13). By late winter, pregnant and wearing her topcoat all the time to cover up her condition, she flew until it became difficult for her to get the stick back in the PT-19s and other small planes she was ferrying. By the end of April 1943 she was grounded, but rather than releasing her from duty and therefore from the WAFS, C.O. Betty Gillies — who needed to keep her squadron in tact — put Esther on desk duty. "Betty told Esther, 'you're not going home, you're going to run the office,'" says Teresa James.

Esther left that summer to give birth to a son, J.T. Rathfelder, and then returned to the squadron, leaving the baby at home with her family. She did her stint at Officer Training School in Orlando the summer of 1944.

While still serving with the WAFS, she was divorced from her first husband and married fellow ferry pilot, Harold Shively. She finally left the squadron for good October 18, 1944 — due to pneumonia. She also was pregnant again. Since Harold was stationed at Newcastle, she remained in the area after deactivation on December 20, 1944.

Her daughter, Bonnie Shively, born on June 7, 1945, followed in her mother's footsteps and became a pilot. Bonnie was killed in the crash of her experimental aircraft on July 20, 1998.

It appears that Esther was born September 6, 1914, and died in December 1975, but this is unconfirmed.

## *Lenore McElroy*

Lenore McElroy's flying career began in 1930 with a ride in a Ford Tri-Motor that took her over Niagara Falls. Too frightened by the experience even to look out the window, she decided to do something about it. To come to grips with her fear, she started spending time at the Indianapolis Municipal Airport. Eventually pilot and friend Elvan Tarkington persuaded her to take a ride in his Rearwin. He assured her that she was flying when all the time he was operating the aircraft with his knees. That accomplished what they wanted and she decided to learn how to fly. She soloed one week later — as promised by Mr. Tarkington on May 30, 1931. She obtained all of her aviation certificates at Indianapolis and got her ground and flight instructor ratings as well.

According to her daughter, Sherrill Arnet, "My mother learned to fly before meeting my step-father, Clarence McElroy. They were married in 1935." They both taught CPT for university students in Parkersburg, West Virginia, and then flew for Hartung in Detroit.

When she interviewed with Nancy Love at Romulus, Lenore had 3,500 hours and was given a check ride in an AT-6. Clarence was, by then, a ferry pilot for the 3rd Ferrying Group and the family was living in Ypsilanti, Michigan. Lenore had not been willing to leave her three children to go to Wilmington because her husband, as a ferry pilot, frequently had to be gone overnight. But when the WAFS came to Romulus, she was there with her ratings and her flying ability and became number twenty-eight, the last of The Originals. She was appointed Operations Officer under squadron leader Barbara Donahue in the summer 1943 and served in that capacity until deactivation.

Lenore went back to instructing and, after the war, taught primarily under the G.I. Bill. Sometime after that, she and Clarence were divorced and, in 1950, Lenore took advantage of the Air Force's offer — based on her WASP service — and joined with the rank of captain. She served three years at Kelly AFB in San Antonio, then was transferred to West Palm Beach, Florida. In 1955, she was sent to Tokyo with the First Weather Wing and served until August 1959. In 1967 she received documentation that she had been transferred to Major-Retired-Reserve.

Following her AF discharge in 1959, she entered Riverside Baptist College, Riverside, California, and worked on her Bachelor of Science degree with a secondary in education. She taught sixth grade at Winton Elementary School in Winton, California, until her retirement in 1973. She flew in at least one Powder Puff Derby and was a member of the Ninety-Nines.

In addition to Sherrill, Lenore had two sons, Warren and Dick, both now deceased. Lenore taught Dick to fly — all the way through his commercial flying license — and she taught Sherrill's husband, John Arnet, to fly when he was in high school. When John earned his private pilot's license, Sherrill was his first passenger. He went on to graduate from West Point and served as a career pilot with the Air Force.

Lenore was born February 18, 1907, in St. Paul, Minnesota and was one of the oldest of the WAFS. She was also the only one of The Originals who did not start off in Wilmington with the 2nd Ferrying Group. She died February 28, 1997, in Connecticut.

�

### *Helen McGilvery*

Helen McGilvery is a bit of an enigma. Her closest friend in the WAFS was Nancy Batson and much of what we know of "Little Mac" comes from her. Teresa James, too, was her friend and she has supplied additional insight.

Helen McGilvery was married to Mac McGilvery, also a ferry pilot with the 2nd Ferrying Group stationed at New Castle Army Air Base. They lived in town.

Little Mac was given her check ride on January 3, 1943, along with Sis Bernheim, and was accepted on January 8 as number twenty-seven of The Originals. They promptly began their thirty-day indoctrination period and Helen served her entire two years with Betty Gillies' squadron. She attended one of the earliest classes at Pursuit School in Palm Springs with Nancy Batson and Gert Meserve and after that split her time between Republic's factory on Long Island and the modification center in Evansville — ferrying P-47s and occasionally the other pursuits. She also attended

Officer Training School in Orlando and was one of The Originals who flew the P-38.

In the days immediately after deactivation when Teresa James came down with a thyroid problem and needed surgery, Mac got her in to see her physician father-in-law on Long Island. "I had three good friends named Helen in the WAFS and WASP," Teresa says, "Helen Mary Clark, Helen Richey and Helen McGilvery, God bless her."

Little Mac was divorced from Mac after the war and went in business with another woman pilot in a Luscombe dealership in Annapolis. Then in late summer 1948, Helen McGilvery died in a mid-air collision. "Mac always had a horror of burning — and she did," said Nancy Batson Crews.

Helen McGilvery was the first of The Originals to die after the war.

### *Gertrude Meserve (Tubbs, LeValley)*

Young Gertrude Meserve made model airplanes as a kid. Not the fancy plastic ones found in kits today, but the ones of balsa wood. She got her first ride in an airplane in 1936 at age 16. "It was a coffee promotion. You had to guess how high this airplane was and send your answer in with a proof of purchase." She won a thirty-minute flight.

Gertrude was one of twin girls born April 28, 1920, in Boston, Massachusetts. She also had a brother who was three years older. "Ever since I was knee-high to a grasshopper, I wanted to fly. Nothing else interested me. I had a few hours of instruction before I graduated from Winchester High School in Winchester, Massachusetts." She excelled in math and science courses in high school.

"After graduation, I was able to concentrate on getting all of my flying licenses — private, limited commercial, commercial and flight instructor." She got her instrument rating in 1939.

The Civilian Pilot Training (CPT) program gave Gert her break. "We had a little trouble with the insurance company. They had never insured a female pilot before, but they needed instructors. I taught eight classes at Logan Airport (Boston) then transferred to Canton-Norwood. My first class was a group from MIT. You could tell which school the young men came from by their dress. The MIT boys had to wear a suit and tie, but the boys from Harvard wore sport coats." She also taught students from North-eastern University and Tufts.

"I dated a couple of them — after training," she says, twinkling blue eyes belying her taciturn Bostonian humor. "They told us never to date someone while he was your student. Then when World War II started, all private flying ceased on the East Coast and we were moved to Athol-Orange Airport in Athol, Massachusetts."

By the time her WAFS telegram came, Gert had 1,964 hours in her log books. "You build up time fast when you're instructing. I descended on New Castle Army Air Base in Delaware and reported to Nancy Love. Flying for the WAFS was like flying on Cloud Nine — which is an under-statement." Accepted September 30, 1942, she was number twelve in the final squadron listing.

Gert was stationed at New Castle throughout her WAFS career, but "I had temporary duty at Republic Aircraft on Long Island, New York, for practically the entire year of 1944." Reason, of course, was the P-47s were built there and Gertrude flew a lot of P-47s. She attended pursuit school in Palm Springs, California, in December 1943 and then attended Officers Training School in Orlando, Florida, as part of the second class that began May 3, 1944. In all, she flew the L-4, PT-19, PT-26, F-24, AT-9, C-56, C-60, P-39, P-40, P-47 and P-51.

What was her favorite airplane? "A P-47. I delivered two hundred of them." Any close calls? "I was bringing a P-51 back from Long Beach. When I took off from Dallas, the engine coughed, so I took it back to Love Field. A test pilot took it up. It coughed on him on the downwind, so they grounded the plane. Otherwise, I'm here. One landing per takeoff."

In April 1944, she married fellow ferry pilot Major Charles J. Tubbs. "His license was signed by Orville Wright."

"After deactivation, I did a little flying, but it was so tame just flying around the airport, I gave it up. When our three sons came along, I let my husband do all the flying as an executive pilot with Curtiss-Wright at Caldwell, New Jersey." Gert did volunteer work with the PTA, drove for the Red Cross, worked for a catalog store and a pharmaceutical company while her boys were growing up.

In November 1969, she and Charlie moved to Florida. He died in 1974. In April 1990, Gert married Russell LeValley, a farmer from Akron, Michigan. He died in March 1998. Now she volunteers with the Neighborly Senior Services, helping people coordinate Medicare and their co-insurance.

Gertrude was one of six WAFS who attended the 1999 reunion in Birmingham, Alabama, hosted by Nancy Batson Crews. In an interview there, she said: "Flying military airplanes was beyond my wildest dreams. Just looking out and seeing that Air Force star and insignia on the wing was a thrill to me. We couldn't believe our luck. First we flew all over the country in Cubs and PT-19s, then later the bigger stuff, and we got paid for it!

"I feel we were the forerunners of today's women in the military and especially the Air Force."

*Florene Miller (Watson)*

Florene Miller, born December 7, 1920, in San Angelo, Texas to Thomas LaMonte and Flora Theis Miller, was the second of four children. She grew up in the small oil town of Big Lake. Then her family moved to Odessa in 1937. Her father owned and operated several jewelry stores in West Texas. Flights in barnstormers' open-cockpit airplanes first stirred eight-year-old Florene's fascination with airplanes. But that was only the beginning.

"During spring of my sophomore year at Baylor University, my father called to tell me that he had bought the family a silver Luscombe airplane.

I wanted to go home fast so that I could learn to fly." And she did. Florene did not return to college that fall. She soloed when she was nineteen and by age twenty had obtained her private, commercial and flight instructor, as well as ground instructor, ratings.

"My father once told a newspaper reporter that he bought the plane because he thought that America would get into the European war and he wanted his children to be able to contribute to the war effort." Florene made him proud when she began teaching men to fly in the War Training Government Program in Odessa, Texas. She met her future husband there when he volunteered to learn to fly.

Then on July 4, 1941, Florene's father and older brother, LaMonte, were flying the Luscombe when it crashed and both were killed. Florene was on the scene minutes after it happened. That, however, did not stop her from flying. The following year, her younger brother, Dolph, also volunteered to teach flying to military cadets.

In late September 1942, Florene joined the WAFS in Wilmington, Delaware. She was number thirteen of The Originals and served as a member of the 2nd Ferrying Group through the end of December. Transferred to Dallas Love Field in January 1943, she was named women's squadron commander and served in that capacity until December. She left for Pursuit School in Palm Springs November 30, started training with the first class there but — in mid-session — was told to report to the 6th Ferrying Group in Long Beach. She was then sent back to pursuit school and she graduated with the second class. From there, she went to Long Beach permanently and remained a member of that squadron for the rest of her WAFS service.

Although Florene was one of the sixteen original WAFS who flew pursuit aircraft, and one of the ten originals who flew the twin-engine pursuit, the P-38 Lightning, she did not continue flying after the war. By then she had married George Christie "Chris" Watson, a petroleum engineer with Phillips Petroleum. They had two daughters. After the girls were in school all day, Florene went back to college and earned her Bachelor of Business Administration degree from Lamar University in Beaumont where Chris was working for Phillips. "Then I drove two hundred miles a day to commute to the University of Houston to work on my MBA. I made straight As and graduated with honors."

When Chris was transferred from Beaumont to Houston, she began teaching business and secretarial classes at the University of Houston. Florene has taken additional graduate work at six different universities including the University of Aberdeen in Scotland and has taught at Howard College in Big Spring as well as Frank Phillips College in Borger, Texas, where she and Chris now live.

Since retiring from teaching, Florene has made herself available to speak on the subject of the WAFS and WASP and has been tireless in her efforts to tell the world of the accomplishments of these women who flew for the Army during World War II. Among her honors are: membership in the Kritser Aviation and Space Museum Distinguished Flying Corps, Amarillo, Texas; inducted into the International Forest of Friendship in Atchison, Kansas in 1995; a speaker at the Experimental Aircraft Association's Aviation Museum at the 1995 Oshkosh, Wisconsin, International Air Show; the first woman inducted into the [Texas] Panhandle Veterans Hall of Fame, August 1996.

She is a member of the Ninety-Nines and serves as Chaplain for the WASP organization, The Order of Fifinella. She was on the program with Attorney General Janet Reno when a bronze statue representing the WASP was dedicated and placed in the Honor Court of the Air Force Academy in Colorado Springs, September 19, 1997. She is also a member of the Texas Aviation Historical Society, the Confederate Air Force, the Women's Military Aviators, and the Air Force Association. Most recently, she represented the WAFS at the dedication of a plaque in the memory of Cornelia Fort. The plaque is located near the site of Cornelia's fatal March 1943 crash in Taylor County, Texas. This ceremony took place October 6, 2000, as part of the WASP 58th reunion held in nearby Sweetwater, where most of the WASP trained.

### Esther Nelson

At age twenty-one, Esther Gebbert of Los Angeles, enamored of flying, began to take lessons in North Hollywood from a flying instructor named Arthur Nelson. Six years later, in June 1936, the two were married. By 1938, Art and Esther had established a flying school in nearby Ontario and in 1939, Esther, too, became a flight instructor — making them well known in the southern California communities east of Los Angeles.

So when Art joined the Ferrying Division of the Air Transport Command, Esther wasn't far behind. She was thirty-three years old and one of the earliest arrivals in Wilmington on September 15, 1942. There is a small controversy regarding the number of hours Esther actually logged prior to her arrival. A news article quotes Esther as having 532 hours. In her book, *On Final Approach*, WASP Byrd Howell Granger (43-W-1) says that Esther had only 429 hours — not enough to qualify — but that Nancy Love went to bat for her with Colonel Baker. Either Esther had the requisite hours or Nancy was not about to turn away someone who had come clear across the country at her own expense to join — providing she was able to show sufficient flying skills. Esther got her flight test, which she passed, and is ranked as number seven in the WAFS original squadron.

October 22, Second Lieutenant Arthur G. Nelson, an officer in the ATC's California Group, got word that his wife had graduated from her initial thirty-day WAFS training. An article appeared in the local newspaper under the headline, "Man, Wife Commissioned as Pilots With the Ferrying Division of Army." A photo of the two of them — him in uniform and her in a stylish, belted jacket and slacks suit that was well ahead of its time and could be popular today — ran in a later edition headlined "Mr. and Mrs. Pilot."

Esther was quite tall — almost as tall as Del Scharr — and statuesque in build. She was a full head taller than tiny Betty Gillies. She was on the quiet side, but friendly. Teresa once commented that she looked like "she had just stepped out of the pages of *Vogue* magazine."

When the original WAFS squadron was split up in January 1943, Esther remained in Wilmington ferrying trainers and other single-engine light planes. In September of that year, Esther and Dorothy Fulton were sent from Wilmington to Palm Springs for what was rumored to be pursuit training, but nothing happened. They were then sent to Long Beach and, from there, reassigned.

Esther went to Fairfax Field in Kansas City for training as a B-25 co-pilot. She also attended Officer Training School in Orlando, Florida. From there, she was sent to Dallas. By then, Art was also stationed in Texas. In the photograph taken at the women's squadron final banquet in Dallas the night of December 19, 1944 Esther Nelson and Delphine Bohn are the only two Originals in attendance. Esther took a Reserve commission as a captain in the U.S. Air Force when it was offered after 1948. However, her name is listed as Carpenter in the Official WASP Roster so apparently she had gotten divorced and remarried by that time.

Esther died February 22, 1991.

*Barbara Poole (Shoemaker)*

Barbara Poole learned how to play bridge while a member of the WAFS squadron in Romulus and has gone on to become a Life Master. "I play a lot of bridge — mostly duplicate, because of the competition. It's a sophisticated game. I play two or three times a week. I love it — it's my hobby."

Her first lesson was the hardest one. She and WASP Margaret Ann Hamilton — who later married General William H. Tunner — were playing against Barbara Donahue and a male officer who was a highly ranked, competitive bridge player. "Playing for a quarter a point, in a hour we had lost $75."

Barbara says she vowed never to let that happen again.

Barbara Poole was born January 28, 1917, in the Bronx, New York. "But we were actually living in West Virginia at the time." Her father was Bert Sabin, a manufacturer. Her mother was Garnette Poole. When her parents were divorced, Barbara took her mother's name by choice. "After the divorce, my mother took a job as a salesgirl in Gimbel's basement to support herself and me. Six months later, she was an assistant buyer. In a year, she was head buyer in ready-to-wear. She had a very successful career in retail, worked there for many years and then went to The May Co."

The day she saw a JN4-D make a forced landing in a nearby field in New Jersey, Barbara became enamored of airplanes. She was three. "I remember it was yellow and a biplane. It looked like a Stearman. Years later I found out it was a Jenny. When I was growing up, my parents would tell me that if I was a good girl I'd grow wings and fly. I used to dream about growing wings and flying above the family car."

She did better than that, she learned to fly an airplane that soared far above earthbound automobiles. And then when she was flight instructing in Detroit she heard about the WAFS. "I was making ten dollars an hour, which was a fortune back then!" She had already gone to Montreal to try to join the group going with Jackie Cochran to fly in England for the ATA. She and Sis Bernheim were there at the same time and got the same disgruntled instructor who flunked all six American women that day. Barbara was the one responsible for notifying Sis when an opening in the WAFS squadron occurred late in the year.

Barbara had 1,800 qualifying hours but did not have certification of a 200-horsepower rating when she arrived in Wilmington and had to leave the squadron to go get it. She returned a day later and was accepted by Nancy Love and Colonel Baker. She is number nine of The Originals.

In January 1943 Barbara went to Romulus and ferried trainers. She left the squadron late in 1943 for health reasons. She eventually married Charlie Shoemaker and they had two children. A widow now, Barbara lives in Sarasota, Florida. And she still answers to her WAFS nickname, Puddles.

&

## Aline "Pat" Rhonie

Aline "Pat" Rhonie learned to fly in Reno, Nevada, in August 1930, earned her private license a month later and bought her first plane in January 1931. By December 1931 she had her transport license.

In 1933, she helped found the Luscombe Airplane Company in Kansas City, Missouri, and in 1934 was the first woman to make a solo flight from New York to Mexico City and back. Pat also flew gliders, test-flew Coupes, Luscombes and Monocoupes, and eventually got her twin-engine as well as seaplane ratings. She earned an English pilot's license in 1936 and in 1938 was the first American to obtain an Irish commercial pilot license. In 1940, in addition to working with the French Aero Club, Pat was also chair of the Aviation Committee, British War Relief Society in New York City. As a volunteer, using her own plane, she flew 26,000 miles around the United States in 1940/41 organizing committees and arranging benefits for relief of the Royal Air Force.

Pat is perhaps best known for her aviation artwork: "The Pre-Lindbergh Era of Aviation on Long Island" — the fresco done for the wall of hangar F at Roosevelt Field depicting the history of flying on Long Island, from the Wright Brothers and Glenn Curtiss up to Lindbergh's Paris Flight. It took her four years to complete the 1,400 square-foot mural.

Initially, Pat turned down the opportunity to fly for the Air Transport Auxiliary in England when Jackie Cochran was looking for volunteers in 1942, hoping for a similar opportunity in the U.S. She got it with Nancy Love's telegram on September 5, 1942 inviting her to try out for the WAFS. Pat was the fourth woman accepted, but she only served until the end of December 1942 when she resigned. By then, she had taken part in several ferrying missions, flying Cubs and PT-19s.

On November 30, 1943 Pat joined the ATA and her release date was November 19, 1944. She was the only woman to fly for both Nancy Love's Originals and Pauline Gower's ATA.

### *Helen Richards (Prosser)*

When Gary and Dean Prosser were growing up, they thought everybody's mother flew bombers and fighters. "But we had to pry the stories out of Mom. The P-51 was her hands-down favorite," says Gary, "particularly the P-51D with the Rolls Royce engine."

Helen Richards was the tenth Original — and the youngest, arriving in Wilmington in the latter half of September, 1942. Born August 2, 1921 to Arthur L. and Sedenia Dunford Richards, Helen had already earned an associates degree in liberal arts from Pasadena Junior College in California and was teaching flying at the Floating Feather Airport just outside Boise, Idaho when word came of Nancy Love's intention to form a women's squadron. She had 975 hours to her credit.

In January 1943, Helen was sent to Dallas where she and another young West Coast WAFS, Dorothy Scott, became best friends. They both entered pursuit school on December 1, 1943. Sadly, Dorothy was killed the third day of training but Helen became one of the earliest graduates in January 1944. Reassigned to Long Beach, she flew all the pursuits and once proved her mettle in a contest with a male pilot, flying a P-47 — out-maneuvering him, she came up behind him for the kill. Helen also did a flying sequence in a BT-13 for *Ladies Courageous*, the movie about Nancy Love and the WAFS starring Loretta Young. And once she received a letter from General George commending her for flying more airplanes than anyone else in a given month.

Helen and future husband, Don Prosser, met in CPT class at Pasadena in the fall of 1939 — they were the top male and female graduates. Don ended up in Arizona instructing US Army and RAF cadets. "Early one Sunday morning, I was blasted out of my bed by a roaring BT-13. It was Helen on a ferrying mission. Then she flew a P-38 in and told the mechanic that it had an oil leak. He told her he couldn't find it. She said 'keep looking, you'll find it.' I proposed to her that night. It rattled her so much, when she took off the next morning, the cover was still on the pitot tube. She flew the first leg without knowing her airspeed." Helen told Del Scharr that once, ferrying a P-51 east, she was admiring her diamond ring and became "so engrossed in my dreams along the way, when I came to, I had drifted forty miles off course and was over Mexico!" Helen and Don were married Christmas Day 1944.

After the war they went into the flight service business and both earned teaching degrees at Fresno State. They lived in Taft and Helen taught some special education classes, mostly kids with muscular dystrophy. In 1968, Don was offered a position teaching aviation in high school in northern California and they moved to Clear Lake.

On October 23, 1976, Helen was giving a bi-annual flight check to a friend who owned a Beechcraft Bonanza. Something happened during the simulated forced landing — it rolled into an inverted dive and crashed. This tragedy took place one day after the death of Helen's hero, Nancy Love.

"In lieu of flowers, I requested that a fund be set up for high school scholarships for students that, although not otherwise qualified, perhaps were still deserving of the honor," Don says. "To this date, more than twenty scholarships have been awarded. It is set up so that it will continue indefinitely."

Naturally, Helen and Don taught Gary and Dean to fly. Gary now flies

Boeing 777s for United Airlines.

"My parents' love of planes was contagious," says Dean. "It's in our genes. Mom gave me my primary instruction in our Cessna 140. Here I am in this family of flying aces and I just wasn't getting it. But she kept saying 'it's gonna happen.' And one day it did — it all came together. She was my best friend. I miss her everyday."

✒

## *Adela Riek Scharr*

Adela Riek Scharr was actually the seventh woman to join the WAFS squadron, immediately following Catherine Slocum. But when Slocum was called home after the thirty-day training period and did not return, Del became the sixth member in the final active listing. Born August 10, 1907, she was one of the oldest of The Originals when she was accepted.

Tall — five feet nine-plus inches — and slender, Del Riek was the tomboy daughter of a St. Louis police officer. Her parents expected her to be a schoolteacher from the time she started kindergarten. She graduated from Harris Teachers College not long after Lindbergh made his historic Atlantic solo flight in 1927. She entered the classrooms of the St. Louis public schools and began to fulfill her destiny, also earning a Master of Arts in psychology from the University of Missouri.

Then yet another destiny began to beckon. Inspired by Lindbergh's feats, Del put on a pair of borrowed white coveralls and climbed into the cockpit of a biplane. That was on Easter Sunday, 1935 and, in her own words: "I haven't been the same since." She soloed on July 24 of that year in Great Lakes #NC11318. Through flying at Lambert Field in St. Louis, she met and married Harold Scharr. Harold was, by then, in the Naval Reserve.

Unfortunately, at that time the St. Louis Board of Education forced married women employees to resign or be fired. Now out of a job, Del put her aviation skills to work. She taught ground school and also hopped passengers. Later that year, she earned her instructor's rating and became

Lambert Field's first female flight instructor. And so yet another teaching career, that of flight instructor, was born.

Among her many students was her husband, Harold. She soloed him, and took him through his private license. By the time Del received her telegram from Nancy Love, the Scharrs were expecting Harold to be shipped overseas any day. A patriot to the core, Del knew that the WAFS was where she belonged. With her husband's full support, she left immediately for New Castle Army Air Base. As it turned out, Harold wasn't shipped out until 1944.

In Wilmington, Del was checked out in a PT-19 by Lt. Joe Tracy. She felt pretty good about flying the 165-horsepower, low-winged trainer and passed with no problem. By then she had 1,429 hours to her credit.

Del served in Wilmington through the end of 1942. In January 1943, she was sent to Romulus as commander of the WAFS squadron that was part of the 3rd Ferrying Group. On June 28, 1943, she became the first woman to fly the dangerous single-engine pursuit, the P-39 Airacobra. Nancy Love relieved Del of her command in Romulus, summer 1943. She returned briefly to Wilmington in August and, in the fall of 1943, was transferred to Long Beach where she became almost exclusively a pursuit pilot ferrying P-51s to the east coast and P-39s or P-47s back west.

Del experienced physical problems throughout 1944, including anemia. In September, doctors finally diagnosed her underlying problem and, eventually, she underwent a hysterectomy. On November 30, 1944, she left Long Beach for home. Since the WASPs were being deactivated December 20 and she would not be sufficiently recovered in time to fly before then, she was given permission to leave early.

After the war, Del returned to teaching. The St. Louis Board of Education by then took a more enlightened view of married women teachers. And she was more fortunate than her close friend Teresa James. Harold came home from the war alive, bearing all the letters she had written him — several each week. Del used those letters, her orders and other paper work she had preserved, and interviews with fellow Originals to write about her wartime experiences. *Sisters in the Sky Volume I — The WAFS* was published in 1986; *Sisters in the Sky Volume II — The WASP* was published in 1988.

On July 17, 1986, Del received the Spirit of St. Louis Aviation Award. She died March 11, 1998.

❧

## *Dorothy Scott*

Dorothy Scott's life was cut short when the BC-1 (AT-6) trainer she was flying, with her instructor, was overtaken during landing by a much faster P-39 flying above and behind her. The sun was low, blinding both pilots. They collided in mid-air and all three pilots died. She was not held responsible for the accident. The blame was placed on the tower and the P-39 pilot. The date was December 3, 1943. It was her second day of training at pursuit school in Palm Springs, California. Dorothy was twenty-three — the second of Nancy Love's original WAFS to die on active service.

Dorothy and her twin brother, Edward, were born February 18, 1920, in Seattle. They grew up and went to school in Oroville near the border with British Columbia.

She attended the University of Washington and, there, learned to fly floatplanes at Lake Union. She and her father, who was also learning to fly, competed to see who could solo first. She won. She was a flight instructor at Washington State College in Pullman when word of the WAFS squadron reached her. She was shy of the required five hundred hours and lacking her 200-horsepower rating as well, so she went to work and brought both up to the necessary levels, earning her horsepower rating just in time to head east.

Dorothy's arrival in Wilmington on November 21, 1942, and her acceptance as number twenty-five put the squadron at full strength. Catherine Slocum had left a month earlier after completing the 30-day indoctrination training. In mid-November, Nancy Love accepted four more women pilots — Dorothy Fulton, Betsy Ferguson, Bernice Batten and lastly Dorothy Scott — to get her magic number of twenty-five. The four took their preliminary training together.

On January 1, 1943, having only been in Wilmington six weeks, Dorothy was one of five Originals transferred to Dallas Love Field and the 5th Ferrying Group. Her closest friend was Helen Richards. In Dallas, she checked out in the BT-13, AT-6, C-78, AT-17, AT-9, C-47, A-24 and C-60. She also was sent to instrument school at Love Field in September 1943 and did so well, she was slated to be an instrument instructor, but her assignment to pursuit school came along and changed that. She left Dallas on November 30, for Palm Springs.

The local airport near Oroville, Washington is named The Dorothy Scott International Airport in her memory. It is a port of entry into Canada on highway U.S. 97. Her brother, Edward, lives in Oroville.

## *Evelyn Sharp*

Evelyn Genevieve Sharp began life as Lois Genevie Crouse on October 1, 1919, though October 20 was, for years, given as her birth date. She was adopted by John and Mary Sharp on December 22, 1919, and given the name by which, ever after, she was known. She died April 3, 1944, in New Cumberland, Pennsylvania, as the result of a crash of the P-38 she was ferrying from California to Newark. Her story is told, briefly, in Chapter 28 and in great detail by Diane Ruth Armour Bartels in *Sharpie*.

Bartels was researching the book when Hillary Rodham Clinton's *It Takes a Village* was published. Bartels notes that Mrs. Clinton's premise — "that it takes more than a mother, a father, or a grandparent to bring up a child; it requires nurturing, discipline, and unconditional love from neighbors next door, the community, and indeed, society itself. . ." — was well borne out by Evelyn Sharp. Evelyn had all of those things going for her. She was raised by not only loving parents, but an entire village — the town of Ord, Nebraska. She and her parents moved there in March 1930 and Evelyn entered Miss Lucille Witter's fifth grade class at South School. In fall 1933, she enrolled in Ord High School and graduated as a member of the class of 1937. In four years time, Evelyn proved herself the All-American girl — excelling at everything she tried, including flying airplanes.

The town of Ord, led by community-minded optometrist Dr. Glen Auble, helped her buy her first airplane and helped her raise the money to go to school to get her transport license. Evelyn gave freely of herself, her talents and her time to her town and her town, in return, gave back to her their love and support. It was a love affair of the highest order. Indeed, when Evelyn died, the whole town mourned. They buried her with dignity and sorrow. Plans were announced the day of her funeral to rename the airport in Ord and to erect a fitting memorial.

On April 8, 1947, a crate arrived addressed to John Sharp in care of the local Postmaster, Alfred L. Hill. Inside was the disassembled, three-bladed propeller from a P-38 and the parts to put it back together. And so on September 12, 1948, Evelyn Sharp Field was dedicated, with flyovers by P-51s, B-26s and new F-80 jets flown by the Nebraska Air National

Guard. The Ord High School band played for one of its own. The silver blades of the P-38 propeller topped a concrete pyramid-shaped monument. Twenty years later, glass-enclosed cases were built to display much of Evelyn's memorabilia that John Sharp had sent to the Nebraska State Historical Society soon after her death.

A white wooden cross marks Evelyn's gravesite, located a half mile southeast of Evelyn Sharp Field.

As of 1996, she was the only woman to be inducted into Nebraska's Aviation Hall of Fame. The first Evelyn Sharp Day was held in Ord, June 1996. Nancy Batson Crews, the fellow Original who had accompanied Evelyn's body home for burial in April 1944, drove from Alabama to Ord for that occasion.

In addition to *Sharpie*, Nebraska Public Television, with Diane Bartels' help and the on-camera participation of WAFS original B.J. Erickson London and WASP Iris Cummings Critchell (43-W-2), has produced a half-hour video, *Sharpie: Born to Fly*, that is well worth watching.

> *I have laughed, shared tears, and put my arms around those who knew and remembered her, and those who have only heard the stories about this young aviatrix. The persona of Evelyn Sharp has left "indelible footprints" on their hearts as well as mine.*
>
> Diane Ruth Armour Bartels, August 1996

᠊ᠥᢩ

## Katherine Rawls Thompson

"Katherine Rawls — or as we called her, Katie — was by far the best all-around swimming and diving athlete of the time," says WASP Iris Cummings Critchell (43-W-2), who swam with and against her in national and Olympic competitions from 1935 to 1939. Both were members of the 1936 U.S. Olympic swimming team. "She was a champion at short and long distance events and in diving as well — one of the few who excelled at all three. She qualified for the

1936 Olympic team in four events — three swimming plus springboard diving."

Katherine Rawls was born June 14, 1917, in Nashville, Tennessee, but the family moved to Florida by the time she was five. "My father had a job helping build roads, until the Depression when he became one of the original farmers in Belle Glade," she told a reporter interviewing her for a newspaper article January 14, 1982. "When he was building roads, the families all lived together in camps. The camps were built next to lakes and there was nothing else to do but swim."

The entire family — she had three sisters and a brother — swam competitively and Katie's father coached her early efforts. She was the first woman to win four national championships in a single meet, a feat she accomplished twice. The first time was in 1933 when she won what one newspaper called "an unlikely combination of springboard diving, 200-meter breaststroke, half-mile freestyle, and 300-meter individual medley."

"She was a fine sportswoman, one of the best sports I've ever known. Competitive athletics was something she handled gracefully and yet was supportive of others," says Iris.

"She had a killer instinct that has softened considerably in her later years," Alicia Komlo, a close friend, told the reporter in that January 1982 newspaper article. "She was so highly competitive, she put 120 percent effort into everything. She was determined to be the tops."

By 1937, Katherine had met and married Ted Thompson, who then became her coach for the remainder of her time in competition. But, according to Iris, all the young swimmers and divers knew the war in Europe spelled the end of the Olympics — at least for the duration. There would be no games in 1940. All, including Katie and Iris, turned their energies elsewhere. As it happened, they both turned to flying and eventually ended up as part of the WASPs.

Ted Thompson also was a pilot and an instructor who ran a flight school. He taught Katherine how to fly. With her superb coordination and athletic conditioning, she took to it like an eaglet to flight. They owned a hangar and a rough-cut landing strip in Fort Lauderdale and stayed in the flight school business until the war came. Then the Navy took over Ted's flight school and he joined the RAF as a ferry pilot.

In September 1942, Katherine also got her chance to fly for her country when she joined Nancy Love's WAFS as number twenty-one and went to Romulus in January 1943. Then on September 30 of that year she was sent to Palm Springs with a small group under Evelyn Sharp's command. Rumor was they were to transition into pursuits, but nothing happened. In the meantime, Ted had returned from the service and wanted his wife home.

"She left Palm Springs soon after we arrived and went home," says WASP Mary Lou Colbert (43-W-1), who was part of the Palm Springs group. She did stay long enough to be in a photograph taken of the group — a treasure still in Colbert's possession. (see page 237)

"When Ted finished, he wanted her to stay at home and be a cookie-baking momma, which she wasn't about to be," Alicia Komlo said in the 1982 interview.

"I fell in love with flying," Katherine told the reporter. "I didn't really enjoy swimming as much because it was practice, practice, practice. It was work. So many hours put into it."

Eventually Katherine and Ted were divorced. She married again but chose to use her maiden name. She also returned to the water and became the swim pro and pool manager at The Greenbrier in White Sulphur Springs, West Virginia. When she retired January 1, 1978 she moved to Royal Palm Beach, Florida.

Until Tracy Caulkins came along and broke her record in 1981, Katie Rawls had won more national swimming and diving championships (thirty-three) than anyone. And she brought the United States a Silver Medal in the 1936 Olympics.

In 1981, she had three surgeries for a brain tumor. Katherine Rawls died of cancer on April 8, 1982, in Florida.

*ఇ*

### *Barbara Towne*
### *(Dickson, Fraskin)*

Barbara Towne became the eleventh woman accepted into the WAFS in late September 1942. Barbara's arrival, along with that of Barbara Poole and Helen Richards, marked the beginning of the entry into the squadron of the younger women flyers.

Barbara Towne was born December 21, 1916, to Gardner Bowers and Gladys (McLachlen) Towne in San Francisco. Unbeknownst to her father, she began taking flying lessons and had actually soloed a Taylor Cub in 1936 by the time he discovered what she was doing. He promptly sent her to Ryan School of Aeronautics in San Diego. Upon graduation, she was hired to teach in their Civilian Pilot Training program.

Barbara had recently married Army Air Forces pilot Robert Dickson. She read about Nancy Love and the formation of the WAFS in a San Francisco newspaper in September 1942. Not content to sit home and do nothing with a war on and her husband in the service, Barbara went east to Wilmington to join the WAFS. She spent four months as part of the 2nd Ferrying Group at New Castle ferrying PT-19s and Cubs. In February 1943, she was transferred to the 6th Ferrying Group in Long Beach, California, where she remained for the rest of her service time, and immediately began to transition into bigger airplanes, beginning with the BT-13.

In June 1943, she, Evelyn Sharp and B.J. Erickson were sent to Palm Springs to check out in the swift new pursuit plane, the P-51. Nancy Love had flown it four months earlier, paving the way for them. Even though Barbara was pregnant with her first child by then, she was such a supremely competent pilot that she checked out and began to ferry the pursuits without a hitch. According to B.J., "She flew the P-51 until she could no longer get the stick back."

Once she reached that point, Barbara did administrative duties for B.J. for awhile, then left and went home to give birth to her son, Roger, on December 13, 1943. She returned briefly in 1944, but, not satisfied with the care she had arranged for her infant son during her absence on ferrying trips, she resigned in August 1944 and went home permanently.

Barbara and Robert Dickson had a second son, Robert, on May 21, 1948. Eventually divorced from Robert Dickson, she married David Fasken in London, England, in 1982.

At the time of her death — December 19, 1995 — Barbara still owned three aircraft — a fixed wing and two helicopters. She had continued to fly the smaller of the helicopters, an MC 500, up until two years before her death at the age of seventy-eight.

## *Alma Heflin McCormick and Catherine Slocum*

Two of the earliest women accepted into the WAFS — Alma Heflin and Catherine Slocum — never ferried.

Alma Heflin McCormick was a test pilot for Piper and also the author of several books about her adventures flying Cubs over very unforgiving terrain in Canada and Alaska. She passed her initial flight test for the WAFS but, like Barbara Poole, was sent back to get the 200-horsepower rating she was missing.

In *On Final Approach,* Byrd Granger writes of Alma: "Sadly, her years of flying Cubs made it impossible for her to transition easily onto the 165 horsepower Fairchild PT-19 trainer used in the women's flight check."

Catherine Slocum qualified for the thirty-day orientation training and commuted daily from Philadelphia, leaving her four children in the care of a nurse. However, when the woman sustained an injury, Catherine felt she must leave the squadron and return home.

Betty Gillies commented on Slocum: "She completed training at NCAAB and was ready for orders, but felt that the job would keep her too far away from home for too long. So she resigned to go home and take care of her four small children. Catherine left October 20, which was two days before we received our first orders. So Catherine didn't do any ferrying — to the best of my knowledge."

And, finally, the woman who started it all . . .

## NANCY LOVE

Nancy Harkness Love — the architect of the Women's Auxiliary Ferrying Squadron of World War II — was not a diary keeper. She downplayed the historical implications of her work and left little in the way of a paper trail — two boxes of assorted documents and letters, a scrapbook kept by her father, and a couple of dozen photos. She died young, at sixty-two, of cancer — before reaching the age when many begin to think memoir, act on their instincts, and write.

She was born Hannah Lincoln Harkness to Robert and Alice Harkness on February 14, 1914, in Houghton, Michigan. But the name Nancy, bestowed on her by her father, stuck. She married Bob Love in January 1936, was part of the Golden Age of Aviation in the 1930s, and continued her flight to destiny into World War II where aviation came of age. And Nancy was an integral part of that, too.

Through talking to the women who flew with her, a picture of enigmatic Nancy Harkness Love emerges — a friend, a role model, a mentor, a woman with an open and innovative mind, a woman who learned to fly while still a girl, and who continued her love affair with aviation throughout her life. She also was tough —outwardly —when she had to be and "could cuss like a sailor," according to Nancy Batson Crews when she felt the need to do so.

In 1942, the other WAFS had the same technical piloting skills as Nancy Love, and several had considerably more hours of flight time, but no one else had the vision — or the opportunity. She took her 1,100 hours — dating from those first ten hours in Jimmy Hansen's Fleet Biplane in late August 1930, her close call with the bell tower at Milton Academy, her Airmarking Project experience, and her first ferrying job to Canada — and when war came to the United States, she volunteered for service. Calling on her flying ability and on her gifts of vision and organization, Nancy Love parlayed those attributes — and the ability to talk to and get along with high-ranking military men — into a program that put women in the cockpits of Army planes for the first time and changed the way those military men thought about women pilots.

On November 14, 1944, Brigadier General C.R. Smith, U.S. Army Chief of Staff, wrote the following to Ferrying Division commander General Robert E. Nowland, General Tunner's successor:

> Before Mrs. Love gets out of the service, if that comes to pass, I would like to see her get a trip to some of our foreign stations. This should have been done a long time ago, as we wanted some of the WASPs to make foreign ferries, but you know the reason why that could not be done.
>
> Within the next two or three weeks we will have either one or two B-24s to be ferried to India-China. If you would want Mrs. Love to go along on one of these airplanes as a passenger, there is no objection to that.

On November 20, 1944, General Smith wrote to General Tunner at headquarters in Hastings Mill outside of Calcutta:

> Would like for Nancy Love to go to Calcutta for the purpose of looking over our operation. Will be necessary that permission of Theater Commander be secured. Would you secure that permission and inform us.

Immediately after the deactivation of the WASPs on December 20, 1944, Nancy Love — Assistant to the Assistant Chief of Staff, Operations, Ferrying Division, Air Transport Command and grade CAF-9 — had one last assignment awaiting her. Armed with the required security clearance and a passport — issued on December 23 — Nancy reported to the New York Aerial Port of Embarkation on December 27. Destination Calcutta. The purpose of her trip was stated as: "TDY for purpose of coordinating Ferrying Division matters and upon completion thereof will return to Cincinnati, Ohio." Her per diem, for travel outside the continental limits of the U.S., was boosted to $7 per day — up from the $6 issued to pilots ferrying airplanes in the United States.

Her scheduled flight out of New York's LaGuardia was on the "Crescent" run to Karachi, India. Crescent was the name for one of several worldwide air routes established early in World War II for the movement of military personnel and materiel. The Crescent route was from Bermuda across the Atlantic to the Azores, to Casablanca, Tripoli, Cairo, Abadan, Karachi, and on to Calcutta. Over that route, airplanes and cargo were ferried to India to supply the China-Burma-India Theater of War, or "The Hump."

The Hump, 550 miles long and 50 miles wide, was the route over part of the Himalayan Mountains (flying above 20,000 feet in bad weather) and the jungles of Burma and into Kunming, China — elevation 6,000 feet. Through The Hump airlift, the U. S. supplied the Chinese Army so that it could keep the Japanese busy fighting on a second front. It was to that command that General Tunner was sent in August 1944.

Following several postponements due to mechanical difficulty with the hydraulic system of the airplane she was scheduled to fly, Nancy finally left New York on a contract carrier. Flying via Bermuda and the Azores, she arrived in Casablanca on December 29. She was due out of Casablanca the following morning on a C-54, but instead spent two days in that North African city as that ship, too, was grounded with hydraulic trouble.

Among other things, Nancy's job on this trip was to check up on the efficiency of the ATC's Crescent run. As Nancy wrote to General Nowland in her Trip Report:

> The entire attitude toward Crescent, insofar as its Karachi run is concerned, seemed to be one of mild derision. This was true both at LaGuardia and at Casablanca. Much of this is undoubtedly due to normal inter-division competitive spirit, but is also founded on some truth, if my experience was a representative one.

Passengers at New York were put off several times, then finally canceled, thus missing several other possible flights.

I saw and talked with several Crescent crews at Bermuda and Lagens, and the attitude of operations personnel at these two stations was very favorable toward the efficiency of the Crescent operation. However, these ships were all going to UK and to Paris. My conclusion was that the India run was being necessarily neglected in favor of the European runs. However it would seem desirable that some attempt be made to maintain even a reduced schedule if the Indian run is to be called a regular airplane service. The reluctance of operations personnel along the route to book passengers or cargo on Crescent is the inevitable result of its unreliability and is resulting in a bad name for the Ferrying Division.

Nancy continued on to Calcutta on a regular North African Division twin-engine C-46. There she was reunited with her former commanding officer, General Tunner and spent the rest of January interviewing pilots and staff. She concluded her Trip Report by writing, "After several side trips to China and the Assam Valley stations, I left Calcutta on 29 January with General C.R. Smith and his Aide, Captain Wiseman, and returned to Cincinnati via Australia, arriving here on 6 February."

Little else is known about Nancy's trip over The Hump and around the world in January 1945. Her daughters relate that she "flew" part of the trip in either the left or right seat. But it was unofficial, in fact wouldn't have been allowed except that she was flying with men of command status who knew her capabilities. Her Trip Report to General Nowland is dated February 9, 1945.

With that, the name Nancy Love faded from the duty rosters of the Ferrying Division, Air Transport Command, U. S. Army Air Forces.

In 1946, Colonel Robert M. Love and Mrs. Nancy H. Love became the first couple in history to be simultaneously decorated by the U.S. military. Colonel Love received the Distinguished Service Medal for "exceptionally meritorious" service as deputy commander of the European Ferrying Division of the ATC and later the West Coast Wing, ATC. He also received three Bronze Battle Stars for combat in the Asiatic Pacific Theater of Operations and the Air Medal for achievement in flight in China. Nancy was awarded the Air Medal, along with an accompanying citation signed by President Truman noting her "operational leadership in the successful training and assignment of over 300 qualified women fliers in the flying of advanced military aircraft." Lieutenant General Harold L. George, chief of the ATC, presented both of their medals.

When the war was over, Nancy Love did what most young American women who lived through World War II did, she went home and had babies — three of them. She had her children late — more like the career-minded women of today — consequently she was still being a mother well into her fifties. Nancy's three daughters further enhance the image of the woman their mother became in the 1950s and '60s: "We had a wonderful childhood," says Marky. "From 1952 on, soon after my younger sister Allie was born, we lived on Martha's Vineyard and an airplane was often the only way to get to the mainland. I used to tell my friends that my mother flew us to the doctor and dentist." She laughs, "Didn't everybody's?"

Nancy did not "work" outside the home, other than helping out her husband with some management details in his airplane and boating businesses. And she never again took on anything remotely like the scope of what she was involved in during the war. She devoted herself fully to her husband and her three daughters, continuing to fly until the early 1970s when she first became ill with cancer. She died October 22, 1976 in Sarasota, Florida.

Updated information on each of the WAFS was our goal; however, some of the biographies are incomplete. The International Women's Air and Space Museum, located in Cleveland, Ohio and The Woman's Collection at Texas Woman's University located in Denton, would appreciate having more complete information on all the WAFS and WASPs. TWU is where the WASP archives are housed. If anyone can enlighten them — or this author — with missing details about any of these women, please use the addresses below. Additional information can be placed in the archives of the two facilities for future researchers to access. And, should this book be reprinted at a later date, updates could be made to individual biographies.

Joan Hrubec, Museum Director/Trustee
International Women's Air and Space Museum
Room 165, Burke Lakefront Airport
1501 North Marginal Road
Cleveland OH 44114
USA
Phone: 216-623-1111
Fax: 216-623-1113
Website: www.iwasm.org

Dawn Letson, Director
WAFS/WASP Collection
Blagg-Huey Library
Texas Woman's University
P.O. Box 425528
Denton TX 76204-5528
Phone: 940-898-2665
Fax: 940-898-3764
E-mail: dletson@twu.edu

Sarah Byrn Rickman
Disc-Us Books
4010 Sawyer Court
Sarasota FL 34233
Phone: 941-927-1063
E-mail: books@disc-us.com

# GLOSSARY

**AAB** — Army Air Base

**AAC** — Army Air Corps

**AAF** — Army Air Forces

**AF** — Air Force

**Alert Room** — Where pilots await flight orders.

**AT** — Advanced training aircraft, flown in the third of three-stage flight instruction.

**ATA** — Air Transport Auxiliary (to the British Royal Air Force — see RAF)

**ATC** — Air Transport Command

**AUS** — Army of the United States

**B-4 Bag** — Canvas luggage that converts into a hanging bag.

**Base Leg** — Part of the landing pattern — the short leg lying at right angles to, and downwind from, the landing strip. The base leg follows the downwind leg and precedes the final approach in the landing sequence.

**Beam** — The sound made up of the combined Morse Code sound for A (dot-dash) and N (dash-dot), making a solid hum. This led a pilot to the airport. The signals became increasingly strong when flying to the broadcasting point and diminished when flying away from the station. It narrowed to a "cone of silence" directly over the emitting station. The sound of the beam is loudest immediately prior to that point.

**Biplane** — An airplane with double wings, one above the other.

**BOQ** — Bachelor Officer Quarters

**BT** — Basic training aircraft flown in the second of three-stage flight instruction.

**Buddy Ride** — Two pilots: one practiced instrument flying "under the hood" while the other served as the safety pilot and kept an eye out for other aircraft.

**CAA** — Civil Aeronautics Authority

**CAP** — Civil Air Patrol

**Ceiling** — Vertical distance from ground to cloud cover.

**CO** — Commanding Officer

**Commercial License** — A federal certificate that allowed a pilot to carry passengers for hire or to haul freight.

**Control Tower** — Tower at an airfield with air traffic controllers who stay in radio contact with pilots in the area, giving them orders until the plane leaves the area or turns off onto the taxiway and is under ground control via radioed orders.

**CPT Program** — Civilian Pilot Training Program; a federal program that subsidized individuals learning to fly 1939-1941.

**Downwind Leg** — The first leg of the flight path of the landing pattern. It parallels the runway opposite the direction in which you plan to land.

**FERD** — Ferrying Division

**FG** — Ferrying Group

**Final Approach** — The last or third leg of the flight pattern where the pilot descends from pattern altitude to the runway, normally into the wind.

**Gosport** — A tube with earphones at one end and a voice cone at the other, used in planes with no interphone system (no radio) to enable instructor to give orders to student.

**Ground Loop** — A high-speed skidding turn by an aircraft on the ground after landing. It is usually caused by loss of control.

**HQ** — Headquarters

**IFR** — Instrument Flight Rules or flying without visual reference to the ground.

**Instrument Conditions** — When there is no visible horizon or when the ceiling is lower than allowable for visual flying.

**Link Trainer** — A simulator with actual aircraft instruments and controls that allows a pilot to practice instrument flying without leaving the ground.

**P** — Designation for pursuit or fighter aircraft, as in P-47.

**Pitch** — The up-and-down motion of the nose of the airplane over its lateral axis.

**Private License** — A federal license earned by a pilot who has demonstrated sufficient skills to be allowed to carry passengers, but not for hire.

**PT** — Primary trainer, the first stage of three-stage flight instruction of military flight training in World War II.

**RAF** — Royal Air Force

**Roll** — An airplane's motion around its longitudinal axis (one wing is lowered to begin the roll).

**RON** — Remain Over Night

**Stick** — A control device usually found in single-engine aircraft, which operates the ailerons and the elevators.

**SNAFU** — Situation normal, all fouled up.

**TDY** — Temporary duty away from home base.

**Transition** — Instructing a pilot on how to fly an aircraft in which the pilot lacks experience.

**VFR** — Visual Flight Rules or clear weather where the pilot can see the ground and the ceiling is high enough to allow the pilot to maintain cruising altitude without flying into clouds.

**WAAC** — Women's Auxiliary Army Corps

**WAC** — Women's Army Corps

**WAFS** — Women's Auxiliary Ferrying Squadron

**WASP** — Women Airforce Service Pilots

**WFTD** — Women's Flying Training Detachment

**WTS** — War Training Service

**Yaw** — An airplane's motion from side to side around its vertical axis (the wings stay level and the nose moves from side to side).

# BIBLIOGRAPHY

Bartels, Diane Ruth Armour. *Sharpie: The Life Story of Evelyn Sharp, Nebraska's Aviatrix*, Lincoln, Nebraska: Dageforde Publishing, 1996.

Bohn, Delphine. *Catch a Shooting Star* (WAFS 1942-1944), Unpublished book-length manuscript circa 1985. Copies available at The Woman's Collection, Texas Woman's University, Denton, Texas and the International Women's Air and Space Museum, Cleveland, Ohio.

Cochran, Jacqueline and MaryAnn Bucknum Brinley. *Jackie Cochran: Autobiography / Greatest Woman Pilot in Aviation History*, New York: Bantam Books, 1987.

Cochran, Jacqueline. *The Stars at Noon*, Boston and Toronto: Little, Brown and Company in association with Atlantic Monthly, 1954.

Cole, Jean Hascall (44-W-2). *Women Pilots of World War II*, Salt Lake City: University of Utah Press, 1992.

Curtis, Lettice. *The Forgotten Pilots: A Story of the Air Transport Auxiliary 1939-45*, Cheltenham, England, Westward Digital Limited, Fourth Edition, 1998. (First published 1971)

Goodwin, Doris Kearns. *No Ordinary Time — Franklin and Eleanor Roosevelt: The Home Front in World War II*, New York: Simon & Schuster, 1994.

Gott, Kay (43-W-2). *Women In Pursuit: A Collection & Recollection*, Self published, 1993.

Granger, Byrd Howell (44-W-1). *On Final Approach: The Women Airforce Service Pilots of World War II*, Scottsdale, Arizona: Falconer Publishing Company, 1991.

Keil, Sally VanWagenen. *Those Wonderful Women In Their Flying Machines: The Unknown Heroines of World War II*, New York: Four Directions Press, 1979.

Kershner, William K. *The Student Pilot's Flight Manual*, Seventh Edition, Ames, Iowa: Iowa State University Press, 1993.

LaFarge, Oliver (Lt. Colonel Air Force Reserve). *The Eagle in the Egg*, Boston: Houghton Mifflin Co., The Riverside Press, 1949.

Lomax, Judy. *Women of the Air*, New York: Ivy Books, Ballantine Books 1986.

Makanna, Philip. *Ghosts: Vintage Aircraft of World War II*, Charlottesville, Virginia: Thomasson–Grant, 1987.

Marx, Capt. Walter J. "Women Pilots in the Ferrying Division Air Transport Command" (In accordance with AAF Regulation No. 20-8 and AAF Letter 40-34), 1944-45, Nancy Harkness Love Private Collection.

Morrissey, Muriel Earhart and Carol L. Osborne. *Amelia, My Courageous Sister: Biography of Amelia Earhart*, Santa Clara, California: Osborne Publisher Inc., 1987.

Oakes, Claudia M. *United States Women in Aviation 1930-1939*, Washington and London: Smithsonian Institution Press.

Scharr, Adela Riek (WAFS). *Sister in the Sky, Volume I The WAFS* and *Volume II The WASP*, St. Louis: The Patrice Press, 1986 & 1988.

Simbeck, Rob. *Daughter of the Air: The Brief Soaring Life of Cornelia Fort*, New York: Atlantic Monthly Press, 1999.

Thaden, Louise. *High, Wide and Frightened*, New York: Air Facts Press, 1973.

Tunner, William H. (Lt. General, USAF) and Booton Herndon. *Over the Hump: The Story of General William H. Tunner, The Man Who Moved Anything, Anywhere, Anytime*, New York: Duell, Sloan & Pearce, 1964.

Verges, Marianne. *On Silver Wings: The Women Airforce Service Pilots of World War II 1942-1944*, New York: Ballantine Books, 1991.

## Magazines, Journals and Newspapers

*Aviation Heritage* magazine, May 1992: "WASPs of War" by Deborah G. Douglas, Pre-doctoral fellow at the National Air and Space Museum, The Woman's Collection, Texas Woman's University.

*Journal, American Aviation Historical Society*, Summer 1995: "What's All the Fuss About... My WAFS/WASP Flying Experience" by Kathryn (Sis) Bernheim Fine, as told to Sam Parker, The Woman's Collection, Texas Woman's University.

*N.A.A. Magazine*, August 1936: "Five Women Tackle the Nation" by Louise Thaden, Air Marking Pilot, Bureau of Air Commerce and Secretary, N.A.A. International Women's Air and Space Museum Collection, Cleveland, Ohio.

*Official WASP Roster*, Published biannually by the WASP.

*The Sportsman Pilot,* May 15, 1938: From the Nancy Harkness Love Private Collection.

*Tennessee Historical Quarterly*, Winter 1981, Spring 1982: "Cornelia Fort: Pioneer Woman Military Aviator" Parts I and II, by Doris Brinker Tanner, International Women's Air and Space Museum Collection.

*Woman's Home Companion* magazine, July 1943: "At Twilight's Last Gleaming" by Cornelia Fort, published posthumously. From The Woman's Collection Texas Woman's University.

## The Internet

The Ninety-Nines web site — http://www.ninety-nines.org/airmark.html

History of North American Aviation — www.boeing.com/company/offices/history/bna/p51

## Personal Interviews

WAFS:

> Nancy Batson Crews
> Teresa James
> Barbara Jane Erickson London
> Gertrude Meserve Tubbs LeValley
> Florene Miller Watson
> Barbara Poole Shoemaker
> Phyllis Burchfield Fulton

Others:

> Hannah Lincoln Love Robinson, Margaret and Alice Love (Nancy
> Love's daughters)
> W. Gerould Clark III and William Goodman Clark (Helen Mary
> Clark's sons)
> Donald, Gary and Dean Prosser (Helen Richards Prosser's husband
> and sons)
> Honey Fulton Parker (Dorothy Fulton's sister)
> Iris Cummings Critchell (WASP 43-W-2)
> Mary Lou Colbert Neale (WASP 43-W-1)
> Ann Hamilton Tunner (WASP 43-W-2)
> Kay Gott Chaffey (WASP 43-W-2)

## Written correspondence

WAFS: Barbara Donahue Ross and Bernice Batten
Sherrill Arnet (Lenore McElroy's daughter)

## Archives

The Betty Gillies Collection of Private Papers, International Women's Air
and Space Museum
Teresa James Collection of Private Papers, including articles written by Teresa
for *World War II Times*
Nancy Harkness Love Collection of Private Papers
Nancy Batson Crews Collection of Private Papers
Nancy Batson Crews, assorted photos and papers, Southern Museum of Flight
Dorothy Scott Letters, The Woman's Collection, Texas Woman's University
Taped interview with Betty Gillies by Dawn Letson, September 1996, The
Woman's Collection, Texas Woman's University
Taped interview with Betty Gillies by Rob Simbeck, September 1996, The
Woman's Collection, Texas Woman's University
Assorted papers belonging to members of the Women's Auxiliary Ferrying
Squadron, The Woman's Collection, Texas Woman's University

## Videos

"Nancy Batson Crews" — Program given for the Birmingham Aero Club, Birmingham, Alabama, August 19, 1999 (Taped by Dr. E.W. Stevenson, Aero Club member).

"Women's Auxiliary Ferrying Squadron" — Press Conference at The Southern Museum of Flight, Birmingham, Alabama, June 22, 1999.

"Women In Aviation" — WASP/WAFS panel, International Women's Air and Space Museum Lecture Series, Taped at Miami Valley Cable Council, Centerville, Ohio, January 13, 1992.

"Woman In Aviation: Nancy Batson Crews" — *A Sense of History Program*, Centerville-Washington Township Historical Society, with Sarah Rickman, interviewer. Taped on May 24, 1999, and produced by John Moraites for the Centerville-Washington Township Historical Society, Centerville, Ohio, and shown by Miami Valley Cable Council beginning October 2000. Included miscellaneous film footage shot by Nancy Batson with her 16-mm movie camera — 1943/1944.

৵৵৵

**Photos in this book come from several sources:**

The International Women's Air and Space Museum (IWASM)
 Teresa James, Betty Gillies, and Helen Thomas Collections
The Nancy Harkness Love Private Collection
The Nancy Batson Crews Private Collection
The B. J. Erickson London Private Collection
The Evelyn Sharp Collection belonging to *Sharpie* author Diane Ruth Armour Bartels
The Southern Museum of Flight
Photos from individuals: Gertrude Meserve LeValley, Phyllis Burchfield Fulton, Florene Miller Watson, Sherrill Arnet (Lenore McElroy's daughter), Honey Fulton Parker (Dorothy Fulton's sister), Don Prosser (Helen Richards' husband), William Goodman Clark (Helen Mary Clark's son), and Sarah Byrn Rickman

**Special thanks to:**

WASP Nadine Canfield Nagle (44-W-9) for the loan of her WASP Roster as well as the loan of several of the books mentioned above.

WASP Betty Stagg Turner (44-W-9), author of *Out of History Into the Blue* (Aviatrix Publishing Inc., Arlington Heights, Illinois, 2001), for sharing with me what biographical data she had on the WAFS as of summer 1999.

Sandy Spafford, secretary to Robert Dickson, son of Barbara Towne Dickson Fasken, for biographical data.

H.O. Malone, aviation historian and author, for his insight, support, and for introducing me to Ann Hamilton Tunner.

Samii Yakovetic, of Yakovetic Productions, Corona, California for her help with historical photographs from the B.J. Erickson London Private Collection.

Cathy Simonson, reference librarian at the Centerville Library, Centerville, Ohio, for checking innumerable facts and finding copies of reference books.

Mimi Collins, director of the library in Taft, California, for answering my e-mail about finding Don Prosser, Helen Richards' husband. Thanks as well to the several sleuths — old friends of Don and Helen Prosser — for responding to her call.

Marcia Rajkovich and Brenda Mullins for professional and personal support.

# ACKNOWLEDGEMENTS

A number of people have had a hand in this book, either in helping me gather information or by inspiring me to continue writing when I wondered if it was worth all the sweat and tears. The danger here is forgetting someone, but here goes.

Thanks to:

My husband, Richard — for putting up with me and my writing for 38 years and counting.

My son, Major James E. Rickman, USAF — for the quietness of his house in which I do much of my creative writing.

My son, Charles Byrn Rickman — for serving as my first reader, finding the stupid mistakes, questioning the flights of fancy I occasionally took in my prose, and telling me when something wasn't clear; and my daughter-in-law Susan, for marrying into this crazy family and taking it in stride.

Liz Trupin-Pulli — for recognizing this marvelous story, encouraging me to get on with it, and then publishing it when it was done.

Joan Hrubec — Director/Trustee, International Women's Air and Space Museum — for asking me to write this story because IWASM has no single resource that tells who the WAFS were and what they did.

WAFS Teresa James and B.J. Erickson London for reading the manuscript and finding errors I never would have found.

WASP (43-W-2) Iris Cummings Critchell — Aeronatuics Professor Emerita, Curator Special Aviation History Collection, Harvey Mudd College, Claremont, California — for reading the manuscript and sharing her superb knowledge of WWII airplanes.

Nadine Canfield Nagle (44-W-9) — the first WASP I met back in 1990 — for inspiring in me a fascination for, and a love of, the story of ALL the women who flew for the Army in World War II.

All the living WAFS. In addition, I've been able to contact families of some of the Originals and I thank them for sharing information.

The WASPs I have met personally and so much admire. Some are mentioned in the book. Many are not.

Dawn Letson and Nancy Durr at The WASP/WAFS Archives at Texas Woman's University, Denton, Texas.

Dr. Don Dodd at the Southern Museum of Flight, Birmingham, Alabama.

James Pittman, MD, of Birmingham, Alabama, for taking me up in his Stearman PT-17 and turning me inside out and upside down so that I knew what flying a WWII trainer felt like.

Dr. Lillie Howard at Wright State University, Dayton, Ohio, teacher, mentor, friend — for believing in my writing all along the way and encouraging me when I doubted.

And, finally, the family of the late Nancy Batson Crews. Knowing that their mother was totally dedicated to the publication of *The Originals*, Nancy's three children have graciously and enthusiastically supported her wishes. My only regret is that she didn't live to hold a finished copy in her hands.

Photo: Daniel Cleary

Sarah Byrn Rickman is a former journalist who also wrote and did television work for the International Women's Air and Space Museum when it was based in Centerville, Ohio (now housed in Cleveland). Her actual aviation experience is twenty-two hours in a Cessna 152.

Current writing projects include two novels about the WAFS and WASPs, both of which won first place in the Historical Fiction category at the Pikes Peak Writers Conference in 1999 and 2000. Sarah and husband Richard live in Centerville and have two grown sons.

# INDEX